Deng Xiaoping and the Cultural Revolution

— *A Daughter Recalls the Critical Years*

By Deng Rong
Translated by Sidney Shapiro

FOREIGN LANGUAGES PRESS   BEIJING

First Edition   2002

Home Page:
http://www.flp.com.cn
E-mail Addresses:
info@flp.com.cn
sales@flp.com.cn

ISBN 7-119-03040-X
©Foreign Languages Press, Beijing, China, 2002

Published by Foreign Languages Press
24 Baiwanzhuang Road, Beijing 100037, China

For sale and distribution in the People's Republic of China only

Printed in the People's Republic of China

Acknowledgements

In order to be able to write this book I had to refer to numerous archives and related books and documents. I also needed and obtained the help of many individuals who were closely involved in the events described. To them I wish to express my heartfelt gratitude. They granted me interviews and gave me valuable information.

My appreciation also goes to Li Ping, from the Central Archives Research Office. He went through the whole draft and provided important guidance. Members of the Deng Xiaoping Research Group at the Central Archives made a great deal of reference materials available and offered their help.

I want to express my deep gratitude to Sidney Shapiro, one of the world's leading translators of Chinese literature into English and an established writer, who translated my book into English. His precision and speed were extraordinary and he has offered his own interpretation of the book in his Translator's Introduction and notes.

I also wish to thank Li Xing, senior feature writer and editor of the Features Department of *China Daily*, who found time during her busy newspaper work to proof-read the English manuscript. Also Lü Wei, who has coordinated the publication of the English version of this book with her dynamic and overall vision.

And finally, my thanks to Huang Youyi, deputy director-general of the Foreign Languages Publishing and Distribution Administration, and to all the people who have lent selfless help to make it possible for this book's publication in English.

Deng Rong

Translator's Introduction

Maomao wrote the biography of her father Deng Xiaoping during the Cultural Revolution, 1966 to 1976, and asked me to translate it into English. I read the book and enjoyed it, but realized it would present difficulties to the average foreign reader.

For it is a book about remarkable persons in a land called China, people with their own history, culture and customs, under extremely trying circumstances. How to interpret their actions, their motivations? How to faithfully reproduce what the author says, while at the same time conveying her style, her spirit?

A daunting task, severely straining my limited capabilities. Let me try at least to offer a few subjective opinions regarding China and the Chinese during the two millennia prior, and leading up, to the Cultural Revolution.

China was a huge, primarily agricultural, imperial country, in which a small number of wealthy landlord families ruled over the vast majority of the population, consisting mainly of serfs and tenant farmers. A wealthy elite controlled the government, the army, the judiciary, the law enforcement agencies, at every level. The depredations of the rulers were sanctified by an absolutist philosophy positing unquestioned obedience to authority in a paternalistic, male chauvinist, autocracy. When oppression reached unbearable proportions, as it frequently did every few centuries, the people revolted and brought the emperor down — only to bring in a new emperor, a new dynasty, without any fundamental, substantive change in the social and political system.

As in Europe, and in feudal countries generally in the same period, there was little thought of "freedom" and "democracy" as we understand the terms today. The traditional concepts were not only accepted by the general public, but were, indeed, considered morally admirable.

They served China well enough for two millennia — from the time of Confucius around 500 BC until roughly the 16th century, when China led the world not only culturally but even scientifically. But then imperial arrogance and complacency began closing Chinese eyes and Chinese doors to the advances in other lands. China fell behind, a weakened prey to internal corruption and incursions from abroad.

By the 19th century, when their unsuitability to a modern world became increasingly evident, there was a great deal of discussion and soul-searching on how to "save China". The Japanese model? The American? Inept experiments all failed.

Finally, in the early 20th century it appeared that conditions in Russia, and its epochal revolution, bore considerable resemblance to the situation in China. A handful of intellectuals in a secret meeting in Shanghai in the 1920s formed a Chinese Communist Party. After a long and bitter struggle under the leadership of that Party, strongly influenced by the Soviet experience, the People's Republic of China was formally established in October 1949. Mao Zedong was chosen Chairman of the Party.

Most decisive in these victories was clearly Mao's analytical powers and vision. He defined the fundamental problems as feudalism and imperialism — China's main internal and external obstacles. Moreover, he developed the magic formula for overcoming backwardness and rallying a vast impoverished populace to create military and economic miracles. Namely, a selfless Chinese Communist Party, dedicated to serving the people, whom it treated with the utmost respect and admiration on a democratic basis.

The success of this formula astonished the world and sent shivers down the backs of certain major powers. Worried about the effects it might have on other lands in which they had "special interests", they increased harassment in and around China's borders.

Mao was superbly confident in the country's ability to cope with military attacks by "paper tigers", and sure of China's ability to "leap forward" economically. But he was erratic and subjective. He pushed ambitious projects without feasibility studies, with disastrous results.

He saw all problems in terms of "class struggle". Other members of the Party leadership expressed doubts and opposition, but Mao simply over-rode them.

What particularly concerned him was the fact that the Communist Party of the Soviet Union decided in the 1960s to opt for what Khrushchov hailed as "goulash communism", an euphemism for thinly disguised capitalist enterprise. By unhappy coincidence, within the Chinese Communist Party many distinct evidences surfaced of a growing elitism, use of power for personal gains, corruption, moral frivolity, and a neglect of the public's interests. Mao felt this was very dangerous, that it could lead to an abandonment of Party principles and a slide into capitalism, or even fascism.

Mao therefore called for an examination of all Communists in positions of authority, for an appraisal of their qualities, and for the correction of their errors, as well as a corresponding reformation in the cultural field. The formal implementation of this policy, starting in 1966, became known as the Cultural Revolution. At that time most Party leaders, including Deng Xiaoping, and the majority of China's intellectuals, supported these reforms. They seemed reasonable and necessary.

The tragedy was that none of us, including Mao Zedong, was able to see that the Cultural Revolution would be taken over and manipulated by nefarious persons for their own purposes, causing enormous social and political damage. Mao, when he woke up to the seriousness of the situation, was unable to control it.

I have tried to faithfully render the content of the original, condensing a bit here and there, and to convey as closely as possible Maomao's refreshing literary style.

Where I feel that certain points would not be clear enough to the foreign reader, I have taken the liberty of adding comments. These appear in footnotes. They are entirely my own opinions, obtained from various Chinese and Western sources, and do not necessarily represent the views of the author. I cannot vouch for their authenticity. Only that they seem plausible to me.

Sidney Shapiro
Beijing

Contents

1. Crowded Events of 1966   1
2. Trouble Begins at Home   10
3. "Bombard the Headquarters"   20
4. Criticize Liu and Deng   25
5. Go All Out Against "Persons in Authority Taking the Capitalist Road"   33
6. Down with Liu, Deng, Tao!   41
7. The Chill of Autumn   50
8. A Lonely Craft on a Bounding Sea   56
9. The "Deng Xiaoping Case Team"   66
10. The Enlarged 12th Plenary Session of the Eighth Party Central Committee   74
11. May Terror   80
12. Calamity Drops from the Skies   86
13. The Performance of the Deng Xiaoping Case Team from Beginning to End   95
14. The Ninth Party National Congress and "Continuing the Revolution"   99
15. A Strategic Exodus   106
16. The Lonely Flight South   113
17. Early Days in Jiangxi   120
18. Working Life   125
19. A Visit Home   133
20. Feifei Returns   140
21. A Quantitative Change   148
22. Shock Waves from the Lushan Conference   156
23. Uneasy "Quiet Days"   161

24. What Happened to Pufang   169
25. Heaven Doesn't Forget People with Hearts   177
26. Winding Back Through Precipitous Heights   189
27. Spring Comes Early South of the Yangtze   195
28. Correcting the Extremist Errors   207
29. Breaking the Fetters and Climbing the Jinggang Mountains   214
30. Old Places Revisited   223
31. Farewell, Infantry School   230
32. Summer, and Back at Work   240
33. The 10th Party National Congress Continues the Line of the
    Cultural Revolution   249
34. Into the Military Commission and the Politburo   257
35. The Storm over the Special Session of the United Nations   264
36. An Ugly Battle   270
37. The Struggle for a New Cabinet at the Fourth National
    People's Congress   275
38. The Deep Significance of the Fourth National People's
    Congress   285
39. Prelude to All-out Rectification   290
40. The Railway Restoration Confrontation   295
41. Mao Zedong Criticizes the Gang of Four   302
42. All-out Rectification   311
43. Documents on National Rectification   322
44. Great Accomplishments   332
45. A Critique of *Outlaws of the Marsh*, and the Last Days of
    Zhou Enlai   342
46. Wicked Persons First Accuse   349
47. Difficult Days   358
48. Tragic Misery   371
49. "Criticize Deng, Oppose the Right-deviationist Attempts to
    Reverse the Judgments"   380
50. The Great April 5 Movement   389
51. The "Two Resolutions" and Deng's Second Overthrow   396

52. Fearlessly Confronting the Waves   405
53. Heaven Angered, the People Enraged   415
54. Mao Zedong, a Great Man, Passes   426
55. Thoroughly Smash the Gang of Four   436
56. A Splendid Restoration   444
57. In Conclusion   450
Glossary   455
Index   472

1

Crowded Events of 1966

O<small>N</small> May 16, 1966 the Political Bureau of the Central Committee of the Chinese Communist Party (hereafter called the Politburo) issued a circular (which became known as the famous "May 16 Circular"). It launched the explosive "Great Proletarian Cultural Revolution".

This was no accident. It was the inevitable result of "leftist" errors within the Party carried to an extreme.

After the People's Republic was established, we had more than seven years of successful socialist reform and construction. But then, the domestic and international situation, plus the combined influence of our victories, inflated self-confidence, and over-heated brains, engendered inside the Party a kind of joyous arrogance. An exaggerated estimation of our accomplishments, plus an eagerness to speed up the progress toward communism, further stirred unrealistic thinking and opened a broad avenue for impetuous surges in violation of the laws of economics. A number of "leftist" theories evolved, and finally found prominence inside the Communist Party.

At the same time democratic foundations within the Party weakened, worship of the top leader and arbitrary decision by the individual grew. Internal Party relations were already abnormal. Mao Zedong made wrong appraisals of the domestic and international situations, particularly in regard to class struggle. He had already set himself up as an absolute authority, and was increasingly impatient with any disagreement. Now he adopted extreme measures in matters of policy and organization, and ultimately even regarding personnel. He brushed aside all hindrances and obstacles, determined to push through a revolutionary line he insisted was correct.

At first, 1966 seemed no different than any other year. We had the usual icy winter weather, the usual cold north winds. The winter sun illuminated the broad land, bringing new strength to all living things.

After three years of hard work between 1963 and 1965, and thanks to unrelenting efforts from the Central Committee down to the grassroots Party organizations, the economy was much improved. The great difficulties brought on by natural calamities and other problems [1] had at last been conquered.

Gone was the pressure on our hearts, frowns were smoothed from our brows. The Central Committee had begun discussing the Third Five-Year Plan. Although grain was still rationed and goods were in short supply, most people had enough to eat, and could live and work in a fairly relaxed manner. Their warmest wish was that in the coming year the country would be still more peaceful, their lives would have still more meaning, and that socialist construction would progress better still.

But events frequently turned out very differently from what we had envisioned, contrary to our good intentions and simple desires.

People hadn't paid much attention to certain things which happened at the end of 1965, things we had not anticipated.

On November 10, 1965, the Shanghai newspaper *Wen Hui Bao* published an article by Yao Wenyuan criticizing Wu Han, the author of a new historical play called "Hai Rui Is Dismissed from Office", claiming that, by allegory, it sought to justify Peng Dehuai's "attempt to reverse the judgment". [2] The article had been secretly conceived by Jiang Qing

---

[1] The "other problems" were due less to the natural calamities than to the rash impractical measures adopted during the commune and "Great Leap Forward" period of the late 1950s. At the same time the Soviet Union, in order to pressure China to yield to exploitation and control, in 1960 suddenly pulled out all her experts and engineers. The combination of these factors caused a sharp drop in agricultural and industrial production, resulting in severe privation and hardship.

[2] At the Communist Party Conference in Lushan in 1959 Marshal Peng Dehuai wrote a letter to Mao Zedong, concerning the failures of the communes and the "Great Leap Forward." Peng was removed from his posts and forced into retirement. The play told of a Ming Dynasty emperor who arbitrarily dismissed a good official named Hai Rui. Mao believed that he was being portrayed as the wicked emperor and Peng Dehuai as the wronged official, and that this was all part of a general vendetta of forces opposed to him.

and Zhang Chunqiao, and written by Yao Wenyuan.

Jiang Qing was Chairman Mao's wife. Nominally, she was head of the Motion Picture Division of the Propaganda Department of the Central Committee. Actually she seldom did any work, saying she was ill.

Zhang Chunqiao was the newly appointed chief of the Shanghai Party Secretariat. He was in charge of propaganda and culture.

Yao Wenyuan wielded a poison pen for the Political Research Section of the Shanghai Party Committee.

In February, 1965, Jiang Qing arrived in Shanghai. With the support of Ke Qingshi, First Secretary of the Shanghai Party Committee, she connived with Zhang Chunqiao to have Yao Wenyuan write his critical article. After it was drafted, it was submitted to Mao Zedong three times for his examination. He approved it, and it was published.

Highly political in motivation, the article had a strong influence on the Cultural Revolution which later followed. In the lengthy process from its conception to its publication the article was kept secret from the members of the Politburo. None of them knew anything about it. Even after it was published in Shanghai, leaders in the Central Committee in Beijing didn't realize its implications, and paid little heed. The Secretariat reserved judgment.

My father, who was General Secretary, completely disapproved of criticizing Wu Han. Peng Zhen told him Wu Han was worried.

Papa said: "I saw that play. Ma Lianliang played Hai Rui. There's nothing wrong with it. Some people try to climb on others' shoulders. They have only half-baked understanding, but they nit-pick and squawk, hoping to make a name for themselves. I can't stand that sort. Tell the professor there's nothing to it. We'll still play bridge together. Political and academic matters should be kept apart. It's dangerous to mix them. It blocks free expression."

My father often played bridge with Wu Han. "Professor," he said, "Don't be so gloomy. What are you afraid of? Is the sky going to fall? I'm 61 this year. From the time I joined the revolution to this day I've survived plenty of storms. I've learned two things: One, fear nothing.

3

Two, be optimistic. Take the long view. When you do that, you can cope with anything. You have my support, so relax."

Papa wanted to protect him. He didn't realize the situation would get out of hand so rapidly. When the Secretariat learned that Mao was behind Yao Wenyuan's article, it had no choice but to let the Beijing papers carry it as well. Their original reluctance seemed ordinary enough, but it irritated Mao, and turned out to be the fuse that was to ignite a huge political storm.

In November 1965, Yang Shangkun, alternate member of the Central Committee Secretariat and Chief of the Central Committee General Office, was removed from his posts. His "crime" was "installing a listening device without the knowledge of the Central Committee." [1]

Yang's family and ours had been quite close. Papa thought what Yang did wasn't very serious. During the Cultural Revolution when Papa was compelled to make a "self-criticism", he said for a long time he didn't consider Yang's action to be "spying", and that his own response to it, as General Secretary, had not been "timely" or "conscientious".

Papa clearly disapproved of the criticism of Yang Shangkun, and felt it without foundation. Yang was transferred to a post in Guangdong Province. His daughter Niuniu was then going to school in Beijing. My parents took her into our home for a time.

If one were to say the criticism of Yang Shangkun was an isolated incident, what happened after that certainly was not.

In December, Lin Biao, Vice-Chairman of the Central Committee and the Central Military Commission in charge of the national military operations, for reasons best known to himself, accused Luo Ruiqing, Vice-Secretary of the Central Committee Secretariat and Chief of Staff

---

[1] According to one foreign journalist, Mao Zedong did not like having secretaries present taking notes when he was receiving foreign visitors. In order for the government to be informed of any casual policy statements he may have made, Yang, as Director of the Communist Party's Central Committee General Office, had a tape recorder installed. This was done openly, in 1964. Several officials knew about it. During the Cultural Revolution Jiang Qing perverted this into an allegation that Yang Shangkun had dared to record the top-secret words of Chairman Mao, that he was a Soviet spy, conveying to his Russian masters the innermost thoughts of Mao Zedong.

of the PLA, of attempting to usurp control of the armed forces. [1]

On hearing Lin's accusations, Mao Zedong convened an enlarged session of the Standing Committee of the Politburo in Shanghai, to expose and criticize Luo Ruiqing. Luo was not invited to attend.

My mother was in Shanghai at the time. As she recalls it, the atmosphere was very tense. There was none of the usual friendliness and smiles among the people she knew who had come to take part. At the meeting not even the secretaries were allowed to look at the documents. Mama was sure something bad was brewing, but she didn't dare ask.

Papa said nothing at all. His face was solemn, and unusually serious.

On December 10, a special plane carried Luo and his wife from Beijing to Shanghai. Mao directed Zhou Enlai and Deng Xiaoping to talk to Luo.

"You come along, too," Papa said to Mama. "And comfort Hao Zhiping (Luo's wife)."

In the car on the way she sat with Papa and Zhou Enlai. No one spoke. The men looked serious. Mama didn't know why. She felt very tense.

When they got to the house where Luo was being detained, Zhou Enlai and Papa spoke with him on the ground floor. My mother and Hao Zhiping went upstairs.

"Try to relax a little," Mama urged. She herself began to sob.

Later, during the Cultural Revolution at a criticism session of Papa, his accusers said the women had embraced each other and wept. They seized upon this as evidence that Deng Xiaoping had protected Luo Ruiqing.

Papa had always disliked Lin Biao. He didn't believe Lin's vicious smear of Luo Ruiqing. He was passive about it, obstructive. As he said when under fire during the Cultural Revolution, "I never could see the seriousness of the charge against Luo. In fact, I forgave him."

---

[1] Actually, it was Lin Biao who was trying to usurp control of the armed forces, and beyond that all of China. He considered Luo Ruiqing one of the persons in his way, and attacked him before the Central Committee on framed charges verging on treason.

After the Shanghai meeting, the Army held another one in Beijing. Mao ordered my father to act as chairman. Papa's attitude was distinctly passive.

"I was named as one of the chairs for the meetings," he told us later, "but I spent most of my time in the Northwest, checking military installations. I told Peng Zhen to take charge. I made it plain I didn't want any part of the attacks on Luo."

Many high-level leaders were shocked and puzzled by the criticisms of Yang Shangkun and Luo Ruiqing. They didn't know that bigger and even more disastrous charges were even then being secretly fomented. Things happened so fast people had no time to comprehend or respond.

At the beginning of 1966 a series of events erupted one after another.

January. Lin Biao convened a full session of all military units involved in political work. In order to lay a theoretical basis for his planned activities he spoke at length about "stressing politics."

February. A "Forum on Literature and Art in the Armed Forces", sponsored by Jiang Qing and Lin Biao, opened in Shanghai.

March. The "Highlights" of the "Forum", after review and editing by Mao Zedong, were distributed nationwide. This was to be the springboard for the armed forces' intervention in the Cultural Revolution.

March. Luo Ruiqing was dismissed from office. He was subsequently imprisoned.

That same month Mao had several discussions with Kang Sheng [1] and Jiang Qing. He said if the offices of the Central Committee impeded him, he would call on the regional units to rebel. The leftists should be supported, Mao said, and organized into factions to start a Cultural Revolution.

Looking back after more than 30 years at the above incidents, no one today can imagine how strong the smell of gunpowder was. Most of the high Party leaders had no inkling of the terrible storm about to break.

---

[1] Kang Sheng exercised a Machiavellian influence on Mao Zedong for many years, starting in the 1940s in Yan'an and extending through the Cultural Revolution. Of the same generation, like Mao, he was a classicist and a scholar. Underneath, he was narrow, bitter, vicious. He perverted Party policy, and hurt a great many people. Unfortunately, Mao trusted and respected him.

There were things they didn't approve of, or which made them suspicious. But they had absolutely no conception of what would follow, the madness, the uncontrollable chaos.

Deng Xiaoping, member of the Standing Committee of the Politburo and General Secretary of the Central Committee, felt the same as other high Party leaders. He disapproved of what was going on, but he was not alert to the dangers which were impending. And he certainly was not mentally prepared.

April 8. Kang Sheng telephoned Deng Xiaoping to notify him that he was urgently wanted in Beijing. At that time my father, together with Vice-Premiers Li Fuchun and Bo Yibo, and ministers of the State Council, was investigating work in the Northwest. All during the trip they discussed and thought only about how to improve the economy in Northwest China and build up the military installations. Hurriedly, they took a special plane back to Beijing. Only then did Papa learn that Peng Zhen was in trouble.

What caused it was that Peng Zhen had not agreed with the publication by Shanghai's *Wen Hui Bao* of Yao Wenyuan's attack on Wu Han. A distinguished historian, Wu Han was also a vice-mayor of Beijing. Peng Zhen, First Secretary of the Beijing Party Committee, as well as Mayor, naturally wanted to know why Beijing was not consulted beforehand.

Jiang Qing, Kang Sheng and Zhang Chunqiao, without first informing the Central Committee, flew to Shanghai, where Mao was staying, and complained that Peng was "checking up on the Chairman". Mao became very angry, and ordered that Peng be criticized.

From the 9th to the 12th of April the Central Committee Secretariat held several meetings.

Kang Sheng, alternate member of the Politburo, and member of the Central Committee Secretariat, read out the criticisms Mao had leveled against Peng Zhen. Namely, that Peng, by his opposition to the publication of the article, had muddied the line between classes; that he had made no distinction between right and wrong; that he had committed serious errors. And, Mao had continued, the Central Committee Publicity Department was a "palace of demons", and the Publicity Division of the Beijing Party Committee was shielding bad people (meaning Wu Han).

Mao's anger was far from abating. In Hangzhou from April 16 to April 22, 1966, he convened a series of enlarged sessions of the Standing Committee of the Politburo aimed at criticizing the "anti-Party crimes" of Peng Zhen.

Papa had not agreed with the criticism of Luo Ruiqing, and neither did he agree with the criticism of Peng Zhen. Not only had he had close contact with them in his work; their personal relations were also very good. In mind and deed he opposed their persecution.

But this latest attack was particularly fierce. Mao's rage was obviously out of control. At a time when democracy within the Party had reached a low ebb, high-ranking Communists like my father, despite their opposition, were not able to state it openly.

As he later recalled: "Peng Zhen's question was not serious. I didn't go along with the criticism. I sent him half a crate of oranges to show him how I felt. Under the circumstances that was the best I could do."

An enlarged session of the Politburo was held in Beijing from May 4 to May 26. Its agenda, arranged by Mao Zedong, linked Peng Zhen, Luo Ruiqing, Lu Dingyi and Yang Shangkun, charging them with "anti-Party activities" and "abnormal relations among themselves." In a speech, Lin Biao painted a shocking scenario, ranting that some persons within the Central Committee were planning a political coup. The session concluded with the passage of a document drawn up by Chen Boda, after several amendments by Mao Zedong.

Known as the "May 16 Circular", it called for the castigation of "reactionary bourgeois thinking" in the fields of academia, education, news media, literature and art, and publishing, and urged a purging of the "bourgeois leadership" in these areas. In a hint of what was to come, the Circular warned that "representatives of the bourgeoisie" had wormed their way into the Communist Party, the government, the armed forces, and all aspects of the cultural field. It said that these were "counter-revolutionary revisionists" who, when the time was ripe, would seize political power, moving it from the hands of the proletariat to the hands of the bourgeoisie. "Some of them we have already recognized, some we have not. Some are receiving our trust, and are being groomed as our successors. Khruschov-types are slumbering in our midst. Party committees at all levels must give this their strictest attention.''....

The "May 16 Circular," in solemn and dangerous terms, heralded the advent of an enormous political storm.

Political and public opinion preparations had been completed. The curtain was about to formally rise on the "Great Proletarian Cultural Revolution", replete with political criticisms and political anarchy. [1]

---

[1] There were indeed ideological hindrances to the development of socialism in New China. These were mainly hangovers from the reactionary mentality and methods of two thousand years of feudalism. These were manifest everywhere, in education, in customs and habits, in the arts, in attitudes and operations in the government and within the Communist Party. Bourgeois influences were small. By concentrating the attack on the bourgeoisie Mao diverted attention away from the main danger — feudal mentality.

But the abuses were real, although mislabeled, and resentment was widespread. People, particularly the young people, responded quickly to what they saw as a call for them to take action. Their own impetuosity, fanned by exhortations from Mao and radical extremists, led to the organization of factions.

With an almost religious fervor they savagely tortured, mentally and physically, any and all persons — especially Communists — in positions of leadership or authority, while brawling noisily, and often bloodily, among themselves. Violence led to more violence, with many parts of the country debuting into anarchy.

How could people normally so self-disciplined, so decent, so law-abiding, behave so chaotically? Ironically, the majority were firmly convinced of their pious orthodoxy according to "the thought of Mao Zedong."

It was Mao who had opened the Pandora's Box. Some said that later he regretted the horror he had unleashed, but then it was too late.

2
Trouble Begins at Home

MAO Zedong was not in Beijing, but he ordered the convening of an enlarged session of the Politburo, to be chaired by his successor, Vice-Chairman of the Central Committee and President of the People's Republic, Liu Shaoqi.

Liu didn't realize that everything Mao did at that time, and the many, many things which displeased and angered him, were not simply brought on by the immediate matters of Peng Zhen, Luo Ruiqing, Lu Dingyi and Yang Shangkun.

After the failure of the "Great Leap Forward" in 1958, and particularly after the rectification of the rash policies in the 60's, Mao started being dissatisfied with Liu Shaoqi and Deng Xiaoping. They shared the responsibility for general work in the Central Committee, but in many respects their ideas were not in harmony with his own. Naturally, he was most angry with the higher-ranking Liu Shaoqi.

In keeping with his goal of "continuing the revolution under the dictatorship of the proletariat" so as to prevent "revisionism" and a "return of capitalism", Mao had already made up his mind. He decided to replace Liu Shaoqi by Lin Biao as his designated successor as leader of the Communist Party. Lin always made a point of posing as being assiduously "faithful" to Mao and all of his theories.

Liu Shaoqi was not aware of Mao's intention, nor was Deng Xiaoping, nor were the high-ranking Party leaders.

Nor were they prepared for the thunderclap events which rapidly followed, and Mao's completely irrational thoughts and deeds. And when they finally did realize what was happening, they couldn't understand it. It was this "slow-wittedness" on their part which made them "unable to keep up" with developments, and commit "errors" which, of course, resulted in their being drowned in the mad floodwaters of the "revolution".[1]

On May 25, the day before the meeting scheduled to criticize Peng, Luo, Lu and Yang, a large poster was put up on the campus of Peking University. It was signed by seven persons, including a woman named Nie Yuanzi, who was secretary of the Communist Party's general branch of the Philosophy Department. The poster attacked the University's Party Committee, plus the Party Committee of the Beijing Municipal Government. Instigated and planned by Kang Sheng, this was the notorious "First Marxist-Leninist Poster". It launched the Cultural Revolution.

The poster threw Peking University into an uproar. My sister Deng Nan, who was a student there, after reading it, immediately phoned my mother. "Nie Yuanzi is a bad person," Mama said. "She behaved badly in Yan'an. Don't tell anybody I said so!"

She was reflecting what my father thought. He was very much against this sudden assault.

The storm had begun. No one could stop it. A thousand more posters went up at the university expressing a broad diversity of opinions. Posters criticizing the deans of nearly every college and middle school and voicing declarations of revolt proliferated throughout the city. After June 1 a flurry of posters flew in all of Beijing's schools and academies. An irresistible surge spread like the plague. The schools were chaotic. Revolts multiplied and became more intensive. In some schools the principals and teachers were excoriated, even beaten.

On May 28 the Central Committee officially established a Cultural Revolution Leading Group. On the instructions of Mao Zedong, it was headed by Chen Boda, with Kang Sheng as advisor. Jiang Qing and

---

[1] These were epithets cast at victimized leaders who disagreed with the turmoil deliberately engineered by the self-professed "revolutionaries".

Zhang Chunqiao were vice-leaders. Yao Wenyuan was named a member. These people, who formerly had been scheming in private, could now openly play major roles. In full armor and war paint they took the stage.

Mao's fundamental principle was "smash first, then build". He believed that "only chaos under the heavens can bring stability throughout the land." From his vantage point away from the scene of action he found the destruction and turmoil in Beijing eminently satisfactory.

But in Beijing, Liu Shaoqi, Zhou Enlai and Deng Xiaoping, responsible for running the major affairs of the Party and government, were put in a very difficult position by the sudden anarchy.

May 29. Liu Shaoqi, Zhou Enlai, and Deng Xiaoping, the three Politburo Standing Committee members who were handling the general affairs of the Central Committee, summoned all of the concerned departments to discuss developments in the Cultural Revolution. It was decided to send one work group under Chen Boda to the *People's Daily*, and another under Zhang Chengxian, the vice-minister of education, to Peking University. Zhou Enlai telephoned Mao Zedong in Hangzhou, telling him of the decision, and requesting approval. A formal request, signed jointly by Liu Shaoqi, Zhou Enlai, and Deng Xiaoping, was formally dispatched by telegram to Mao on the 30th. His reply came the same evening: "I agree to this course of action."

While the Central Committee top leaders were busily trying to cope with the confusion, the movement suddenly changed. On June 1, Mao Zedong stated his approval of Nie Yuanzi's poster. He directed the Xinhua News Agency to broadcast it in its entirety, and ordered its publication by all newspapers and periodicals. He said: "This marks the commencement of the smashing of Peking University's reactionary fortress."

People's Daily on June 1 immediately published an editorial entitled "Sweep Away All Ox Demons and Venomous Spirits".[1]

---

[1] Symbols of evil in Chinese mythological superstition. The term was indiscriminately applied during the Cultural Revolution to smear intellectuals and moderate Party and government leaders.

The editorial called on the masses to "sweep away the ox demons and venomous spirits smothering our ideology and culture", to "squeeze the juice out of the so-called 'experts', 'scholars', 'authorities' and 'venerables' of the bourgeoisie, and drag their prestige through the mud."

A draft of the editorial was whipped together overnight by Chen Boda, and published the next morning without prior notice to the Central Committee. That night, the Central People's Radio Station broadcast the poster of Nie Yuanzi and her six collaborators.

Liu Shaoqi, Zhou Enlai and Deng Xiaoping were completely taken by surprise. In the days that followed, *People's Daily* issued a series of provocative editorials, reports and articles. The situation veered sharply downward, and the movement spread swiftly throughout the land.

On June 3, Liu Shaoqi hastily convened an enlarged session of the Standing Committee of the Politburo to discuss how to deal with the situation, and invited responsible members of related ministries and commissions to attend. The meeting reached a general consensus on Eight Principles to govern participants in the Cultural Revolution: distinguish between internal and external matters; keep confidential matters secret; do not put up posters in the streets; no linking of revolutionary groups in different organizations; no parades and demonstrations; no large denunciation meetings; no surrounding of the homes of accused persons; and no beatings or vilifications.

Most of the capital's schools and academies were virtually paralyzed. It was decided to send work teams to them, or any place where trouble erupted — quickly, like fire brigades.

Deng Xiaoping said the Eight Principles should be disseminated immediately. They should be announced at a huge mass meeting. We must delve to the heart of the matter, he said.

The Beijing Municipal Party Committee promptly dispatched work teams to a number of colleges and middle schools. But because persons behind the scenes were backing the rebels, not only were the work teams unable to stop the spread of the turmoil, they found it increasingly difficult to control the situation. Liu, Zhou and Deng met repeatedly to analyze the numerous complications that were emerging.

Many important policy questions could not be decided because Mao was not in Beijing. On June 9, Liu, Zhou and Deng traveled to Hangzhou and reported to Mao Zedong. From the 10th to the 12th Mao conducted two meetings where the Cultural Revolution was discussed. They were quite informal, and touched on every aspect, including speculation that it might go on for another half year or so. But there were no specific proposals on how it should be conducted.

As to the work teams, Mao said it wasn't good to send them too quickly. They weren't prepared. It was better to let things bubble for a while and have some pitched battles. That would clarify the situation. Then the work teams could be sent in.

Liu, Zhou and Deng returned to Beijing. Zhou was due to go abroad. He entrusted responsibility for guiding the movement to Liu Shaoqi and Deng Xiaoping. Starting from the 6th of June, the new Beijing Municipal Party Committee, learning from the experience of the group which had gone to Peking University, now sent work teams to a number of colleges, academies and middle schools.

Liu and Deng hoped in this way the Party could maintain leadership of the movement and halt the turmoil and restore order. They supported the work teams, and met separately with various members of the teams to keep tabs on what was happening and provide guidance.

On June 4, Deng met with the work team which was operating in the Girls' High School affiliate of Beijing Normal University. They talked about the current wave against the teachers accused of being "bourgeois academic authorities"..

"If they really are cultured, you should welcome them," Deng said. "Girls' High has a pretty fair record in math and physics. Good schools are famous; everybody knows about them, they have standing. It takes good teachers to cultivate good students. You, the work team, should make distinctions. Your job is to educate the kids, help improve their ability to analyze. Have they beaten anyone? Hitting shows you have no brains, that reason isn't on your side.

"Criticisms should be well prepared. Facts must be checked, and presented in a calm and reasonable manner. Some people may be part of a 'black gang'. Most are not. If everyone who said anything wrong was marked bad, there wouldn't be any good people. Don't call a struggle meeting if there isn't sufficient evidence. Don't permit any torture in disguise, or putting on dunce caps. Later, you should apologize for things you've done wrong.

"Political questions must be solved in a political manner. There are plenty of good Party committees in the schools. Most of the principals and assistant principals are good, too. What sense would it be to wreck the Party, and the Youth League? Would you call that victory? After all, our country is a dictatorship of the proletariat led by the Communist Party. The vast majority of the teachers are good. I don't agree that all the teachers are bad!"

I've reported these words in detail because they show two things: First, that Deng Xiaoping ideologically and as a matter of policy rejected the theory of "rebellion". Second, that he didn't see the point of the political movement Mao Zedeng had launched, to say nothing of going along with it in word or deed.

Because of his criticisms of the way the work teams were performing, the turmoil in the schools and in society generally subsided a bit. Anarchy was halted. On June 28, he and Liu Shaoqi convened an enlarged session of the Standing Committee of the Politburo. They stressed that the movement must be orderly, and called for specific principles easier to enforce.

Although completely unprepared for this sudden insane movement, Liu and Deng made rational decisions, correct decisions. Like the vast majority of Party and government functionaries, they hoped the schools would return to normal, that the students would go back to class, that the capital would be peaceful again.

They didn't know that their methods were basically at variance with Mao Zedong's intentions. Or that the clique in the Cultural Revolution Group was even then gathering itself to spur on the students and support their rebellion. For Jiang Qing and her gang thought a state of utter confusion provided the best stage they could come forward on and perform.

15

The Cultural Revolution was contrived from top to bottom. Lin Biao, Jiang Qing, and the rest of their clique grabbed the "revolutionary" enthusiasm and naïveté of the students, inflaming them with a lot of demagogic flummery. As a result, the work teams sent in by the Central Committee were unable to calm things down. In fact in a number of schools they were hotly opposed by the "revolutionary masses", and driven away.

Because of their different attitudes toward the work teams, the students split into two factions: the "conservatives" and the "rebels". These were, in essence, a manifestation of the opposing stands between the top leadership in the Central Committee headed by Liu Shaoqi and Deng Xiaoping, and the Cultural Revolution Group under Lin Biao and Jiang Qing.

In July, the situation was tense. The Central Committee convened three meetings, on the 13th, the 19th, and the 22nd, to discuss the work teams. Chen Boda, speaking on behalf of the Cultural Revolution Group, said the work teams suppressed democracy and threw cold water on the masses. He demanded that they be withdrawn.

Liu Shaoqi, responding angrily, got into a heated argument with Kang Sheng. Deng Xiaoping, usually so restrained, jumped to his feet.

Pointing a finger at Chen Boda, he shouted: "You fellows say we're afraid of the masses. Go and see for yourself! Pull out the work teams? Nothing doing!"

The open clash between the Central Committee and the Cultural Revolution Group, from ideology to language, grew white hot.

The turmoil continued for more than a month. In some schools Red Guard units were formed. Meetings excoriating the schools' leaders, the "black gang", the "ox demons and venomous spirits" grew in intensity. Some victims were tormented and beaten. Work team advocates clashed with those opposed. Factionalism gave rise to the formation of factions.

There were no more classes in high schools and colleges. Debates went on day and night. Members of the Cultural Revolution Group visited all the schools, fanning the flames, urging rebellion. Liu and Deng had no choice but to go to the schools personally and reason with the students.

I remember one time when Papa went to a college to join in the discussion and answer students' questions. Other Central Committee leaders and Jiang Qing and members of her group were also there. The hall was crowded, slogans shook the heavens. Student emotions ran high.

Beneath the blinding floodlights Jiang Qing screeched: "Learn from the young Red Guards! Salute the young Red Guards!"

With Wang Li, then a member of the Cultural Revolution Group, translating, Chen Boda made a speech in his incomprehensible Fujian dialect. He looked very proud of himself, absolutely elated.

Liu, Deng, Zhou Enlai, and other high leaders spoke to the students and urged moderation. They sounded rather weak and helpless. These old veterans who had devoted their lives to the people's revolution were flabbergasted by the "revolutionary rebels" and their twisted ideas.

Mao Zedong had instigated the Great Proletarian Cultural Revolution. He supported the rebellion. While "all was chaos under the heavens" in Beijing, he was in Hangzhou by the shining waters of West Lake voicing concepts opposed to those of the leaders in Beijing.

On June 21 he said the Cultural Revolution was a political struggle, a class struggle. This is not the time to send work teams into the schools, he said. Let there be more upheavals for a while.

In a letter to Jiang Qing, dated July 8, he wrote: "Complete confusion leads to complete stability. The task today for the entire Communist Party, for the entire nation, is to fundamentally destroy the rightists."

Another "battle cry" by Mao Zedong in the Cultural Revolution!

After grandly swimming across the Yangtze at Wuhan on July 18, Mao returned to Beijing.

Mao shunned Liu Shaoqi, who came to report to him, on the excuse he needed rest. But he listened to reports by members of the Cultural Revolution Group.

From the following day till July 23, in response to Mao's instructions, Liu convened a meeting to report on the progress of the Great Proletarian Cultural Revolution. There were strong disagreements. The Cultural Revolution Group asserted the work teams sent by the Central

Committee were suppressing the students.

Mao said he felt very badly by what he found in Beijing. It was cold, quiet. Some people were even suppressing the student movement. This was wrong, he said. It must be changed immediately.

On July 24, Mao called a joint meeting of the Politburo Standing Committee and the Cultural Revolution Group. He said the work teams had a bad effect; they hindered the movement. He ordered that they be removed.

With the work teams thus labeled, Liu and Deng, who had deployed them, of course had "committed an error".

On July 29, at a meeting of ten thousand called by the Beijing Municipal Party Committee in the Great Hall of the People, the work teams were officially dissolved.

Liu Shaoqi, Zhou Enlai and Deng Xiaoping all spoke.

"It must be made clear that the dispatch of the work teams to the colleges and middle schools by the Beijing Municipal Party Committee was done in accordance with the decision of the Central Committee," Deng said. "Some comrades say old revolutionaries are faced with new problems. That certainly is the case."

Zhou Enlai said: "The majority of the comrades in the work teams are good. Old revolutionaries are indeed faced with new problems."

To the huge audience Liu Shaoqi said: "You're not very clear on how to conduct the 'Great Proletarian Cultural Revolution'. You're asking us. Frankly, I don't know either. I believe many comrades in the Central Committee, and many members of the work teams, don't know either."

Liu, Zhou and Deng, although accepting responsibility, were speaking from their hearts.

As one of the Red Guard representatives from my school I also attended. I remember it very clearly. A hush fell on that broad presidium; you could have heard a pin drop in that spacious hall of ten thousand. We were members of our school's pro-work team faction. As we listened, we wept. Deep inside we could sense the opposition and frustration behind the words spoken by my father's generation.

I remember, too, when the meeting was ending, how Mao Zedong suddenly appeared on the presidium. He bore an aura of incomparable greatness as he waved a greeting to the huge assemblage.

The audience went wild. Young Red Guards excitedly jumped and cheered, tears streaming down their faces. In their eagerness to see Chairman Mao, people in the rear scramble atop desks and chairs.

"Long live Chairman Mao!" they shouted emotionally.

The solemnity and heaviness that had marked the start of the meeting was instantly converted into a sea of joy.

From that day on, all wraps were off Mao Zedong's Great Proletarian Cultural Revolution. Implacably it rolled into the next stage: "To rebel is justified!"

3

"Bombard the Headquarters"

T HE 11th Plenary Session of the Eighth Party Central Committee convened from August 1 to 12, 1966. An enlarged meeting of the Standing Committee of the Politburo started the proceedings. Mao Zedong condemned the dispatch of work teams into the schools.

"This is repression, terrorizing," he said. "The terrorizing comes from the Central Committee." More specifically, he added, "There are ox demons and venomous spirits sitting here among us."

Using typical language, Mao had already written his famous poster, "Bombard the Headquarters". In it he alleged that certain leading comrades, within the Central Committee and right down to the local Party organizations, had taken a reactionary bourgeois stand, and were enforcing a bourgeois dictatorship. Although he didn't mention names, it was obvious whom he was aiming at.

The session then commenced an exposure and criticism of the "errors" of Liu Shaoqi and Deng Xiaoping. Each of the big players in the Cultural Revolution Group took turns in castigating Liu and Deng for everything from suppressing the student movement by sending in work teams, to all of the "errors" by top Central Committee leaders ever since 1962.

Mao said the suppression of the student movement by Liu and Deng was a question of orientation, of line, of erroneous line.

People came away from the session with the impression that in addition to the Central Committee headed by Mao, there was also a bourgeois headquarters commanded by Liu Shaoqi.

At the last moment, at Mao's suggestion, a new item was added to the agenda: A re-election of the Politburo and its Standing Committee. Liu was dropped from his position in second place to eighth. Deng, although he moved from seventh to sixth, was actually demoted. Lin Biao floated straight up and landed in second place, replacing Liu Shaoqi. As the only vice-chairman in the Central Committee, he became in effect heir to the position of the highest leader of the Chinese Communist Party.

Liu Shaoqi and Deng Xiaoping, who had been in charge of the major duties in the Central Committee, from then on no longer led it.

Papa still had to go to some of the schools to attend their mass meetings and answer questions. If he hadn't understood the Cultural Revolution when "old revolutionaries were confronting new questions", now, after having been criticized, he understood it even less. Despondent and silent, he was disgusted by the madness of the Cultural Revolution Group and the stupidity of the rebel factions.

At times he ignored where he was and spoke openly on his own behalf, and on behalf of others. On August 2, he was notified to attend a large meeting of teachers, students, workers and employees of People's University of China. A student sent up a slip asking him about the "February Mutiny". Father knew very well that this was a trick to get him to say something which could be used against Marshal He Long, who was then being vilified. He knew too that Chen Boda and other Cultural Revolution Group bigwigs were in the audience. But his response was straightforward.

"That matter has been investigated, and there's nothing to it," he snapped. "I can also tell you this: Peng Zhen cannot mobilize the Army, and neither can I!"

His brief reply clearly revealed his anger. He wanted to rebut in detail the assaults on his old comrades-in-arms, but he was in no position to say more.

At Mao's direction, Lin Biao called an enlarged meeting of the Standing Committee of the Politburo. The original plan was to continue criticizing Liu Shaoqi. But Lin Biao and Jiang Qing felt Liu had already been demolished. The main danger, the main impediment, they insisted, was Deng Xiaoping. And so, Deng was designated as the target of the meeting. Not only were critics selected, it was decided that Lin Biao himself would take the field. Deng was to be treated as an enemy.

The charges were unfair and slanderous. Papa must have been very upset. He didn't say anything when he came home, but at night he didn't go to bed. Mama saw the light still burning in his bedroom.

"It's after three. Why aren't you asleep?" she asked.

"The focus of the attacks this evening moved from Liu Shaoqi to me."

"Who attacked you?"

"A military man."

Papa said no more, and Mama didn't press him. She only said soothingly: "Get some sleep. Otherwise you won't be able to get up in time for the meeting tomorrow."

My father knew the criticism of his "errors" now would not be limited to having sent work teams to "suppress" the students. He would be called to account for his entire history.

As a result of the meeting, Papa was compelled to step down. Some of the duties he has been performing in the Liaison and Investigation (Intelligence) departments of the Party he turned over to Kang Sheng.

"I'm handing these jobs to you," he said. "I cannot continue."

Papa had always been a taciturn man. He had been busy with scores of problems after the Cultural Revolution burst on the scene. Now, having to quit because of his "errors", he became more silent than ever. He attended fewer and fewer meetings and activities. At home he only examined the few documents which were occasionally sent in.

No longer occupied with Central Committee duties, Papa was strict with us children. We were all involved in the Cultural Revolution movement in our colleges and middle schools, and were seldom home. After the work teams were withdrawn, although we knew Papa had committed some sort of "error" in connection with them, we didn't realize what he was really coming up against. We just kept busy with the movement in our respective schools.

In early August Red Guards in some of the schools put up couplets reading: "If the old man's a hero, the son's a true man; if the old man's a reactionary, the son's a rotten egg." [1]

Immediately, everyone began arguing about the 'inheritance theory". The Red Guard unit in my middle school, including me, agreed. My big sister Deng Lin was studying in the Central Academy of Fine Arts. She and her Red Guard unit renounced it. Red Guard units all over Beijing were involved, and we traveled from school to school day and night and joined in the debates. No sooner had we finished our noisy arguments at the Central Conservatory of Music than we turned to the Central Academy of Fine Arts. Deng Lin and I disagreed violently.

It was already very late at night. I called home from a public phone outside the assembly hall. I asked Mama for her opinion. She became quite agitated.

"That couplet is wrong," she cried. "Don't argue with your sister. Come home immediately!" Her tone was strong. She kept repeating: "That's what your father says!"

I was very displeased with my parents' decision. Later, when I found out what was behind the so-called "inheritance theory" I was glad I listened to them.

On August 18 at a mass meeting to celebrate the Great Proletarian Cultural Revolution, Lin Biao exhorted the Red Guards to "smash all the old concepts, culture, customs and habits of the exploiting classes". On the 20th Beijing took the lead in an unprecedented Red Guard assault against the "Four Olds". It quickly swept the country.

Coming out of the schools, the Red Guards blanketed the land in a "revolutionary Red Terror". It inflicted severe damage. Instigated by Vice Grand Marshal Lin Biao, and spurred on to a frenzy by the Cultural Revolution Group, it debauched into a wild spree of home searches, property destruction, free-for-all fights, and even murders.

Countless naive adolescent Red Guards, in the name of "defending

---

[1] Another aberration of the Cultural Revolution. Children were discriminated against, politically and economically, if not of worker, peasant or soldier descent, or if their father was attacked as a "capitalist roader".

Chairman Mao's revolutionary line", blindly, heatedly, threw themselves into lunatic "revolutionary" activities.

My parents saw that the situation was out of control. My younger brother and I were in middle school. They called both of us home, and forbade us to leave. They said we were not to take part in any more searches and fights. By then, we brothers and sisters had some understanding of the precariousness of my father's position. We obeyed and stayed home. One learned to knit, another assembled a radio set, another practiced Chinese calligraphy, using a brush pen to write quotations from Chairman Mao. It was very quiet at home. We were far from the madness outside. Looking back, I am grateful to my parents for their restraints in that crucial period.

The Cultural Revolution and the mass movement turned society upside down. After the removal of Liu and Deng from office it hurtled forward with increased passion.

Mao Zedong, in military uniform, and wearing a Red Guard armband, on August 18 gazed down from atop Tiananmen Gate on a million Red Guards. By the end of November that year, on eight occasions he received a total of over 11 million of them. With his personal support the Red Guard movement rapidly expanded with added heat and intensity.

Even before the mad "smash the Four Olds" had subsided, a "spread the revolution" craze began. Responding to the call of Mao Zedong, young Red Guards, dressed in pseudo old military garb, clambered by the thousands on trains and buses (fare free) and wandered all over. They claimed to be spreading the flames of rebellion to every corner of the land.

Social stability was ruined. Industry, agriculture and commerce were badly disrupted, causing widespread public resentment. Disturbances and conflicts increased. At the same time, since understanding and concepts varied among the numerous Red Guard organizations, they developed serious factional differences, and constantly argued and debated heatedly among themselves. The vast land of China rumbled and seethed.

It had indeed reached the "ideal" stage of "chaos under the heavens" so earnestly sought by that revolutionary seer.

4

Criticize Liu and Deng

ALTHOUGH rebellion "of course was justified", although "revolution" had become the criterion for truth, impediments to the movement existed from the moment the Cultural Revolution erupted.

At the same time the movement broadened and deepened, more and more people grew doubtful about the direction it was taking, its methods, its theories. Mao Zedong had launched it, the powerful Lin Biao and Jiang Qing supported it, but many forms of opposition were stubbornly entrenched. There were constant new disturbances.

All of this, essentially, was due to the erroneous nature of the Cultural Revolution itself. Mao Zedong believed Liu and Deng were the cause of the opposition, that they headed a small group of leaders who were "taking the capitalist road". He felt that for a time a capitalist line had virtually assumed command, and that it still was influential within the Communist Party. To guarantee the smooth progress of the Cultural Revolution, it was essential to clear away all obstacles in its path.

From October 9 to October 28, Mao convened a work meeting of the Central Committee. Again it criticized the "reactionary capitalist line" represented by Liu Shaoqi and Deng Xiaoping.

Despite the fact the meeting had been called by Mao himself, it was clear from the start that a number of comrades, both in the Central Committee and on the local levels of the Party, still were a trifle "slow", "not terribly clear", and "unable to keep pace" with developments.

Mao was irritated. "The opening speeches were not very correct," he said.

Some of the chieftains of the Cultural Revolution Group rode forth. Chen Boda spoke. After boasting windily of six important "accomplishments", he turned to the main targets.

"The erroneous line of Liu and Deng has its social basis," he said, "namely, capitalism. There is a market for this line within the Party, because a small clique of Party leaders is taking the capitalist road. And also because we have a considerable number of mixed-up Communists who haven't rectified their world outlook, or haven't rectified it enough."

Lin Biao, from a position of obvious importance, made a summation in which he stressed the necessity for the Cultural Revolution and its great significance. Liu and Deng, he said, implemented a "counter-revolutionary line suppressing the masses."

"For a short time," he asserted, "that line attained almost total dominance."

Kang Sheng and other Cultural Revolution Group worthies joined in a noisy chorus of denunciation, suffusing the meeting with the smell of gunpowder.

Xie Fuzhi, who had served under Deng in the Second Field Army, and who now headed the Public Security Ministry, jumped up and charged his former commander. He said: "Deng gives the impression he hasn't been wrong in 30 years. He's very influential in the Party. This, in no small part, is why opposition to criticism of the bourgeois reactionary line is so large."

Chen Boda said Deng was the spearhead of the erroneous line, and listed all of his "sins" since the 60s.

Effortlessly lying, Lin Biao said Deng had sought to take credit away from Lin's Fourth Field Army and give it to his own Second Field Army. Not only that but, in the Seventh Red Corps period, Deng had been a deserter!

Mao also manifested his displeasure. He said Deng was rather deaf, but at meetings he always sat a long distance from where Mao was speaking. He claimed Deng never sought him out. In six years not once had Deng reported to him on his work.

On October 25, Mao gave the official concluding address. He said the purpose of the meeting was to "sum up experience, work on political ideology" and solve the "ideological confusion". He said he initiated the Cultural Revolution because in the past he had put too much trust in certain persons. After the establishment of a first and second line of command, quite a few independent kingdoms had emerged. He couldn't get his ideas implemented in Beijing. It was impossible.

As to the movement itself, Mao spoke with some heat.

"It started only a short time ago, and it came on very strong," he said. "I hadn't expected that the Peking University poster would rouse the whole country.... When the Red Guards went into action, they shook you up pretty badly.... I was the one who lit the flames of the Cultural Revolution!"

Then Mao turned conciliatory. He said the questions of the Central Committee had been solved. Liu and Deng's problems, and those of many others, were contradictions among the people. We must allow people to make mistakes. Liu and Deng acted openly. They should be permitted to continue taking part in the revolution.

To the conference participants, he said: "I don't want to crush you. It seems to me the Red Guards don't necessarily want to either. You can't satisfy your critics, I'm just as anxious about it as you. Time has been too short. It can be forgiven. You didn't violate the correct line on purpose. Some people say they went wrong because they were confused. We can't put all the blame on Comrade Liu Shaoqi, or on Comrade Deng Xiaoping. There was a reason for their making mistakes."

Mao said: "This movement has been on only five months. We probably need two more five-month periods or a little more." He then predicted that the movement in a year, or a bit longer, would attain its goal.

Mao genuinely seemed to believe this. Unfortunately, future developments proved he was wrong.

Liu Shaoqi and Deng Xiaoping had both made self-criticisms at the meeting on October 23. Mao had read over Liu's prepared statement. First, Liu said he had made "errors" during the first 50 days of the

Cultural Revolution, as well as in the past. He offered no excuses, and accepted full responsibility.

This was not at all the way he felt but, under the circumstances, he could say nothing else.

Deng's self-criticism was also forced. Although he criticized his own "errors", he tried to avoid affecting others.

"In this Cultural Revolution," he said, "among the leading comrades in the Central Committee, in the entire Communist Party, the only representatives of the bourgeois reactionary line are Comrade Liu Shaoqi and me."

"I want to state this clearly," he went on, "the vast majority of the comrades in the work teams are good. Although one or two may have made mistakes, any blame should rest mainly on me and Comrade Liu Shaoqi."

Deng's speech had also been read in advance on October 22 by Mao, who made this handwritten notation on the draft: "Comrade Xiaoping, you can make this speech. After the first line, where you say: 'I will correct my mistakes and start anew...' why not add a few more positive words, such as, 'Through my own strenuous efforts, plus the aid of my comrades, I am confident I can correct my errors. Please give me time, comrades. I will stand up again. I have stumbled after half my life in the revolution. Surely I can recover from this one mis-step?'"

Everyone knew that Mao had been angry with Liu and Deng since the start of the Cultural Revolution, but his notation on my father's draft was reassuring. Our whole family was relieved. We heard Papa had committed errors, and we were concerned about his political future. Second Sister Deng Nan had been traveling around the country with her Red Guard group. Mama ordered her to return home at once.

Deng Nan sneaked into Mama's bedroom every night and got in with her under the covers. Pulling the quilts over their heads, they conversed softly. Mama told her all about Papa's history, about his work in the Central Committee before the Cultural Revolution, about his relations with Peng Zhen, and Luo Ruiqing....Mama wanted her children to know their Papa was clean, he had done nothing wrong.

Papa never talked about himself. Although I loved him, I knew nothing of his history; I hadn't heard any of the many stories connected with his earlier life and his work. After hearing what Mama said, I was confident, like her, that Papa was blameless.

We even simplistically believed that Chairman Mao was against certain situations, not against specific individuals; that he wanted only to criticize "errors' committed during the Cultural Revolution. We felt that at most Papa would be demoted. We never expected he would be expelled completely.

The meeting was over; the self-criticisms had been made. Innocently, we thought all we had to do was wait for a good result. True, charges had been made against Peng, Luo, Lu and Yang; true, the Cultural Revolution had already revealed its anarchic side; true, we were all uneasy about what clearly was a serious situation. Most of the top Party leaders, including my father, were far from mentally prepared — nor could they have been — for the chain-reaction explosions that were to follow.

The meeting had ended, but that wasn't, as we had hoped, the end of the criticisms.

On November 2, a flood of posters suddenly went up in the Organization Department of the Central Committee criticizing Liu and Deng. On November 8, a poster by Nie Yuanzi appeared in Peking University entitled "Deng Xiaoping is a person in authority taking the capitalist road inside the Communist Party". It accused him of being opposed to "worship of an individual" (meaning that he opposed accepting uncritical obedience of Mao in all things), of advocating a restoration of private farming, of being against the Cultural Revolution, of being the behind-the-scenes supporter of Peng Zhen....

I was pretty upset, seeing the way the wind was blowing. My two sisters and I got on our bikes and made the rounds of schools and offices to read the posters, to see exactly what they had to say about Papa. We found that except for the "errors" he was alleged to have committed during the Cultural Revolution, none of his other so-called "questions" were particularly serious. The worst the posters could say was that he hadn't had a deep understanding of Chairman Mao's "revolutionary" line, that he hadn't adhered to it closely.

What I found most reassuring was that no one had claimed Papa had any political question in his background, as these were automatically treated as criminal during the Cultural Revolution.

But the vicious tone of the posters, their effort to paint Papa in the worst possible light, made my hair stand on end. The criticisms were not over. Nothing could be clearer than that. The only comfort was that, for all their efforts the posters hadn't been able to raise a single fatal question about Papa.

It was autumn. The weather turned cooler. Winds blew the falling leaves. A desolate silence prevailed between heaven and earth.

Like Liu Shaoqi, Papa no longer took part in any work, or attended any meetings. He sat at home reading documents which were occasionally delivered. Of course, whether in number or in content, these couldn't be compared to what he used to receive before. What would his political fate be? Papa could only wait.

We children couldn't figure out what his "error" was supposed to be. Big Sister Deng Lin asked him: "How should we understand the movement?"

What could he say? His only reply was: "Analyze it yourself."

Papa had committed an error, and therefore we were tarred with the same brush. All of us were criticized and had to make self-criticisms in our respective schools. Sometimes we were locked up and deprived of our freedom.

Would these criticisms ever come to an end, when would they cease, how far would they go? Our family didn't have a clue.

Mao Zedong criticized Liu Shaoqi and Deng Xiaoping. But he hadn't yet decided to overthrow them completely, as he had Peng, Luo, Lu and Yang. Moreover, he was considering how to make a distinction between Liu and Deng.

He had replaced Liu with Lin Biao as his successor, so, of course, Liu had to go. The only question was how severe to make his downfall.

Mao Zedong originally had held Deng Xiaoping in high regard, and wanted to appoint him to important posts. But after the failure of the "Great Leap Forward" Deng and other Central Committee leaders distanced themselves from radical "leftist" methods, and Mao became annoyed with these leaders, including Deng. His annoyance grew with the changing times to a point where it affected his appointments.

In the early stages of the Cultural Revolution, when he replaced Liu Shaoqi with Lin Biao, he still wanted to use Deng Xiaoping, and hoped Deng would support the changes he was making. He had summoned Deng for a talk.

As Papa later recalled: "He asked me to have good relations with Lin Biao. I agreed. But when I tried talking with Lin Biao, it was a failure."

The reason was simple: Lin Biao was afraid Deng would impede his upward climb. He knew there was a difference both in nature and degree in Mao's irritation with Liu on the one hand and Deng on the other, and that this would be very important when Mao determined how to dispose of them. With Liu out of the way, Deng was still Lin Biao's greatest worry.

The crafty schemer knew it would require all of his skills to topple Deng. He kept heightening the intensity of his attacks. At a meeting on December 6, Lin Biao spoke. He said the errors of Liu and Deng were not merely restricted to the first 50 days of the Cultural Revolution, they extended over a 10-year, a 20-year period. He greatly increased the level of their culpability.

Since Mao showed no indication of going forward with their overthrow, Chen Boda, Kang Sheng, Jiang Qing and other worthies of the Cultural Revolution Group joined together with the Lin Biao clique and plotted to raise a still larger storm and destroy Liu and Deng .

On December 18 Jiang Qing publicly called for the overthrow of Liu Shaoqi.

That same day Zhang Chunqiao summoned Kuai Dafu, leader of the student rebel faction in Tsinghua University, to Zhongnanhai. They discussed detailed tactics to be used against Liu and Deng.

During the last few days of 1966, on December 25, 5,000 teachers and students of Tsinghua University braved the bitter cold and marched to Tiananmen Square. There they stood and vowed to strive for the overthrow of Liu and Deng.

On December 27, the Red Guard groups from colleges and universities in Beijing gathered in the Workers' Stadium in a mass meeting to "denounce the bourgeois reactionary line of Liu and Deng". Nie Yuanzi and other rebel leaders viciously slandered them in the most poisonous language. Rebel factions whipped up a huge tidal wave against Liu and Deng all over China.

1966 was a most unusual year. It will occupy a special page in history as a "great revolutionary rebellion" which was "great" and "without precedent" — and completely imposed from the top down.

It was a year when Mao Zedong, venerating the ideal of continuous revolution, and exercising his boundless imagination and skill, let the whole world open its eyes wide and see what was meant by the power of a "mass revolution."

There isn't going to be an end to revolution. In the final days of 1966, Mao Zedong predicted, in what virtually was a vow, that next year — 1967 — would be a year of class struggle throughout the land.

This prediction, like a curse, loomed in an ominous cloud over the vast plains and heights of China.

5

Go All Out Against "Persons in Authority Taking the Capitalist Road"

"**W**AGE the Great Proletarian Cultural Revolution to the End" was the title of editorials appearing in Communist Party newspapers and periodicals on January 1, 1967. They called for a general offensive against the "small clique of persons in authority taking the capitalist road" and those "ox demons and venomous spirits" lurking in our society.

As a result, more Party leaders, from the Central Committee down to local levels, were criticized and overthrown. On January 11, credentials to attend meetings of the Politburo were withdrawn from Liu Shaoqi, Deng Xiaoping, Tao Zhu, Chen Yun, and He Long. The Group labeled Tao Zhu, member of the Standing Committee of the Politburo, the "worst royalist". Lin Biao called Marshal He Long the "biggest bandit".

Many high-ranking provincial and military leaders were overthrown. In the course of the cruel struggle sessions, a number of them were tormented or beaten to death. Many levels of governmental authority, created since the establishment of New China, were "wrecked overnight". Leaders on every level were toppled. It truly was a season of madness.

But just to overthrow the government and the Communist Party leaders on all levels was not enough to satisfy the ambitions of the Lin Biao clique and the Cultural Revolution Group. In January, at the instigation of Zhang Chunqiao and Yao Wenyuan, rebels took over all

Party and government organizations in Shanghai. Mao Zedong approved. The seizure of power then spread nationwide. "Cultural Revolution committees", headed mainly by rebel factions, replaced all original Party and government organizations.

Mao gave his full support. He considered it an important step in implementing his ideal of continuous revolution. His dream was by means of "the greatest revolutionary change in the history of mankind" to smash the old world controlled by "Party persons in power taking the capitalist road", and create a completely new revolutionary world. This ideal world would be modeled on the Paris Commune. Proletarian revolutionaries would head a new governing body to be called the Revolutionary Committee.

Mao Zedong said the "Great Proletarian Cultural Revolution" would go from "great chaos" to "great stability". Would the creation of a Revolutionary Committee bring the "great stability" he longed for? "Great stability" could not conceal reality — the continuation of chaos — an out-of-control, impossible-to-dissolve, much more serious, chaos.

Rebels raided schools; they raided local organizations of the Party and government. They entered and assaulted Army headquarters units. A whole series of confused events followed.

At the end of January 1967, in Shihezi, Northwest China's Xinjiang Uygur Autonomous Region, a rebel raid on an Army unit ended bloodily. In Chengdu, capital of Southwest China's Sichuan Province, army and rebel forces clashed; each claimed the other was "counter-revolutionary". In Xining, capital of Northwest China's Qinghai Province, an army unit was forced to open fire to repulse a rebel armed attack; there were several casualties. Rebel raids on newspaper offices and military units brought about arrests by the Army. All sorts of actions and counter-actions erupted in Guangdong, Anhui, Henan, Hunan, Fujian and Inner Mongolia.

The Cultural Revolution began with the denunciation of individuals and raids on private homes. Next, large numbers of administrators were slandered and forced out of office. And finally, there were big battles in which much blood was shed. As these stages unfolded, people went from being confused, to being disturbed, to being opposed, to being very angered, by the Cultural Revolution.

By February 1967, China's veteran Communist leaders who fought fascists bravely during World War II stood on one side. Representatives of the Cultural Revolution Group stood on the other — Kang Sheng, Chen Boda, Jiang Qing, Zhang Chunqiao, and Yao Wenyuan. They faced off in a hand-to-hand struggle.

At meetings of the Politburo and at the Central Military Commission meetings courageous veterans who had performed outstanding feats for, and devoted their lives to, the revolution, who had given their hearts' blood to the building of socialism, angrily exposed the plots and treachery of the Cultural Revolution Group. The heat of their language, the intensity of their emotions, the blast of their fury, was blunt and sizzling, truly reflecting their outraged sense of justice.

Unfortunately, their righteous cries did not awaken Mao Zedong. On the contrary, he regarded them as interference and obstacles to what he considered a revolutionary movement he had launched personally. Mao sharply criticized this so-called "February Countercurrent". He decided to sweep away all opposition, and press forward with his "revolutionary" movement, so unprecedented, yet obviously so difficult for people to comprehend.

At a work meeting of the Central Committee convened in March, Mao again criticized Liu and Deng. He organized a "Liu Shaoqi Case Team". Its function was to investigate Liu's "crimes". As the severity of the criticisms of Liu and Deng escalated, it was clear that they — particularly Liu — would soon formally be denounced.

On April 1, *People's Daily* and the magazine *Red Flag* published an article by Qi Benyu entitled "Patriotism or Treason". It referred to "the biggest capitalist roader inside the Communist Party", and to "another biggest capitalist roader inside the Communist Party". Although the names of Liu and Deng were not spelled out, everyone knew they were the targets, and that the article heralded their dismissal from office.

It was no longer necessary to obtain permission from higher authorities to conduct an ordinary denunciation session. Anyone the rebels chose to summon could be denounced at any time. Nor did removal from office require advance approval. Higher authorities — of course that meant Lin Biao or Jiang Qing's Cultural Revolution Group — had only to drop a hint, or some rebel faction claim it necessary, and the accused could be hauled before a denunciation meeting. The session would commence, slogans would be shouted, and the accused would be "overthrown" — in other words, dismissed from office.

If however the target was a very high official in the Party or government, a formal procedure had to be instituted. That meant either the person's name had to be openly stated in a newspaper or periodical, or he had to be identified by a special appellation. Public identification of the accused was very important. Whether or not to identify, whom to identify, when to identify, how to identify — these were all reflections of status.

Describing Liu and Deng in the leading Party publications as "the biggest capitalist roaders inside the Party" signaled that the criticism of them was about to be greatly intensified.

On April 3, Papa wrote a letter to Mao Zedong. In it he said: "Since January 12, I have been hoping to see you and get your advice. But I wondered whether this would be appropriate at a time when the masses were hotly denouncing our reactionary line and its bad results. And so I hesitated. Recently, I read Comrade Qi Benyu's article. I gather that the nature of my error has already been decided. Under the circumstances, I urgently feel the need to be enlightened by you, personally. If you consider this suitable, please notify me at any time."

The letter was sent, but there was no reply. All my father could do was wait — in unfathomable danger, helplessly wait.

Rebels charged into Liu Shaoqi's home on April 6, 1967. They denounced this man the National People's Congress had elected the President of the People's Republic of China.

The next day, within a few hours, all of the posters Liu had put up in Zhongnanhai replying to charges against him, were removed.

On the 10th of the same month, the rebel faction of Tsinghua University assembled a mass meeting of 300,000 to denounce the wife of Liu Shaoqi — Wang Guangmei.

The denunciation of Liu had gone quite mad. Papa and our family prepared for the worst.

One day in May, Wang Dongxing, head of the Central Committee General Office, came to speak to Papa. He said Chairman Mao had recently returned to Beijing and directed him to relay to Papa three recommendations: 1) Be patient, don't get excited. 2) Understand that a distinction will be made between Liu and Deng. 3) Write to me directly if you feel it becomes necessary.

Papa told Wang that many of the allegations in the posters did not correspond to the facts. He requested a chance to speak to Mao. Wang relayed the request.

Not long after, late at night, when the courtyard was deep in darkness and the family was sound asleep, the phone rang in the west wing where we children slept. I stumbled to answer it. The operator said Mao's secretary wanted to speak to Secretary Wang Ruilin, but Wang was not in his office. He had no home phone, and lived near us. Could we call him to the phone?

We went over to Wang's place and escorted him to our house. A few minutes later Mao's secretary, Xu Yefu, also arrived. We lived in a villa by the side of Huairentang in Zhongnanhai. Wang and Xu went to Papa's bedroom and awakened him. They told him Chairman Mao wanted to see him.

Papa quickly got up and dressed. Xu said he wouldn't be needing his bodyguard. He and Papa went off together.

My mother was very tense. Since the start of the Cultural Revolution, and all during the criticisms of Liu and Deng, Chairman Mao had never called Papa in for a talk.

It was almost dawn before Papa returned. He told Mama the Chairman had questioned him about an incident in the 1930s when Papa had left the Seventh Red Corps and gone to Shanghai to report on his work to the Central Committee, which was then in that city. Papa responded in detail. The Chairman then reprimanded him for having sent work teams into the schools. Papa said he told the Chairman he accepted the criticism.

Papa asked whom he should contact if he had anything to report to the Chairman in the future. Mao said he could tell Wang Dongxing, or he could write to him, Mao, directly.

The Chairman's attitude had been quite warm, and his criticism had not been severe. Our family felt considerably relieved.

Provoked and supported by Lin Biao and the Jiang Qing clique, the wild charges against Liu Shaoqi grew even more serious. By September 1967, over 150 articles attacking him had appeared in newspapers and student tabloids. At the beginning of July, a rebel faction camped outside Zhongnanhai demanded that Liu write a self-criticism.

On September 13, the rebel faction of the Architectural Engineering Institute established what it called the "Summoning Liu Vanguard" outside Zhongnanhai's west gate. Encouraged by the Cultural Revolution Group, it rapidly expanded. Zhongnanhai was soon ringed by a sea of banners, written slogans, tents and command posts. Ear-shattering high-frequency loudspeakers blared forth announcements. Tens of thousands surrounded Zhongnanhai — the site of the Central Committee of the Chinese Communist Party and the State Council of the national government.

Their broadcasts demanded that the "black gangs" and the "capitalist roaders" within the national ministries and the provincial governments come forward and be denounced. They also issued, with the support of the Cultural Revolution Group, calls to assault all of the main gates of Zhongnanhai.

The criticisms of Liu Shaoqi were loud and vociferous. The criticisms of Deng Xiaoping were clearly milder. Liu was the "biggest capitalist roader". He obviously had to be overthrown first. The pressure on him was therefore greater. Mao, moreover, felt that a distinction had to be made between the two men in the disposition of the charges against them.

Mao's "proletarian rage" was directed primarily against the man he originally had designated as his successor — Liu Shaoqi. Mao found Liu unable to carry out his line of thoughts to its core. He had to replace Liu with somebody else. Liu must be purged.

As to Deng Xiaoping, although Mao's dissatisfaction with him increased in the 60s, it could not be compared with his anger against Liu. We can see from Mao's words and deeds that he always maintained a measure of appreciation for Deng. After Liu and Deng committed "errors" during the Cultural Revolution Mao criticized them both, but his spearhead was aimed mainly at Liu.

Regarding this, Deng later said: "Mao always want to 'rectify' anyone who didn't obey him. But, in each case, he weighed the degree of severity".

On July 16, 1967, after Deng was removed from office, Mao, speaking privately, told Wang Li, then a member of the Cultural Revolution Group: "If Lin Biao's health gets worse I intend to call Deng back. I'll make him at least a member of the Standing Committee of the Politburo."

There was a deeper reason why Mao distinguished between Deng and Liu: He wanted to keep Deng where he could use him again if he needed him in the future.

Papa probably didn't know this at the time. After he was denounced, and particularly after he was removed from office, he stayed at home all day. He had no work to do; no one came to see him. We children could at least leave Zhongnanhai whenever we wished. Through us he was able to obtain some news of the widespread denunciations then going on, and the ensuing widespread confusion.

Like other high leaders under charges who lived within Zhongnanhai, he was required to read the posters put up by rebel factions. But they did not insist that he write a self-criticism, as they demanded of Liu Shaoqi. Nor did they denounce and attack him with the same vehemence. Only once, when Papa was reading posters outside our house, was he surrounded by some of the "revolutionary masses" in Zhongnanhai and verbally assailed. Someone must have intervened, because the attack didn't go beyond that.

Confronted by wave after wave of criticism, implied identification in the press, all manner of attacks, slanders, and vituperous inventions, Papa read and listened, patient and forbearing. How could he be so calm?

Perhaps because as a thorough revolutionary he was without weakness or fear. Perhaps because in his more than 60 years of life he had traveled many a bumpy road. While he couldn't avoid thinking about the abnormal situation, the unjust treatment, his uncertain future, he could bear the prospect stoically.

We saw no change in Papa's usual behavior or demeanor, no difference in his spirits. He remained his usual quiet, taciturn self.

We children were teenagers then. Alarmed, confused, angry, we felt abused. But from Papa, to a greater or lesser extent, though only half-comprehending, we derived a strength which enabled us to stay on keel. Daughters and sons, we all loved Papa. We were absolutely certain he was not part of a "black gang" opposed to the Party and socialism.

The rebel faction in Zhongnanhai ordered us to expose and criticize our father. We couldn't refuse to write, but we couldn't invent something out of nothing. In the end, we three sisters penned an article and hung it up. The rebel faction said we refused to expose Papa, that we avoided the important and included only the trivial.

Posters and slogans were plastered all over Zhongnanhai. The "Summon Liu Vanguard", camped outside, was now insisting that Liu and Deng both be hailed before them and denounced together. The atmosphere was very menacing. Our family — Papa, Mama, Grandma, and we children — felt as if we were on a little craft on a bounding sea. Buffeted by wind and waves, we could only cling together. But our mutual faith and love gave us comfort and support, and put iron in our souls.

Although none of us could guess what future the criticisms would bring, the stepped-up proceedings against Liu Shaoqi warned us to be mentally prepared for a further deterioration of the situation.

6

Down with Liu, Deng, Tao!

IN 1967, the movement had already been in existence for over a year. Chairman Mao had started it, pushed its development, supported the rebellion of the "left" factions, criticized and eliminated all "reactionary" forces impeding the movement's expansion, and established new "revolutionary" governing bodies. All achieved success exceeding his expectations. If that was his goal, he should have been satisfied.

Wasn't his aim to guarantee that China would not go revisionist, to preserve forever the revolutionary spirit and a revolutionary line, to inject by revolutionary methods fresh forces into organizations, personnel, and even high governmental authority?

But, as Mao himself often said, things sooner or later turn into their opposites. From the start the movement kept accelerating, like an overloaded truck hurtling forward at full speed. Nothing in the world could resist the fierceness of its spring, the surge of its impetus. Not even Mao himself. Its rhythm, its direction, could no longer be controlled — even more so because it was an incorrect movement based on erroneous ideology and a wrong appraisal. Because of its flawed nature it could only stagger along on a twisting path beyond the will of any individual.

Mao wanted the criticisms of Liu and Deng to be different from the criticisms of Peng Zhen, Luo Ruiqing, Lu Dingyi and Yang Shangkun. This displeased Lin Biao and the Cultural Revolution Group. They wanted the immediate complete overthrow of Liu and Deng, and began preparations for huge mass denunciation meetings, intending to thereby hasten Mao's support of their approach.

41

On July 15, the Central Committee General Office submitted a request for instructions to the Cultural Revolution Group regarding proposed denunciations of Liu Shaoqi. Chen Boda, as head of the Group, put a check beside Liu's name, and added the names: "Deng, Tao and their wives."

In preparation for a mass meeting denouncing Liu Shaoqi, Jiang Qing, Kang Sheng and Chen Boda, on July 18 ordered a search of Liu's home, and decreed that he be deprived of his freedom. Our old orderly Wu Hongjun called our mother to a hallway in the rear of our house and said softly: "They searched Liu Shaoqi's place today, and went off with a whole truckload of stuff. I hear they'll be coming here tomorrow. Better get your things in order, fast!"

People today cannot imagine how frightening it was to have your house searched. If a rebel faction found something they called "criminal evidence" in the house of an innocent person it might lead to his death. Although we children had heard a lot about these searchers, we had not taken part in them ourselves, nor had we seen them in operation. After Liu Shaoqi's house was searched, we knew we had to prepare. We examined everything carefully. In those troubled times there was no limit to your trepidation. Whether or not you were being investigated it was better to check through your things again and again, and be prepared for the worst.

Our furnishings were simple, no luxuries, no special frills. Mama had a few bottles of perfume given to her by Russian friends when she was in the Soviet Union. They had never been opened. My two sisters and I took them to the bathroom and poured them down the sink, carefully opening the taps and flushing them away. The mixture of the water and the perfume must have caused some sort of chemical reaction, for the drain gurgled and spewed up a lot of white bubbles.

Looking back, the incident was laughable, and very stupid: we got rid of the perfume but kept the bottles. It wouldn't have been too bad if the rebels found bottles filled with perfume, but if they found empty bottles they could have claimed we made lavish use of perfume in a typical affluent bourgeois manner! Fortunately, the bottles escaped the search party's notice.

My greatest regret is that we destroyed photos we were afraid the rebels would seize upon as "criminal evidence". They showed various members of our family together with Peng Zhen, Luo Ruiqing and Yang Shangkun, and pictures of Mama when she was a young student at Peking University. We consigned all of them to the flames. They are gone forever.

The next day, July 19, the rebel faction in Zhongnanhai summoned Papa and Mama to Huairentang, which was next door, saying they needed to question them. After my parents left, members of the rebel faction came to our house and began to search.

They went first to my father's office and his reception room, then to our living quarters. They searched high and low, but found nothing.

Papa took no notes at meetings, or any place else, ordinarily. He never wrote out his speeches in advance. At most he jotted a few words on a slip of paper. He did write on documents issued to him, inscribing his comments and handing the documents to his secretary to be returned the same day he received them. He retained no documents. His office was always clean and neat. Except for a few books, there was nothing in it.

A half-day's search produced not even a straw for the rebel faction. "Not a single note," the searchers fumed. "How can a General Secretary operate that way!"

They couldn't leave with absolutely nothing. So they came to where we children lived. Again a thorough search ended in failure.

My brother Feifei was home that day. They asked him what he was doing. He said he was reading *Journey to the West* (a Chinese classical novel). In fact, he had in his pocket the cards my father played bridge with. Luckily, they didn't search Feifei or they would have discovered criminal evidence — Deng Xiaoping's playing cards! (I remember one poster which listed among Papa's "crimes": "He liked to play bridge and enjoy himself.")

The rebel faction demanded that we produce our money and our deposit books. They thought our family was rich. It never occurred to them that because we had a large family with lots of expenses, we didn't have a penny put away, in fact we owed the Office 200 yuan we had borrowed. Instead of unearthing evidence of Deng Xiaoping's corrupt life-style, the rebels had to leave empty-handed.

The house search meant that Papa was formally "overthrown". On July 29, "revolutionary masses" in Zhongnanhai in the name of his Party branch denounced Papa, and gave him three days within which to present a "request for punishment". It announced that from that day on, Papa and Mama had lost their freedom of movement.

The slanders and denunciations were more than Papa could bear. He wrote a letter to Wang Dongxing as follows:

"You are no doubt aware of the meeting of my Party branch this morning. In addition, the Foreign Languages Institute wants me to hand in a confession before July 30. My Party branch has given me three days. It is only reasonable that I should request instructions from Chairman Mao and the Central Committee on how to deal with such matters. Phoning you is not convenient. I enclose a letter to Chairman Mao asking to see him. Please forward it for me."

In his letter to Mao Zedong, Papa said: "When we met in May, Chairman, you said I could write to you directly if it became necessary. This morning, July 29, Party branches in several organizations held meetings at which they exposed and denounced me for errors and crimes. They ordered me to submit requests for punishment within three days, and thoroughly reveal how I committed the crimes of opposing the Party, socialism, Mao Zedong Thought, and Chairman Mao. They also imposed certain restrictions on me. I am truly at a loss as to what to do. I sincerely hope for a chance to seek your instructions personally. I know this request may not be appropriate, but I have no other way to express the feelings in my heart. If you are too busy, Chairman, perhaps some other comrade can come and talk with me."

Mao Zedong did not receive Deng Xiaoping again. It was already impossible to divert the surge to overthrow Deng.

On August 1, Papa's secretary Wang Ruilin, and his bodyguard Zhang Baozhong, were both transferred. A new "secretary" was dispatched.

The first thing he did was to summon Mama to his office. A slogan on the wall read: "Leniency to those who confess; strictness to those who refuse." The "secretary" sternly demanded that Mama expose my father.

"Comrade Xiaoping never tells the family anything about his work, or regarding Party matters," Mama said. "I know nothing about them. As to documents, the ones that require immediate attention he disposes of the same day. The rest he sends back to the General Office. If you want to see them, you can look at them there."

Clearly the "secretary" couldn't fish anything out of Mama. He brought his inquisition to an end.

The searches were over. The next step was the denunciation meetings.

On August 5, to celebrate the first anniversary of Mao Zedong's poster "Bombard the Headquarters", Xie Fuzhi and Qi Benyu went to the "Summon Liu Vanguard" and proposed that the rebels assemble a huge mass denunciation meeting on Tiananmen Square. At the same time they urged the rebel factions in Zhongnanhai, site of the Central Committee and the State Council, to organize criticism and denunciation sessions against Liu Shaoqi, Deng Xiaoping and Tao Zhu.

Today, more than 30 years later, I remember the situation very well. Our family already knew what was coming, and we were ready. Mama instructed us children not to leave the house, no matter what happened.

The Zhongnanhai rebels swarmed into our home. They took Papa and Mama out to the garden and surrounded them. Rebels pushed their heads down and forced them to bend at the waist, demanding that they confess. Roars of "Down with them!" shook the air. A string of shouted accusations followed, and a babel of voices yelled questions. I remember it clearly. During the meeting, a girl rebel, who had been brought in from Shanghai to work in the Central Committee Secretariat, screeched in a voice that was piercingly shrill.

Mama's eyeglasses had been removed. With her head down, she tried to steal a glance at Papa, but she couldn't see clearly. Papa was rather deaf. Standing half-bent, he could hardly hear anything, and could answer none of the questions. He tried to offer an explanation, but the words were barely out of his mouth when he was rudely interrupted. The rebels said he had a bad attitude, that he was feigning ignorance to avoid replying. Again there was a clamor of shouts and criticisms.

The rebels had rigged up a loudspeaker in the garden, and were broadcasting the proceedings at the mass denunciation meeting in Tiananmen Square, to let Papa and Mama hear.

My two sisters and I were in our room, pressed close to the window curtains. My sisters' hearts were in their throats when they heard the wild shouts. They didn't dare look at the cruel scene. I stood on the table and peeked out through an opening between the curtains. I said I wanted to see; I wanted to see it all, to engrave it in my memory forever!

When the denunciation session ended, Mama helped Papa back to the house. He was very pale. I quickly poured him a glass of water and took him by the arm to lie down and rest. Thus ended that day's noisy confusion.

I heard later that our ordeal was relatively "civilized". The sessions against Liu and Tao were much crueler. Liu Shaoqi was savagely beaten.

After the denunciation session, and the house having been searched, it could truly be said that Papa had been completely "overthrown."

My parents were under virtual house arrest. Although we children could continue to live at home we were not allowed into the north wing where they lived. Fortunately, there were no rebels camped in our compound, and we frequently managed to slip into our parents' quarters.

Papa, though quiet, silent, unsmiling, showed not a shred of agitation or dismay. Thanks to his steadiness, none of us was particularly discouraged, though we seldom left the house. We were aware that many of the people we knew were much worse off. It sounds strange to say, but compared to them we had no complaints.

Some things that happened in our most difficult period our family will always remember.

We lived near Huairentang in a small lane containing the homes of four families from north to south. Li Fuchun was in the first, Tan Zhenlin was in the second, we were in the third, and Chen Yi was in the fourth. All were old Army veterans, old comrades. Our relations were very close. The children grew up together, and played together like brothers and sisters.

After the Cultural Revolution broke out, with its plethora of posters and slogans, every one of the families was kept busy answering charges, and had no time to be concerned about anyone else. We were even less inclined to go out after Papa was dismissed. We didn't want to meet people.

One day my big sister Deng Lin and I walked to the end of the lane, and saw Uncle Chen Yi and his bodyguard coming toward us. We guessed from his depressed expression that he had just been reading posters. We hadn't seen him in a long time. He was much thinner. The infectious smile we had known since childhood was gone. But he still stood ramrod straight. We knew he had been charged with involvement in the "February Countercurrent". We didn't want to get him implicated in our troubles as well, and deliberately avoided him.

His eyes lit up when he saw us. His frown vanished. Calling our names, he strode over. He bent from the waist, as if in a bow.

"Is everybody well?"

We were stunned for a moment. Then we realized who he was referring to. My eyes filled with tears,

"We're all fine," I quickly replied.

"That's good, that's good," Uncle Chen Yi said.

Again his face fell. He walked slowly deeper into the lane.

We were very moved. We didn't know this was the last time we would see Uncle Chen Yi alive.

Another time, our orderly Old Wu came back. He gave Mama a pack of cigarettes for Papa. He said he had met Young Kong, Li Fuchun's bodyguard in the lane. After looking around to make sure no one was near, Young Kong slipped him the cigarettes. "Comrade Fuchun says they're for Comrade Xiaoping," he whispered.

When Mama and Papa saw the cigarettes, they didn't say anything for a long time. In days of trouble, their old comrades had not forgotten them! A year earlier Papa had sent Peng Zhen oranges. Today, Li Fuchun sent cigarettes to Deng Xiaoping. How the world had changed.

A little more than a month later, on September 13, Old Wu suddenly came rushing in. He said Liu Shaoqi's children had been driven out of their home, driven out of Zhongnanhai! The three middle school students were allowed to take one bedroll each and a bicycle, and were forced to return to their schools. The maid was given charge of the little girl who was in primary school and compelled to take her away. Old Wu urged us to prepare.

Only Deng Nan and I were at home then. We talked it over with Mama and agreed: We would not be driven out as the Liu children were. If we had to go, we would all go to the same place. Our old Grandma, Papa's stepmother, lived with us. If we children had to move to our schools, what would happen to her? She had been with us since Liberation. At her age we couldn't leave her with nowhere to go. Liu Shaoqi's children were younger than we were. Driving them away was brutal. We couldn't be like them. We couldn't let others manipulate our lives!

Our minds made up, we steeled ourselves for whatever would come.

Before long people from the rebel faction and the Central Committee General Office came. In an ugly manner they ordered us to return to school, and ordered Grandma to go back to her village. They gave us two hours to "get out of Zhongnanhai!"

Papa and Mama, under house arrest in their rooms, could not come out, but my sister and I argued with the rebels: "We'll leave, but you have to find us a place to live. We absolutely refuse to return to school. Grandma can't go back to her village. There's no one there to look after her. Do you want her to die? You'll have to tie us up and drag us away, otherwise we won't go!"

The rebels shouted, we shouted back. They got tough, we got tougher. We yelled with all our might, tears streaming down our cheeks. Unable to do anything with us, the rebels left temporarily.

And then we really wept, crying aloud. All of the unhappiness we had felt, all of the anger we had suppressed since the day Papa was criticized, plus our latest misery over the impending separation from our parents, now gushed forth in an irrepressible flood.

48

Since leaving was inevitable, we phoned Big Sister Deng Lin to come home from school. We girls began going through our things in the west wing. Mama got busy in the north rooms. We examined every nook and cranny. Every time Mama found anything useful, she gave it to us. She and Papa wanted us to take along everything we could carry.

In the end, we won. The rebels notified us they had found two rooms in a one-storey building near Zhongnanhai. They ordered us to "clear out" within two hours.

Each of us, in turn, slipped into the north wing to say goodbye to our parents. Mama hastily brought more things from her room and gave them to us. There were tears in her eyes. When she handed me something, her hands felt burning hot.

Papa was in a corridor in the rear. I quickly kissed him and left. We children were his greatest love. I didn't dare look at him too long. I knew that he was strong, fearless, that he rarely showed joy or anger. But to be separated from the children who had been constantly at his side, perhaps never see them again, would be an enormous blow. No political misfortune could floor him. But could he withstand a final separation from his loved ones?

7

The Chill of Autumn

THAT autumn, in September 1967, we left our parents, left the home we had lived in for 10 years in Zhongnanhai.

From then on our parents led an enclosed existence, cut off from the outside world. We children began lives that were entirely new to us. We knew the road ahead was far from smooth. In Zhongnanhai we had been sheltered in a secluded lane. Now we were cast into a harsh world, vulnerable and open to hardships, unable to dodge, with no place to hide.

In the two years which followed, the two "biggest capitalist roaders" Liu Shaoqi and Deng Xiaoping were kept under house arrest in their homes in Zhongnanhai. Because Mao Zedong made a distinction between them, Deng's situation was somewhat easier.

Liu was held in Zhongnanhai, but his wife Wang Guangmei was locked up in prison. Her servants were exchanged for jailors. Liu Shaoqi — elected by the National People's Congress, China's top legislature, as President of the People's Republic of China according to the State Constitution — was very ill. After endless torments, he finally passed away. He died a miserable death in Henan Province, in the city of Kaifeng.

Deng Xiaoping, although restricted to our house, was never separated from Mama. In difficult times remaining with your loved one is the greatest boon. As long as Papa and Mama had each other, they didn't care how savagely Papa was overthrown and denounced — they could always give each other comfort and support.

Papa's secretary was long since gone. The rebels sent someone else — I don't know what his title was supposed to be. Actually he was a kind of warden.

We never had many in help in our house. Papa's bodyguard and driver had been removed, but our cook Yang Weiyi and our orderly Wu Hongjun were allowed to stay. They had both been with us over 10 years. Although they were compelled to criticize the "capitalist roader" and declare a class distinction between him and them, they and our family were quite attached to each other. They were able to look after Papa and Mama, and the house was less lonely with them around.

Old Wu was especially helpful. He came from our old home in Sichuan. Although he was uneducated and didn't understand politics, even he learned a lot about them in this so-called Cultural Revolution. Whenever he heard anything he felt important, he would wait until no one was around, and then go to the rear corridor and tell my mother about it secretly. In this way our parents, supposedly cut off from the outside world, could occasionally get a bit of news.

While still subjected himself to noisy denunciations, Papa was sometimes asked by rebel factions to write appraisals of other individuals. That meant the persons in question were being investigated and denounced. It angered Papa to see old comrades and fellow battle veterans subjected to unjust treatment. He always did his best to clear their names.

Three rebel factions from the Ministry of Health demanded to know why he highly rated Dr. Qian Xinzhong, the Minister they had overthrown. On November 3, 1967 Papa wrote this statement:

"Qian Xinzhong worked closely with our Second Field Army for a long time. We, and I in particular, trusted him. We felt he was quite competent in organizing health work. The surgery he performed under those difficult conditions was first-rate. He worked very hard, especially when doing rescue work on the battlefield. I always felt he had a lot of small faults, but was good on big matters, and earned merit in battle. Premier (Zhou Enlai) proposed that he be appointed Minister of Health, and discussed it with me. I approved. I had no secret scheme with An Ziwen (then head of the Organization Department of the Central Committee) regarding this."

Papa's endorsement showed his sympathy and support for comrades who were being persecuted.

Those who had been denounced and overthrown were compelled to do punishing labor in the name of rectification. Some rebel factions used this as a means of hurting and torturing people.

Confined to our own home, Papa and Mama hadn't really much to do. At first, the rebels ordered them to cook their own meals, but after two days, they called it off. Probably it occurred to them it wasn't a good idea to let a "capitalist roader" have access to implements like knives.

Finally, they ordered Mama to sweep the courtyard. At first, she did it alone. But then Papa got a broom and swept with her. For two years, every day, wind or rain, hot or cold, they methodically swept. In their lonely restricted environment, they were glad to have even this light work to keep them occupied. But no matter how carefully they swept, it didn't last long. The rest of the time they could only stay in their room and read books and newspapers, or listen to the radio, or just sit in silence.

In order to economize, for two years they added no new clothes. Papa had a cashmere sweater, given to him by a friend, who had been working in the underground in Shanghai, just after the city was liberated. He had worn it for 20 years, and there were big holes in the elbows.

What to do? Mama knew how to mend woolen garments. She found some heavy yarn nearly the same color and separated it into threads as fine as cashmere. Then, with a needle and this thread, she wove patches. They looked the same as the original. If you didn't know, you wouldn't have been able to tell the difference. She did the same with the frayed cuffs and edges. The sweater looked as good as new.

Papa wore it for a long time. Later, even when he was given a new one, he hated to change. Of course, it now wasn't in order to save; it was because every stitch of the old sweater reminded him of those long days in confinement.

In the evenings the courtyard was silent and dark. Only a dim light glowed in the empty rooms. Papa sat quietly smoking. Mama at first only watched him, then she too took up smoking. As a saving, she collected his half-smoked cigarettes. Papa urged her to quit. He knew she had a bad heart.

"You already have the habit worse than I," he said. "How are you going to cope?"

"I smoke because I'm thinking of the children," said Mama. "The minute I can see them again, I'll quit."

Their isolation was difficult for them but, fortunately, they didn't have to suffer the torments inflicted on other "capitalist roaders". It was not good luck which kept Papa from being mistreated. The decision was Mao Zedong's. In fact you might say it was one of Mao's political provisions.

When Deng Xiaoping was denounced and overthrown, he was protected by Mao, both physically and politically. During the time Papa was under restraint, Mao had put Wang Dongxing, whom he trusted, in charge. He did not let Lin Biao or the Cultural Revolution Group intervene.

On November 5, 1967, when members of the Cultural Revolution Group were discussing the Ninth Party National Congress and Party rectification, Mao apparently lumped Liu and Deng together.

"Liu and Deng cooperated," he said. "The Eighth Party National Congress resolution was adopted without first passage by the presidium, and without asking my opinion. In 1963 we promoted a Ten Provisions program. Only three months later they held another meeting and put out a 'Post Ten Provisions', again without asking my opinion. I wasn't at the meeting. Deng Xiaoping must be criticized. Let the Military Commission please prepare a document."

Yet, at the same time, Mao said: "My idea is that he should be distinguished from Liu Shaoqi. Their cases must be treated separately."

Just that one statement, but it was of deep significance. Superficially, it determined the fate of Liu and Deng. But underneath, it involved numerous, and very complicated, questions.

Mao Zedong had designated Lin Biao his successor. At public functions Lin always followed close behind him. But elsewhere, or in private sessions, Mao never manifested any intimacy with Lin Biao.

Why? He knew that Lin didn't get along with Deng Xiaoping, yet he insisted on protecting Deng. What for? He treated Liu and Deng differently. Was that only because Deng's "question" wasn't as serious as Liu's? Lin Biao was at the height of his revolutionary "redness". What was Mao thinking? Was he preparing something new? Mao's mind was as deep as the sea — and just as unfathomable.

Mao predicted that 1967 would witness a vast class struggle throughout the land. And the events of that year were indeed many, and swift, and chaotic.

After the power grab by rebel groups in January, and the "countercurrent" in February, a tide of "seize the traitors" spread across the land. Countless innocent people were slandered and condemned. In April, the press greatly upped the level of denunciations against Liu and Deng — particularly against Liu Shaoqi.

Lin Biao, in July, called for arresting "the small clique inside the Army". Many officers were overthrown. That same month Jiang Qing cried: "attack peaceably, defend by force". This led to a sudden escalation nationwide of the brawls among the factions and a large increase in bloody clashes. In August, at the instigation of the Cultural Revolution Group, rebel factions set fire to the British legation in Beijing, and created a number of other international incidents.

By then, leaders at every level, including all ranks of the Army, had been ousted. The Communist Party and government organizations were paralyzed. Rebel factions fought among themselves. Large bloody battles constantly erupted. Industry and agriculture suffered severe setbacks, production continued to fall. The whole country was in a state of turmoil and civil war.

From July to September, Mao Zedong made a tour of North China, and the South-Central and East China areas. He was not in the least alarmed by what he saw. In fact, he said: "China's Great Proletarian Cultural Revolution is not merely pretty good, it's in excellent shape....Some places, in the early stage, were chaotic. But it was a chaos against the enemy, it served to temper the masses."

Mao thought he saw his prediction coming true, that he was truly witnessing "great chaos under Heaven". And as long as there was chaos, it should be a thorough chaos, a chaos that turned the universe upside-down.

He once analyzed himself thus: "There is a tiger quality in me; that is my main quality. I also have a monkey quality, but that is secondary."

The tiger quality was imperial, tyrannical. The monkey quality was pugnacious, rebellious. The blend of those qualities in Mao Zedong gave him a dual personality. He was both a ruler and a rebel who used his role as a rebel to attain a new imperial realm. No one, be it in ancient or modern times, in China or abroad, ever matched his unusual character and methods in the creation and pursuit of his ideal of "continuous" revolution.

Mao Zedong was a great man, a powerful figure for all times. His thoughts and deeds cannot be discussed in the same manner as those of an ordinary person. Perhaps that is one of the reasons for the huge gaps which constantly appeared between his ideals and their realization.

8

A Lonely Craft on a Bounding Sea

O<small>F</small> the many families assailed during the Cultural Revolution, ours was not the hardest hit. My parents were certainly not pampered, since they were political figures, principals on the political stage. The ups and downs in the political situation were their normal milieu. In a way, it was harder for us children. We were only teenagers. To be suddenly plunged from our simple schoolroom existence into the depths of being insulted and denounced was indeed a severe trial.

The Central Committee General Office found us a place outside Xuanwumen in the southeast part of Beijing. It was in a compound at a small lane called Fanghuzhai (Square Kettle Studio). It contained a few simple one-storey dwellings and a small building said to have been erected during the Japanese occupation. We were given two rooms in the building, in the deepest part of the building. Workers from Zhongnanhai lived in the rest of the area, plus a few families of General Office cadres accused of having committed "errors".

Grandma and my kid brother Feifei slept in one room. We three sisters and a girl cousin who was going to school in Beijing occupied the other.

The building was very dilapidated. The floorboards squeaked when you stepped on them. Only a thin wall separated our rooms from the ones next-door. We could plainly hear our neighbor every time he coughed.

Water was drawn from a tap in the courtyard. Toilets were in the lane outside. We bought a stove and put it in our hallway. It burned coal, ignited by wood shavings that emitted lots of smoke. On this, Grandma cooked our first meal in our new home.

We considered ourselves very lucky — lucky because we weren't forced to live in our schools, as Liu Shaoqi's children were, lucky because we had a place to rest, a home to return to. Crude as it was, it hadn't come easy, we had to fight for it.

Settled in at last, when night fell and all was still, we lay crowded together on our wooden bed, unable to sleep. We thought of our father, we thought of our mother. We knew they too were unable to sleep, they surely were thinking of us.

Whatever else you might say about our place in Zhongnanhai, it was a kind of "ivory tower". Here in Fanghuzhai we definitely were part of the real world.

All the residents in our compound were General Office workers and employees and their families. Word must have come down from above, and they were quite nice to us. When we just arrived, many asked whether we needed anything, was there anything we were short of? We were given a few scallions, a bit of soy sauce.

Fresh from Zhongnanhai, the place looked old and run-down to us. But workers and their families had always lived in places like this. They didn't feel there was anything wrong with it. We began to see that this was how the ordinary people lived. Their wages were very low — around 20 yuan per month. Forty, at most. And that often had to support a family of three generations. Many of the wives and children pasted cardboard boxes, or matchboxes, to help make ends meet. Some families had no beds. A few boards laid across two long benches made do for one big bed for everybody.

Meals consisted of cornmeal muffins and salted turnips. Fried soy sauce noodles with a bit of shredded meat were a treat. Clothes were covered with patches. They were fortunate if they had enough to wear to ward off the cold.

What had we to complain about? We had no right to be dissatisfied.

We learned to live like the ordinary worker families in our compound. We drew water from the spigot in the yard. We used the public toilets in the lane. We handed in ration coupons to buy grain at the grain store, and showed our ration booklet at the coal depot to buy coal. At holiday time, we queued with the others to buy *mu er* (edible black fungus), and *huang hua* (edible day lily), and five-flavor condiments. Once a week, we rose at four or five in the morning and lined up in the vegetable market for bean curd. When word came to the courtyard that the meat market was selling soup bones, we hurried with the others to buy our share.

We adapted quickly to this kind of life. People are all the same. As long as you have no conflict in your heart, you can always get along, you can adjust to anything. That was how the workers survived. Compared to them, we were "prosperous".

Nominally, our parents were still being paid their salaries. Actually, it was entrusted to their Communist Party units. They had to make a request each time they wanted to draw any money.

Those of us living on the outside had no source of income. The General Office decided that each child should be given 25 yuan per month for expenses. Grandma received only 20. The money was deducted from our parents' salaries. We had to go to the West Gate of Zhongnanhai every month to pick up our "pay".

Mama knew we were having difficulties, and she kept finding excuses to get us a little more money. She told the General Office we needed padded clothes for the winter, or that we didn't have enough quilts and had to buy more, or that a growing boy had a big appetite — he needed more grain coupons. Every month she managed to eke out something extra. Whether money or grain coupons, every little bit helped.

Second Sister Deng Nan and I went to the West Gate every month at the appointed time to draw our grain coupons and money. Sometimes we found folded within the wad of cash Mama's handwritten list of items or a notation slip. Seeing Mama's familiar, elegant writing was like touching her warm loving hands. How we missed her!

We grew bolder as time went on. We would ask for a bit more money and, most important, we would demand books from the library room in our old home. At first, the men at the gate ignored us. Deng Nan and I argued with them loudly. We refused to leave. They didn't know what to do with us. We weren't afraid, we dared to stand up against them.

With Mama on the inside of Zhongnanhai, and us on the outside, cooperating, we not only obtained additional money and grain, we also were able to take away many of our books. These books later stayed with us for many lonely days and nights. For two years we were able by these indirect means to maintain at least some slight contact.

Here, I want especially to talk about my Grandma.

Her name was Xia Bogen. She was our father's stepmother, the mother of my two aunts, the daughter of an old boatman on the Jialing River in Sichuan. After she married my grandfather she became our family's sole working force and support. She was famous for miles around for her capability. She could cook, do farm work, make clothes, and raise pigs and chicken. Grandpa died early, leaving her to look after a large family.

Under Kuomintang rule, she was known as "part of that Communist family". She concealed the revolutionary books Papa shipped back home, protected the wounded from the Communist guerrilla band in the Huaying Mountains in Sichuan, and supported her daughter's local Communist underground activities. One thing she was sure of — the Communist Party was good.

In 1949, the moment Sichuan was liberated Grandma packed a bedroll, locked the door, left the village, and headed for us in Chongqing. From then on she was a major member of our household. She was of enormous help to Mama, who was busy with outside duties. Mama turned all the household affairs over to her.

Grandma raised me and my kid brother Feifei. Later, she also brought up the four children of my two aunts. She also cooked, and made our shoes and clothes. Grandma had small bound feet. She had no education, and couldn't read. But she was very intelligent, and could calculate sums accurately. Every day she listened to the news broadcasts. She knew all about domestic and international affairs.

When we were a little older, she taught us girls how to stitch a hem and sew on buttons, to salt turnips and pickle vegetables, to do many, many other household chores. Imperceptibly, over time, we absorbed more knowledge from Grandma than I can say. Raising all those kids, handling so many of the household duties. As Papa and Mama often said, Grandma was our family's "Major General".

Expelled from Zhongnanhai, separated from our parents, yet in our misfortune we had the greatest good luck, namely, we still had Grandma. She came from a working family, and had a hard time half her life. She had been through everything. Nothing frightened her, nothing fazed her. Although Grandma didn't understand politics, she was not upset by the big changes and turmoil going on all around. When the neighborhood committee denounced her in our Fanghuzhai compound, she silently listened to their curses and insults, unperturbed. Grandma was tough. She had only one thought in mind: "I've got to see how all this ends!" Having her, we children — particularly me and Feifei — had a solid anchor. She made it relatively easy for us to withstand our trials.

Around us were many other "black gang" children who also had been driven from their homes. They had no one to look after them, had no experience. They couldn't light a stove and cook, they didn't know how to handle money. They'd eat one meal, and miss the next. They couldn't patch their clothes. The rooms of some of them were so dilapidated and dirty they looked like dog kennels. We always had Grandma to fall back on.

Grandma was not only our bastion in daily life, she was our staunchest spiritual pillar. Without Grandma, how could we have survived so well? Where would our first meal have come from after being kicked out of Zhongnanhai?

Grandma had a warm, generous heart. Besides looking after us, she was very kind to Luo Ruiqing's three children, and Ulanhu's little daughters. They all loved Grandma. With no home of their own, they sometimes came to see us, or stay a few days. She always fed them. Grandma was everybody's Grandma.

Our parents sent us expense money whenever possible. Because we didn't know how long the situation would last, or what was coming next, we had to watch our pennies. Grandma was a great cook, and knew how to economize. We had no meat, and little oil, but our food was always fragrant with her home-made condiments.

Feifei and I, living together with Grandma, had a fairly peaceful existence. Big Brother and my two older sisters had to move back to college to face criticism under supervision. Their lives were not so pleasant.

Big Sister Deng Lin was locked up by the rebel faction of the Central Academy of Fine Arts. Any time anything happened inside the Academy or out, regardless of whether she was connected with it in any way, she would be brought out and denounced. When someone else was denounced, she was required to "accompany" the accused.

Deng Lin is an honest person. Under questioning and hectoring she never argued back. On one thing she was firm — if she didn't know, she said so, and stuck to it. The rebels subjected her to "rectification through labor" — she was made to clean all the women's toilets, without any help. Every day she left them spotless.

She was very homesick, and she worried about Grandma and her younger brother and sisters. Every time I went to see her, she plied me with questions, trying to make our talks last, hating to see me go.

At college, the rebels limited the freedom of Big Brother, Pufang. He wasn't allowed to go home. He missed us, and arranged with Second Sister, Deng Nan, who was also a student at Peking University, to meet secretly every Sunday beside Weiming (Nameless) Lake. It was also on campus. They would meet at night, when it was dark and few people were around, after escaping from the vigilance of the rebel faction. There they would exchange news and views.

Brother knew a lot about history and politics, and was quite sensitive to what was going on. He told Sister at length his analyses of the situation. She was allowed to leave the school and go home, and so she was able to tell him something of the outside news. They don't remember how many times they met at Weiming Lake, but they both say that from childhood to this day there was never a time when their thinking was more in harmony.

Although Deng Nan was criticized at college, the rebel faction allowed her to come home on weekends. She was a good math student, and knew how to keep accounts. She took full charge of our finances at Fanghuzhai. In the two years we lived there, she handled all of the main problems of us younger children.

She would pick up some things on the way home from school. Fruit was too expensive, and she would look for bargains, like bananas that were just starting to spoil. She was delighted when she could "take the edge off our cravings". Once she saw some old boards, and bought several big ones. It was a long walk home. She was exhausted and panting by the time she got to Fanghuzhai. But those old boards really came in handy. Later, Big Brother made a small stand for crockery out of them.

Feifei and I were around sixteen or seventeen. With Grandma looking after our daily needs, and Second Sister managing our money, we had few livelihood problems. We spent most of the day at home, reading. Outside, everything was chaotic. People far and near knew we were the "whelps" of Deng Xiaoping. Whenever we ventured out, we might be sworn at, or stoned. We were lucky if we got off with a detailed censure.

Because of this, we preferred to stay at home. It was quiet, and we could read. We devoured any book we could get hold of. We read a great many. Our schools were not conducting classes. We studied the textbooks ourselves. Feifei was in second year junior high when the Cultural Revolution began. He liked science. He finished studying the texts for junior high and started on the senior high books. He was crazy about *weiqi* or *go* chess. He used to spread the plastic sheet marked out as a chessboard on the bed, place the pieces, and try different maneuvers against himself. He would exult softly whenever one worked successfully.

I liked the arts better than the sciences. Anything on literature, history and politics — I read. I plunged heart and soul into the sea of knowledge. It didn't matter what the season of the year. In our little enclave at Fanghuzhai, Grandma's care and older brother's and sisters' help made us immune to poverty and hardship. All we wanted was to live in peace.

But where could you find a quiet refuge during the madness of the Cultural Revolution? Rebels, when they heard that members of Deng Xiaoping's family lived here, came, uninvited, many times. Why? If not to criticize then to search the house. They wanted to overthrow Deng Xiaoping. If they couldn't find him in person, they could vent their spleen on his children. They barged in at any hour of the day or night. Shouting slogans and denunciations, they forced us "whelps" to stand with our heads bowed. Not even our old grandmother, then nearly 70, was spared. They shoved her and yelled insults.

Whenever they came they ransacked the house, turning everything upside-down, throwing things on the floor, stamping on them, as proof of their "rebellious spirit". They plastered the walls with slogans and posters, and usually smashed some glass before they triumphantly departed, still shouting slogans.

When they first started coming, we couldn't suppress our fury, and even argued with them. One time Feifei trembled with rage at their savage behavior. He demanded they pick up the things they had thrown on the floor. A "whelp" of the "black gang" had dared to resist! Several big brutes wearing red armbands menacingly closed in on Feifei. He stood defiantly, his face flushed red. I rushed over and threw my arms around him, weeping loudly. The rebels saw that neighbors were gathering around the house. They cursed Feifei roundly, but they didn't strike him.

Looking back, I realize we barely escaped disaster. They could easily have beaten Feifei to death. Life was cheap during the Cultural Revolution, particularly among the children of the "black gang". Later, after many searches, we got used to them. We didn't argue with the rebels, we didn't protest. After they left, we would look at the wreckage, and the posters and slogans all over the walls. Gradually we would put our belongings back in place, and tear down the posters and slogans. Our hearts were miserable, and chilled, and filled with hatred for the rebel factions.

While we younger children were open to frequent raids at home, Big Brother Deng Pufang, and older sisters Deng Lin and Deng Nan in their schools were subjected to endless demands for self-criticism and "exposure" of Papa. We were the family of the "Second Biggest Capitalist-Roader" in China; we were the blackest of the black, "children of the black gang". We could be denounced and cursed with impunity. There was no talk of humanity or reason where we were concerned.

All of this we suffered in silence. Little did we know that greater misfortune still lay ahead.

Autumn of 1967 came and went like any other autumn. Spring goes and autumn comes; autumn goes and is followed by winter. Nature's steps proceed in an orderly manner. Nature has its fixed rules, beyond the control of any man. Why doesn't human society have laws and regulations that ought to be respected, that must be respected? Surely it wasn't meant to be completely without bounds, so full of disorder and strife? Why can't we have peaceful days?

Why, in the midst of turmoil, do some people show themselves so weak and worthless? Why is that the justice, humanity, fairness, and respect that humans believe in and talk so much about, can at one blow be smashed to smithereens? Why have the creeds and codes established by human society itself become pallid and flabby?

A crack of winter light could be seen in the high compound wall close behind our dim rooms in Fanghuzhai. North wind whistled through it against our battered wooden window. Dressed in padded tunics and trousers, we huddled around our small stove. I was reading. Feifei was learning how to make a radio. Grandma, bifocals perched on her nose, was stitching and mending. The coalballs in our stove burned cherry-red. The only sound was the hissing of the kettle. That little stove produced a lot of heat, bringing warmth into our trouble world.

1967 thus departed. 1968 thus arrived.

Winter was long, and cold. The days were frigid, and so were our hearts. We longed for winter quickly to pass, for spring to come soon.

And come it did, calm and unhurried. It was typical northern early spring. The biting north winds were gone, but the grass was not getting green, and the sprouts had not emerged. The space between heaven and earth was still. A spring chill continued to seep into human breasts.

9

The "Deng Xiaoping Case Team"

On March 5, 1968, Zhou Enlai, Chen Boda, Kang Sheng, Jiang Qing, Yao Wenyuan, Yang Chengwu, Xie Fuzhi, Ye Qun, Wu Faxian, and Wang Dongxing sent a report to Mao Zedong and Lin Biao saying there was no depository for a mass of material exposing Deng Xiaoping. They proposed that a sub-team be established under the existing "He Long Case Team" to receive the material about Deng Xiaoping's "question". Mao noted his consent. Lin Biao indicated his agreement with a circle.

That marked the formal creation of the "Deng Xiaoping Case Team".

A "Liu Shaoqi Case Team" had come into existence a year earlier. The formation of a special team for Deng at this time indicated that Mao agreed to intensify the investigation of Deng Xiaoping.

The Deng Team convened a meeting in the Great Hall of the People on May 16. Kang Sheng, big wheel in the Cultural Revolution Group, and Huang Yongsheng and Wu Faxian, activists in the Lin Biao gang, were in charge of the proceedings. Kang Sheng was the principal speaker. He said they couldn't directly adjudicate Deng's question, but they could conduct a thorough search for evidence.

According to Kang Sheng: Deng's history still was not clear. He ran when the old Seventh Red Corps was faced with battle; he was passive in the opposition to Wang Ming during the Yan'an Rectification; he was on good terms with Peng Dehuai; he pushed the Wang Ming line in the Taihang Mountains; he promoted the Three Unities and One Deletion policy while in Moscow in 1962. In brief: historically, Deng Xiaoping enforced the Wang Ming line; organizationally, he stood for surrender and treachery; militarily, he tried to usurp the army and oppose the Party.

Kang Sheng's speech gave the Deng Xiaoping Case Team a boost, and set the tone of its operations. Later, it was expanded in size to nine members.

It was weird. Within the Party Deng was accused of being the "Second Biggest Capitalist Roader". Yet his case team was only a subsidiary of the He Long Case Team. There was really no end of inexplicable situations during the Cultural Revolution.

Deng didn't know about the formation of his case team. On May 21 he wrote a letter to Wang Dongxing requesting an opportunity to see Chairman Mao or, if that wasn't possible, to see Wang. Wang delivered the letter. Mao directed that it be read aloud and discussed at a meeting of the Cultural Revolution Group on May 23. Mao said he wanted the opinions of "everyone" as to whether he should speak with Deng. Of course it was impossible that an "everyone" embracing Lin Biao and the Cultural Revolution Leading Group would agree. Deng's request was turned down.

Deng Xiaoping had already been overthrown, yet Mao asked "everyone" to discuss his request. It showed that Mao hadn't forgotten Deng and, to a certain extent, was still concerned about him. To Lin Biao and Jiang Qing and their ilk, this wasn't good news at all.

Yes, Mao consistently intended to treat the criticisms of Liu and Deng differently. It was a significant decision reached after deep thought. Lin Biao, Chen Boda, Jiang Qing and the other stalwarts of the Cultural Revolution Group were dissatisfied, and not a little worried. Girding their forces for battle, they ordered the Deng Case Team to speed up its search for evidence, and nail the proof against Deng iron-solid.

With beating drums and clashing cymbals the team swung into action. They probed everywhere with the greatest "work enthusiasm", even requesting permission from the Organization Department of the Communist Party to review Deng's documents. What they found wasn't nearly enough to establish guilt.

Moreover, the Central Committee wouldn't let them directly adjudicate. What could they do? Finally, they hit upon a plan: Deng Xiaoping had to write his life history, starting from the age of eight. The history would have to comply with the following conditions: It would be detailed, specific, and accurate, contain a list of witnesses of each stage of his life, including their present addresses, and be submitted piecemeal as each section was completed. The whole history had to be handed in by the beginning of July, at the latest.

Huang Yongsheng approved the plan, and Wang Dongxing, head of the Central Committee General Office, transmitted it to Deng Xiaoping.

Papa didn't know it was the Case Team's idea. He thought it was something the Central Committee wanted. Without any hesitation, he took his pen and began to write.

During more than half a year of confinement, solitary and alone, he had given a lot of thought to this Cultural Revolution which had brought him down, and to the many things he had not had time to review carefully in the tumultuous days preceding it. From 1922 when, at the age of 18, he joined the revolution, a full 46 years had elapsed.

Before Liberation, beset by dangerous enemy forces, he was involved in constant military operations. After Liberation, he was given a high position and kept busy with his work. He had no time to recall past incidents, to say nothing of reflecting on and summarizing them. Now, he was asked to write his autobiography — it didn't matter by whom, or why. He decided to do it. In the course of writing, he would be able to think back calmly in detail, and analyze and sum up his entire life.

Papa finished in 15 days — from June 20, 1968 to July 5. He titled it "Self Appraisal." It was 26,500 characters long.

He recalled his birth, his family, his childhood in a private school, the father he hadn't thought of in years. He recalled the courses he took in Chongqing in preparation for going to France for a combined work-study program, his trip across the ocean, his hard work and study in France, his introduction there to revolution, and the revolutionary comrades he met.

He recalled his tense days in the Communist underground in

Shanghai at the start of the revolution. He recalled the formation, battles, defeats and maturing of the Seventh and Eighth Red corps, the ups and downs of the Central Soviet Area in Jiangxi, the Long March. He recalled the battles in the War of Resistance Against Japan, and his comrades in the 129th Division. He recalled the campaigns in the Dabie Mountains and Huaihai, and the liberation of the Southwest. He recalled his efforts during the 17-year construction of New China and his 10 years as General Secretary of the Chinese Communist Party....

Papa's "Self Appraisal" clearly reflected his dignity and sense of responsibility. Every incident in his past seemed to have come to life again in his mind. He remembered every step. He replied in a strictly factual manner to every suspicion and doubt raised against him. He spoke not of his accomplishments, but only of his mistakes. Like everyone else accused of "errors" at that time, he was obliged, reluctantly, to apologize for alleged misdeeds.

At the same time, his politically sensitive antennae told him of the "distinction" being drawn by the subtle Mao Zedong. Decades of political experience made Papa very aware of life's twists and turns. He voiced only one plea in his awkward political situation: to stay in the Party. It would be his one last line of political defense.

Knowing that Mao would read his "Self Appraisal", Papa wrote, in conclusion: "My greatest hope is that I be allowed to remain in the Party as an ordinary member. I request that at an appropriate time I be given a small assignment where I can labor to the utmost of my ability, and thereby redeem myself."

A veteran Communist who had been in the Party more than 40 years could not forget his obligations, even under the most difficult circumstances. Being wronged never shook his faith, his hope. He seized every opportunity to retain his ties.

While Papa was writing his "Self Appraisal", the Deng Xiaoping Case Team was not idle. It began drafting an "Overall Report" on the "crimes" of Deng Xiaoping. Lin Biao and the Cultural Revolution Group were burning with eagerness to demolish Deng Xiaoping. The "Second Office of the Central Case Bureau" — immediate superior of the Deng

Case Team — was controlled by the Lin Biao clique. It kept phoning the Deng Case Team every few days, asking how it was progressing with the report, and urging the members to hurry. Kang Sheng, that master of harassment, called a series of meetings to hear reports on the various case investigations then in progress.

During the Cultural Revolution if a person was alleged only to have been a "capitalist-roader", or to have committed an error of "line", it wasn't easy for the rebels to overthrow him. To do that, it was necessary to prove he had a "history question", such as having been a turncoat, or an enemy agent. This was considered unshakable criminal evidence. Anyone overthrown on the basis of such proof had no hope of restoration.

But Deng had never been arrested by the enemy, had never quit the Party. For all their probing, the rebels had been unable to unearth a shred of misconduct.

Looking back, later, Papa smiled. "I'm a very lucky man," he said. "I was never wounded in battle, and I was never arrested when working in the underground."

Since Papa didn't have any "history questions", they had to be invented. It was the duty of the Deng Case Team to wrack their brains and find some. On June 18, Jiang Qing spoke at a meeting regarding the "crimes" of Deng Xiaoping.

"I want you to carefully examine the evidence," she said. "He probably is a turncoat. I've been analyzing his material right along. I'm with you in your struggle against him. You must concentrate on his past record and his present actions at the same time."

After the meeting Kang Sheng summoned the head of the Deng Case Team and gave him 10 large folios of documents written by the "Criticizing Deng Group" which he had personally been keeping. He also handed him material veterans of the Seventh Red Corps had been required to produce, and some photographs.

The Deng Case Team worked hard for a month and a half and concocted a "comprehensive report" on the "crimes" of Deng Xiaoping. On July 25, the team assembled in the East Hall of the Great Hall of the

People and read the report in full to an impressive audience, which included: Kang Sheng, Huang Yongsheng, Wu Faxian, Ye Qun, and Li Zuopeng.

Kang Sheng said they now had a great deal of evidence. The question was how to use it. The material on Deng's history was weak.

Wu Faxian claimed there was something wrong with Deng Xiaoping's entry into the Communist Party. But the men who had introduced him were all dead. There was no way to check.

When the meeting was over, Huang Yongsheng, Wu Faxian, Li Zuopeng, and the Deng Case Team repaired to the fourth floor of the Jingxi Hotel for a council of war, and reviewed the project from start to finish. By dawn of the following day they had worked out a final draft of what they called: "The Main Crimes of Another Biggest Person In Authority Within the Party Taking the Capitalist Road — Deng Xiaoping". It was divided into seven parts, and was over 15,000 characters long.

The Deng Case Team took the fruit of this difficult labor and immediately delivered it to the Second Office of the Central Case Bureau. In less than 24 hours Kang Sheng, Huang Yongsheng, Ye Qun, Li Zuopeng, Qiu Huizuo and Zhang Xiuchuan all had read it.

Kang Sheng inscribed this notation: "Send as quickly as possible to the Chairman, Vice-Chairman Lin (Biao), the Central Committee and the comrades of the Cultural Revolution Group. Print 52 copies".

Two days later, Kang Sheng's office sent word to the Deng Case Team several times that Kang was very pleased with the document.

Nevertheless, the Deng Case Team people felt the evidence on Deng's "history question" was still insufficient. They doubled their efforts to "correct weaknesses" and "fill the holes". The only possible "breakthrough" they could see in Deng's more than 40-year revolutionary record was in regard to his so-called "defection" in the Seventh Red Corps period. They said they had to dig deeper, to establish this as fatal proof of Deng's guilt.

On September 11, 1968 the Deng Case Team sent a report to Huang Yongsheng, Wu Faxian, Ye Qun and Li Zuopeng, requesting that Deng be ordered to supply additional material concerning two occasions, in 1930 and 1931, when they alleged he took unauthorized leave from the Seventh Red Corps and went to Shanghai. Huang asked Wang Dongxing to help. Wang then directed Wang Liang'en, Vice-Director of the Central Committee General Office, to demand, in the name of the Political Department, that Deng add supplementary material.

Papa complied. He wrote again about the situation in the Seventh Red Corps at that time, and added that he went to Shanghai twice to report on his work to the Central Committee, which was then in that city. He gave a full and factual explanation. Again the Deng Case Team flubbed, unable to find even a straw to clutch at.

The Deng Case Team, that same day, sent a report to Zhou Enlai requesting his "guidance" regarding several questions in Deng Xiaoping's past. It claimed there were inconsistencies in Deng's statements about the date of his entry into the Party, and that he was vague about the persons who introduced him. It said he had falsely slipped into the Party and was not a real member.

The Deng Case Team also asked Zhou Enlai for leads on various "suspicious points". It said that Deng went to Shanghai in 1930 and 1931 not to report on his work to the Central Committee, but for other purposes. Deng had said that in 1931 the Central Committee in Shanghai had sent him to Wuhu in Anhui to check on the work of the provincial Party committee, but that he found the committee had been smashed, and had returned to Shanghai. "We believe," the Team cried, "that it had been destroyed long before that, and suspect that Deng had probably sold it out."

This report had first been read and approved by Huang Yongsheng, Ye Qun, Wu Faxian, Li Zuopeng, and Kang Sheng before being submitted to Zhou Enlai. They pressed him for a reply. Zhou found the report unreasonable and unreliable. He ignored it, and it sank like a stone in the sea.

The Deng Case Team still didn't give up. It searched here and searched there, and finally pieced together "revelatory material" from former comrades in the Seventh Red Corps. Compiled in the form of "special criminal evidence", it was handed over to higher authorities.

At the same time, the Central Case Bureau was hastening the determination of guilt of all the so-called "black gang members" and "capitalist-roaders". The reason was that the Central Committee had decided to convene the 12th Plenary Session of the Eighth Party Central Committee and the Ninth Party National Congress.

The Second Office of the Central Case Bureau met to discuss 15 cases under investigation. Huang Yongsheng had words of praise for the work of the Deng Xiaoping Case Team. But Wu Faxian was dissatisfied. He said: "Deng Xiaoping is mustering his cronies and covering up for bad eggs. It's very serious. We've got to move on."

On September 22 and 24 the Central Case Bureau met twice in the Great Hall of the People. The Bureau's "First Office" was investigating 14, and the "Second Office" was investigating eight, major cases. They made determinations on all. Liu Shaoqi was labeled "The Biggest Person in Authority Taking the Capitalist Road Within the Party" and was slandered a "renegade", "hidden traitor" and "scab". Deng Xiaoping's "question" was described as having been "deeply hidden", and his crime was that of being another biggest person in authority within the Party who had taken the capitalist road.

After all the sweating and straining, Deng Xiaoping's "question" was deemed a present one. As to his "history", that was "hidden" really much too deeply.

10

The Enlarged 12th Plenary Session of the Eighth Party Central Committee

THE Enlarged 12th Plenary Session of the Eighth Party Central Committee was held in Beijing from October 13 to 31 in 1968. Its purpose was to prepare for the Ninth Party National Congress.

Mao Zedong convened the meeting, and gave the opening address. He first raised these questions: Do we or don't we want the Cultural Revolution? Has it been successful in the main, or have its successes been too few and its failings too many? His reply was specific:

"The purpose of this Great Proletarian Cultural Revolution is to strengthen the dictatorship of the proletariat, prevent the restoration of capitalism, and build socialism. It is absolutely necessary, and extremely timely." Mao again expressed his unswerving support for the Cultural Revolution, which he initiated.

Lin Biao and Jiang Qing, and their Cultural Revolution lieutenants, had strenuously attacked the veteran revolutionaries who had participated in the so-called "February Countercurrent". They said it was an "anti-Party incident of the utmost gravity", a "rehearsal for a capitalist restoration", and had compelled the veterans to confess and criticize themselves time and again.

Now they trotted out a document concocted by Kang Sheng and his cronies, entitled "A Proclamation and Report on the Crimes of Renegade,

Hidden Traitor and Scab Liu Shaoqi". The meeting approved it, and decreed that Liu Shaoqi was expelled from the Party for life and removed from all of his posts within and outside the Party.

They handed out another document they had prepared in advance. This one was called "The Main Crimes of Another Biggest Capitalist Roader Within the Party — Deng Xiaoping". Deng was thus removed from all Party and government posts.

Major decisions at a meeting of such importance naturally had to be approved by Mao Zedong. Lin Biao and Jiang Qing were displeased. They busily tried to stir up dissent, hoping to create an atmosphere in which they could create a demand for Deng's expulsion.

Mao wouldn't have it. He said Deng had fought well against the enemy in wartime, and nothing wrong had been discovered in his past. He should be treated differently from Liu Shaoqi. You all want to kick him out, Mao said. I'm not keen on the idea.

Mao Zedong had the typical stubbornness of people from Hunan. Once he made up his mind, nobody could budge him. It was one of his most obvious traits.

The meeting was an abnormal one, in an abnormal period, convened under very abnormal circumstances. Many members of the Central Committee had been overthrown and deprived of their political rights. Seventy-one percent of the members and alternate members of the Eighth Central Committee had been declared "turncoats", "spies", "in touch with foreign countries", or "anti-Party elements". Of the 97 members of the Central Committee, not counting the 10 who had died, only 40 were able to attend. Since this was not enough to comply with the Party Constitution requirement that at least half the membership had to be present to constitute a quorum, 10 more persons had to be added from among the alternate members. The unofficial participants in the meeting were more than half of those attending, and they had the same voting rights as the full Central Committee members. Even stranger, after the meeting it was discovered that one of the voters wasn't even a Communist!

More than two years had elapsed since the Great Proletarian Cultural

Revolution burst upon the scene. It had rioted long enough; there had been sufficient turbulence, a surfeit of rebellion and seizures of power. Now what? I'm afraid Mao himself wasn't very clear. In the beginning he said the Cultural Revolution needed a year. Then he said probably three years.

In other words, by the following summer it should have been over. In April 1969, the Ninth Party National Congress was convened. The Communist Party Constitution was amended, and the assignment of posts were settled. Everything had proceeded according to plan.

But there was no stopping the Cultural Revolution.

Probably, at the very beginning, Mao Zedong had something else in mind. But, by this time, the Cultural Revolution had become the opposite of his original intention. Like a wild horse that had slipped its tether, it was galloping madly, out of control. Before old contradictions had been solved, new ones had emerged. Factionalism, armed clashes, struggles for power, and the seizure of positions not only had not ceased; in fact they had grown worse, more insoluble.

In our two-room flat in Fanghuzhai in the Xuanwu District of Beijing, we children lived together with our grandmother. Mutually dependent, we managed to get by. Big Sister Deng Lin, because of Papa's "question", had been criticized and kept under surveillance at her academy. It was difficult for her to get permission to leave. But now the factions were brawling among themselves, and nobody bothered with "black gang" and "ox demons and venomous spirits". Deng Lin took advantage of this to sneak home on weekends.

Big Brother Pufang and Second Sister Deng Nan, because of the strife among the factions in their school, Peking University, were able to "slip through the net". Deng Nan, especially, rarely failed to return to us on weekends.

A battle broke out between two factions in Peking University on March 29, 1968, in the middle of the night. The campus was filled with helmeted figures carrying cudgels and spears. The factions tore fiercely into each other. There were heavy injuries on both sides. Neither would give in. They prepared for the next encounter.

The whole university was gripped by fear. Deng Nan and some of her classmates had watched the bloody clash from the windows of their dormitory. They hastily put their things together. At four in the morning, just before dawn, they escaped through a break in the campus wall.

Deng Nan worried about Pufang, who was still there. She sent Feifei, with instructions to bring Pufang home. In the confusion, he was able to do so. Many had been killed in the battle. One of Deng Nan's classmates had watched, without taking part. A flying spear pierced the classmate's middle. It didn't kill him, but it ruptured his liver and left him a permanent invalid.

We brothers and sisters were together at last. The five of us, plus Grandma, for the next month or so were truly a united family group at Fanghuzhai. It was much livelier than when there had been just Grandma, Feifei, and me. Grandma, Pufang and Feifei had one room. We three sisters had the other. There was a hallway between us, with the doors facing each other. We had a girl cousin going to school in Beijing. She moved in, and we four girls shared one single big bed. It was too crowded. I pulled two large crates together and made myself a bed on top of them. I felt really free and roomy.

The searchers stopped coming. They seemed to have forgotten our little corner. Though life was hard, we weren't lonely. Actually, it wasn't too bad. The hardship was the way we felt inside. In our most difficult times, we tried to find things we could enjoy. We had few means of amusement. We would put a small open cardboard box on the bed, stand back a distance, aim chess pieces, and see who could toss in the most. It was good fun. One thing we had all learned from Papa was to remain optimistic, always.

Our life was relatively uneventful, except for two times when we were careless with our stoves and were nearly asphyxiated. (Poor people couldn't afford chimney pipes, and burned coalballs, which gave off lethal fumes. Many became ill, or died, if they forgot to keep a window or door open, particularly when going to bed.)

The first time Grandma and Feifei were affected, though not seriously. Their only reaction was headaches for a couple of days. The second time Grandma and I were in our room, sleeping soundly. I heard Grandma calling. Remembering our first experience, I jumped out of bed, rushed blindly to the door, and pushed it open. I fell to the floor in a swoon, unable to rise. We had a real dose of coal fumes. If Grandma hadn't been a light sleeper because of her age, we both would have been goners.

We had our dangers, but we had our laughs, as well. One day, Grandma wanted to spend a little extra to prepare something better than our usual fare, and give us a treat. Deng Nan, who ran the family budget, refused to give her the money. They got into a heated argument. Grandma was illiterate, and certainly hadn't read any famous foreign novels. But she had an excellent memory, and apparently recalled a foreign movie she had once seen.

Angrily, she turned on Deng Nan and called her a "Grandet"! It was the miser in Balzac's novel *Eugienie Grandet*, which had been made into a film and shown in China dubbed in Chinese. Grandma had never forgot him. He was the worst figure of stinginess she could think of to fling at Deng Nan, as the two of them quarreled and wept. Later, we all laughed and rejoiced at Grandma's display of "literary scholarship".

Brother Pufang had been confined to Peking University ever since Papa was criticized. This was his longest time at home. With nothing else to do, he took his saw and plane and did some carpentry work on the old boards Deng Nan had bought. He made a small bookcase for Feifei, and shelves for Grandma's crockery. He spent most of his time helping Feifei with his lessons. Feifei was in the second year of junior high when the Cultural Revolution started. Unable to go to class, Feifei could only keep reviewing his textbooks. Pufang helped him. Pufang liked to teach and Feifei liked to learn. He made good progress in math, physics and chemistry. These were an essential basis for going on to college and studying for a master's or doctor's degree.

Big Brother was six or seven years older than Feifei and I. When we were smaller, Pufang was always busy at school. Although we respected him, we had little chance to talk with him. But now, at Fanghuzhai, we were with him all the time, and we could ask him about anything that was on our minds.

I remember I once asked him: "Why do they want to overthrow Papa?"

Looking off in the distance, Big Brother replied: "To clear the way for Lin Biao."

Pufang was well attuned to political affairs. Although a lot of us were enthusiastic about the Cultural Revolution when it first began, he sensed it was going to bring trouble, and kept a low profile. But that didn't keep the rebel faction from confining and criticizing him.

And now, he was actually home, away from the rebels' grasp, free of the long pressure on his spirits. One day when we were eating together he was so happy he drank too much. His face flushed, he rambled on about everything under the sun, and recited a classical poem. We watched him sadly. It wasn't the wine that was making him drunk. He was intoxicated by his own emotions. You should know we were drinking bitter wine, a wine of the bitterness of life!

For the time being our family group had distanced itself from the raging tide, seeking small pleasures wherever they could be found. Little did we know that a truly terrifying time would soon be upon us.

11

May Terror

ONE day in May several big trucks from Peking University drove into our courtyard. A rebel faction gang, carrying cudgels, jumped down and swarmed into our house. They seized Pufang and Deng Nan, blindfolded them with strips of black cloth, pushed them out and dragged them on to one of the trucks. Fiercely shouting "down with Deng Xiaoping" and "down with the counter-revolutionary whelps", they revved up the motors to a thunderous roar. Grandma, Feifei and I stared, stricken dumb, as the trucks rolled off in a cloud of dust.

We had been through not a few house searches and criticism sessions since the start of the Cultural Revolution, but to see the seizure of our brother and sister in this horrible manner shriveled our bones. We were gripped by an unspeakable fear, our throats choked with sobs.

We were raided a number of times more. Completely ignorant of what happened to Pufang and Deng Nan, or even whether they were still alive, we were in a perpetual state of worry and despair.

As we later learned, on reaching the university campus they were first locked in a dormitory, which had been converted into a battle base. Then they were moved to the Physics Building, into two adjoining rooms. Rebels stood guard outside. They were forbidden to speak to each other.

They were frequently questioned, separately, after first being blindfolded and pushed into a special interrogation room. They were cursed and yelled at, and suddenly hit with blows of a cudgel. The line of questioning was always the same — "expose" Deng Xiaoping.

This was at a time when the "Deng Xiaoping Case Team" was speeding up its investigations in an effort to patch together a report on Deng's "crimes". Lin Biao and Jiang Qing and their cohorts, frantically seeking a breakthrough, felt sure Deng's children, particularly the older ones, knew something. They instructed the notorious leader of Peking University's rebel faction, Nie Yuanzi, radical vanguard of the Cultural Revolution, to seize Deng Xiaoping's children and extract "evidence".

Nie Yuanzi faithfully obeyed her masters' orders. She first sent flunkies to Fanghuzhai to make sure we were home, then loaded trucks with Red Guards, and sent them to grab Pufang and Deng Nan, take them to the school, and extract "proof".

In the nearly two years since the start of the Cultural Revolution, no matter how fiercely it raged, or how dangerous the situation was, we children of the Deng family, except for making a few pro forma criticisms of Papa, never agreed to break with him politically, and "expose" him or Mama. We were convinced Papa was innocent. We loved him, and were willing to face all risks together. Words cannot describe the deep love between parents and children in our family.

After it was all over, Papa said to Mama: "Our children behaved wonderfully during the Cultural Revolution. They went through a lot for us. We should show our appreciation more." It was this precious love which gave our family the spiritual sustenance to bear the most dangerous trials.

At Peking University, following the orders of the Cultural Revolution Group leaders, the rebel faction used every dirty trick at its command to pressure Pufang and Deng Nan — threats and fright and beating and torment.

Deng Nan later told us: "I was very scared. But what good did being scared do? I had to stand up to them. I said at home my father never spoke about his work, I didn't know anything. I just gritted my teeth and refused to talk."

Pufang said to the rebels: "I'm the only one who knows about family affairs. My younger sisters and brother don't know anything. If you've got any questions, ask me!"

Pufang and Deng Nan were concerned about us. Pufang managed to sneak a note to her, so that their statements would be the same. Deng Nan immediately thought they ought to let the rest of us know. But how? The guards kept a close watch. Deng Nan had a bright idea. She told her captors that when they arrested her she hadn't had time to take things she needed for feminine hygiene. Could they have someone bring them from home?

I had been very worried about them. When the rebels notified me, I put some things together and immediately headed for the university.

Peking University was a famous institution of higher learning. It had a place of special importance in our family. Our mother was admitted to study in its Physics Department in 1936. Pufang and Deng Nan, no doubt influenced by her, also went there, and also majored in physics. Ever since primary school, I had hoped to enter the university some day and study history. In my imagination it was a holy palace where dreams came true.

But now, when I arrived at the school, it looked entirely different from what I had pictured. Posters were plastered all over the campus, layer upon layer, thickly covering the walls. Some had already been torn down, and were twisting along the ground in the breeze, and being trampled underfoot. Many doors and windows were nailed shut with boards and iron strips. Stakes had been planted and foxholes dug outside the entrances of several buildings, as obvious defenses for impending battles. Cudgel-carrying warriors marched quickly by in ragged lines, wearing wicker safety helmets in lieu of army headgear.

Very few people were around. The ones you saw looked grim. The atmosphere was very different from what it had been at the start of the Cultural Revolution, when crowds of excited spectators came to view the first posters. The big beautiful campus was sunk in chilly gloom.

I hadn't been anywhere for months. This was the first time I had ever seen such a large battlefield. I felt pretty tense. The entrance to the Physics Building looked menacing, with its walls of dark gray. There was no one outside. All the windows of the ground floor were boarded shut. The big entrance doors were barricaded with iron plates. Only a

82

small narrow space was left for passage in and out. Sandbags were piled high in front. The walls were dirty and scarred. It reminded me of lines in a Mao Zedong poem: *"Furious battles once raged there/The village walls were pitted with bullet holes."*

I learned later that the Physics Building was one of headquarters of Nie Yuanzi's rebel faction. That was why it was so strongly fortified.

I stood at the entrance for a while, and someone brought Deng Nan out. Fortunately, the rebel escort let us talk privately. Deng Nan asked how things were going at home. Quickly, she whispered what she and Pufang had been saying when they were questioned. She told me to go to the Central Academy of Fine Arts and inform Deng Lin. Urge her to keep steady, just say she didn't know anything, and stick to it.

Deng Lin's health wasn't very good. We were afraid she might become too depressed. We discussed how best to encourage her. Deng Nan exhorted me to look after myself, and Feifei and Grandma, and to be sure to keep safe.

As I watched the tough-looking rebel lead Deng Nan back into that dark doorway, the tension and fear that gripped me when I first arrived, vanished, replaced by a limitless sadness.

I left immediately, and hastened to the Arts Academy. I found Big Sister Deng Lin, led her to a secluded place out of earshot of the rebels who were watching her, and relayed Deng Nan's message. Much relieved, Deng Lin said emotionally: "You don't have to worry about me. I'm not afraid of anything. I'll stand firm!"

Two weeks later, Deng Nan was moved to the battle detachment headquarters in the Physics Department. She lost touch with Pufang. At first, the rebel faction questioned her every day. But when they found they really couldn't learn anything from her, they gradually slackened off. Finally, they permitted her to go to the mess hall by herself at meal times.

Springtime passed. It was followed by an oppressively hot sweltering summer.

Nie Yuanzi's rebel faction at Peking University was determined to take advantage of its seizure of the children of Deng Xiaoping. It hoped to win glory for itself in the campaign to overthrow him by reporting success to its masters in the Cultural Revolution Group. But after several months of effort, it was unable to obtain any evidence. Pufang was Deng Xiaoping's oldest son. He surely knew a lot, the rebels thought. It must be possible to squeeze at least something out of him. It was said that Nie Yuanzi issued an order that Pufang must be made to talk.

The rebels increased the pressure. They questioned him every day, blindfolding him both during the inquisitions, and when he was being led from one place to another. Jiang Qing had screeched a rabble-rousing speech in the outdoor stadium of Peking University in the early days of the Cultural Revolution. Pufang had been present in the audience, and had been heard to say: "Let's see how long you'll be able to rant!"

Now the rebels maintained he had cursed "Comrade Jiang Qing", and should therefore be labeled a "counter-revolutionary". They demanded that he expose the "questions" and "crimes" of his "black gang" father Deng Xiaoping. In addition to these political steam-roller tactics, the rebels beat and cursed and insulted him, and used every means to torment him physically.

They kept changing his place of confinement. For a long time he was locked in the shower room of the swimming pool in the school's gymnasium. It was dark and damp and had no sunlight. Once, Deng Nan walked through the gym to get to the mess hall, and she saw Pufang in the distance. Although it was summer, he still had on the heavy old corduroy jacket he was wearing the day he was arrested. In the dimness he looked pale and weak.

For Pufang, it was a rare day. He actually felt warm, after the cool damp of the shower room!

The only thing he craved was to be able to smoke. He induced his guard to buy him cigarettes at 20 cents a pack. Using only three matches a day, he chain-smoked morning, noon and night.

Once, over the loudspeaker system, he heard that the rebel faction had named him and a number of people he had never met as members of an "anti-Party clique". It was clear the rebel faction would never let up. They had imprisoned him, questioned him, tormented him. Now they wanted to label him an "anti-Party element", a "counter-revolutionary", to destroy his last vestige of political respectability.

Peking University became a fascist concentration camp, a place of bloody violence and torture. One professor, tormented beyond endurance, made four different attempts at suicide, until he finally succeeded. A student who opposed Nie Yuanzi had nails driven through his kneecaps, slivers of bamboo shoved under his fingernails, his fingers broken by pliers. Then he was tied in a gunnysack, kicked downstairs, and beaten almost to death.

Lu Ping, president of Peking University and secretary of the school's Party committee, was hung by his thumbs from a rafter and tortured to force a confession that he was a "false Communist" and a "turncoat". Famous philosopher Feng Ding was so abused that he tried to kill himself three times.

These are only examples. During the Cultural Revolution three people were killed in battles at Peking University. Among teaching staff, workers, employees and students, over 60 other people were driven to their graves. These included the historian Jian Bozan, physicist Rao Yutai, and many other top-drawer professors. The horrendous deeds committed at Peking University by Nie Yuanzi's rebels are too numerous to record even if we use up all our writing material. Whether from a moral or a legal point of view, their acts were absolutely evil, completely unforgivable.

But in that period, they were the masters. It was a time when the tigers and wolves of the rebel factions ran amok. Peking University's lovely gardens were ruined; its beautiful lake was filled with sludge.

The summer of 1968 was indeed unusually hot, unusually long, unusually cruel!

12

Calamity Drops from the Skies

A day which is deeply engraved in our memory occurred at the end of August.

Second Sister Deng Nan telephoned me from Peking University. She said: "Brother has had a fall. The school wants to send him home." She had already cried herself hoarse. She said she would come soon to talk it over. I hung up. We at home were so shocked we didn't know what to do with ourselves. What had happened? We could only wait tensely for Second Sister.

Deng Nan came home and told us: Brother had been tormented unbearably. He couldn't take any more. He chose a moment when the rebels weren't watching and jumped from the window, as a final gesture of protest. Before that, he had written a letter, in which he said: "The rebels insist that I speak. I cannot. Under the circumstances, I have no other way out."

When Pufang was injured, the rebels went into a flap. They took him to a hospital. On learning that the victim was the son of the "Second Biggest Capitalist Roader", the hospital refused to accept him. Several more hospitals all turned him down. Truly, an inhuman black period! Life was cheaper than a blade of grass. Later we heard that Nie Yuanzi was frantic. The rebel faction in the Third Beijing Hospital was the same as hers, and she compelled them to admit Pufang.

Although they admitted him, the hospital rebels wouldn't even take him to the emergency room. He had to lie in the hallway. After a whole night his condition had clearly become critical. The doctors decided to

My parents during the summer of 1964.

A family photo, also summer 1964. From left: Mama, younger brother Feifei, me (Maomao), Papa, older brother Pufang, older sister Deng Nan, and oldest sister Deng Lin.

Mao Zedong and Deng Xiaoping in 1960.

Deng Xiaoping on an inspection tour of Northwest China in March 1966, just before the Cultural Revolution.

Hundreds of thousands of Red Guards rallied several times in Tiananmen Square in summer of 1966. Chairman Mao, on August 18, 1966, waves from the rostrum.

On November 8, 1966, Nie Yuanzi and her supporters put up posters calling Deng Xiaoping "the capitalist roader in the Party."

Autumn 1966, Liu Shaoqi (middle), Zhou Enlai (right) and Deng Xiaoping on the Tiananmen rostrum. Liu and Deng were purged shortly thereafter.

Deng Xiaoping's three daughters, Maomao, Deng Nan, and Deng Lin, in Red Guard uniforms, at the beginning of the Cultural Revolution.

Grandma held the whole family together after my parents were put under house arrest.

Feifei was 15 when the Cultural Revolution started.

Three sisters in 1968, living away from home.

Deng Pufang was one of the best students in the Physics Department of Peking University before the Cultural Revolution. In 1968, political persecution forced him to jump from a dormitory window. The resulting injuries left him permanently paralyzed.

Posters in Peking University during the Cultural Revolution.

Deng Nan and I in Beijing after I returned from Shaanxi.

Before leaving for farm work in Shaanxi in 1969, Deng Nan (left) visited Deng Lin, who was working in a factory.

tap his spinal fluid. That required his family's written consent.

The university rebel faction went to where Deng Nan was confined and told her about it. She nearly fainted when she heard that Pufang had fallen and fractured his spine. She hurried with them to the hospital and saw Pufang in the emergency room. Her originally healthy brother was lying with a fractured spine, running a high fever, his life in danger. Deng Nan's mind went blank. Her eyes filled with tears, she took up the heavy pen and signed. The rebels immediately led her away.

Because of the incessant abuse and inhuman treatment by the university rebels, Pufang had long since made up his mind. Hesitation and doubts were gone. He was reasonable, entirely too reasonable. Clearly, fearlessly, he made his choice. A talented fourth year student in the Technical Physics Department of Peking University, Pufang had been a strictly law-abiding Youth League branch secretary, a probationary member of the Communist Party. Only 24 years old, he had possessed great faith, had cherished many aspirations, ideals, hopes. In the end, all he had left was a firm determination, an unshakable determination. Calmly, he leaped.

He lost consciousness. He remembered waking temporarily, lying somewhere that was very cold, but immediately passed out again. The next time he awoke, he was in the hospital, surrounded by people gazing at him with icy eyes. Above him a drip infusion bottle pulsed. Everything was very blurred, very unreal. In the emergency room of the Third Beijing Hospital, Pufang lapsed between unconsciousness and waking for three days and three nights.

Whether it was due to divine intervention, or some unavoidable fate, or because the instinct to live was too strong, in any event Pufang defeated the spirit of death. Life or death is an eternal question in this world. It is a wicked battle, a fierce struggle. What misery for the person who doesn't want to live, but cannot die!

When Pufang woke again he found himself staring at the ceiling. He was drained of emotion. He was not unhappy. There was nothing in his mind, no regrets. The shouts of the rebels, the doctors' questions, breezed past his ears, unheard.

Pufang's fall had inflicted compound fractures of his 11th and 12th chest vertebrae and his first waist vertebra. Although he couldn't move his lower limbs, he still had sensation above his abdomen. Ordinary medical procedure required immediate surgery to clean the wound and lessen the pressure. Otherwise blood would be forced upwards inside the spinal column and would congeal, increasing the paralysis. If the doctors had felt a shred of humanitarianism, and had operated in time, Pufang would not have been as disabled as he is today.

But a "child of a black gang counter-revolutionary" who had "defied the people" by committing suicide, had himself thereby become a "counter-revolutionary". In that political atmosphere, if the hospital had not allowed him to die it would have been considered a "generous" deed. They could not have given him any treatment whatsoever.

And so, Pufang's paralysis spread upwards, from the 11th chest vertebra to the seventh chest vertebra. As a result he had no feeling from the chest down. He lost his urinary and bowel functions, and was doomed to an irreversible high area paralysis.

After about 10 days in the hospital, it was apparent Pufang would live. The rebel faction notified Deng Nan the danger had passed, and they would no longer intervene. They intended to send him home.

Worried and upset, Deng Nan retorted: "You can't do that. I have to talk it over with the family first." The rebels agreed. Deng Nan took the bus and hurried home.

Grandma, Deng Nan and I sat in our sunless little room in Fanghuzhai, our faces wet with tears. We felt the Peking University rebels had tormented Pufang into this condition. They couldn't push the responsibility for looking after him on to us. And they certainly shouldn't send a person home who wasn't entirely out of danger. How could just the few of us and an old grandma take care of him, give him medical treatment? No! We'd have to talk to someone, take it up with the Central Committee General Office!

I went with Deng Nan to the West Gate of Zhongnanhai, and said we wanted to talk to a leader in the Office. The guards ignored us. We said we wanted to see someone who gives us our regular living expenses.

They refused. What to do? We found a public telephone and racked our brains trying to remember the numbers of units connected with the General Office. We called them all. Either they said it had nothing to do with them, or that we should discuss it with Peking University, or they simply hung up.

As a last resort we called the duty office of the Security Bureau of the General Office. Like the others, they said it was not their affair. Angrily, we blasted them:

"You're the ones who put him into this state. It's not the duty of the children to take care of him. Our parents live in Zhongnanhai. Send him to them. If you dare send him to our house, we'll carry him through the streets to the main gate of Zhongnanhai. We'll tell everyone: 'This is Deng Xiaoping's son. This is what they've done to him. Look, everyone!' If you dare send him home, that is what we will do!"

We hung up, so agitated our hands were trembling. Standing outside Zhongnanhai, helpless and alone, we gazed at the high battered red walls. Neither Heaven nor Earth would answer our pleas. Who would help us in this indifferent world?

Now we understood. No one could help us at such a time; it wasn't possible. We had to rely on ourselves. I talked it over with Deng Nan. We decided that under no circumstances would we let the University send Pufang home. On this issue, we would fight them!

Our uncompromising stand finally bore fruit. We don't know who issued the order, but the rebels abandoned their plan to send Pufang home and, instead, moved him into the university hospital.

The hospital didn't give him any treatment. At first, the rebels sent people to see him, but after a week, they didn't bother. They told Deng Nan they had no responsibility; it was up to our family to look after him. They ordered her to send Feifei to stay with him.

Deng Nan and I felt that wasn't a good idea. Feifei was only 17, and he was a stubborn kid. If he got into a row with the rebels, they might beat him to death. We decided that Deng Nan and I would take turns serving as Pufang's nurse.

From then on, I stayed at the university and looked after Pufang with

Deng Nan. His urinary tract became infected, and he ran a fever of over 40 degrees Celsius, often accompanied by chills and spasms. Because his chest vertebra was fractured, he couldn't move, or even sit up. We had to keep helping him roll over a bit to prevent the development of bedsores, which would slow his recovery. Neither Deng Nan nor I had any nursing experience. We could only give him the most elementary care, watching and helplessly worrying.

But the rebels still wouldn't spare Pufang and Deng Nan. They often came to the bedside to criticize them and demand that they expose Papa. Pufang would lie there, his eyes staring. Not a word would pass his lips, no matter how the rebels ranted and swore. On holidays, everyone in the hospital celebrated and the patients were given the traditional *jiaozi* (dumplings). But not Pufang. He was the "whelp" of Deng Xiaoping, he was a "counter-revolutionary". Even his right to eat *jiaozi* had been taken away.

Only when I went to the mess hall for meals was I able to escape the oppressive atmosphere of the hospital. Whether the sky was vast and clear, or massed with somber clouds, I could straighten up and raise my head, and gaze at the limitless firmament. Sometimes I strolled to Weiming Lake. Beneath a canopy of verdant foliage, I walked along the leaf-strewn path, and sat by the lakeside. Looking at the dark reflections of the green trees and blue sky on the placid surface of the water, I immersed my soul in its azure depths, my mind free of turmoil, I enjoyed intensely the solitary peace.

We hated the rebel faction; we loathed the political frenzy all around us. We had neither the will nor the strength to resist. All we wanted was to restore quiet to our hearts, to withdraw, to hide. But where in those mad times could one find quiet, a place of refuge? The heavens didn't care. Human life was of little consequence. We had been cruelly tormented. We felt we were very unfortunate.

But there were many others whose fate was just as bad as ours, in fact worse, much worse. People were mercilessly crushed in the name of the "revolution". Many were overthrown and arrested, many were physically tortured to death, their homes smashed, their families scattered.

It was a lunatic time without order, or reason, or humanity, devoid of even human emotion!

We recall these events in detail with only one hope: that all those who were involved in the tragedy will always remember it, that those who were not will know about it; that all thinking persons will see to it that such a tragedy never happens again!

Summer passed, and autumn came again. In Beijing, chill winds rose in mid-autumn. The weather gradually turned cold.

It was in the latter half of October that the 12th Plenary Session of the Party's Eighth Central Committee, previously mentioned, was convened.

Our family was very concerned about this Plenum. Not whether it would declare some new revolutionary line, or some new changes of office, but whether it would make a political evaluation of Papa. If it did, it would be conclusive. Good or bad, it would be of vital importance to Papa, and to our entire family.

We tried to get news wherever we could. We heard that Mao Zedong was determined that Papa should keep his membership in the Communist Party. I went at once to the Central Academy of Fine Arts to tell Big Sister, Deng Lin. Ever since her capture and forced return to the school, she had been kept in the "Monsters Enclosure" — rooms in which those under attack were confined. Naturally, they were cut off from all news.

When I went to see her, a rebel watched us all the time, afraid we might be making some "counter-revolutionary" contact. I couldn't talk in front of him. I said I was thirsty, and he kindly went out to get me a glass of water. Quickly, I whispered to Big Sister: "Papa has kept his Party membership!"

Her eyes lit up. It was tremendously important. In other words, Papa still had not been pushed to a deadend. We had no illusions or false hopes regarding his political future, but we knew for a veteran Communist like Papa, who had fought for the Party all his life, for him to retain his Party membership was of vital significance. Some might say it was just a turn of the political weather vane, but to a loyal Communist it meant more than life itself.

91

After the conclusions of the Plenum were announced, half the steam went out of the pressure being exerted by the Peking University rebels. They were no longer quite so interested in Deng Xiaoping's children. They gradually came to the hospital less often, and then stopped coming altogether. The recently assigned Army Propaganda Team and the Workers' Propaganda Team dropped by, only once, to check up. Luckily, the rebels had placed Brother's room "off limits." We were able, when no one else was around, to even read the classic novel *A Dream of Red Mansions*, a book that was strictly forbidden.

The Cultural Revolution wasn't over; changes and developments hadn't stopped. Too many unusual things were going on, so much so that Mao Zedong got wind of them. 1968 was drawing to a close. On December 26, the Central Committee issued a notice entitled: "Policies to Be Observed and Implemented During Struggles Against the Enemy". Mao Zedong personally added the following provision:

"Even if they are children of counter-revolutionaries or of unrepentant capitalist roaders, do not call them 'black gang children'. Say rather that they are a part of the majority, in fact the vast majority, of those who can be educated (simply referred to hereafter as 'children who can be educated'), so as to distinguish them from their families".

From then on, our status changed. It was a great boon. Mao's words were magically effective. The rebel factions, who were so harsh with us, had to change their attitude, whether they liked it or not. With the high pressure off, we were much more relaxed.

Gradually, the days passed. Gradually, things settled down. The struggles were over, and in their place came a stirring campaign for educated youngsters to "go up into the mountains and down into the countryside".

Feifei and I, who were both in middle school, were perfect material. In December 1968, Feifei and his whole class at the First Middle School attached to the Beijing Normal University were assigned to a farm brigade in North China's Shanxi Province. Feifei believed in his older brother. He went to see him in the hospital.

"My school wants to send us to the countryside. Should I go, or not?"

he asked.

Pufang felt very badly about it. He thought a moment, then said: "I don't know. Maybe some of the others will be allowed to come back and you won't. But if you don't go, it will be a political burden on your back. They'll say you didn't respond to the call for young people to go the rural areas. It might make things worse for you."

"Alright," Feifei said, "I'll go."

We were really concerned. Feifei was only 17, and he'd be going so far. We helped him pack. We bought him two large cases, one of canvas, the other of wood, and filled them with whatever we had on hand. Quilts, padded clothes, padded shoes, hats, pants, stockings. He liked making radios. We put one in, even adding a small mallet and a hammering block.

Deng Nan loved to pack. She wanted Feifei to take everything. She crammed both cases to capacity, and still she wouldn't quit. It was as if she wanted to pack her heart in, as well. She inserted a list of every item, and where exactly it was located, to make sure Feifei could find it all.

Before departing, Feifei went to see Big Sister Deng Lin, who was still being detained in the "Monsters Enclosure" at the Central Academy of Fine Arts. She felt terrible that she couldn't give him any going-away present, or see him off at the railway station. She wasn't even sure she would ever see her little brother again. Deng Lin wept. The parting was almost more than she could bear.

The day Feifei left, the platform of the Beijing Railway Station was crowded with students and people seeing them off. In the long row hands tightly clasped hands, voices urged endless injunctions. All around were glistening eyes and tear-stained cheeks. Everyone hated to part. Hearts were suffused with worry as the youngsters entered the carriages. The locomotive whistle shrieked, the wheels began to turn, and the train rumbled into motion. Inside the cars and on the platform young and old burst into tears. Their loud laments over-rode the thunder of the train.

Deng Nan and I watched the train till it vanished in the distance. Only then did we leave the railway station. Neither of us spoke. Our tears were still flowing. Pufang was lying ill in the hospital. Deng Lin was confined in the Arts Academy. Feifei was going far away. We had no news of Papa and Mama who were under house arrest. Never in this wide world had we felt more isolated and lonely.

Not long after Feifei's departure, in January 1969, my classmates and I in the Girls' High School attached to the Beijing Normal University were assigned to a farming brigade in the Yan'an region of northern Shaanxi Province. On a train moving west I passed my 19th birthday. Except when Deng Lin and Deng Nan were occasionally permitted by their schools to return, the only occupant of our home in Fanghuzhai was our 70-year-old grandmother, eking out an existence on an allowance of 20 yuan per month.

13

The Performance of the Deng Xiaoping Case Team from Beginning to End

AT the Enlarged 12th Plenary Session of the Eighth Party Central Committee, Mao Zedong, ignoring opposition, preserved the Party membership of Deng Xiaoping. This puzzled and disturbed Lin Biao, Jiang Qing and their cohorts.

Lin had been designated as Mao's successor. But he knew very well his position was risky as long as Deng remained unpurged. Only by knocking Deng out could he feel secure. He and the Jiang Qing clique directed the Deng Xiaoping Case Team to step up operations, first concentrating on efforts to prove that Deng had betrayed the revolution and surrendered to the enemy. With increased personnel the team swung into action and searched all over the country.

One segment went to Shaanxi to investigate Deng's actions when the Party sent him in 1927 to work with Feng Yuxiang, a Kuomintang high-ranking official, as his army's political commissar.

Deng had been working in 1928 with the Party Central Committee, which was then in Shanghai. He returned to Shanghai again on two occasions, in 1930 and 1931, to report to the Central Committee on the situation in the Seventh Red Corps he was then commanding in Guangxi Province.

Now, members of the Deng Case Team hurried to Shanghai to

investigate Deng's alleged "desertion in the face of the enemy". They also asked about him during his combined work and study in France, in the 20s.

In Anhui another group sought clues to his alleged "betrayal" in 1931 while he was checking on the work of the Party in that province.

In Jiangxi information was sought regarding him when he went to the Central Soviet Area there in 1931.

In Sichuan, they wanted information about his family and his "counter-revolutionary activities" in his old hometown.

In Tianjin they wanted to know about Deng during the time he was with the army of Feng Yuxiang.

In Guangdong, Ningxia, Hunan, Liaoning and Jiangsu they sought testimony from his old subordinates.

The investigators were extremely diligent. They made every effort to dig up evidence. The three-man team that went to Guangxi in just two months raced through four prefectures and 22 counties, and interviewed over 200 people.

That was in various parts of the country. In Beijing, the Deng Case Team wasn't idle either. In the summer of 1969 they scurried around in the broiling heat looking for witnesses, questioning Papa's old comrades, veteran administrators, veteran generals. Some answered strictly according to facts. Some avoided the questioners, or ignored them.

Frantic, the probers got Huang Yongsheng and Wu Faxian to arrange a meeting with Marshal of the People's Republic of China and Vice-Chairman of the Central Military Commission, Nie Rongzhen. On July 20, 1969, he received them in a small meeting room in the Jingxi Hotel. A man of high probity and vision, he was seated on a wicker chair. They began asking questions.

Slowly, Marshal Nie replied. He started from the days when he and Papa were young and were in France together on a work-study program in the 20s. He told of their close relations in military campaigns. He knew a great deal about Deng Xiaoping. He spoke patiently for nearly 40 minutes. But nothing he related contained even a hint of any so-called "crime" or "question" in Papa's past.

Finally, he said: "I'm not very well. That is all I can say today." He stood up and, escorted by his secretary, walked out of the room.

The Deng Case Team questioners had failed again. They returned, very disconsolate, to their office on Cuiwei Road.

For a year and a half, starting in June 1968, the Team concentrated on looking for evidence of "betrayal and surrender". They sent out 93 investigative groups containing 223 people, who went to 15 provinces, municipalities and autonomous areas, and over 140 cities and counties, traveling a distance of more than 300,000 kilometers. In Beijing alone they were busily in and out of nearly 100 government, Communist Party, media, military, cultural, social, and scientific research, organizations.

Deng Xiaoping had been a long time in the revolution; he had worked in many places; he had been involved in a wide variety of activities. It was no easy job to check all this out. The Case Team did its best. But despite all its efforts, when it wrote its report to Kang Sheng and the others, it was compelled to regretfully admit: "We still have no direct testimony regarding his entry into the Youth League and the Communist Party, and some aspects of his implementation of a socialist line. On important questions such as whether he was ever arrested, turned traitor and supplied information to the enemy, we have not discovered any clues."

Unable to find anything in Papa's past, the Case Team turned to his present. In the above report they added the following: "We already have considerable evidence that Deng Xiaoping in collaboration with Yang Shangkun placed a counter-revolutionary listening device near Chairman Mao, that he organized a clique, and protected wrong-doers, traitors and spies. We will submit this material for review by the leadership. Our next step will focus on three of Deng's crimes: plotting a counter-revolutionary take-over, scheming to usurp the Party and government, and keeping in secret communication with foreign powers."

Three days later, with Kang Sheng's approval, the report was sent to Zhou Enlai, Chen Boda, Jiang Qing and Xie Fuzhi. It claimed there was some question as to how Deng joined the Communist Party. When the report got to Zhou, he added this notation: "Deng Xiaoping joined the

Youth League and transferred into the Party while in France on a work-study program. I, Li Fuchun and Cai Chang all knew about it."

You can imagine how disappointed the Case Team and their bosses were to read this.

Still, the Case Team did not fold their banners and muffle their drums. In the latter half of 1969 they questioned all of the prominent Communists being held "under investigation" in the numerous prisons and detention centers around Beijing regarding Deng's present-day "activities", and ended with nothing.

The Deng Xiaoping Case Team operated in failure, and dissolved in disgrace.

Its final attempt took the form of a request on November 28, 1970 to Kang Sheng, Huang Yongsheng, Wu Faxian and Ye Qun for permission to inspect documents in various departments for evidence of Deng's "crimes." Wu Faxian forwarded it to Zhou Enlai. A few days later the Case Team saw the response, which Zhou had endorsed on the request. It read: "These documents are all matters of public record. Why review them again? I remember that when Deng Xiaoping and Tan Zhenlin were sent down into the countryside, their matters were removed from the special case teams."

The Deng Case Team was shocked. They hastily wrote to Huang Yongsheng and Wu Faxian asking whether they should continue sending in reports of their investigations. It wasn't until December 24, 1970 that Wu's secretary came to their office and called a meeting of the entire team.

"The leadership has seen the reports you sent in regarding Deng Xiaoping's question, and the Premier's reply," he said. "The leadership told me to instruct you not to submit any more reports. Don't do any more on the Deng case. Hold on to the material, and wait."

There was no need to wait. Everyone on the Team knew their mission had ended. In less than two and half years the Deng Xiaoping Case Team had expired, unheralded and unmourned.

14

The Ninth Party National Congress and "Continuing the Revolution"

IN April 1969, the Ninth National Congress of the Chinese Communist Party was convened in Beijing by Mao Zedong. He considered this an extremely important move in preserving and strengthening his revolutionary line against revisionism.

The Congress made several important decisions: 1) It endorsed Mao's theory of class struggle, calling it "our Party's basic line during the entire period of socialism", and once again affirmed the "necessity" and "timeliness" of the "Great Proletarian Cultural Revolution". 2) It amended the Communist Party Constitution to formally recognize Lin Biao as the close comrade-in-arms and successor of Mao Zedong. 3) It elected a new Central Committee. So many Cultural Revolution Group leaders and heads of rebel factions were absorbed into the Committee that a "leftist" theory, line, and orientation were guaranteed.

After the Congress, the Ninth Central Committee met. Mao Zedong was elected Chairman, and Lin Biao, Vice-Chairman. The Committee members now included Jiang Qing, Zhang Chunqiao, Yao Wenyuan, Chen Boda, Kang Sheng and Xie Fuzhi, from the Cultural Revolution Group. The Lin Biao clique provided Huang Yongsheng, Li Zuopeng, Qiu Huizuo, Wu Faxian, and Ye Qun. Numerous functionaries and supporters of both organizations were also elected. Altogether the two forces occupied more than half the seats in the Central Committee Politburo. Directly and indirectly they exercised strong leverage in all of the leadership units under the Central Committee.

Mao must have felt that the "revolution" he had launched, to the amazement of China and the world, was a political and organizational success; that it was assured of a major niche in history. He had confidently predicted at the 12th Plenary Session of the Eighth Central Committee the previous year, "by next summer it will be more or less finished."

Truly "more or less"? Actually, the Cultural Revolution was a long, long way from being finished!

There were sharp differences of opinion about the Cultural Revolution from the start, and many obstacles. New developments followed wave upon wave. Serious factional struggles erupted everywhere. Because Mao's aims and actions in the Cultural Revolution were wrong in the first place, many questions and contradictions were all tangled together like a big ball of yarn. You couldn't find the thread ends; you couldn't unravel it. How could you expect to clear everything up with one Party congress?

The popular saying was that the Cultural Revolution would be "carried through to the end." Mao asked: "What do we mean by 'the end'?" No one was able to answer. Mao's own response clearly showed his mental contradiction. In the same speech in which he predicted the Cultural Revolution would be "more or less finished", he said:

"Our foundation is not solid. From what I have learned, perhaps in not all, or even the majority, but in a very large number of the factories, the leadership is not in the hands of the true Marxists, in the hands of the worker masses."

Mao continued: "In this revolution there are things we haven't finished, things we have to go on with, such as struggle, criticism and reform. After a number of years, we may even need another revolution."

He called for strengthening the dictatorship of the proletariat in every factory, farm and school. Putting it that way meant not only that the Cultural Revolution was necessary, but that it had to be continued in even greater depth.

The gap between Mao's ideas and reality, his erroneous appraisal of the situation, and the important use he made of the Lin Biao and Jiang Qing cliques, resulted in his complete loss of control over the movement. In the years of the Cultural Revolution which followed he was constantly confronted with things he had not anticipated, with a chaos he had no wish to see.

By the Ninth Party National Congress the Cultural Revolution had been on for three years. No one would have guessed that it had gone less than one third down the road.

Papa knew about the Congress from the newspapers. Although the press still referred to him as the "Second Biggest Capitalist Roader in the Party", and although he had been removed from all his Party and government posts, he had not been expelled from the Party. His over 40 years of political experience told him how important this was. He sensed, too, that there was some secret underneath. As long as he remained in the Party, he still had room; a lifeline still remained.

On May 3, 1969 he sent a letter to Wang Dongxing, head of the Central Committee General Office. It expressed support for the resolutions passed by the Congress, and asked Wang to relay this to the Chairman, the Vice-Chairman and the Central Committee. He said now that the Congress was over, he wondered whether it was time to settle his question, and that he would wait calmly for the Party's decision. He assured Mao Zedong he would accept without reservation whatever political conclusion and administrative disposition the Party might make, and would never seek to have them reversed.

In conclusion he requested an interview with Wang Dongxing, to talk about his impressions.

The letter was put into the hands of Mao Zedong, just as Papa had anticipated. Mao read it, and passed it on to Lin Biao and to those members of the Politburo who were then in Beijing.

Deng Xiaoping's attitude surely made an impression on Mao Zedong. First, he was willing to criticize himself. Mao considered this very important. He mentioned it in later statements. Second, it proved to Mao that his decision not to expel Deng Xiaoping from the Party was correct. This same decision foreshadowed an extremely important political event in the future.

As a result, Papa's situation improved. What mattered most to my parents was that they were allowed to see their children.

By then, my younger brother Feifei and I had been assigned separately to farming villages in Shanxi and Shaanxi. My Big Sister Deng Lin had gone with the other students of the Central Academy of Fine Arts to Xuanhua in Hebei Province for education and labor training under the People's Liberation Army (PLA).

Big Brother Pufang, still in the Peking University Hospital, had his status changed from "counter-revolutionary" to "child who could be educated". A decision must have come down after the Ninth Party Congress, and he was transferred to the famous osteopathic division of the Jishuitan Hospital for treatment. He was no longer kept in isolation. Several of his Peking University classmates — some of whom had also been labeled as "counter-revolutionaries" who had "fallen into the mire" — came to the hospital to see him.

Second Sister Deng Nan was called back to the Physics Department of Peking University to wait further assignment. One day after Pufang had been moved to the Jishuitan Hospital, Xie Jingyi, a big official in the Cultural Revolution Group, suddenly summoned her. What did so important a lady want with Deng Nan? Xie Jingyi wanted Deng Nan to accompany her on a visit to Pufang.

It was common practice for people to be nasty to us "black gang children". Why now so friendly and polite? It was strange, and a bit disturbing. We hoped it would mean a further improvement in Pufang's treatment. At least it wouldn't get worse.

Not long after, Deng Nan was notified by the PLA team in the university that she could see our parents in Zhongnanhai. Deng Nan was overjoyed, but she couldn't believe it. "Aren't we supposed to make a class distinction between us and them?" she queried experimentally. "I won't go."

"This permission has come from above," the PLA man replied. "You can go once a week from now on."

Still doubtful, Deng Nan took the bus and made her way to

Zhongnanhai.

Our parents had also been notified. They were told their daughter would come to see them on Saturday afternoon. They were very excited. They hadn't seen any of us for nearly two years. Day and night they thought of their children.

After lunch they took no naps, but just sat, waiting. At last, Deng Nan arrived. Tremulously, she hailed them. Papa and Mama, very moved, were all smiles. It was a joyous reunion.

As Mama later recalled: "I hadn't seen Deng Nan in two years. She had become a big girl, so slim and beautiful!"

Mama simply doted on her. Papa never spoke when he was moved. Nor did he speak when he was happy. Silently, he watched Mama and daughter. They couldn't say enough to each other. Quietly, he smiled.

Mama had expected all the children would come. When only Deng Nan arrived, she asked: "Where are the others?"

Deng Nan told her that Deng Lin had gone with her schoolmates to work in Hebei Province, that Maomao had been sent to a farm brigade near Yan'an, that Feifei was in another farm brigade in Shanxi Province. She said we frequently wrote letters to her, that we were fine.

"What about Chubby?" Mama asked. Chubby was Pufang's nickname when he was a baby.

Deng Nan didn't answer. "Aiya, my hair is filthy," she cried. "I've got to wash it." She hurried to the bathroom, turned on the water and began washing her hair.

Mama sensed something was wrong. She followed Deng Nan into the bathroom, and questioned her again. The more Mama asked, the more evasive Deng Nan became. Finally, Deng Nan told her the whole story.

Mama burst into tears. She never dreamed such a tragedy could befall her son. The joy she felt when her daughter arrived instantly evaporated. Mama was heart-broken. The more she thought about it, the more she cried. She wept for three days and three nights.

Papa said nothing, but he smoked incessantly. After Deng Nan left, he urged Mama to compose herself. He said as long as things had come to such a pass, they should do their best to ensure that Pufang received proper medical care.

A reunion with dear ones should have been a source of happiness. But in those days, so far as our family was concerned, happiness was always fleeting, likely to be crushed at any moment by suffering and pain.

On learning that his son had been paralyzed, Papa naturally was upset. He wrote a letter to Chairman Mao, requesting the Party to help arrange further treatment for Pufang. Mao Zedong and Zhou Enlai endorsed their approval. Wang Dongxing, of the Central Committee General Office, referred the matter to the No. 301 Hospital of the Logistics Department of the People's Liberation Army.

Qiu Huizuo, head of the PLA Logistics Department, was one of Lin Biao's chieftains. After Lin Biao was designated as Mao's successor, the Hospital's leaders were reluctant to admit any "questionable" patients. They refused even Marshal Chen Yi when he became ill. They certainly didn't want the son of the "Second Biggest Capitalist Roader." Only after Wang Dongxing showed them the endorsement by Mao Zedong and Zhou Enlai did they agree to accept Pufang. It was very difficult to get any assistance from an army controlled by Lin Biao.

Pufang was transferred to the surgical division of the No. 301 Hospital on August 5. He had received virtually no treatment while in the Jishuitan Hospital. A veteran doctor there had examined him. But because the man himself was under attack, charged with being a "bourgeois academic authority", it was impossible for him to prescribe any treatment. Pufang frequently ran a high fever due to a urinary infection. They erroneously gave him an injection of streptomycin, and he went deaf in one ear. That is how confused and irresponsible hospitals were during the Cultural Revolution.

In the No. 301 Hospital he was put in a private room. At first they guarded him closely, and it was difficult for most people to see him. But gradually, security was relaxed. He still suffered from a urinary infection, and still had a high fever. The hospital began a course of treatment, including acupuncture to relieve the pain. Some of the doctors, nurses, and other patients were quite nice to him. In this more normal atmosphere, Pufang felt much better.

Our parents of course were happier after Pufang was admitted to the No. 301 Hospital. They wanted their son to have the best possible treatment. Although they knew he could not have a complete recovery, they hoped that at least he would be able to take care of himself in daily life. Pufang was only 25. He had many long years ahead.

15

A Strategic Exodus

IN March of 1969 two clashes erupted between forces of the regular armies of China and the Soviet Union on Zhenbao (Precious Pearl) Island in Heilongjiang Province on the northeastern border. Relations between the governments and Communist Parties of the two countries had fluctuated between warm and cool after diplomatic relations were first established in 1949. A period of fraternal cordiality was followed in the beginning of the 60s by a debate between the two Parties along ideological lines. This led to a split between the Parties and a serious eroding of governmental relations. There had been a number of border incidents, starting in 1964. This one, on Zhenbao Island, was the largest.

Mao Zedong over-estimated the seriousness of the situation. He thought a new world war was inevitable, that China had to get ready to fight. Full-scale war preparations were commenced throughout the land.

Lin Biao, in Suzhou, on October 17 issued an emergency directive entitled "Strengthen War Readiness Against a Surprise Enemy Attack". Accordingly, on October 18, Chief of the General Staff Huang Yongsheng circulated "Vice-Chairman Lin Biao's Order Number One," and ordered the Army, Navy, and Air Force to begin immediate preparations for war.

In co-ordination, the Central Committee decided to scatter some of its personnel through various parts of the country, including a number of its former leaders currently under attack. Of the veteran comrades, Zhu De and Dong Biwu were assigned to Guangdong Province; Ye Jianying to Hunan Province; Chen Yun and Wang Zhen to Jiangxi; Nie Rongzhen and Chen Yi to Hebei. Of the "capitalist roaders", Liu Shaoqi would go to the city of Kaifeng in Henan, and Tao Zhu to Hefei in Anhui Province. Deng Xiaoping was assigned to the province of Jiangxi.

As Wang Dongxing remembers, after this disposition was decided, Mao sent for him and said: "Put Chen Yun and Wang Zhen near convenient lines of communication. I can't do without them if the fighting starts. They're useful. I still need them."

Mao was also going to leave Beijing. Zhou Enlai asked that Wang Dongxing be allowed to remain to help with the general exodus. Mao said he could stay another 10 days. Thus, the job of talking to Deng Xiaoping fell on Wang.

In October, Wang Dongxing, accompanied by Wang Liang'en, Vice-Director of the General Office, called on Deng Xiaoping. This was both in response to Deng's letter requesting to see him, and to inform him that he and Mama were being moved to Jiangxi. Wang Dongxing told Papa about the war preparations, and the decision of the Central Committee to scatter its people in various parts of the country. In Jiangxi, Papa would be working in a factory.

Papa was surprised to hear about the exodus. He thought a moment, then asked whether they could take his stepmother, Xia Bogen, our grandma, with them. She was old, and had no one to look after her. Wang agreed.

In conclusion, Papa reminded him that the Chairman had said he could contact Wang if he had any problems. Could he continue to do that after he went to Jiangxi? Wang Dongxing said he could.

Papa felt much better. Wang's promise was very important. It meant that even though Papa was a thousand *li* away, he could still maintain his links with the Central Committee.

Because he was preparing to accompany Mao Zedong when the Chairman left Beijing, Wang Dongxing turned his duties over to Wang Liang'en. Not long after, Wang Liang'en again called on Deng Xiaoping to check on how he was getting on with his packing. Mama said they had a lot of old books they wanted to take with them. Could he please supply a few big crates? Also, for many years she and Papa were used to keeping the bedroom dark when they slept. She proposed to take the bedroom drapes along. Wang Liang'en nastily refused both requests.

Papa was very angry. He demanded to see Wang Dongxing. Shortly thereafter, Wang Dongxing arrived. He promptly agreed about both the crates and the window drapes. He told Papa he could take anything he liked. Whatever he left behind would be safe. Nothing would be changed in our compound. He and Mama would still be living there when they came back.

Wang Dongxing was close to Mao Zedong, and was Mao's most trusted confident. At the start of the Cultural Revolution, Mao had discussed Papa's case with him. Later, he put him in complete charge.

It was a positive sign that not only was Wang Dongxing very pleasant but also that he promised my parents they could eventually move back to our original home. In effect he was letting them know that the order to leave Beijing was not being directed against Deng Xiaoping alone. In addition, my parents would be allowed to work in a factory after they got to Jiangxi. It didn't matter whether this would be considered a form of study, or a means of reform — it signified an end to the isolation they had endured in Beijing. It was a positive development. Their minds eased, my parents went on with their packing.

Sister Deng Nan and all of her schoolmates at Peking University, in compliance with Lin Biao's Order Number One, were directed to move to Huairou County in the outskirts of Beijing. My parents requested that Big Sister Deng Lin, who was in a farm brigade in Hebei Province, be allowed to come home and help them pack. The General Office approved, and Deng Lin rejoined temporarily the parents she hadn't seen in two years. But they had little time to talk of family affairs, for the time of departure was fast approaching.

Mama also obtained permission to visit Pufang in the No. 301 Hospital. As she walked toward his room she recalled the tall husky son who loved to jump and run. In only two years he had become paralyzed. It was like a knife in her heart. She burst into tears. The people with her urged her to control herself — it would be bad for her son to see her like this. She sat down on a chair. Gradually, she was able to suppress her pain. Wiping her eyes, she entered Pufang's room.

He was the only occupant. The equipment and furnishings were not bad. Mama felt a little better. At least she was able to see him before leaving Beijing. That was some consolation! She told Papa all about it when she got home. Pufang was getting better treatment in the No. 301 Hospital. There was even a thread of hope his condition might improve. You might say it would be the greatest good fortune to come out of all this tragedy.

In the last-minute packing, my parents had no time for anything else. They were unaware that their old comrade Zhou Enlai was making detailed and careful arrangements for them. On October 18, 1969 he telephoned the office of the Revolutionary Committee of Jiangxi Province and spoke to Cheng Huiyuan, head of the Revolutionary Core Team.

"The Central Committee has decided that some of the leaders shall go down and familiarize themselves with the local situations," Zhou Enlai said. "They will also take part in appropriate labor and learn from the masses. Comrade Chen Yun will be going to Jiangxi. He will be accompanied by his secretary, a guard, and a cook. Comrade Wang Zhen, his wife and his whole family will also be going to Jiangxi. They are both over 60. Physical labor would not be appropriate for them. They will have difficulty in adjusting to the sudden change of environment, moving from the north to the south. You must look after their living conditions. Naturally, they will pay for their own food, but their rent mustn't be too high....

"The second thing, Comrade Wang Dongxing has probably already told you. Deng Xiaoping and his wife will also be coming down. As Chairman Mao said at the Ninth Party National Congress, Deng Xiaoping's question is different from other persons'. He will be steeling himself in labor. Of course he mustn't work full time. He's also over 60, and not in very good health. The rent should be reasonable.

"Telephone Comrade Wang Dongxing and discuss with him where specifically these old leaders will live and when they can move in. Let me emphasize: you must help them, and appoint people to take care of them. Talk it over and provide a concrete proposal."

Cheng Huiyuan hurried by car to Wuyuan to see Cheng Shiqing, covering over 350 kilometers that same night. Cheng Shiqing was Director of the Revolutionary Committee of Jiangxi Province, and the First Political Commissar of the Provincial Military Area. He had seized power during the Cultural Revolution and had become quite an important figure. Although known as being closely allied to Lin Biao, he dared not delay enforcing Premier Zhou Enlai's telephone instructions. He thought it over, and said to Cheng Huiyuan:

"We resolutely support the wise decision of the Central Committee, and will firmly carry out the Premier's instructions. We will welcome Comrades Chen Yun and Wang Zhen and Deng Xiaoping and his wife to Jiangxi to live and work. They can come whenever they wish. We will first put them up in the Binjiang Guest House. Later, we will move Deng Xiaoping and his wife to Ganzhou.

"As to where Chen Yun and Wang Zhen will stay, we will talk it over with them, and then decide. Wherever it is, we promise to install steam heat. We absolutely guarantee their safety, and will not permit rebel factions or Red Guards to disturb them.

"But there are two questions on which we request instructions from the Central Committee: One, will it be appropriate for Deng Xiaoping and his wife to live together with the others? And, two, shall we send people to Beijing to escort Comrades Chen Yun and Wang Zhen here to Jiangxi?"

On October 19, in response to a telephone call from the Revolutionary Committee of Jiangxi Province, Zhou Enlai expressed general agreement with the arrangements. But he did not think Deng Xiaoping should be housed in Ganzhou.

"It's too far from Nanchang," Zhou said. "It's in the mountains, travel is difficult, and the conditions are very poor. He's an old man over 60. What if he gets sick? My idea is that you put him near Nanchang where it will be easy to look after him. The best thing would be for him and his wife to stay in a small two-storey house. They could live upstairs, and a helper live downstairs. It should be a single house in a courtyard. That way they would have space to move around in, and it would be safe.

Tell my idea to Cheng Shiqing."

The Premier's proposal was very detailed and very specific. The Jiangxi people discussed it back and forth, but couldn't agree on a common conclusion. Finally, they requested Beijing to send someone down to look things over and help them decide.

Wang Liang'en, Vice-Director of the Central Committee General Office, summoned the Deng Case Team to a meeting in Zhongnanhai. He told of the situation in Jiangxi and the Premier's instructions.

"I want you to send a man down and help the Jiangxi comrades find Deng a suitable place to live," he said. "It would be better if it had steam heat. Deng Xiaoping is an old man. He shouldn't live too far from where he works. They would have to send a car for him every day, and that wouldn't be good. Or if he had to walk to work, or take the bus, it wouldn't be safe. Although Comrades Chen Yun and Wang Zhen will also be in Jiangxi, they are different from Deng Xiaoping. Both of them were elected to the Central Committee at the Ninth Party National Congress, Deng was not. They're not likely to have any problems. There were photos of Deng even before the Cultural Revolution, and now he's charged with being the 'Second Biggest Capitalist Roader Within the Party'. He's easily recognized. People might want to call him out for a struggle meeting. Do you understand me? Alright, then. Go home and get ready. Be at the Shahe Airfield tomorrow morning at 8:00."

In the meantime, my parents and Big Sister Deng Lin were packing. Ordinarily, my folks lived simply. It was easy for them to get their daily necessities together. But since it was permitted, they thought they'd take along a little more. From the library in the rear of our courtyard they pulled out the Marxist classics, plus books on history and literature they had accumulated over the years, and placed them one by one in the crates the General Office had supplied. They knew these volumes would help them pass the many days and sleepless nights, which might lie ahead.

The day before departure, that is, October 21, Papa sent a letter to Wang Dongxing. He said he accepted the Central Committee's disposition, and reiterated his vow to Chairman Mao and the Central

Committee to do his utmost as an ordinary Communist and a socialist citizen at work and in labor. He said he hoped the letter would be relayed to the Chairman and the Central Committee.

Papa knew that while leaving Beijing would free him of his constrained existence, in distant Jiangxi he would be separated from the Central Committee and Chairman Mao by more than 1,000 *li*. He wanted, through his letter to Wang Dongxing, to make his attitude clear to Chairman Mao.

Just as Papa wished, Wang did indeed transmit the letter to Mao Zedong, and Mao personally read it.

16

The Lonely Flight South

MY parents rose early in the morning on October 22, 1969. With Grandma and Deng Lin, they got into the jeep which came for them. Their luggage went in another vehicle. It was a dull day. Although the sky was already light, there was a somber feeling to Beijing. Heavy clouds hung low, capping the pervasive autumn chill.

The windows of the jeep were shut tight; the thick curtains were drawn. After leaving Zhongnanhai the vehicle twisted and turned along Beijing's bumpy roads. The passengers couldn't see a thing. They were only aware of winding through the streets for a long time. None of them spoke. Finally, the car stopped, and they got out. They were at a large military airport.

The smaller pieces of luggage were loaded on to the plane. For fear of over-weight, they were told the crates would have to wait for later shipment.

With men bustling all around them, Deng Lin felt utterly distracted. Pufang lay paralyzed in the No. 301 Hospital, Deng Nan and her classmates had been moved to the outskirts of the city; Maomao and Feifei were in farm brigades in Shaanxi and Shanxi. Deng Lin was the only one of the children able to see our parents and Grandma off. She watched them climbing a rickety temporary ladder into the plane. It was hard for Grandma because of her age, and her small feet.

At the cabin entrance, Papa stopped and turned around for a last look at Beijing. In the three years since he had first been criticized in 1966, he had not been a step away from Zhongnanhai. He wanted to see the ancient city where he had lived for nearly 20 years. But all that was in view was an empty airfield. He turned and entered the plane.

At three minutes after 9:00 am the engines began to roar, the noise steadily increasing in intensity as the plane raced along the runway. It lifted off and headed toward the low-hanging clouds. It seemed to become smaller and smaller, until it vanished completely into the distance.

The plane was an old Ilyushin 14 military aircraft. There were five passengers. Accompanying Papa, Mama, and Grandma were the head of the Deng Xiaoping Case Team and an orderly. Near the door at the front of the cabin a folding cot with a mattress was placed for Grandma, who might find flying a strain. Mama and Grandma were seated on the cot. Papa sat beside a folding table near the window. The two men from the Deng Case Team sat in the rear of the cabin.

It was impossible to be heard above the roar of the engines. The plane was not soundproofed. An attendant brought a thermos of hot water. He banged with his hand on the metal wall of the cabin to query whether anyone wanted to drink. The passengers either nodded, or waved negatively.

No one spoke. What was there to say? Would this trip bring misfortune, or good luck? Although it was a strategic transfer, was it also conclusive in nature? They were traveling south. When could they return north to Beijing? Life in Jiangxi would be different from their confinement in Zhongnanhai, but in what way? During their two years in Zhongnanhai they had not even been able to see Beijing. What would Jiangxi, a thousand *li* distant, look like? The children were so far away. How were they getting on? Would they be able to come to Jiangxi?

It was impossible to know the answers to these questions which filled their minds as they flew toward Nanchang in Jiangxi. The outcome of the Cultural Revolution, the future of the nation, political developments — all were unfathomable, to say nothing of personal fates. Their sudden, sometimes farcical, changes brought unexpected, damaging, political tragedy to individuals, to society, to the nation as a whole.

After several hours' flight, the plane slowly descended on the Xiangtang Airport in Nanchang, Jiangxi.

A group of people was already waiting. When Papa stepped down from the plane, the Director of the Office of the Jiangxi Provincial Revolutionary Committee, Cheng Huiyuan, came forward and shook hands. Smiling, he introduced himself and said: "Comrade Deng Xiaoping, Chairman Mao has sent you to Jiangxi. We're delighted to have you."

The long shunned term "Comrade", the long discouraged smile, started the stay in Jiangxi.

A convoy of three cars — sedans, not jeeps — rolled across Jiangxi's reddish terrain. The three arrivals sat in the middle car. Its windows were open, its curtains were not drawn. They could look out and see the world around them. Another new sensation.

How familiar those broad fields of red earth were to Papa, how dear. More than 30 years before he had begun his fighting career in this area, then a soviet, from here he had set off on the famous Long March. Thirty years had gone by in a flash. Human life is indeed fleeting!

Before long, the cars arrived in Nanchang and stopped at the Provincial Communist Party Committee's First Guest House (also called the Binjiang Guest House). Yang Dongliang, the vice-chairman of the Provincial Revolutionary Committee and commander of the Jiangxi Military Area, greeted the just-arrived Deng Xiaoping. He spoke volubly of how Papa should work well and accept reformation. It was a "welcome" of sorts and, at the same time, a statement of official duties.

With the three newcomers settled in the Guest House, it was time for the two escorts from the Case Team to get busy. They had to find them suitable living quarters and a place to work without delay. That same day, with the Jiangxi people, they inspected several houses, but didn't like any of them. The next day, they looked again, without success. The third day, the provincial people took them to what had been the Nanchang Infantry School of the Greater Fuzhou Military Area. They examined the small house where the principal had lived, and the newly built county tractor factory, only two or three *li* away. The Case Team men thought these places were ideal.

That night, they telephoned their findings to their superiors in Beijing. These approved, and relayed the report to the Central Committee

General Office, which also gave its consent.

Their mission accomplished, the Deng Case Team escorts came to the Guest House and talked with Papa for 10 minutes or so. They told him about the housing and work arrangements, and asked whether he had any requests. They would report them to the Central Committee in Beijing.

Papa said: "I agree with the arrangements the Central Committee has made for me. I'm here in Jiangxi, now, but I'll be coming out eventually. I can still work for the Party for another 10 years."

The reply took the Case Team men by surprise. So clear and positive, it didn't sound like what a person under investigation for so-called "errors" would say.

"There is one thing, however," Papa added. "My oldest daughter is 28 this year. I'm a little concerned about her."

"As to your first point," the head of the Case Team said, "that depends on you. It's up to the Central Committee to decide whether you'll come back to work. Regarding the second question, all children are the nation's responsibility. You must be confident she can handle her own affairs. At the same time, the nation will look after her."

This was the first time the Deng Xiaoping Case Team spoke formally face-to-face with the man they were investigating. Although the Team had been in existence for over a year it had not even met Papa, to say nothing of questioning him directly. That 10-minute meeting was the first and last time the Deng Case Team spoke with Deng Xiaoping. Only in the irrational years of the Cultural Revolution was it possible for such absurdities to happen.

Actually, his situation was not unique. On the one hand, Mao Zedong wanted to criticize him, to have him overthrown via the machinations of Jiang Qing and Lin Biao and their gang. On the other hand, Mao preserved his Communist Party membership, and had the Central Committee General Office — that is, Wang Dongxing — take direct responsibility for Papa, and did not permit Lin Biao and Jiang Qing to intervene. You might say that all during the period when Papa was being criticized and purged, to a certain extent Mao protected him, including guaranteeing his personal safety. Looking back, it is obvious that if Mao hadn't wanted to protect him, and if Lin Biao and Jiang Qing had been given authority to handle the case, Deng Xiaoping's fate would have been very different.

During the Cultural Revolution Mao Zedong protected, or better say preserved, not only Deng Xiaoping, but a large number of old comrades, for a variety of reasons.

Let us talk first about Mao's choice of a successor. He picked Lin Biao after much deep thought. During the war years, starting with the Jinggang Mountains period, Lin Biao was one of Mao's favorite generals. He knew how to wage war; he won battles. In the political in-fighting inside the Party and in the Army, Lin always stood on Mao's side. After Liberation, at the Lushan Conference in 1959 he joined in the criticism of Peng Dehuai. In the 60s he called for the study of Mao Zedong Thought. At the Conference of Seven Thousand in 1962, while Liu Shaoqi, Deng Xiaoping and many of the leading comrades strongly attacked, the "leftist" policies, Lin Biao praised Mao and unctuously flattered him.

Mao Zedong was a great man. At the same time, he was highly subjective and emotional. He remembered slights, and he remembered favors. His opinions of people and the way he dealt with problems were invariably tinged by his emotions. Mao felt that historically Lin Biao was his man; that he did not veer toward the conservative like Liu and Deng, that he would uphold Mao's ideology and be faithful to his revolutionary line. Mao believed that when the decision-making power was slipping away and class struggle was extended into the Party itself, Lin Biao was his obvious successor; that he could utilize Lin Biao's control of the Army to launch his Cultural Revolution.

But he didn't entirely trust him, particularly after Lin's expanding ambitions became increasingly apparent. Mao grew cautious.

His approach to Jiang Qing and the Cultural Revolution Group was still more subtle. From start to finish he applied "revolutionary" methods to attain "revolutionary" goals. He used Jiang Qing, Chen Boda, Kang Sheng, Zhang Chunqiao and Yao Wenyuan as planners, initiators, and the basic forces of the movement. He at first considered them the real leftists, the true warriors defending his line and ideology. But they soon demonstrated quite obviously an unbridled political divisiveness. Mao sensed this, and began treating them with circumspection and restraint. He never permitted them to control the State Council, or handle foreign affairs, or take over the armed forces. He allowed them to be the lead vanguard in the Cultural Revolution, shields of his theory and practice, but never an elite guard or rulers of the nation. On these matters Mao preserved a steady clarity.

Mao attached importance to the two main forces he was utilizing, but never relaxed his vigilance. He both used them and watched them. The man who doesn't consider tomorrow will surely have problems today. Mao was a statesman. Even while ardently promoting the movement, he never lost his cool appraising eye — which is why he preserved Deng Xiaoping and a number of veteran leaders.

The revolution had to continue but, in addition, the economy had to be strengthened, China had to attain communism, possibly a big war had to be fought — the road ahead was long. Continuing the revolution and building the economy were both arduous tasks. With so many serious problems, just depending on a successor like Lin Biao would never solve them. Adding Jiang Qing and her gang wouldn't do it either.

One thing was clear in Mao's mind: It wouldn't do to bring down all the old leaders — including Zhou Enlai. Some had to be retained. There was still use for them. Mao therefore ordered that, although a strategic exodus was to be carried out, special consideration should be given to the veteran comrades. He directed Zhou Enlai to take charge, for he knew that Zhou was the only man who could do the job properly. He gave special instructions regarding Chen Yun and Wang Zhen. He said he still needed them, that he couldn't do without them. He said they were useful, that he would soon be calling for them. Mao spoke very frankly.

In this complicated political situation, in the special circumstances engendered by an ideal of continuous revolution, in the open and hidden struggles between the two major factions, now splitting, now joining together, at the height of the revolution's burning fever, Mao Zedong remained cool and thoughtful. When anarchy brought on by "the great chaos brings great stability" slogan became chaotic beyond all bounds, Mao clamped fetters on the mad savagery. To a large extent this halted the widespread purging and brutalizing of leaders. Some of them were returned to their jobs.

These sober actions on Mao's part at this critical juncture, whatever his intentions might have been, provided a valuable basis and vital strength for China of the future. His saving of the veteran leaders showed a rare wisdom in the political actions of his late years.

17

Early Days in Jiangxi

P APA, Mama and Grandma left the Binjiang Guest House at 4 pm on October 26, 1969 and headed for the house in Nanchang provided by the Provincial Revolutionary Committee. They rode in a sedan, followed by a truck carrying their belongings. After driving through Nanchang, they crossed the big August First Bridge.

Through the windows of the car they could see the sparkling Binjiang River below. Shimmering like silver it hastened east, never ceasing, forever flowing beneath the bridge linking the hills on either side. You had the feeling it was the waters of life itself, surging in your heart, unforgettable.

Crossing the river, they continued west about five kilometers to Xinjian County in the outskirts of Nanchang. The car turned in to a gravel road leading to a large gate which opened automatically. They had reached the former Nanchang Infantry School of the Greater Fuzhou Military Area. Both sides of a narrow but straight gravel road were lined by tall French poplar trees, closely spaced, their dense foliage providing deep shade. Behind them stood a large office building, from which a path led up a hill to a high green compound wall. Inside, a small red brick building could be seen, with a gray roof.

They were "home". Though unfamiliar, at first glance it gave them a feeling of warm intimacy.

The two leaves of the gray wooden compound gate were opened, and the vehicles drove in. A small two-story house stood in the center of the round compound. Four cassia trees screened the front door. Immediately inside was an empty entrance hall. A door on the right led to a dining room, and a kitchen.

On mounting the creaking wooden stairs you came to a hallway, two bedrooms, and a bathroom. A long verandah faced south. Standing there, you could see far into the green countryside. The verandah also opened on another apartment, similar to the present one. Since it was not intended for their occupancy, they didn't bother to inspect.

The quarters were not bad, in quiet surroundings. Their first impressions were quite satisfying.

With some help, they unloaded the things on the truck and moved them upstairs. The combined age of Papa, Mama and Grandma was 180 plus. But, under the stimulation of having a new "home", they rolled up their sleeves and went quickly up and down the stairs. Before they knew it, it was dusk, and they turned on the lights. In the virtually empty infantry school area, in the dark stillness, light glowed from the small house. Although it wasn't very bright, it was alive. It brought a touch of excitement, absent from the former school for so long.

The Deng Case Team and the Jiangxi people who had escorted the Deng family, their duty done, had already departed. Only two persons remained. One was a man named Huang Wenhua, a functionary in the Provincial Military Area, who had been sent by the Jiangxi Revolutionary Committee. The other was a young soldier called Young He.

Huang's duty was to ensure that the daily life and work of Deng Xiaoping and his family went smoothly. He had to watch them, and protect them. He had to report on them, and also transmit to his superiors whatever messages or requests Deng might wish to send. Huang had a telephone in his room, enabling him to contact the security team of the Provincial Revolutionary Committee at any time.

Young He did the shopping for the food and other things which required leaving the compound. He also swept and cleaned the house and washed Huang's clothes. The two had separate quarters downstairs in a different part of the building. They became additional members of the small household during the months that followed in Jiangxi.

By the time all of the family's belongings had been put in place and the beds made, it was 10 o'clock at night. They were too tired to cook dinner. Huang and Young He walked over to the artillery regiment's canteen and bought a dozen muffins, and then boiled up a pot of egg soup. That was the family's first meal in their new home.

Papa and Mama and Grandma turned off the lights and went upstairs to rest. In their first night in their bivouac quarters the bedding they slept in was still slightly damp.

While they continued putting their things in order and preparing for their new life, the head of the Deng Case Team, on returning to Beijing, made this report:

"On October 22 we delivered Deng Xiaoping, Zhuo Lin, and Xia Bogen to Jiangxi. We returned today, the 28th. We delivered them to a former infantry school 13 kilometers northwest of Nanchang. It is looked after by caretakers from an artillery unit and the former infantry school. The Provincial Revolutionary Committee has dispatched an artillery squad of 12 men to act as guards. The Deng family lives alone in a small building. A functionary and a young soldier who take care of them live downstairs. Deng will work during the day. He will continue to use the name Deng Xiaoping."

A short time later, Cheng Shiqing, chairman of the Jiangxi Revolutionary Committee and political commissar of the Provincial Military Area, called on Papa. He didn't adopt any hectoring tone, but instead spoke grandly of the "great improvements" that had come to Jiangxi, and of his "policies", after the Cultural Revolution began. Although Cheng was a famous figure in the Lin Biao gang, he was surprisingly pleasant to the "Second Biggest Capitalist Roader".

As Cheng Shiqing was leaving, Chen Changfeng, his second in command in the Provincial Revolutionary Committee and head of the Security Department, noticed a soldier on guard at the door.

"We don't need to have a man standing guard," said Chen. "He can 'sit guard' instead."

Thereafter, the guard squad which had been posted outside the compound was ordered to stay concealed, out of sight. Chen Changfeng had been one of Mao Zedong's guards during the Long March, a Red

Army veteran. The safety of some of the old comrades who had been sent to Jiangxi was mainly his responsibility.

Jiangxi in October is autumn, but not really autumn. It's not cold, the trees are still green, the broad leaves of the poplars still shield against the sun. The Dengs quickly adapted to their new life. Although when they arrived at the airport Papa had been greeted with the word "comrade", he was still the "Second Biggest Capitalist Roader Within the Party". In Jiangxi he remained under a sort of loose house arrest and semi-restraint. He could go to the factory, but not any place else. He could not even freely leave the small compound.

In addition to the two living with them, the family was aware of a detachment of soldiers stationed outside, although they didn't know how many they were. Papa had promised the Central Committee he would not make contact with outsiders. But security was so tight he couldn't have, even if he so desired. If we children wanted to visit we first had to obtain permission from the Provincial Revolutionary Committee.

Their lives were not entirely free but Papa, Mama and Grandma were quite content. They felt the atmosphere of the infantry school, the little compound, the small house, was much more relaxed than the strictures of Zhongnanhai had been, much more natural.

They assumed household chores according to their age and physical capabilities. Papa, although he was 65, was the only "stalwart" among them. He took on the relatively heavy jobs — such as mopping floors, chopping kindling, and breaking the big chunks of coal.

Mama was the youngest, only 53. But she had high blood pressure and a bad heart. She did the lighter tasks like sweeping, wiping the table, washing clothes, sewing and mending.

Grandma was nearly 70, but she was accustomed to hard work, and was still strong. Because she was a good cook, she assumed full charge of tending the stove, cooking, and all the other kitchen functions.

Mutually caring and solicitous, the three oldsters were determined to conquer all difficulties. They cheerfully strengthened their resolve and made a warm, lively home out of their simple, limited environment.

In Jiangxi, they were allowed to communicate with their children, and Mama wrote a letter to every one of us, telling us all about them. I remember receiving Mama's letter on the high loess plateau of northern Shaanxi. Every word in her fine elegant handwriting breathed her thoughts and concern. I couldn't stop crying. How I longed to sprout wings and fly to their side.

With their own lives settled, my parents' main worry was their children scattered in different parts of the country. They received their wages regularly, and were not short of money. But for our sakes, they were very economical. Deng Lin and Deng Nan had graduated from college. They had jobs and were self-supporting. But Pufang lay paralyzed in the hospital, with no source of income. I, Maomao, their youngest daughter, and Feifei, their youngest son, had been assigned to agricultural brigades. We could satisfy our ordinary needs through our labor. But we hadn't enough to buy clothing, and certainly not enough to afford fare home.

As a result, while life in the small house in the former infantry school appeared placid on the surface, our parents' hearts were beset with several insoluble problems. They talked it over with Grandma, and the three of them decided on strict frugality. They wouldn't buy new clothes; they'd eat little meat. Their only indulgence was Papa's cigarettes. He had smoked for many years, and cigarettes were his only solace against loneliness. Now, to economize, he cut down sharply. Sometimes he smoked only half a cigarette, and kept the other half for later.

They saved every possible penny. The total expenditure for the three of them every month was only 60 yuan. The rest of the money, they saved for their children.

18

Working Life

T HEIR living arrangements settled, my parents began working at the Xinjian County Tractor Factory. It was only one kilometer away.

Actually, it was engaged in repairing agricultural machinery implements. The total work force was around 80. After inspection by the Beijing and Jiangxi people, the provincial authorities notified Luo Peng, who doubled as chairman of the factory's revolutionary committee and Party secretary, that Deng Xiaoping and his wife would be coming to work under supervision.

Their complete safety had to be assured. There were to be no public denunciation meetings. If anything went wrong, Luo Peng was to notify the Provincial Revolutionary Committee immediately. Deng was not to be addressed as "comrade", nor was his full name to be spoken aloud. He was simply to be called "Old Deng". Because of his age, his work should not be too heavy, and be suitable to his physical capabilities.

During the War of Resistance Against Japan, Luo Peng had been a functionary in the Ji(Hebei)-Lu(Shandong)-Yu(Henan) military area under the command of Deng Xiaoping. He had listened to talks by Political Commissar Deng Xiaoping several times in the Taihang Mountains. He knew a lot about him.

After Liberation Luo Peng had been an assistant bureau chief in Beijing's Ministry of Public Security. But because he had been accused of "committing an error" during the 1959 campaign against Peng Dehuai for his criticism of the "Great Leap Forward" movement, he had been sent down to Jiangxi. When the Cultural Revolution started he was assigned to the small county factory.

Learning that Deng Xiaoping would be working there came not merely as a surprise — it was a shock. Deng may have been the "Second Biggest Capitalist Roader Within the Party" but he was, after all, an old comrade, and Luo Peng still admired him. He promptly called a meeting of the factory's Party committee, and made all the necessary arrangements. Moreover, he set aside a special small room where Papa and Mama could rest.

They set out for the factory very early, right after breakfast, in the morning of November 9. With Huang's help they had prepared two sets of blue khaki work clothes, and Mama had stitched elastic bands into the openings of the sleeves to make them snugger for work. They both wore grass-green Army sneakers as they stepped through an opening in the big gray compound gates and started down the red gravel school path. Listening to it crunch beneath their feet, they gazed around at the shades of jade and amber green, and their hearts were glad.

From the school grounds they entered upon the main road. The rice in the fields on either side had been harvested, its stumps standing erect in the moist earth, waiting to be plowed under. Blue sky, white clouds, green trees, wide fields, the whole surrounding scene was fresh and bright, very intimate and dear. This was the first time they were out on their own since the Cultural Revolution erupted, the first time they were free and easy, out in the world, walking along the highway on their way to work, ready to check in and mix with ordinary people. After three years of confinement they had a feeling of nothing less than liberation, a new life.

A 40-minute walk brought them to the factory. Luo Peng gave them a general briefing in his office, then led them to the workshop and introduced them to the foreman Tao Duanjin. In keeping with the custom at that time the factory sections were designated in military terms, like company, and platoon. The workshop was a platoon, and its head was called lieutenant. An honest, straightforward fellow, Lieutenant Tao was very cordial, very painstaking. He welcomed Deng Xiaoping to his workshop. He was genuinely happy to have him.

Tao was a worker. In this small county factory no worker could have been more typical. When he worked he wanted what he turned out to be good. Like all the other workers in the factory, to him the Cultural Revolution movement was one thing; doing his job, working, supporting his family, was another, and much more important. When the Cultural Revolution was sweeping the nation, in this factory there were no Red Guards, and very little disturbance. It was a quiet place, with no waves, a little island apart from the rest of the world.

Lieutenant Tao's mind was calm. Some "capitalist roader" has come to work here? That makes him just like the rest of us. The other workers felt the same. Old Deng was getting on in years. They gave him a chair to sit on when he got tired. Old Zhuo (Mama) wasn't in good health. Just do as much work as you feel up to, they told her.

What could they ask this old leader to do? Tao really had to ponder. At first he gave him a light job, cleaning spare parts with gasoline. But Deng's hands trembled with age. He couldn't grip things very well, and he had trouble bending. Tao switched him over to reading charts. But Deng's eyes were bad, he couldn't see clearly.

Finally, Deng himself proposed: why not let him do something that required a little more exertion? Would you like to try using a file? Tao asked. Deng immediately agreed. The fitter's bench was in a corner of the building. A variety of tools hung on the wall. Deng was very pleased. He took a file and set to work. Tao was puzzled. Deng's technique didn't look like a beginner's.

The fact was that 40 years before, during his work-study period in France Deng had worked as a fitter in the Renault Automobile Plant. Although many years had passed, his hands hadn't lost their skill. He laughed on hearing Tao's praise. He himself hadn't expected that what he had learned decades ago in France would be of use in a small factory in Jiangxi. A pleasant surprise!

Finding work for Mama was easy. Since she was in poor health she was given a job with women cleaning coils of wire. The head of the electrical section was a young woman named Chen Hongxing. She cordially asked Mama to be seated. Talking and demonstrating, she showed Mama how to uncoil the wire and clean it. The whole section was composed of young women, who watched, smiling. It was a pleasure to be with them. Mama was happy.

Before my parents came the workers were warned to keep their distance. At first, they only observed the newcomers curiously. Most of them originally had been simple farm folk. They had never seen anyone so important, even their own provincial leaders, to say nothing of big "capitalist roaders" or "black gang" chieftains.

But after a few days, the workers got used to them. Old Deng and Old Zhuo were the same as they. They came every morning and worked just like them. Before long, they all felt quite natural. The atmosphere of caution and curiosity vanished, and the factory returned to normal.

For my parents, being with the workers daily, far from the political whirlpools, with no slogans, and no criticisms, and no exhortations, brought an end to their loneliness. Away from the turmoil of the Cultural Revolution, they could mix naturally with other human beings on a one-on-one basis, working together, chatting and laughing together. It was a joy they formerly could only long for but never hope to attain.

From the house to the factory took them over 40 minutes. At one point they had to cross a stretch of motor road and pass a bus terminal. The trip took time, and wasn't entirely safe. Luo Peng, Lieutenant Tao and our household manager Huang talked it over, wondering whether some more direct route couldn't be found.

They climbed the earthen back wall of the factory compound and looked toward the old infantry school. A walk in a straight line would be much shorter than the present one. They immediately set to work and opened a small door in the rear wall. Proceeding across the cultivated fields and open land, they leveled bumps and filled holes, and created a small path. A walk along that path required only about 20 minutes to get to the factory from the infantry school.

From then on, rain or shine, hot or cold, unless they were sick, my parents could be seen setting out along the path every morning, followed by Huang, heading for the factory. In their three years in Jiangxi, their contact with the workers, and the work itself, were an indispensable part of my parents' lives, indeed, an extremely important part.

They worked every morning, and returned home at noon. After lunch they rested a while, then started family chores. Other than the factory, they were not allowed to go any place else. Mama and Grandma ran the household. They had Huang and Young He buy kitchen utensils and the necessary basic cooking ingredients. Coal and wood were kept in a shed in the rear of the compound.

Papa found a big wooden block and used it as a base for chopping kindling. On a hard piece of ground, he hammered large chunks of coal into smaller usable bits. He and Mama put the kindling and the coal into big bamboo hampers, and stored these in the shed. When winter came they would have enough for cooking and heating bath water.

They had a division of labor on doing the wash. Mama did the every-day clothing herself. When she washed big items like sheets and comforters, Papa would rinse them in clean water, and then the two of them would ring them out and hang them up together.

The busy afternoons would pass, and the dense shadows of the trees would slant across the courtyard in the fading sunlight, small birds fluttering in their branches. After a simple dinner, the three oldsters would wash the dishes, wipe the table and sweep the floor. Any leftovers were put in a small cabinet with a screen door. They would bank the fire, turn out the lights and go upstairs.

Every night, without fail, they would listen to the news broadcasts from the national Central People's Radio Station. At 10, they got ready to retire. Papa liked to read in bed for an hour before sleep. They had always led a regular life. In Jiangxi they continued their habits in the same manner.

The infantry school had been abandoned during the Cultural Revolution. There was no one in it. Some of the doors and windows were gone. Those that remained banged and clattered in the emptiness when the wind blew. There were no streetlights at night. All around was a stygian blackness. Only in the small house on the hill did a few dim lights glow. After they were extinguished the whole school compound was plunged into darkness, except for a few silvery beams if a moon rose. No human voices, no call of birds, no soughing of the wind. Between heaven and earth only a heavier silence, a more oppressive atmosphere.

With my parents and Grandma occupied with their new life, Huang ordinarily did not come upstairs. Young He, who shopped for the food, was in and out several times a day. Most of the time Huang and He kept to their own quarters, or played ping-pong on a table in the entry hall.

Deng Xiaoping was in Jiangxi to work and steel himself, under observation. He couldn't just work and, at the same time, not be observed. On November 23, after instructions from above, Huang came upstairs. He asked Papa and Mama to write their reports after a month of work and study. Papa's reply was brief.

"If I have anything to say I'll write a report to Chairman Mao and the Central Committee."

Stymied, Huang left without another word.

True, a month had slipped by. It was time to write to the Central Committee.

On the 26th of November, Papa took up his pen and wrote a letter to Wang Dongxing. It said:

"We left Beijing on October 22 and arrived in Nanchang the same day. After four days in the military area guesthouse we moved to our new quarters on the 26th. The house is very nice. We were busy putting things in order for a few days, buying food and daily living utensils. On the 9th Zhuo Lin and I started work at the factory. We get up at 6:30 every morning, and leave the house at 7:35. We get to the factory in 20 minutes and work for about three and a half hours. We return home at 11:30. We take a nap after lunch. When we get up, we read the works of Chairman Mao (we try to read for an hour a day), and also read newspapers. At night, we listen to the radio news. We also do some household chores. Time passes very quickly. We do our own cooking (my stepmother does most of it, Zhuo Lin and I help.) We are quite happy."

Papa was speaking from the heart. Their new life, steeling themselves at work — everything was so fresh and new. Overall, they were indeed happy. His letter continued:

"We are in Xinjian County (in the suburbs of Nanchang, about 20 *li* away), and work in a tractor factory. Originally it was a county tractor repair station. Now, it has been expanded to build and repair tractors. It has over 80 people. Aside from work, we took part in two Party meetings and a meeting urging a big push in production during the last 40 days of the year. The comrades in the factory are very cordial, very kind. Our work is not heavy. Zhuo Lin's heart is a little worse. Her blood pressure is 200 over 100. Though it's an effort, she tries to work every day."

Papa's letter vowed he would be worthy of the Chairman and the Party's concern, and do nothing to hurt the Party and the socialist motherland; he would strive to live out his final years honorably. In conclusion, he wrote:

"Because I wanted to familiarize myself with things here first, I waited a month and four days before sending you this letter. Hereafter, I will report to you periodically. If you think it necessary, please convey this report to the Chairman, the Vice-Chairman and the Party Central Committee."

Although a thousand *li* away in Jiangxi, Papa wanted to use letters to keep in touch with the Central Committee, just as he did in Beijing.

Along with the letter, Papa added a note which said: "To prevent overloading the plane we brought only half of our things. Some of our clothing and our books still haven't arrived. We have almost no books at all, here. They were supposed to be sent by train, but they have not come yet. Please ask the comrades in charge to check. It would be best if they could be delivered. If it is decided that they be left in Beijing, please let us know."

Wang Dongxing relayed the letter to Zhou Enlai, Chen Boda and Kang Sheng. He forwarded the note to Wang Liang'en, vice-director of the Central Committee General Office. Not long after, the luggage and books were shipped to Jiangxi.

This indicated to Papa that Wang Dongxing had received his letter. It proved that his channel of communication was still open.

With the help of others, my parents hauled the heavy crates of books upstairs. They pried open the boards, removed the folded newspaper cushioning, and there were their books — new and old, precious volumes which had traveled from Beijing a thousand *li*. Their arrival added much color to my parents' lives.

Our family had all kinds of books. Chinese history like *Twenty-four Histories*, and *A Synopsis of History Since the Zhou Dynasty*; literature like *A Dream of Red Mansions*, *Outlaws of the Marsh*, and *Journey to the West*; poetry from the Tang, Song and Yuan dynasties; works of modern Chinese authors like Ba Jin and Lao She. Foreign literature included the writings of Leo Tolstoy, Nikolai V. Gogol, Anton Pavlovich Chekhov, Balzac, Hugo, Romain Rolland, Moliere, George Bernard Shaw, and Hemmingway. And lots and lots of foreign histories, memoirs, biographies, and philosophical works. And, of course, many Marxist classics.

Those heavy crates indeed contained our family's treasures. In my parents' years of isolation books helped dispel their loneliness, enriched their lives, increased their knowledge, lightened their moods, soothed their spirits. They loved to read. In their free times in the afternoon, in the stillness of the night, books were their constant companions.

19

A Visit Home

Iɴ the yellow soil highlands of northern Shaanxi Province the mountains are linked together. Their summits form a single plateau, locally called a *yuan*. Walking without a stop you couldn't cross the big, flat surface in two full days. It is pure yellow earth, no stones, no water. If you want to build, you have to tamp it into hard walls. For drinking water you must dig down through it 60 or 70 meters. No trees or grass grow on the *yuan*. The only place you can find trees and a few patches of green is around the villages. Fuxian County, where I was sent to live with the peasants, is located on the *yuan*, the yellow soil highlands.

Autumn and cool weather came in October 1969 to that yellow plateau, endlessly stretching beneath the white clouds in the lofty sky. Harvesting had ended. In every village and hamlet the grain had been threshed. There was joy in every household. Little donkeys treaded around creaking grindstones in family courtyards, crushing the fat yellow kernels of millet and wheat.

When we reaped the buckwheat, we bound it into sheaves with grass rope. They weren't a bit heavy. Even a child could shoulder a big bundle.

We lived in Fuxian County. *Fu* means prosperous, but it was anything but prosperous. Northern Shaanxi is really poor. Instead of saying "to eat dinner," they said, "to drink gruel". It usually was a millet soup, in which you rarely saw a grain of millet. Or you might have a muffin of dark hard millet that had chaff mixed in.

If they had a good harvest, you could eat fresh cornmeal muffins, or even one of white flour that wasn't very white. Or fresh buckwheat noodles, or flatcakes flavored with locust tree bark, plus fried spicy peppers. One big bowl after another, hot and fragrant.

The Shaanxi farm folks are warmhearted people. They felt sorry for me, a young girl from Beijing, alone in the village, and the women took turns inviting me into their homes to eat. They added fuel to their stoves, and worked the bellows until the flames were dancing. They made sweet cakes of the yellow grains, and boiled mixed noodles, peppery and hot. The girls and women plied me with food, endlessly urging: "Have a little more, have a little more!"

I watched the young fellows pulling the big stonerollers on the threshing fields, and the young wives tending the gristmills, and the children running all over the slopes, everyone joyous after the good harvest, and my heart was glad. I also had another reason to be happy. I had just received a letter from Mama in Jiangxi.

I kept reading it, and putting it in my pocket, and taking it out and reading it, again and again. During the day I read it in the sunlight, at night I read it beside my small oil lamp. I read it in the fields, even in the moonlight. What made me happiest was that Mama said they would be allowed to see their children, in other words, their children would be allowed to visit them in Jiangxi.

I was very excited. At night, I couldn't sleep. I wanted to go home and see the parents I hadn't seen in several years, and the old Grandma who raised me.

But here I was "under control", a "child who can be educated", the daughter of the "Second Biggest Capitalist Roader". I couldn't leave without the permission of the brigade and the commune headquarters. I had to get permission even to go to the commune office, only five *li* away. What chance had I of going home to visit my "capitalist roader" parents?

I took Mama's letter and went to the brigade office and requested leave. Brigade said they couldn't decide, I would have to ask commune. At commune they said I would have to ask the county. County said I would need permission from the Yan'an Prefecture Administration.

Finally, word came down from Yan'an: In order to go to Jiangxi I needed a certification of approval by the Jiangxi Revolutionary Committee.

To go home and visit family you had to have your approval certified! After all my running around, that was the result. Angry and upset, I immediately wrote to Mama and urged that she get proof from the Jiangxi Revolutionary Committee that it agreed to permit the children to come home and visit.

After receiving my letter, Mama asked Huang to request a certification from the Provincial Revolutionary Committee. The committee said it couldn't decide; it would have to ask instructions from the Central Committee General Office in Beijing. Mama waited anxiously for a reply. When it came, to her surprise it said although the children were permitted to visit, the Jiangxi Revolutionary Committee would not issue a certification. That was the last straw. Mama burst into tears.

My parents again applied. Finally the Jiangxi committee issued what amounted to a certification of approval of the children coming home to visit.

In northern Shaanxi I waited day and night. After more than a month I was informed — I could go home. With smiles all over my face, I packed rapidly. I shouldered my backpack, ready to go. The farm folk with whom I labored every day, when they heard I could go home to see my parents, were almost as happy as I. "Capitalist roader" and "black gang" meant nothing to them. The mamas and the aunts lit up their cook stoves and made me noodles from freshly ground flour, and stacks of big flapjacks, and wrapped them in their homespun kerchiefs, and added just-made sweet cakes of glutinous rice ... and shoved them all into my backpack.

The day I left, all the girls and women I worked with walked with me to the entrance of the village. Holding their kerchiefs to their tear-reddened eyes, they urged me to take care on the road.

I toted my heavy backpack and walked rapidly through an arroyo in the yellow earth plateau, covering some 30 *li* in almost a single breath. I spent the night in the county town, took a bus the next morning and rode nine hours through clouds of dust to Tongchuan. I stayed over that night.

The following day I took the train to the city of Zhengzhou in Henan Province. From there I got another train to Zhuzhou in Hunan, where I spent another night. The next day a train brought me to Xiangtang in Jiangxi, where I changed for a small train which brought me, two hours later, to Nanchang, at last. The total journey had taken me exactly seven days and seven nights. I didn't bother to ponder whether that was fast or slow. I was burning to get home.

But Nanchang City still wasn't home. Where was it? I finally managed to find the Jiangxi Revolutionary Committee office building, and get someone who agreed to take me there. We took a local bus in the city, then changed for a long-distance country bus, crossed the August First Bridge, kept going for a long time, and finally reached the Wangchenggang bus station, and got off.

We were almost there. I hurried into the former infantry school compound, circled past its big office building, marched up the gravel path. There, ahead, was the small house. I pushed open the gray wooden gate and stepped in, yelling at the top of my voice: "Ma! Mama! Pa! Pa!" I flung my dusty backpack to the ground, ran to the house, through the door, up the stairs, into the room.

Papa and Mama were sitting there. Papa had a blanket over his knees, and was reading. Mama was sewing something. I threw my arms around them. Only then did they realize it was me. They rose quickly. One on the left, one on the right, they kissed my dusty cheeks, their tears falling upon my face, mingling with my own, as we stood locked in a tight embrace.

Mama said I was fatter, darker, not like before, uglier! Grandma asked how could I wear such a tattered tunic, with the stuffing sticking out. She immediately started heating water so that I could take a bath. Papa was wearing an old blue-gray quilted tunic, and a blue cloth skullcap, which I could tell at a glance Grandma must have made. He watched Mama and Grandma fondly teasing me, and saw that I was darkly sunburned and strong, but still, before them, girlishly mischievous. Papa said not a word, he only smiled — a smile of deep happiness and contentment.

It was early December 1969. Winter had already come to the yellow soil highlands of northern Shaanxi. Although it hadn't snowed yet, the north wind was biting. Here down in Jiangxi it was still sunny and warm, and the leaves of the French poplars were jade green. Fragrant cassia trees stood before the house. Behind, was the woodshed. All had an endearing, intimate appeal.

I was home. My home was here. My papa and mama were here. This was my home. Mama and Grandma took me on a tour of the house. Everything was so different. Sunlight filtered through the cracks in the board walls of the woodshed. The freshly chopped kindling was pleasantly fragrant. Pieces crackled as Grandma fed them into the cook stove, and dancing flames dazzled the eyes. Fat clucking hens outside the kitchen window scratched and pecked in the courtyard.

Papa chucked coal in the heater of the water boiler in the kitchen, to hasten it along. Grandma poured a lot of oil into a round-bottom pan, and beat a noisy tattoo upon it with an iron spoon, getting ready to prepare a lot of tasty dishes. Mama put all the clothes I had brought in the washtub, and added scalding water, and boiled them. She said she was afraid they had lice. Ai! Even the pretty sweater Big Sister had knitted and sent me parcel post over hundreds of kilometers didn't escape. All the colors washed away. It came out faded almost white, much tighter, and much shorter. A heart-breaking sight.

After my bath, I put on some of Mama's clothes. I was a new person. I tucked into Grandma's food, really delicious. Papa, Mama, Grandma, and I, one on each side of the square table. They didn't even pick up their chopsticks. They just sat there, watching me eat.

The excitement I stirred up by coming home subsided slightly after dinner. We all repaired to the living room, and I sat closely beside Mama. They asked and I answered. I asked and they answered. It was as if we were trying to spill out at once all the things we had wanted to say during our long separation, and ask all the questions we had wanted to ask.

They asked what my life was like in the farming brigade in northern Shaanxi. I told them the country folk treated me fine. That made them very happy. When I said I had taught myself acupuncture, and sometimes went out in the middle of the night to give people treatments, Mama became very upset. She kept repeating that I must be more careful. Grandma shook her head skeptically when I boasted I had learned to roll out superb noodles.

I said I was the only Beijing student assigned to my brigade, that in northern Shaanxi it was considered relatively affluent. In fact after a good harvest each of us could earn 12 to 13 cents per workday. Papa, who was listening, frowned.

Mama told me Deng Lin and Deng Nan had not been granted home leave. They would not be coming. Feifei should be able to, though. She and Papa had asked the Jiangxi Revolutionary Committee to get in touch with Shanxi. But Feifei hadn't written. They weren't sure when to expect him. Pufang was still in the No. 301 Hospital in Beijing. They didn't know whether he was improving.

As to themselves, Mama said, they'd been fine. Their only concern was about their children.

Grandma issued a complaint. "Your papa and mama are too frugal," she said. "They don't let me buy meat, and they don't eat meat. They want to save everything for you kids for emergencies. Luckily, I've been raising a few laying hens, and I can feed them eggs every day. All that work in the factory, and the chores around the house aren't easy, either. What can we do if they get sick?"

Papa smiled. "There's nothing wrong with us. I've put on weight since coming down here!"

We talked and talked in the soft lamplight. It grew late, and we lowered our voices but we still had so much to say. Sitting beside Mama, I ran my hand over the thick padded tunic Grandma had made for her after coming to Jiangxi, so soft, so warm. Their words sounded dreamy, like music in my ears. The stimulation I felt upon arrival gave way to a languid contentment. The seven days and seven nights on bus and train faded into a distant memory, floating off to the horizon.

That night, I doubled up with Grandma in her bed. The freshly aired comforter smelled faintly of sunlight. Outside the window there was neither wind, nor rain, nor sound, nor movement. In an instant, I was deep in dreamland!

20

Feifei Returns

Without the usual holiday firecrackers and the boisterous noise of New Year's Eve, our family nevertheless happily enjoyed a New Year's dinner. Quietly, we said goodbye to 1969, quietly, we welcomed the arrival of 1970.

Three weeks after the winter solstice, winter really starts in south China.

Southern winters are very cold. You don't have the eternal white snows and moaning winds of the north, where dripping water instantly turns into icicles. It is rather a dim dampness that seeps into your bones, where the temperature indoors and outdoors is the same, and you can't escape the unrelenting cold. In the north, no matter how cold it is outside, you can always warm up a bit inside, even if it's over a small coal-ball stove. In the south, if the sun comes out, it's warmer outside than it is indoors.

I had never slept under such a thick quilt, or wore such heavy cotton-padded clothes and shoes before. My hands and feet nevertheless became frost-bitten. When I got up in the mornings I could see my frigid white breath in the sunlight streaming through the window. If you let a cup of boiled water stand for a few minutes, a film of ice quickly formed on the surface.

What you longed most for during the day was sunshine. If it was sunny, you could run into the courtyard and sop up warmth in your upper and lower body. At night we all huddled around a small charcoal brazier — our only weak source of heat. Southern winters were truly hard to bear. It was difficult for people who had lived in the north a long time to adapt. All you could do was keep adding clothing.

Papa was different. His way of coping was to "fight cold with cold". Every day, he washed with cold water — a habit he had formed during the war years when he was young. At that time, he just doused himself with a bucket of cold water. He couldn't keep doing that now that he was nearly 70 — instead he used a big washcloth soaked in icy water, rubbing himself briskly till his whole body was red and glowing. Not only was he warmer, but he felt very alert.

"Washing with cold water in the winter helps me ward off the cold," he said. "It also improves my resistance. I rarely catch colds or get sick." He urged all of us to try it.

That may have been alright for him. We didn't object to him doing it. But none of us had the nerve to do it ourselves. It took more than enough courage just to undress and creep into that icy bedding every night, to say nothing of washing down with cold water! We admired Papa's bravery, but definitely had no desire to follow his example.

Early in January, Feifei arrived. The Provincial Revolutionary Committee had delivered him from Nanchang to the former infantry school. Our family was overjoyed. He was only 16, skinny and not very tall, when expelled from Zhongnanhai two years before. Now he stood before our parents, big and sturdy, a real man.

Unfortunately, the "real man" was not a very attractive sight. His darkened face was sweat-stained and dirty. The old padded army uniform he wore was also dirty, its stuffing sticking out in several places. A grass rope bound his waist. The uppers and soles of his muddy padded shoes looked about to part company. A small army knapsack hung slantwise across his shoulders. Floppy and empty, it had a number of holes.

Mama was happy and tearful to see him. Then cold reason took over, and she forbade him to set foot in the door until he had removed all of his dirty clothing. Only after that was done, did she allow him to come in and sit down. Grandma told us to bring out the apples we had been keeping.

"How many can you eat?" I asked Feifei.

"Let's start with five!"

We fed him one after another. When he finally rested, we counted. He had finished off 12 at one go.

Surrounding him, we bombarded him with questions: Why hadn't we heard from him? Why hadn't he come until January?

He said he and his schoolmates had not been permitted to join the big students' tour around the country because they were too young. They decided to visit some of China's scenic mountains during the idle farm season. With three other boys Feifei set out from their Shanxi farm brigade and scaled the beautiful heights of Mount Wutai, Mount Huashan and Mount Tai. Carrying their small knapsacks, they made a broad sweep.

"What did you do about money?" Mama asked.

"Hei! Who needed money?" Feifei scoffed. "We hid what little money we had. I put my 10 yuan in a small plastic bag, and then hid it in a cornmeal flatcake. See, here it is!"

We peeled open the cake, which was as hard as a rock. Inside, folded and re-folded small, was a 10 yuan bill.

"We poor students were pretty broke. We never bought any train tickets. Everything was in a mess. Sneaking on trains was easy. We went from station to station. When ticket collectors came round, we hid. If we couldn't hide we simply said: 'We don't have any money. If you don't believe it, search us.' They never could find anything.

"One student hid some money in his cloth shoe. When the conductor couldn't find anything in his clothes, he told him to take off his shoes. The boy was really scared. But when the conductor picked up the shoe it was so dirty and smelly he threw it aside. Since we hadn't bought tickets, they made us get off. But all we did was wait for the next train.

"After visiting the mountains we decided to split up and go home. I came to Jiangxi. At Jiujiang I ran into trouble. I was picked up by a workers' patrol. The place is full of them, and Jiangxi has more regulations than other provinces. They said I would have to work till I earned the price of a ticket home. So I worked, under detention, for a week. Luckily, home wasn't far away. I bought a train ticket for a few yuan and went to

Nanchang. I was very tired, so I took a nap on a park bench. In other places, no one bothers you. But here, again I was arrested, this time again by a workers' patrol. I said I wanted to go to the Provincial Revolutionary Committee. They took one look at me, and snorted. Finally, the committee identified me, and the patrol let me go."

Between apples, Feifei spoke animatedly, his brows dancing, with a rather self-satisfied air. I'm afraid I egged him on. "As a girl," I said admiringly, "I wouldn't have dared to make a long trip the way you did. With just a little bit of money, you were right not to spend it all on train tickets!"

Feifei and I got into an excited exchange of news: Where were there pitched battles? Where were rebel factions using guns and even armored cars? Where had students assigned to farm brigades seized farmers' noodles and muffins because they were hungry?...To students like us working in the countryside, such banditry did not sound strange or unusual. The more we talked the more stimulated, the prouder we became.

Mama and Grandma were listening, wide-eyed. They had been isolated since the start of the Cultural Revolution. Although they had heard about such things as "rebellion" and "revolution", and knew there were factional battles, they had never seen with their own eyes or heard about the broad chaos into which all of society had been plunged. Their impressions and conceptions were still of the period before the Cultural Revolution. The higgledy-piggledy, lawless wildness Feifei and I were describing was completely beyond their comprehension.

Papa hadn't said a word. When we finished blathering, and had poured everything out, he spoke sternly.

"Don't you know," Papa demanded, "these things you have been talking about are extremely bad!"

His words punctured our inflated chatter. Feifei and I looked at each other and stuck our tongues out in embarrassment.

Mama and Papa had been under restraint for a long time. After coming to Jiangxi, the factory was their only contact with the outside world, and even there they couldn't mix freely. When I arrived I told them only things I thought would please them. I said nothing about the denunciations, curses, insults, and even the hunger we sometimes had to endure.

The Cultural Revolution had been going on for over three years. Papa had been criticized, overthrown, had been labeled the "Second Biggest Capitalist Roader in the country." He was a veteran revolutionary who had fought for the ideals of communism all his life. To him his creed was sacred. His heart was pure. A man of such integrity and faith could never have imagined the extent to which the unbridled savagery of the Cultural Revolution had devastated China.

Feifei and I stopped our mindless chatter. We told our parents from the beginning everything we knew about the madness, the ugliness, the cruelty of the Cultural Revolution.

We said that in addition to the persons they already knew about, the vast majority of the Central Committee and national government leaders had been overthrown and removed from office. Some had been struggled against, some had their homes raided, some had been tried by "people's courts", some had been locked in "Monsters Enclosures", some had been sent to "functionaries farms", some had been tormented to death. Many were people we knew personally, friends of the family. We listed those who were imprisoned, or killed. Some of their children were also imprisoned. Families were broken up and scattered.

Many of the rebel organizations formed at the start of the Cultural Revolution had split into factions, and were fighting among themselves, often in pitched battles with arms and ammunition. In some places the army had been forced to intervene. Jiang Qing's rallying cry "attack peacefully, defend with force" exacerbated the strife. The fighting became so bad that Mao Zedong finally had to put a stop to it, personally.

Army propaganda teams and worker propaganda teams were sent into the schools again, just as they had been at the start of the Cultural Revolution. The public security organizations, the procuratorate, and the judiciary were a shambles. Many factories were closed down. Farmers in some places had quit tending their fields to join the "revolution".

Conditions were worse now than they had been during the "three bad years". In northern Shaanxi, where I had been assigned to a farm brigade, in poor counties a day's work paid only 8 or 9 fen (cents). Twenty years after Liberation, they still had no toilets and no pig pens. In the Ansai-Mizhi area, there was often only one pair of padded pants for the whole family, and they all had to sleep under a single quilt. Chaff and weeds were common fare. By springtime, they usually ran out of grain, and the government had to issue relief flour and emergency funds. Now, because of the "universal chaos", no one bothered about farming. People were lucky if they could stay alive.

We talked and Mama and Papa listened, as we gave them the whole picture. Now they understood. Papa frowned, but did not speak. What could he say? Such a huge unexpected change in only three years. The economic improvements so painfully wrested by the strivings of the entire Party and the entire people were utterly ruined in only three years. The Party organization, government at every level, Party and government leaders at every level, were all smashed and overthrown. Why had millions of Communists given their blood and lives for the revolution? Why had the Party led the masses in bitter battles to win the rivers and mountains of our vast land? What was the good of the labor, the creativity, the construction, the constant experimentation, which the people of China so diligently contributed? A mad, chaotic world, run by villains — is that all we had to show for it?

Papa was a statesman, an old Communist with a strong sense of responsibility to the Party, the nation, and the people. In such a situation he was bound to listen, bound to observe. But he said nothing because he could say nothing. In distant Jiangxi, restricted and restrained, he could only think and ponder, and bury his thoughts deep in his heart.

No matter how the world changed, no matter how the movement developed, life for our family in Jiangxi went on as usual. The only difference was that since Feifei returned it was much livelier.

He clowned around like a child to make us laugh. Once he said to Mama: "Aiya, your floor here is cleaner than our platform bed on the farm." He flopped down, stretched out, and pretended to snore.

Or he tightened the straw rope around his waist and puffed up aggressively. In the thick accent of a Shaanxi farmer he cried: "Any hard work around here just leave it to me!" He took the mop and sloshed the floor soaking wet.

Once he announced that he would do the washing. So enthusiastic were his ministrations that the whole room, and he himself, soon were drenched.

We were all amused by his antics. Mama and Papa went to work as usual every morning. In the afternoon we gathered in the kitchen to discuss the evening meal. That grandma of mine was a great cook. She could do fish, and meat. Even the humblest potato in her hands, with a little vegetable added, became a delicious dish.

Actually, Papa was also a very good cook. His Sichuan-style family dishes were attractively done, and very tasty. He left home when he was 16. I don't know where he picked up the ability.

Mama couldn't cook, she could only help fan the flame in the stove. But she was strong on theory. She usually stood beside Grandma as she cooked, and gave instructions. It was something like those cooking class lessons you see today on television.

January in south China is very cold. Mama's health was poor. Her blood pressure usually stood at around 220 over 110. That, plus the fact that she added too many clothes to ward off the cold, made it difficult for her to climb the stairs. When we cleaned up after dinner, she would stand at the foot of the stairs and shout up to Papa: "Give me a hand, old brother!"

With Papa pulling her with one hand, and clutching the banister with the other, the two would slowly mount the stairs together.

Sometimes Feifei would run over, tug his straw belt and say: "Ma, you see how strong I am. I'll carry you on my back!"

Mama would laugh and retort: "You wild devil. You won't be satisfied till you've pulled all my bones out of their sockets!"

My parents had been taking sedatives before retiring for many years. Under the pressures of the Cultural Revolution, they increased the dosage. In Jiangxi, Mama asked Huang to get some more from the hospital to replenish her supply. He did so, but gave them only a small amount each day. In the beginning, he insisted on being present when they swallowed it. After a while, thanks to the increased physical activity, and labor in the factory, Papa's health improved. No longer thin and haggard, he put on weight, and was in much better spirits, especially after some of us children returned. Starting on January 1, 1970, he quit using sedatives. After all those years, breaking the habit was quite an accomplishment.

21

A Quantitative Change

T HERE'S an old saying: "Behind good fortune, trouble lies in wait." In other words, unhappy things are bound to happen just when you are happiest. Unfortunately, that old saying is very true.

When Mama and Papa first arrived in Jiangxi, they were paid the same monthly salary they had been getting before Papa was overthrown. Of second administrative rank, he received 404 yuan. (Before the Cultural Revolution that was the figure for Central Committee members from the first to the fourth grade.) Mama was grade 12, and her monthly salary was 120 yuan per month.

But in January 1970, the money they were issued came to a total of 205 yuan. Mama had Huang inquire, via the Jiangxi committee, at the Central Committee's General Office. Word came down: Their salaries had not been cut, but they were being given only enough for living expenses. The rest of their pay was being held for them temporarily by the General Office.

During the Cultural Revolution everything was political, everything was an expression of politics. The manner in which the wages of overthrown leaders was handled was a measure of how serious their political questions were deemed to be. It was divided into three categories: Salary stopped or changed into living expenses, or only a small amount granted as living expenses to those of their children who had no jobs, or not even living expenses.

Among the people we knew, they received only living expenses instead of salaries. Some received not even that, and were reduced to selling off their possessions, or depending on help from relatives.

For children of the "black gang" it was especially cruel. In one family the father was put in prison and the mother committed suicide. The children had no one to help them. A terrible dilemma. It was the same for children of former members of the Politburo and the Secretariat. We had grown up together with some of those kids. In the cases of Peng Zhen, Luo Ruiqing and Yang Shangkun, all members of the Secretariat, both husband and wife were arrested. Bo Yibo, Li Jingquan, and Liu Lantao were thrown into prison and their wives were hounded to death.

Compared to them, our family was a lot better off.

We children, after being expelled from Zhongnanhai, did occasionally have to sell things when we ran out of money, but we always received living expenses. Once Feifei and I joined the farming brigades, the living expenses were halted, but we were able to earn enough through our own labors to feed ourselves. Our two older sisters were drawing wages at the university, and they usually managed to spare a bit for us younger ones.

All in all, our family's situation wasn't desperate. Our parents were being paid as usual, and they could keep in touch with us children. In fact, those were our most comfortable days since the start of the Cultural Revolution.

But just at that time, our parents' salaries were halted. We were taken completely by surprise. We knew it couldn't possibly be only a question of money. Did it signify some political change? We all were a little uneasy. On February 9, Papa took up his pen and wrote a letter to Wang Dongxing.

"More than two months have passed since my last letter to you," Papa said. "Our life, our work, and our study, are still the same. We go to the factory every day (we now work an hour less). We read books and newspapers, and listen to the radio broadcasts. Except for the factory, Zhuo Lin and I have never been anyplace. We write to our children, but have had no contact with any of the people we knew well before."

In his letters to the Central Committee during the Cultural Revolution, Papa spoke only about politics and never asked for anything personal. This time, however, he said: "My youngest daughter Maomao came early last December. At the beginning of January my youngest son Feifei also arrived. (They will soon return to where they are working.) Zhuo Lin and I hadn't seen them in over two years. You can imagine how happy we were. We were hoping our other two children (Deng Lin and Deng Nan) would join us for a family reunion, but their application was not approved, although they do have permission to visit."

Papa continued: "In a letter to me my oldest daughter Deng Lin says the students in her school are about to be assigned to jobs. She has asked permission to change her profession (that is, to give up art work, since she is not very good at it,) and be assigned to a factory. We share her desire. She is already 28 and her health is poor. She still does not have a boyfriend. Because she has many ailments, working on a farm would be difficult for her. Putting in eight hours work in some factory workshop would also be hard. Some technical job — such as receptionist, or secretary, or caretaker, might be more suitable for her. I spoke to you about this in Beijing. Zhuo Lin and I will be grateful if you are able to help. Our greatest wish is that she be assigned to some place near us (assuming that we are going to remain in Jiangxi a long time)."

He then raised the question of expenses: "Starting this January the Central Committee is giving us a total of 205 yuan as a monthly allowance. We asked the provincial committee to check with you whether this is a long term arrangement. As yet we have had no reply. A few days ago we received the February installment. It is still 205 yuan. We understand the decision and will adjust our lives accordingly.

"Of course, to be frank, such an amount is pretty tight for nine persons (my wife and I, my stepmother, five children, plus the children of Zhuo Lin's older sister, who are also our responsibility). Deng Lin has wages, but because of her many ailments she has only enough for herself. My oldest son Pufang, in the hospital, costs us around 35 yuan a month (25 for the hospital's fixed meals, plus 10 for cigarettes). The two college students cost us about 30 yuan a month each — bringing the total for the three of them to between 90 and 100 yuan per month. That leaves only about 100 yuan for the three of us here.

"Our youngest daughter Maomao and our youngest son Feifei are both working in communes. They earn only enough money for food, and need a little help from us. We also had to lay out some money when they came to see us. (They are quite far away, and need about 100 yuan each for round trip fares.) We had to spend more on food after they came, and we have to pay something each year for their clothes and petty expenses.

"Adding it all together, our budget is tight. Since the Party has decided on a total amount, we have no reason to ask for more. Zhuo Lin and I will economize and save 30 yuan out the 100 left for us, and put it aside so that the children can come and visit us once a year. We just have to get used to our new life down here!"

Get used to their new life! Papa said those words to the Party, and he said them to himself.

He still had one more thing to add. Papa wrote: "It's quite expensive for us each time a child comes home. We hope Maomao can be transferred to some place nearer to where we live."

The letter finished, Papa signed his name.

Reading that letter today, nearly 30 years later, I can imagine what Papa must have felt. It was better than being locked up in prison. At least he had the luxury of being able to see his children. But the uncertainties of the political situation, plus being responsible for the livelihood of the whole family, were a heavy burden. He couldn't help thinking about it; he couldn't help pleading for help.

The letter went off. There was no reply, but neither were there any bad political developments. Although that much was good, our changed financial situation necessitated changes in the way we lived.

First of all, Mama and Papa further economized on their already frugal ways. There was meat in the table when the children visited, but once we left it seldom appeared. They raised a few hens, which meant they could eat chicken and eggs. Any rice and vegetables that were left over, were kept for the next meal. They cut out tea, which Papa had been drinking for years, as too expensive. For wine, they switched to a cheap local brand, and he had only one small glass after lunch.

Papa had been smoking for dozens of years. He couldn't quit cold, but he could cut down. He had the provincial committee buy him one carton of inexpensive filterless cigarettes a month. He limited himself to one pack every three or four days. He didn't smoke all morning when he went to the factory, and had only a few cigarettes in the afternoon and evening. He adhered very strictly to his self-imposed regimen.

And, if this wasn't enough, he decided to "open up virgin land"!

Spring had just come when my parents began "opening wasteland" in our compound and planting vegetables. They had done this during the war years in Yan'an, and in the Taihang Mountains. Only by depending on their own efforts did they have enough food and clothing.

Feifei and I were able to put to use the things we had learned in the farming brigades. Feifei was strong, a self-professed "veteran planter". We naturally let him do most of the hard work. Tightening the rope belt around his waist, he raised his hoe high, and plied it in a heroic manner, making the clods of earth fly and spattering himself at the same time.

"You don't have to dig so deep," Grandma scolded. "We're only planting a few vegetables."

Before long all the ground was loosened. Papa took the hoe and shaped it into rows and ridges. Mama sat down on a small bench she had brought into the field, and cast aside unearthed stones and bits of brick. Grandma dumped all of our dirty dishwater into our future vegetable plot. With the whole family working together, it soon was ready for operations.

Young He helped us buy vegetable seeds. We bought seeds for peppers, two kinds of beans, tomatoes, eggplants and little *bai cai* (Chinese cabbages). We sowed the seeds in separate rows, covered them with earth, and watered them. The fresh soil emitted a heavy fragrance. In the backyard, before the woodshed, we planted two kinds of melons. A few small chicks we had bought trotted chirping behind our big mother hen. The quiet courtyard came to life. I thought of the green vegetables which would soon be poking up through the earth, and could almost hear the clucking of the grown up chicks as they laid lots of eggs, savoring well in advance the fruits of our labors.

Our family was always able to make the best of a bad situation. We children learned from the behavior of our parents under the rigors of the

Cultural Revolution. You had to seek your own happiness, fight for it. You had to overcome difficulties and hardships by your own stubborn efforts. And you must be forever optimistic. Just as the *Internationale* proclaims:

Nobody'll bring us liberation,
Nobody, no God, no hero great.
We will achieve emancipation,
With our own hands decide Man's fate.

Frugality, hard work, naturally are good. But my parents, especially Papa, sometimes overdid them both, and this gave rise to arguments and dissension. For example, we always finished any leftovers at meal time. But if the gruel went sour, Papa insisted on finishing that, too.

"What difference does it make?" he said. "Boil it again. That will kill the germs. I've got a good stomach. That stuff won't hurt it!"

All we could do was to glare at him. And then there was his insistence on helping our greens and sprouts grow strong. No one had any arguments with that. But when he proposed that we make "farmers' fertilizer" from our own urine and stool, we flatly refused. He certainly knew how to stir the normally placid surface of our family harmony. Ai! What could you with him!

Spring time in Jiangxi. If it wasn't overcast, then it rained. Not a bit like the sunny brightness of the north. The compound of the former infantry school, so quiet and lonely all winter, suddenly came to life. The endless spring rain bathed the leaves, saturating the earth. Fresh tender little leaves appeared on the dark green winter trees. The withered yellow grass in the red soil quickly sprouted new green blades.

On the slopes, on the hillocks, the mountain peach trees, usually unnoticed, produced early buds, which abruptly changed into blossoms. Soft, red, alluring, the blossoms hung like clouds and mist, unrestrainedly joyous in the fine rain.

Oh, and then there was jasmine, snowy white tips emerging from dark green pods, ready to burst open at any moment. Delicate raindrops clung adoringly to sweet smelling petals of translucent jade.

153

That is how spring comes to the south.

We had been together for three months. You can imagine how happy we were. Several times the Jiangxi revolutionary committee hinted that we children had been staying too long. We ignored them.

But it couldn't last.

March came, which meant that spring in the north was about to begin, and with it plowing and planting. The students who had been assigned to the commune farming brigades started to return.

Feifei also had to go. Mama and Grandma washed and patched his padded jacket and pants, and helped him pack. The day of his departure, Feifei was spotlessly clean, the grass rope tied around his waist. The sun-blackened complexion he had acquired working in the fields had faded somewhat, and his face glowed with ruddy good health. His black brows met above the bridge of his nose, forming a single line. A faint down adorned his upper lip. He said goodbye to Mama and Papa, and marched away with a firm stride.

Their son was fully grown, a man, but my parents hated to see him go. Mama burst into tears. Papa kept his feelings bottled inside. Silent, as usual, he insisted on going to the factory.

While at work, he suddenly felt uncomfortable. His face went white, and he broke into a cold sweat. Mama was informed, and she hurried over with some workers and helped him to a seat. She knew he was having an attack of his old ailment — low blood sugar. She said white sugar in water would bring him round. Hong Xing, the woman squad chief, ran home, which was nearby, mixed a glass of sugar water and hastened back. Papa drank it, and felt a bit better. The factory didn't have any cars, but Lieutenant Tao commandeered a tractor cart, drove Papa home in it, and helped him up the stairs to lie down in the bedroom.

We pulled the window curtains closed to let him rest quietly. We knew the reason for the attack was entirely because his son had left. The family, his dear ones, his children, were his most precious, and right then his only, possessions. His son was gone, who knew when he would see him again. Although Papa didn't speak, he couldn't help thinking, he couldn't help worrying.

Not long after Feifei left, I also had to return to Shaanxi. I really didn't want to go. I would have to make the trip alone, and the road was so long. I was the only educated girl in my brigade. I didn't mind the hard farm work and the rough food. What bothered me was leaving those three old people on their own, confined in that small compound. When Feifei and I left, all we were able to leave them was our sadness at parting, our boundless concern.

I had only one wish as I walked upon Shaanxi's vast high plateaus of yellow soil: Let the time pass quickly, quickly, and when autumn comes, after the harvest, let me quickly go home again. Like a bird in the sky, let me spread my wings and fly home.

22

Shock Waves from the Lushan Conference

F AR from Beijing and cut off from news in general, Papa had no information on the dissension inside the center of political power.

The days flew by. In the flash of an eye it was the summer of 1970. The Cultural Revolution had been on for exactly four years. According to Mao Zedong's plan, this should have been the time for its "harvest". He intended to convene the National People's Congress, and amend the State Constitution, and thereby solidify the "accomplishments" of the Cultural Revolution.

But political developments took a sudden unexpected turn.

Mao never anticipated that in 1970 a new political struggle would erupt, a struggle which like a dagger would rip a great hole in a political arena already gasping for breath from the battering it had endured.

It came about like this: Mao proposed that the Constitution be amended to eliminate the post of Head of State. Summing up the "lessons" learned, he sought to avoid a recurrence of a struggle for power. Lin Biao not only wanted the office retained but proposed that it be assumed by Mao.

Mao saw through this immediately: Lin Biao was hoping that he himself would get the post, sure that Mao would refuse it. Mao repeatedly turned the offer down. He said: "I cannot do this job. The suggestion is inappropriate."

Lin Biao's coterie nevertheless continued to insist. By spring of that year the differences between Mao Zedong and Lin Biao on this matter had already become clear.

On the surface this was only a question of whether or not to retain the post of Head of State. Actually, it concealed a host of emotions and contradictions.

Many people at that time did not understand. Mao Zedong was at the peak of political status and power. How could Lin Biao not have comprehended his meaning, and dared to go against his wishes? In the Party Constitution Lin Biao had already been named as Mao's successor as chairman of the Communist Party. Why should he strive to become governmental Head of State as well?

Actually, it was clear enough: Precisely because he was secure in his position as Mao's successor, Lin Biao felt strong enough to try to take over as Head of State. His present post of Vice-Chairman of the Party could not compare in power.

Lin Biao's coterie was eager for him to get the job. As his wife, Ye Qun, said: "If there is no office of Head of State, what will happen to Lin Biao? Where should he be in the government?" Lin Biao's health wasn't good. His gang, especially his wife Ye Qun, was afraid he wouldn't outlive Mao, and urged him to upgrade his power now. The Fourth National People's Congress was an opportunity to reshuffle the top government ranks.

From the start of the Cultural Revolution, the gangs of Lin Biao and Jiang Qing had periods of unity and periods of clash. Later, there was more clash than unity. Harsh words were exchanged, and they scrambled for advantage. Their hottest disagreement was over whether Lin Biao should be made Head of State.

To Lin Biao and his coterie it was a crucial moment, an opportunity not to be missed, a time which would never come again. And so, they dared to oppose Mao Zedong, and take the field, united.

The second plenum of the Ninth Communist Party Central Committee opened in Lushan on August 23, 1970.

Lushan, a beautiful mountain resort area, was the scene of many important political happenings. It had suited Lin Biao's evil purposes. Here, he had attacked others. He didn't know that Lushan was to portend bad luck for him.

The contradictions burst forth immediately.

Lin Biao opened with a speech hinting at the intention to create the office of Head of State. His clique vociferously voiced their support. Then Jiang Qing and her gang took the initiative. They visited Mao privately at his residence and reported to him what they called Lin Biao's "unusual activity." Mao summoned an enlarged meeting of the Politburo. He sternly criticized Lin Biao and his coterie, thus dooming Lin Biao's scheme to failure.

The plenum ended on September 6. Mao's concluding speech struck his auditors like a thunderclap. With that sharp, yet pungently relaxed eloquence so uniquely his own, Mao ridiculed the farce Lin Biao and his gang were attempting to stage.

Some of Lin Biao's lieutenants were also criticized, and were compelled to make self-criticisms. Perhaps the most pitiful of these worthies was Chen Boda, who had just switched his allegiance to Lin Biao. He hadn't expected when he voiced his support at the meeting that he would be swept up in the general anti-Lin antipathy, and be criticized and examined like the others.

The stormy meeting, and its unexpected results, ended. Although Mao hadn't mentioned Lin Biao by name, it was now clear that a new battle was impending, that it had only just begun, and that the main contenders in this battle were Mao Zedong and his recently appointed successor, Lin Biao.

While encouraging a movement to expose and criticize Chen Boda, at the same time Mao adopted a variety of measures aimed at limiting and weakening the Lin Biao clique. On a number of occasions he criticized several of the lieutenants directly, and indirectly criticized Lin Biao himself.

The gang had over-played their hand, and they suffered badly. Their leaders were exposed by name, criticized, forced to make self-criticisms, or removed from office. The power of the gang was considerably weakened. They could sense that the next battle would be even fiercer.

In Mao's eyes what the Lushan conference revealed was not a simple political "error", but the ambitions of the Lin Biao clique. Mao was angry, and disappointed. Even more, he considered the matter dangerous. He himself had chosen Lin Biao to be his successor, to serve as a major political figure guaranteeing that Mao's revolutionary line would be continued. He felt that the accomplishments of the Cultural Revolution which he personally had launched were extremely important indicators that this aim was being achieved.

Mao had never expected that Lin Biao would dare to muddy the waters, and openly stand up against him as an equal. Mao was over 76. The sober realization of the way things were moving was a severe blow.

The ones who gained the most in this struggle were Jiang Qing and her cohorts. They and the Lin Biao faction had constantly been jockeying for power, covertly and openly. Going to Mao and bringing charges against them chalked up a good mark for Jiang Qing. After the conference, Lin Biao's power was weakened, and the Jiang Qing gang seized upon this as an opportunity to expand.

Lin Biao's position was in jeopardy. Lin Biao was tense. Jiang Qing was happy. Mao Zedong was concerned.

This is no market fair story-teller's tale, but a true report of the political scene during China's period of chaos.

The meeting over, everyone came down from the mountain. Mao said: "The problems discussed at Lushan have not ended. They still haven't been solved."

Mao decided to deal with Lin Biao. On the one hand he took steps to weaken the hold of the Lin Biao gang on national and local government offices by methods colloquially called "throwing a few stones", "mixing in sand", and "digging away at the foot of the wall". On the other hand, in August and September of 1971, Mao traveled around the country, talking to key people, and stressing how serious the situation had become.

The Lin Biao gang had done many bad things. People were speaking out against them. They were plainly vulnerable — like turtles in a jar. Lin Biao was frantic, and so were other members of his gang. His son Lin Liguo concocted a plan to kill Mao Zedong. It failed, and the plot was exposed. Lin Biao had taken a fatal step from which there was no return.

On September 13, 1971, at the urging of his wife Ye Qun and his son Lin Liguo, Li Biao fled. He commandeered a plane at the Shanhaiguan Airfield. They flew north, heading for the Soviet Union. A wicked road must lead to disaster, as the saying goes. Demons make the spirit stumble. The plane crashed in Mongolia. The lonely desert became the final resting place of Lin Biao, that perpetrator of unforgivable crimes.

In his climb to power during the Cultural Revolution the number of people he wronged, harmed, confined, imprisoned, caused to be beaten, tortured, crippled, tormented to death...was legion. The Central Special Case Office under his command was a gang of sadistic fiends. The crimes of Lin Biao and his bullies were countless. For him to end up in a nameless grave showed that indeed Heaven has eyes!

23

Uneasy "Quiet Days"

DURING 1970 and 1971 the rhythmic flow on the political stage was frequently punctuated by sudden changes flashing by too quickly for the eye to follow. Truly, a remarkably hectic time. But Deng Xiaoping and his family in the old infantry school compound in the suburbs of Nanchang in Jiangxi continued their quiet, circumscribed, existence.

Nanchang is one of China's famous "ovens". In summer it's really hot!

With the temperature sometimes hitting 40° C, it was hot in the open, and hot in the shade, it was hot outdoors, and even hotter in the breezeless rooms. There was no place to escape the heat. For southerners, who were used to it, the weather was not so bad. We northerners had a tough time adjusting. But we had to learn how.

In the privacy of our home Papa could walk around in his underwear shorts and a top. But, going to the factory every day he had to wear a regular shirt and long pants. That already was warm enough. Papa was a fitter. The moment he began filing, his clothes became drenched with sweat. When Mama saw what he looked like, she urged him to sit down and rest.

"I don't mind sitting down," he said. "The problem is once I sit down I can't get up again." After all, Papa was 66.

Every day when they came home from work, the first thing they did was to wash down in cool water. It wasn't really cool — actually only around body temperature. When they went to bed at night, their grass sleeping mats were too warm, and they changed to mats of woven bamboo slivers. First they would wipe them down with water, and also sprinkle the floor. That seemed a bit better. The heat would wake them in the middle of the night, and they would bathe again, and again sprinkle the floor.

To make matters worse, because we lived on a small hill, at the height of summer running water couldn't reach our house. Papa was the strongest one in our family, so the job of toting water upstairs naturally fell to him. Sometimes the water couldn't even get to the foothills. That meant going outside the compound, which Mama and Papa were not allowed to do. We could only ask Young He, our orderly, to assume this "major responsibility".

Not very tall, Young He was a hard worker. Toting two full pails on a carrying pole, perspiring heavily, he would carry the water into the house and up the stairs, and dump it into the bathtub. He certainly was a lifesaver. He wouldn't touch the snacks Grandma offered, or drink a mouthful of water. Young He would wipe the sweat from his face, smilingly refuse with a shake of his head, pick up the empty pails and depart. This good, honest boy for two years virtually never rested. He was of enormous help.

Life is like that. Happiness always contains some hardship; within hardship there is always a little joy. As long as you do your best to adjust to your environment, life will provide you with compensation.

In the courtyard the melons and vegetables we had planted that spring were tall and strong. We had given them plenty of fertilizer, and they came up early. Eggplant hung from their branches, fat and shiny and purple. Half hidden by their oil-green leaves, our tomatoes went from green to yellow, and from yellow to red — an intoxicating red that was almost translucent. Our peppers were the kind that pointed upward. They and their leaves both were pointy.

We had half a dozen varieties of beans, all sizes and shapes, in shades of red and green and purple, and little onions and garlic — no end to them, more than we could gather, more than we could eat.

In the rear garden we had built a bamboo trellis, from which hung an assortment of gourds and melons, growing bigger every day, their vines shiny and green and intertwined. Our bitter melons were white, and of irregular shape.

Our compound was a mass of color. The house was gray; the soil was red; the parasol trees were green. Front and rear, we raised vegetables and melons. They grew in the spring, and flourished in the summer. All the credit belonged to the three old folks for their supervision. Our family was in good shape. Not only were we able to save a lot of money on food — we had built ourselves a living, thriving environment that was a pleasure to the eye and a comfort to the heart.

Near the end of summer Big Sister Deng Lin's request for a vacation was granted. She came to visit our home in Jiangxi.

Deng Lin had always been sickly since childhood. Mama naturally asked all about her life and work. Deng Lin said she and her former classmates were being "re-educated" by an Army unit in Xuanhua, about 100 kilometers northwest of Beijing. Because she had already graduated, she was receiving regular wages, but she had not been formally assigned to any job. This was true of all of the arts academies, thanks to the "solicitude" of "Comrade Jiang Qing", who insisted that everyone in the arts need to be "re-educated".

After six months of temporary work in a paper mill, Deng Lin and her classmates were put on a whole series of odd jobs — planting rice, pulling down bean vines. She didn't mind the hard work, she was able to stick it out. The most difficult part was that they were under Army supervision. The political atmosphere was heavy. They were constantly subjected to high mental pressure.

Once, Deng Lin discovered she had left her wristwatch in a field where they had been working. She borrowed a bike and rode 40 *li* from the dormitory back to the field to bring it back. By co-incidence, someone secretly punched a hole in a portrait of Lin Biao at the dormitory. A "counter-revolutionary" crime! Deng Lin headed the list of suspects, and she was subjected to repeated questioning.

Then investigators from the Central Academy of Fine Arts came to Xuanhua. They said someone claimed that Deng Lin had drawn a map of Zhongnanhai, thus revealing "important state secrets". Lengthy grilling showed there was nothing to it, and the matter was dropped.

Absurd political "investigations" emerged at the drop of a hat. Deng Lin was very depressed, and she shed many a tear. She envied us children in the farming brigades. Although our work was hard, our spirits were free. She thought of us frequently. Except for a few yuan for basic necessities, she used most of her meager 46 yuan monthly salary to buy us things — padded shoes, canned edibles. She longed to see our parents in Jiangxi, but her requests for home leave were ignored.

Now she had come home at last, free from those endless "investigations", free to be with Mama and Papa. It was like a dream come true. Student leaves were short, she couldn't stay long. She tried to do everything she could for the three old people in the time allowed.

Soon, it was time to go. Deng Lin hated to leave. But no matter how she tried to drag it out, the day of departure arrived. She shouldered her backpack, and said goodbye the three oldsters with tears in her eyes.

With Deng Lin gone, the three were left alone. Luckily, the heat of summer would soon end. By September, although the autumn breezes had not yet started, the scorching days of summer were over.

Before we knew it, the four cassia trees in front of the house blossomed. Their golden flowers clung thickly to the branches. Among the leaves, along the branches, all was golden yellow, beautiful, fragrant. The perfume of the blossoms could be savored from afar. A light breeze through the branches wafted it even wider.

Mama and Grandma spread plastic sheets beneath the trees. They shook the branches, bringing the blossoms showering down. They collected these in glass jars, covered them with white sugar, and screwed the lids on tight. When we kids came home, they would make us dumplings stuffed with delicious sweetened cassia flowers.

Papa hadn't known about the Second Plenum of the Ninth Party Central Committee when it was in session. He heard about it later on a radio news broadcast in September. On the 19th of that month he wrote a letter to Wang Dongxing, expressing his support. He requested Wang to forward the letter to Mao Zedong and the Central Committee. Wang relayed it to Mao, who read it and endorsed it over to Lin Biao, Zhou

Enlai and Kang Sheng.

Papa had been in Jiangxi for nearly a year. He used this means of maintaining contact with the Central Committee. Although there was no guarantee Mao would read these letters, or that they would have any effect, Papa persisted in sending them.

The same day he sent this one, he also sent another to Wang Dongxing. The first had concerned politics. The second told of his situation in Jiangxi, and about his family. To him, his family, although of secondary concern, was still very important.

"Zhuo Lin and I are the same as I told you before," he wrote. "We work in the factory every morning. In the afternoon and evening we read, study, read newspapers, listen to the broadcasts, and do some family chores. Except for our home and the factory we never take a step in any other direction. Comrade Huang escorts us to the factory every morning. He and a young soldier help us buy our daily necessities, so we have no difficulties. Work has become our most important need. Although summer has been very hot, we insist on going to the factory.

"We planted some vegetables in our garden. Except for exchanging letters with our children we have no outside contacts. We hear that our oldest son Deng Pufang, still receiving treatment in the hospital, is a bit better. Before he couldn't urinate or move his bowels without special assistance. Now he can urinate naturally, and also move his bowels — though with difficulty. We are very relieved to hear it. The General Office of the Central Committee has been looking after him. (We hear that he gets an allowance of 30 yuan per month, plus 35 for food and 5 for incidentals. That is good.)

"Our oldest daughter Deng Lin is still in Xuanhua, in Hebei. Her school is still involved in the movement. We don't know when they will be assigned jobs. If she is sent to a factory, we hope you will be able to help her out. (I told you about that in my last letter.) The other children are all working on farms. One is in Jinxian, in Shanxi. Another is in Fuxian, in northern Shaanxi. The third is in Ningqiang in Hanzhong (also in Shaanxi)."

Papa talked about himself and his children in his letter. Ordinarily, it was his character to be only concerned about important affairs. Yet here he went into great detail about his family life. He did want to keep the Central Committee informed about his situation. At the same time in the back of his mind was the thought that it was important to maintain contact. If anything went wrong in the family in the future he could turn to the Central Committee for help.

In the absence of anything special, Papa only wrote to the Central Committee every half year or so. This time only a month later, on October 17, he sent another letter to Wang Dongxing.

He had just been notified that the hospital authorities considered Deng Pufang much improved, and that they intended to discharge him. He would be sent, with a nurse, to live with the family in Nanchang.

The news took the three oldsters completely by surprise. How much had Pufang's health really improved? Did he still require medical treatment? Did the family have the facilities to look after him? They were very uneasy. Papa had no choice but to write another letter to Wang Dongxing, pleading for help from the Central Committee.

He wrote: "We have heard from Deng Lin that Pufang is making progress. But from what we understand he is completely paralyzed from the waist down, and still needs help in everything. He can't be improving that quickly. How can we cope if he comes here? We are three elderly people. My stepmother is over 70, I am 67. Zhuo Lin is 55, but she has all sorts of ailments, and is not as healthy as we are. She suffers from severe high blood pressure. (Recently the low went from 100 plus to 116. High was over 180.) Her heart also is getting worse. We have no way to look after Pufang. More important, we sincerely hope he can be cured. Now that his condition is changing if he can continue to receive treatment, he surely will be able to make a big improvement. We therefore earnestly request that he continue to be treated in his present hospital. In our situation today, we don't know what to do. We can only beg you to help, beg the Party to help."

From the letter it was obvious how distraught Papa was. If his son came to Jiangxi not only would it be impossible for the three old people to look after him, but Pufang's one chance of cure would be lost. If Papa wasn't in such a hopeless position he would never have opened his mouth.

After the letter was sent, the three waited anxiously. Fortunately, the heavens were not deaf. Fairly soon, word came down: The decision to send Pufang to Jiangxi was suspended. The three heaved a sigh of relief.

Time passed quickly. It was autumn, the season we loved the most. After harvest, the fields rested, and we students who had been assigned to the brigades flew home like birds released from their cages. Feifei and I both returned to Jiangxi.

Spring Festival, 1971, marked the start of the New Year. This is the time of family reunions, a joy for everyone, when all troubles are set aside.

We had another celebration less than a month later. Second Sister Deng Nan was granted home leave from her job in Hanzhong in Shaanxi. There had never been so many of our family together in the old infantry school grounds at one time. Never had the place been so lively. People say: "Three girls together make a whole show!" Well, there were only two of us there then, but we chatted and laughed and made enough racket for any three. "If the son misbehaves, the father's to blame; if the daughter misbehaves, the mother's to blame." It was all Mama's fault for having always been too lenient with us! Papa was a little deaf. Our noise didn't bother him whether he heard it or not, he was so happy to have us.

It was the first time so many of the family were able to get together since we were expelled from Zhongnanhai in 1967. Deng Lin and Pufang were missing, but we still enjoyed our reunion.

Deng Nan, in Hanzhong, married a classmate, Zhang Hong. She was assigned to a farm production brigade deep in the mountains. It had very few fields. The people were extremely poor. They would sell their annual cloth ration coupons, and use the little money they obtained to buy salt and other necessities.

But the poorer they were, the kinder they treated Deng Nan. A poor family was only able to raise one pig a year. When they slaughtered it, they had to sell half to the government and could keep only half for themselves. That half had to feed the whole family for a year. Meat was very hard to come by. But these mountaineers are wonderfully generous. Any family that had meat was sure to invite Deng Nan.

At work, they took especially good care of her. During the rice harvest, they let her supervise the weighing, and do only the lightest jobs. They weren't interested in any so-called "capitalist-roaders", or "capable of being re-educated children". They demonstrated to Deng Nan the true feelings of the honest ordinary folk. After the days of "putting politics in command" and "class struggle as the touchstone" in Beijing, the mountains of Shaanxi were a great relaxation.

She had only one bad moment. It happened when she was cutting brushwood high in the mountains. She had a big load on her back, and slipped on the narrow trail. If she had fallen she would have dropped into a very deep ravine, and that would have been the end of her. Luckily, she recovered her balance.

Deng Nan was very moved by the pure humanity of the simple mountaineers. Their hard lives made her heartsick and upset. New China had been in existence for more than 20 years, and the ordinary folk still didn't have enough food to eat and enough clothing to wear. Communists had given oceans of blood to free the land. Was it for this that they had sacrificed their lives?

Spring Festival was coming. Our family rejoiced around the festive board, chatting and laughing, and sharing a midnight snack. The oldsters were relieved to see their girls safe and sound. Papa was so pleased he had a few extra drinks. His face shone flushed and ruddy in the lamplight.

24

What Happened to Pufang

W HILE our family was celebrating the holiday in Jiangxi, something nasty occurred in distant Beijing.

According to the "farmers almanac" or the lunar calendar, Spring Festival, the most important traditional holiday, fell on January 27, 1971, that year. Just as everyone was preparing to discard the old and welcome the new, criminal hands reached towards an unfortunate person.

Some people were displeased that Pufang was quietly receiving treatment in the No. 301 Hospital. They wanted to make an issue out of it, and at least have him moved elsewhere. Because Papa had written a letter to the Central Committee, their original plan to shift Pufang to Jiangxi was not put through. But once the holiday passed, they tried another tack.

Pufang had no idea what was afoot. The doctors had him X-rayed. The results showed that only half of his spine was functional. They were considering how to proceed. Pufang didn't know disaster was about to strike.

On January 21, only a week before the New Year, the patients were busily welcoming visitors bearing gift packages large and small. Some were getting their things together in anticipation of going home for the holiday.

That day after lunch the patients returned to their wards to rest. Suddenly, several men from Peking University entered Pufang's room. "The Party has decided to send you to another place for treatment," one of them said harshly.

This notification seemed to Pufang to be very abrupt. Naturally, he didn't want to leave the No. 301 Hospital. But since his callers clearly said the decision was by the "Party", and didn't ask for his consent, what could he say?

"I agree," Pufang replied, his face expressionless. "When must I go?"

"Immediately."

Immediately! They had come only a few minutes before, and they wanted him to leave immediately! Pufang was speechless. He didn't ask where they were going. What would be the use? His fate was in their hands. He had brought nothing when he came to the No. 301 Hospital, and he took nothing when he left.

They carried him from the hospital and put him in a car without another word.

The car traveled a long time from the No. 301 Hospital in western Beijing to a large compound some 20 kilometers to the north from downtown Beijing. Many hands helped Pufang out of the car and carried him into a room. The men from Peking University, not willing to spend another minute, promptly left.

This was the Beijing Social Rescue Home, in the Qinghe section of the city's outskirts. At that time Beijing was still pretty run down, and travel facilities were poor. To people in mid-town, Qinghe seemed far away.

The residents of the Home were mainly disabled veterans and dependents of men killed in action. There also were destitute old people, cripples, and disabled and retarded children. Pufang was put in a very large room, which he shared with 10 other disabled persons. Two small coal stoves provided a little heat against the winter chill. Only two of the inmates were able to walk. One was a 79 year old man, who was half deaf. He tended the stoves, served the meals, brought in fresh diapers and removed the soiled. The other was a retarded boy. He gave some help to those unable to move. Everyone else was immobilized. All had to rely on the old man and the boy.

Pufang's transfer had been so quick he had no time to bring anything with him. The Home issued him a quilt, a mattress, and a set of black cloth padded tunic and trousers. He had no underwear, and the garments were cold against his skin. His room mates were very cordial to the new arrival, and helped him as best they could. They told him about the Home.

During the Cultural Revolution any "welfare", any "humanitarianism", was condemned as bourgeois hypocrisy. A welfare organization could not be described as a "welfare home," it had to be called a "rescue home", or in this case a "Home for Honored Military Persons". With its emphasis on "rescue", its "welfare" naturally was very weak.

At that time China's overall production was low. Ordinary persons had great difficulty in making ends meet, to say nothing of disabled inmates of a "rescue home". They received a monthly allowance of 21 yuan each, out of which 8 yuan was deducted for food. The rest went for medical treatment. They were served rough grain and pickled vegetables for their morning and evening meals. Fine grain was provided at lunch. They had meat only on holidays. Although they had to hand in their personal grain ration coupons, there was no limit to the amount of grain they could eat.

The buildings were old, the sanitary facilities were worse. Pufang was severely disabled, but he had no physical aids. It was a trial for him even to turn over. In the No. 301 Hospital he had a bar suspended over his bed, and he could raise himself and move a bit. But here, he had nothing. Moving, eating, natural functions...all were a problem.

Once, he accidentally scraped his thigh. For a normal person, it wouldn't have amounted to anything. But when a man was paralyzed from the waist down, such a wound was slow to heal. Life had become very burdensome since the day he came from the No. 301 Hospital. To say Pufang was depressed would be putting it mildly. His only consolation was the kindness of the other patients. They were truly "brothers in misery."

My young aunt, Deng Xianqun and her husband, who were working in Tianjin, returned to their home in Beijing for the New Year (Spring Festival) holiday. She was Papa's younger sister. On the first day of the lunar new year, carrying gifts, they went to the No. 301 Hospital to visit their nephew Pufang. They were very upset to learn that he was gone, and hurried to the Home in Qinghe. There they found him, wearing wrinkled black padded garments, lying in a bare crowded room. They were absolutely heartsick. My young aunt questioned him at length. On learning that he didn't even have any underwear, she said she would have new clothes made for him. Pufang firmly disapproved. He said to a man in his situation, clothes didn't make any difference.

On returning home, they immediately wrote to my folks and told them all about Pufang. Deng Xianqun was very concerned about him. She was also worried how my parents would react.

"What's to be done?" she wrote. "If he stays there, perhaps you can get someone to wash his diapers and look after his basic needs. But it still would be very difficult for him. If he came to live with you, there would be some advantages, but the difficulties would be worse. Both of you are old, and he is only 20. You can look after him as long as you live, but what about later? Even now, you're not really able to care for him. Neither of you is very healthy. It's not bad if you can just take care of yourselves! I think the best thing is to rely on the Party. Pufang's situation is complicated. I particularly hope he can be cured enough to be able to take care of his natural functions by himself. Then later find him a job in some small factory."

My young aunt was worried my folks would take the news too hard. As a special postscript she wrote: "Please don't let your feelings run away with you. Give the matter calm, careful consideration and come up with a practical proposal."

I remember in Jiangxi after Spring Festival how life in the family was getting back to normal. We had just seen off Deng Nan, who had come home for the holiday. Mama and Papa were again going to work in the factory every day. Deng Xianqun's letter was like a bolt from the blue. My folks had been relatively happy, but the news of Pufang's miserable conditions plunged them into the depths of despair. Mama couldn't bear to have her son remain in Beijing. She wanted him by her side immediately. She didn't care about the difficulties Deng Xianqun predicted the three old people would have to endure. She wanted her son home. No matter how bad her health was, she would look after him herself.

In the end it was Papa's more rational mind which prevailed. On February 3, the day the letter arrived, he took up his pen and wrote to Wang Dongxing, as follows:

"Comrade Dongxing: Permit me to trouble you again about my son Deng Pufang. My younger sister Deng Xianqun recently went to see him, and wrote telling us about him. I enclose her letter. It speaks for itself. The last time I wrote to you I said we hoped he could continue to receive treatment. Now that is no longer possible. We, as parents, cannot ignore the conditions in the Home at Qinghe.

"After careful consideration, Zhuo Lin and I feel it would be better to have Pufang brought here to live with us. Of course, it will be difficult for three old people to look after him. He must be helped to get in and out of bed. If the Party approves our request, we will be extremely grateful if a person can be sent with him to help us with shopping and other things, in addition to taking care of Pufang. If this request seems unreasonable, we are willing to look after him ourselves. It is something we should not shirk. Regardless of whether the leadership approves sending a person to help us take care of Pufang, we beg that it will at least approve the appointment of a person to bring him to Nanchang. In which case, please notify us soon, so that we can make preparations and avoid any initial confusion. We await your instructions."

Papa's love for his son was very evident. He and Mama decided that even without anyone to help them, and even though Papa was nearly 70 and Mama 60, they wanted their son home. They would look after him themselves, and no difficulty would stop them.

They gave the letter to the Jiangxi revolutionary committee for forwarding to Wang Dongxing.

After it was sent, the Jiangxi people told them not to write any more letters. That meant they could no longer communicate with Wang, even if they had problems. He was their one link with the Central Committee. Was this the Central Committee's idea, or Jiangxi's? They didn't know, and there was no one they could ask.

The son was suffering in Beijing. The parents were worried in Jiangxi. The letter went out, but they couldn't write any more. There was nothing else they could do. They could only wait, helpless and uneasy.

Winters in the south are very cold. Winter passed, but spring was slow in coming.

In February it started to rain. This was the spring rain of the south, sometimes heavy, sometimes light. It rained during the day, it rained at night, it never stopped. The weather was constantly gloomy and dark. Endless dampness made you want to scream. If you weren't careful edibles turned moldy. The kindling in the woodshed got so damp it wouldn't burn. Damp clothes and bedding were chilly and uncomfortable. Even the inside of your shoes sprouted mold.

The only good thing about it was that you could collect basins and buckets of rainwater as it dripped from the eaves of the roof. That was a convenience, but it was only secondary. It rained so much you could never relax. The weather was dark and cold. In May you still had to wear padded clothes. It rained without a halt for a full three months.

We waited and waited for the rain to stop, and at long last it finally did. Typical of the south, the moment the rain ended, a fiery red sun brightly illumined the sky. Everything on the land sprang to life. The cold was gone, summer heat was upon us. We changed our padded tunics for short-sleeved shirts. We seemed to have leaped from winter into mid-summer. Happily we welcomed the sunlight that brightened the land.

We spread our moist clothes and our damp kindling out to dry, as well as our own enervated selves. Little trees and sprouts which had been beaten down by the rain raised their heads. Snowy-white tangerine blossoms burst forth on the trees, perfuming the air with their enchanting fragrance. We owed it all to the sun. Humanity cannot exist without the sun's beams, without its blinding light.

Papa thought constantly of his son in the Rescue Home in Beijing. Three rainy months had passed, and still no word from the Central Committee.

Pufang was gradually becoming accustomed to his new surroundings.

The inmates were the unfortunate of the earth, people without support, or care, or help, people on the lowest level of society. If they were able to get along, so could he. Pufang forced himself to deal with all of the problems of his daily existence.

He hadn't imagined that, even then, there were still persons who wouldn't let up on him. One day, men came from Peking University. They told him the school had decided to cancel his candidate membership in the Communist Party, in other words, to expel him from the Party.

Pufang was ill but could not receive treatment, had a home but could not go to it, and now he had lost his Communist Party membership. In this wide world was there really no place for him?

There certainly was. He would demand medical treatment, he would demand home leave, he would refuse to remain tied down in Qinghe!

One morning, when the sun had just risen, Pufang, with the help of a few room mates, got into an old wheelchair and rolled out of the compound. He was going into town, to Zhongnanhai, to appeal to the authorities.

It was May, and already quite hot in Beijing. Pufang was still wearing his black padded clothes. He had no others. Eager to reach the city, he pushed and pushed on the wheels of the chair. What a long road it was — more than 25 kilometers! His padded clothes were soon soaked with sweat. Not until the sun was directly overhead did he finally arrive at the west gate of Zhongnanhai.

He gazed up at the high red walls, at the massive gate he had not seen for so long. Since childhood, many a time he had passed through that gate. It had been familiar and dear to him. Today it was strange, impassable. Pufang propelled his wheelchair forward and told the guard who he was. He said he had come to ask for medical treatment. He was told to back far away from the gate, and wait.

After a long time someone came out and instructed him to go to a compound in a lane opposite the gate. Pufang managed to push his wheelchair there, and entered the compound. Immediately, he was seized by several men. Without a word, they bundled him and the wheelchair into a jeep, and returned him to the Home in Qinghe.

After all that time and effort, he was back where he started. Pufang lay in his bed. He could no longer feel the misery in his heart. He had not died, but his spirit was dead. Nothing had any meaning any more. Expressionless, saying very little, he lay bending strips of wire into paper-clips and putting them in small cardboard boxes. He was paid three cents per box. In a month he could earn four or five yuan, enough for some cigarettes and a little liquor.

None of his roommates looked down on him, in fact they were very sympathetic. They treated him as an equal, and as a friend. In his period of utmost difficulty, these honest, disabled friends gave him the most precious utmost warmth.

25

Heaven Doesn't Forget People with Hearts

W E don't know whether his visit to Zhongnanhai had any effect, in any event one day in June Beijing finally agreed to send Pufang to Jiangxi.

Mama and Papa had waited for news from February to June. Now their son returned, the son they hadn't seen in five years. But this boy didn't come bounding happily home as other children did. He came home in a wheelchair.

He was back. There should have been no end of things they had to say. But when father and son met, they looked at each other in silence. What could they say? What was worth saying? Papa's stricken gaze said it all.

Of the family, just the three old folks were home. With others assisting they moved Pufang into a room on the ground floor on the north side next to Comrade Huang's room. Before his arrival they had borrowed an iron bed from the provincial hospital. But Pufang had a high area paralysis, and needed to lie on a hard wooden bed. The carpenters in the factory made him a big one. He didn't have the strength to raise himself and turn over. But he had to change his position every two hours; otherwise he would develop bedsores. Every day the three old people, especially Papa, would help him. They did it not only during the day, but had to get up during the night as well.

Pufang thought this was much too tiring for them. Again they turned to the factory. The carpenters, following Pufang's instructions, suspended two rings from the ceiling. Grasping these, he could raise himself and shift somewhat. His comfort was eased considerably.

The three oldsters arranged a division of labor. Papa took on the hardest work, such as helping Pufang turn over, and washing him down. Mama did the dirtiest jobs — emptying the urinals and the bedpans, washing the mattress sheet. Grandma did the cooking and helped Mama wash the clothes. One disabled boy kept all three of the old folks busy. In spite of this Papa and Mama never missed a day at the factory.

Summer comes early in the south, and 1971 again was a scorcher.

It was particularly hard on northerners. Mama and Papa worked in the factory, and when they came home they had chores to do. That would have been difficult enough, but now they also had a bed-ridden son to care for. Of course it was also a great trial for Pufang. If he touched any part of the wooden bed, it was always hotter than his hand. He perspired even when he lay motionless. Whenever he grasped the rings and strained to turn a little, immediately he was drenched in sweat. To prevent bedsores and to keep him clean, my parents washed him several times a day and sprinkled him with talcum powder. It was their busiest and most trying summer since coming to Jiangxi.

But hard or not, busy or not, it was a joy to have part of the family together again. It was much better than having Pufang alone and suffering hundreds of miles away. My parents' bodies were tired, but their minds were at rest.

Human endurance is truly astonishing. In moments of crisis if you grit your teeth you are able to do unimaginable things. But it wasn't easy. Looking back today over 20 years later at that summer in Jiangxi I still feel pressure on my heart.

Gradually, the days passed. They became accustomed to their way of life. The heat slowly diminished, although it was still very warm. The end of summer slowly approached.

Everyone relaxed. Mama and Grandma raised a flock of chickens. Mama had only to step into the yard and the hens and the chicks rushed up and trailed behind her, clucking and pecking at the pebbles in the grass. Mama really looked the part of "Commander-in-Chief of Chickens" of this little army.

After dinner, when the dying sun filtering through the leaves traced a red mosaic on the gravel path, she and Grandma sat in the yard, chatting and wielding plantain fans.

Papa resumed his walks in the courtyard after dinner. He circled the house with quick steps, again and again, deep in thought. He was not concerned about the difficulties of daily life. Nor did his personal political situation trouble him. What unrolled in his mind's eye was a scroll of scores of years of the revolution, the uneven path trod by the Party and the nation, the victories savored, the painful lessons learned. He thought of the past, the present, the future — especially the future. Bathed in the golden haze of the setting sun, he walked around and around, day after day, year after year. His footsteps etched a faint white path on the reddish ground.

As the summer heat dwindled, life in the small house in the old infantry school compound became easier and more orderly. But the three oldsters couldn't handle it all, now that Big Brother was home. They arranged for me to come back from my agricultural brigade in north Shaanxi. There was nothing I wanted more.

My main duty was to help with the family chores. In the village I had learned how to make noodles. I was really good at it. With a long roller I would flatten a lump of dough into a big, round flab, thin as a piece of cloth. I would fold it into accordion pleats, chop with my cleaver, splash into a pot of boiling water, and soon you had genuine north Shaanxi noodles!

Grandma could make her native Sichuan dishes. Although in Jiangxi she had learned to leaven dough and make steamed rolls and dumplings, she didn't know how to do noodles. I impressed everyone when I demonstrated my north Shaanxi expertise. To my surprise, the three oldsters picked it up quickly, especially Papa. In fact he got to be practically as good as me.

I was also put in charge of helping Brother turn over, and other small functions. But I was careless, forever creating mishaps. Because Pufang was immobilized, his lower limbs had shrunk somewhat, and his legs and feet felt cold to the touch. In winter Mama used to put a hot water bottle at his feet to help him keep warm. When I took over, I made a mess of things. One morning we discovered the bottle I had put in the night before had been too hot, and had scalded his feet. The doctor we called said Pufang had suffered second-degree burns. They would heal slowly in a person whose lower extremities were paralyzed. I had forgotten that Pufang had no sensation in his feet.

I felt terrible. Mama and Grandma scolded me angrily. It took three months for Pufang's feet to return to normal.

He lay all day on his wooden bed, reading and listening to the radio. In Peking University he had been one of the brightest students in the mechanical physics department. Besides having done well in his studies, he was very dexterous, and could tinker with radios and all sorts of electrical equipment. Now all this educated, skilled 27 year-old young fellow could do was lie idly in bed.

Papa had an idea. "Does our factory have any electrical repair work?" he asked Lieutenant Tao.

Tao was surprised. Ordinarily, Old Deng, after greeting everyone on arrival, would go to his fitter's bench and start meticulously filing. He spoke very little. Tao knew there must be something on his mind. He said the small factory didn't require any electrical repairs.

"Aren't there any radios that need fixing?" Papa persisted,

"Why do you ask, Old Deng?" Tao queried.

Papa told him Pufang was at home with nothing to do, and that he was handy with electrical repairs. It would be good to keep him occupied.

By then everyone in the factory was fond of Deng. Although Tao would have liked to help him, the factory really didn't have that kind of work.

Papa wouldn't give up. "What about at home? Don't any of you have a radio he could repair?" he asked. "Anything would be better than just lying in bed all day."

Tao was touched by Papa's obvious devotion to his son.

"To tell the truth, my family's income is only 40 or 50 yuan a month," he said. "I have four kids. The oldest is only primary school age. We also have an old parent with us. Our life is very hard. Where would we get the money to buy a radio?"

Papa fell silent. It was not because he had been unable to find something for his son to do. It was because he was upset by what this ordinary worker had said. More than 20 years had passed since the establishment of socialism, yet a worker's family couldn't even afford a radio.

As a leader, Papa had done his utmost for our nation's construction. He had seen how the whole country, at every level, had united to overcome the devastation wrought by three years of natural calamities. He had traveled to every corner of the land and discussed with the people and the local cadres means of strengthening national well-being. After many ups and downs, twists and turns, China had at last evolved a formula for developing the economy.

Now a Cultural Revolution was sweeping the gains away.

Papa himself had been purged. He no longer held any position of leadership. He was miles from the center of political activities. He neither heard, nor saw, nor knew, anything about the latest developments. But as an acutely attuned political person, he could sense that China was still chaotic, that the political situation was still complicated, that the economy remained stalled, that the people were still suffering poverty and hardship.

Whether in or out of office, as a veteran Communist, Papa was concerned first and foremost with the country, the people, the Party. His shock at the commencement of the Cultural Revolution had turned to depression. The frank admission of an ordinary worker like Tao made him sick at heart.

While in the south the last vestiges of the summer heat still lingered, in the political arena in the north a major event exploded. On September 13, 1971, Lin Biao fled in a plane with his wife and son. The plane crashed and shattered in the desolate sands of Mongolia. Our small house in the infantry school compound in Jiangxi was isolated. But however isolated it was, nothing could stop the news from getting in.

Pufang was quite skilled mechanically. He enjoyed tinkering with radios and electrical equipment. Mama and Papa were afraid he would be bored, lying in bed all day. They gave him our family's best radio so that he could listen to the broadcasts. Pufang was delighted to find that it had shortwave capability. He was able to hear shortwave programs, sometimes even including some from abroad.

The three old folks didn't know the difference between long wave and short, but Pufang could tune in both. He heard on a foreign news program that a Chinese plane had crashed in Mongolia. A few days later he heard a foreign analyst speculate that something of major importance must have happened in China. Pufang told our parents about this. Papa said nothing.

On October 1, China held the usual National Day celebrations, but eliminated the usual National Day parade. Even more surprising was the fact that in all the news of the celebration Lin Biao's name was not mentioned. Lin Biao must be in trouble, Pufang said to me. Papa, as usual, made no comment.

Lin Biao's self-destruction was the most shaking political event since the inception of the Cultural Revolution. Five days after it happened the Central Committee, with the approval of Mao Zedong, notified its members of Lin Biao's treasonous flight. Ten days later military leaders of departmental and divisional rank were also informed. On October 6 the Central Committee issued a document regarding the criminal activities of the Lin Biao clique. In the middle of the month the document was sent to all local Communist Party secretaries. On the 24th the Central Committee made it available to members of the Communist Party throughout the land.

On November 6, the factory notified my parents to come and listen to a reading of Central Committee documents. Papa had retained his Communist Party membership after being purged, but the news that he could hear such material amazed him. He and Mama put on their overshoes and took their umbrellas, and headed for the factory in the rain.

Waiting restlessly for their return, I wandered from Pufang in his bedroom to Grandma in the kitchen. What was happening in the Cultural Revolution? Was it good or bad, lucky or evil? Not even the Old Lord of the Sky knew!

My parents found some 80 workers seated quietly in rows in the factory dining hall. At one end two long tables had been pushed together to form a presidium. After greeting the workers they knew, Mama and Papa sat down in the rear. Luo Peng, the chairman of the factory's revolutionary committee, and the head of the county industrial bureau were sitting at the presidium. Spotting my folks in the audience, Luo called out: "You're a little deaf, Old Deng. You won't be able to hear clearly. Come sit closer." Papa and Mama moved up and took seats in the front row.

The Central Committee documents which were read consisted of the notice of Lin Biao's treasonous flight and material regarding the crimes of his anti-Party clique.

The reading took over two hours. The audience listened, scarcely breathing. When the meeting concluded, all the workshops were asked to hold discussions. Papa listened to the unusually animated comments of the workers in his fitters' shop. He himself did not speak. Tao suggested to Luo Peng that Old Deng be allowed to take the documents and read them at home. And so, when Mama and Papa entered our house door, they had the documents with them.

It was after one p.m. by the time they returned. Full of questions I came forward. Mama took my hand and led me to the kitchen. With her finger she wrote on my palm: "Lin Biao is dead." During the Cultural Revolution because we knew "the walls have ears," we used this method to communicate.

Every drop of hot blood in my body seemed to rush to my head. Afraid of being overheard I dared ask no more. I ran to Brother's room, closed the door, and whispered the news. His whole body swelled with excitement.

Papa as usual did not speak. On finishing dinner we all went upstairs and closed the door. Mama emotionally told me what they heard at the meeting. Tears gushed from my eyes. Papa did not sit down. He stood, smoking, watching us. Finally, he broke his customary silence. He was as moved as we were. He spoke only one sentence.

"It would have gone against Heavenly Reason for Lin Biao not to die!"

Two days later, that is on the 8th of November, Papa took up his pen and wrote a letter to Mao Zedong.

"Before hearing the communiqué I knew nothing of Lin Biao and Chen Boda's anti-Party clique," he wrote. "I could only sense that Chen Boda had gone wrong. The revelations about Lin Biao were very sudden. I was shocked and angered to learn of their despicable crimes."

Papa confirmed his support for the Central Committee decision regarding the clique. "Its exposure is a cause for celebration," he continued. "Had it not been for the brilliant leadership of the Chairman and the Central Committee, and the early exposure and quick disposition, the plot might have succeeded. Even if they were finally buried by the revolutionary masses, as the Central Committee communiqué said, who knows how many heads would have rolled, how many twists and calamities our socialist motherland would have endured. But the crisis was averted. I, like all the people of our land, am tremendously happy!"

Papa wrote: "I cannot restrain my emotions!"

It was true. Since the advent of the Cultural Revolution he had written self-criticisms, self-examinations, several letters. Under the compulsion of the political situation and the times, much against his will he wrote blaming himself, using the jargon of the Cultural Revolution. He pleaded for help for his family and his children. He was unable to say what he wanted to say, he was forced to say things he didn't want to say.

The monstrous Lin Biao had ended in a nameless grave. A joyous event! Papa fully supported the Central Committee decision. His words were from the depths of his heart. He could spill out at last things he had been longing to say for years.

Calmer reflection reminded him that he was writing to Mao Zedong. He had not written to him directly after their last talk together. Mao had told him to contact Wang Dongxing about any problem, be it political or family, and have Wang to relay his requests to the Chairman or to the Central Committee. This time was different. Papa wrote directly to Mao, first, because Lin Biao's demise was of the utmost importance, and, second, because he realized this was a critical moment.

One of the main reasons Deng Xiaoping was overthrown in the Cultural Revolution was Lin Biao. Yet Mao Zedong had insisted on preserving Deng's Party membership. There had to be a political reason behind this. In so complicated a political environment, no matter how bad his personal circumstances, Deng never let his emotions run away with him. He did not become depressed; he never gave up hope. While maintaining his self-respect, while sticking to principle, as a Communist should, he sent his self-criticism to Mao.

Papa had no illusions, but he never quit trying. As a Communist who had fought for the revolution all his life, it distressed him to see the turmoil, to see villains usurping power, to see disorder, to see the people suffering. How could he feel otherwise?

His one aim before Lin Biao's fall was to preserve a last line of political defense. Now, with Lin Biao gone, his goal was clearer. He would grasp every opportunity to make a comeback, to work again for the people and the Party. In the past five years he had given a great deal of thought to how China should proceed on the socialist road. If the day came when he could return to office, he would devote all of the knowledge he had acquired during the long stormy years of the revolution to bring order out of chaos. That would be his gift to the country and people he loved so well.

Papa's rich experience told him that although Lin Biao had died China's political scene remained confused. Opposition to the old revolutionaries' returning to office was still very strong. It would be a tough struggle. Mao had to re-think his strategy and placement of personnel. It was an important time, an opportunity not to be missed.

In his letter, Papa wrote also about his private affairs. "I have been in Jiangxi exactly two years now," he said. "Every morning I work in a factory. In the afternoon and evening I read books and newspapers, listen to the radio and do some chores. Except for going to the factory I haven't taken a step away from the house. I am cut off from the outside. In keeping with your instructions I have been reforming myself through labor and study. I am strictly observing the guarantees I have made to the Party. I have had no contact with anyone except members of my family. The Party is looking after us. There is no problem about our living conditions."

Papa continued: "I have no requests for myself, only that some day I may be able to do a little work for the Party. Naturally, it would be some sort of technical job. My health is pretty good. I can put in a few more years before retirement. Every day the press carries reports of the flying advances of our socialist motherland in domestic construction, of our unprecedented international prestige. I am very stirred. I am longing for a chance to pay back by hard work a bit of what I owe."

I remember when Papa first arrived in Jiangxi he said to the men of the Special Case Team: "I will be going back to work." Now, two years later, he clearly formulated his request to Mao Zedong. He believed that at a time like this Mao Zedong would give careful consideration to a request like this.

Papa was a political person. To his mind political questions, major questions, had to be given first priority. He was also the head of the family, a husband, and a father. Family affairs had an important place in his heart. In his very political letter to Mao Zedong he could not forget the members of his family.

"I hope I can be closer to my children," he said in his letter to Mao Zedong, "especially my two youngest, Maomao and Feifei. My daughter Maomao was assigned to an agricultural brigade in northern Shaanxi, and has been there for over three years. Because I am unable to care properly for my crippled oldest son, who is living with us, I have brought her here temporarily to help look after her brother. She is keen on studying medicine, and has already learned a few basics through self-study. My youngest son Feifei has been more than three years in an agricultural brigade in Shanxi. They have not been given good job assignments because of their relationship to me, and they will never get any unless the Party intervenes.

"I am getting on in years, and can't help being concerned about my children. I hope they can be assigned to places near to where I work. It would be fine if they could be given jobs in factories. That would ensure them fixed wages. If Maomao can study medicine, that of course would be even better. These are things I think a lot about, and only mention them to you, Chairman. Of course I understand the disposition of such matters depends entirely on what the Party decides."

Warmth wells up in me as I read this. I think we children were very fortunate because we had a father who loved us, who was concerned about us at a time when he was in extreme difficulty, a father of whom we could be proud.

When Papa wrote to Wang Dongxing the previous February requesting that Pufang be moved to Jiangxi, word came down from Beijing telling him not to write Wang any more letters. Now, he not only wrote, but addressed a letter to Mao Zedong himself.

In it he said: "The Chairman instructed me to seek Comrade Wang Dongxing if I had any problems. Early this year when I wrote to him about my son Pufang, I was advised not to write him any more. For the next eleven months I wrote nothing. If I have any problems in the future, I don't know whether I should write to him or not?"

In conclusion, Papa said: "Chairman, I sincerely wish you long life. Your long and healthy life ensures the greatest happiness for the whole Party and all our people!" Papa solemnly signed his name.

This letter proved to be a very important factor in Papa's political life. Although Papa did not know what happened to it, and though he had no reply, as we later learned, Mao Zedong did indeed receive it.

"Why aren't you handling his affairs?" Mao asked Wang Dongxing.

Wang actually didn't know about Deng Xiaoping's previous letter. "I am," Wang replied. "It's just that I've been with you, away from Beijing. I asked Wang Liang'en, the deputy head of the General Office, to take charge while I was gone."

"Comrade Xiaoping's letter says he wants you to manage his affairs," Mao countered.

His meaning was very plain: Wang Dongxing was still responsible for Deng Xiaoping. On the envelope of Papa's letter Mao wrote this endorsement: "Print and issue to the Politburo. Have Wang Dongxing deal with his family affairs."

26

Winding Back Through Precipitous Heights

LIN Biao's death was indeed a shocking event in the Great Proletarian Cultural Revolution. Viewed from whatever aspect, its explosive effect brought great joy to China's millions. But cool scrutiny also revealed that the Cultural Revolution was open to serious question.

Mao Zedong had adopted a number of measures intended to ensure the implementation of his revolutionary line. One of the most important of these was naming Lin Biao as his successor. Its failure showed not only that Mao had evaluated his choice incorrectly; it also raised doubts about the entire course of action, orientation, and policy followed since the advent of the Cultural Revolution, and the methods employed. The fall of Lin Biao was generally hailed as another great victory for Mao's philosophy and his revolutionary line. Mao himself knew better

A person who worked closely beside him later recalled: "After Lin Biao crashed, the Chairman became very ill. Lin Biao's betrayal had a serious effect on his health. We heard him quote the old adage: 'At 73 or 84, if Death doesn't invite you, you should go to its door!' We felt badly. He was very depressed. When we tried to reassure him, he became angry. 'You're going against the rules of Nature,' he said. 'When there's life, there's death. Everyone has to die. Claims to the contrary are just farts!'"

About the revolutionary line he was pursuing, about the Cultural Revolution he had initiated, he had no doubts, nor would he allow others to express doubts. But the death of Lin Biao forced him to reconsider certain radical measures he had permitted, believing them necessary for the sake of the revolution.

Responsibility for the daily work of the Central Committee was in effect turned over to Zhou Enlai. On October 3 Mao Zedong dissolved the Office of the Military Commission formerly controlled by the Lin Biao clique, and created a new Military Commission Office under Marshal Ye Jianying.

The new set-up was this: The Central Committee and the State Council (including the Ministry of Foreign Affairs) were under Premier Zhou Enlai; military affairs were headed by Ye Jianying. On all major policy discussions in the Military Commission "the Premier was invited to attend." Jiang Qing and her cohorts exercised complete responsibility for all Cultural Revolution activities.

Before, China's main political camp had been divided between the Lin Biao and the Jiang Qing cliques. Harmony or conflict was up to them. Lin Biao's death changed all that. It was Zhou Enlai and Ye Jianying representing the old revolutionaries on one side, and Jiang Qing representing the Cultural Revolution forces on the other.

Mao Zedong was a Marxist, with deep roots in China's traditional culture. He was thoroughly familiar with the nation's classical treatises; he knew China's history from her earliest civilization. The exciting events and striking figures of the past several thousand years were sharply incised in his mind. The benevolence and tyrannies of emperors and ministers, the romanticism and pride of literary creations, the rebelliousness of bravos against convention, and the special wisdom, philosophy and thought patterns with which China's history and culture are so imbued all permeated his very essence.

Mao's creed was the Communist ideal of liberating all mankind. His sentiment was replete with romantic poetic imagery; his mind was a winged steed flying untrammeled through a boundless sky; his deeds were I do what I think is right whatever the cost; his strategy was keep moving forward, there's always a way; his policy was support the good and be prepared for the worst.

As a young man he was a fearless revolutionary. In middle age he was a strategist of vast vision. In his old age, his assurance that he could attain his ideal became gradually eroded by prejudice.

First he chose Liu Shaoqi, then Lin Biao, and he failed in both. As a result it was hard for him to believe in anyone. Never again would he give a relative concentration of power to a single individual. If in the past he had noted the scattering of forces under his command and the balance among them, now he paid close attention to the divisions within the political factions and the restraints they exercised on one another.

To keep the national machine in motion he found he had to depend on the loyal "old guard". To guarantee a "revolutionary" line he would also utilize new forces he thought would be faithful to that line.

Mao Zedong always believed in a unity of opposites. In his declining years he applied this stringently in political matters. As a philosophical rule the principle is correct. But using it to impel mutual restraint in political affairs and among personnel is another matter. It is very risky. If improperly applied, not only will it produce needless conflicts, it will make them very dangerous. The events which followed proved this.

Now regardless of how he placed his personnel, Mao had to reflect on developments since the start of the Cultural Revolution, and his own role. He began to have a new understanding, especially of the wrong measures in the initial stages. At a number of meetings he criticized himself, and took steps to rectify the errors.

He also began to liberate large numbers of cadres who had been purged. Some of them were returned to their posts, their reputations restored.

First, Mao cleared the high ranking cadres who had been attacked for participating in the so-called "February Countercurrent". On the 14th of November 1971, Mao Zedong received delegates who had been attending a conference in Chengdu. Indicating Ye Jianying, who was present, Mao said: "Don't call him part of the 'February Countercurrent' any more. What was the 'February Countercurrent?' It was directed against Lin Biao, Chen Boda, and Wang Li, Guan Feng and Qi Benyu."

Subsequently, Mao issued directives demanding correction of the treatment of Chen Yun, Luo Ruiqing, Tan Zhenlin and other veterans. He sincerely apologized to the old heroes who had stood shoulder to shoulder with him in life-and-death battles, who together helped shape the epochal new China. On several occasions he said their treatment was wrong, that he had listened to prejudiced allegations by Lin Biao.

"It is bad to hear only one side of a story, comrades," he said. " I offer my self-criticism."

By then, Marshal He Long had been killed. "I was wrong about Comrade He Long," Mao confessed. "I bear full responsibility!"

Zhou Enlai seized upon this atmosphere to hasten the liberation of cadres. Thanks to his efforts many were released from restraint, supervision, mistreatment, and forced labor. A few were cleared of all charges and returned to their jobs. Their political lives were restored, their personal safety guaranteed. The cruel murderous environment of the Cultural Revolution at last was ameliorated. Although it was still winter and icy cold, warmth began to flow back into people's hearts. Their tightly knit brows relaxed.

It was this thaw which ushered in 1972.

With the death of Lin Biao and the freeing of many cadres, Mao Zedong surely thought of Deng Xiaoping. In 1967, when the frenzy of the Cultural Revolution was at its height, Mao had said if Lin Biao's health failed, he would have to bring Deng out. Now, with Lin Biao gone, using Deng again was an eminently practical proposition.

On January 6, 1972, one of the founders of the nation, Marshal of the People's Republic of China, Chen Yi, passed away in Beijing.

On January 10, a not particularly cold winter's day, a memorial service was held for Chen Yi at the Cemetery for Revolutionaries. Slandered as a member of the "February Countercurrent", angered and depressed, he developed terminal cancer which took his life. The unhappiness people had been suppressing in their hearts burst forth, pervading the memorial service.

To everyone's surprise, Mao Zedong suddenly arrived, with only pajamas beneath his long overcoat. The greying hair at his temples hung down to his collar. He stood before the bier of the old soldier who had been with him since the Jinggang Mountains days, and bowed respectfully three times. His stricken expression spoke more than words.

"Comrade Chen Yi was a good man, a good comrade," he said afterwards to Chen's widow, Zhang Qian. "Comrade Chen Yi served with distinction." Pointing to Zhou Enlai and Ye Jianying, Mao said: "If Lin Biao had succeeded in his plot, he would have destroyed all of us veterans."

Mao also mentioned Deng Xiaoping, linking him with Liu Bocheng, then a member of the Politburo. He said Deng was different from Liu Shaoqi, that Deng's situation was less serious.

Mao's open reference to Deng Xiaoping was very important news. Zhou Enlai hinted to members of Chen Yi's family to let Mao's appraisal of Deng become generally known, to help muster public opinion for Deng's rehabilitation.

Near the end of the month Zhou Enlai received a delegation from other provinces in the Great Hall of the People. In the presence of Jiang Qing and Yao Wenyuan, Zhou spoke of Deng Xiaoping. He urged the delegates while criticising Lin Biao not to confuse errors which are different in nature. He said the Lin Biao gang wanted to put Deng Xiaoping in an enemy category. This was not in keeping with Chairman Mao's estimation.

Although the news about Deng Xiaoping circulated to a certain extent, our family, sealed off within the confines of the Jiangxi fortress, knew nothing about it. The obvious relaxation all around us, however, gave us a definite sense of a more positive atmosphere.

We had several unexpected guests during the Spring Festival in 1972 — three children of Li Jingquan, former Politburo member and former First Secretary of the Southwest Bureau of the Party Central Committee. They got our address from a high ranking provincial official and an old friend. We were extremely happy to see them. They were the first outsiders ever to visit us. Our two families had been very close; we children had grown up together.

We had heard bad news about each other after the Cultural Revolution started, but hadn't met for years. They told us their father Li Jingquan had been overthrown, and criticized at huge public rallies more than 100 times. Then he had been moved to Beijing and put in an army prison. Their mother had been so tormented she committed suicide. The second oldest son had written a poster expressing dissatisfaction with Mao's extremist methods at the start of the Cultural Revolution, and had been beaten to death by a radical faction. The youngest boy had been locked up in a Beijing detention center. The rest of the children were either working in agricultural brigades or in factories near their old home in Jiangxi.

We all fell silent, very moved.

Mama and Papa brought out the best we had in the house to feed our young visitors. Papa even went to the kitchen and made a few dishes for them personally. They stayed with us for five days. As they were leaving, Mama urged them to come again the next time they were in Nanchang. They did call later, two or three times.

Mama was particularly fond of Huachuan, the youngest boy, who had been let out after being held for a few years in a detention center in Beijing. She treated him like her own son. Afraid he wouldn't be able to cope alone, Mama stuffed some money into his pocket when he left. The Li children no longer had a home of their own, but they had a home with us.

Although Zhou Enlai had already begun pushing the liberation of cadres, and although the political situation of our family had somewhat improved, countless cadres across the land were still being harassed and treated unjustly.

27

Spring Comes Early South of the Yangtze

THERE were many changes in our family in 1972. In my personal life, too, there were changes I never expected.

In the latter half of 1971 when I was still on the yellow soil plateaus of northern Shaanxi, Lü Tongyan, daughter of the famous old general Lü Zhengcao, came to see me. After graduating from the China Medical Academy, she had been assigned as a doctor to a commune hospital only five *li* from our village. Her baby name was Pangpang (Chubby). Since childhood I called her Sister Pangpang. I was naturally delighted, in that remote impoverished rural area, to meet a close friend from Beijing. When I had free time I often went to her commune.

One day when we were reminiscing about Beijing and people we knew there, Pangpang suddenly said: "There's a fellow named He Ping. He'd be just right for you. I'm going to introduce you two!"

When Pangpang said something, she did it. The next time she went to Beijing, she looked up He Ping, and pressured him into exchanging letters with me.

He Ping's father in the old days had fought in the Honghu Lake guerillas, and later became head of the medical department of the Second Front Army of the Red Army. Labeled a "capitalist roader" in the Cultural Revolution, he was criticized and reviled. He was

195

undergoing reform through labor in a May Seventh Cadre School [1] of the Jiangxi Health Department, living in a "monsters enclosure".

He Ping himself had been a student in the Harbin Military Technology Academy. Because of a preposterous charge leveled against him during the Cultural Revolution of being involved in something called the "Extraordinary Committee of the Chinese Communist Party", he was shackled hand and foot and thrown into prison. One year and four months later, a verdict finally came down: "Investigation justified. Dismissed for lack of evidence", and He Ping was freed. He was assigned to an army farm reclamation in Yuanjiang in Hunan Province.

Warmhearted Pangpang dragged together two people who originally had no such thought. Otherwise, with one of us in an agricultural brigade in northern Shaanxi, and the other in an army farm in Hunan, how would we have met? But because we were in similar situations, after several exchanges of letters, we felt we had a lot in common.

Not long after, He Ping was going to visit his parents who were being "reformed" at a May Seventh Cadre School in Jiangxi, and would be passing through Nanchang. I honestly reported this to my parents. Mama, worried that because of Papa's and her own "questions" their children would have difficulty in finding marriage partners, was overjoyed when she heard He Ping would be coming to see us.

I went to the Nanchang railway station to meet him. There had been two months of letters between us, and an exchange of photographs, but we had never met. I'm nearsighted, and He Ping recognized me first. My first impression was that he was terribly tall! I took him home with me on the public bus. We had only just met, and we ourselves had not thought very far ahead.

---

[1] Mao Zedong said on May 7, 1966, it would be good for intellectuals to live and work for a time among the people in the countryside. After the Cultural Revolution began, many organizations bought plots of land from rural communes and set up what were called May Seventh Cadre Schools. To there they sent large numbers — sometimes all — of their personnel to work and study Mao's revolutionary philosophy, make self-criticisms, and criticize the heretics in their ranks. As a result, the bulk of China's finest practitioners in the arts, sciences and professions were put out of action for nearly 10 years, and thus organizations, institutes and schools lay dormant, causing China to fall further behind the rest of the world.

But Papa and Mama and Grandma, seemed to have plunged into a "full alert"! They became very busy. Mama bombarded He Ping with questions, obviously grilling a prospective son-in-law. Grandma, in the kitchen, clattering a loud tattoo on the skillet, was cooking up a horde of tasty dishes, which she loaded on to our small square table. A young fellow of 26, coming all the way from an Army farm in Hunan, had to be very hungry! The more dishes Grandma made, the more He Ping consumed, with no finicky shows of politeness. All the plates and platters on the table ended piled up empty in front of him. When we Sichuanese invite guests nothing pleases us more than to have them eat. Grandma's face, as she collected the chopsticks, was wreathed in smiles.

In the afternoon He Ping helped Mama and Grandma plant melons. He's tall, and he works fast. Before you knew it, he had a trellis up. "That tall fellow gets things done!" Grandma said.

We sat around in the living room upstairs in the evening, and He Ping told us all the news, including the "inside story" of Lin Biao's fall, and that the old cadres were being liberated. Young fellows like He Ping traveled around a lot, and met many different people. Their news sources were much broader than us girls'. What we enjoyed hearing most was Lin Biao's end. What interested us most was the liberation of the veteran cadres.

He Ping is a very down-to-earth person. He was relaxed and intimate with the three oldsters right from the start. They liked him. He stayed with us two days, then left to visit his parents in their May Seventh Cadre School. He had a carton of cigarettes, then very difficult to obtain, and before he left he gave half to Papa.

After seeing He Ping off at the railway station I returned home. I found the old folks sitting on small bamboo stools by the melon patch behind the kitchen. They were talking about something. When Mama saw me she called me over, in a rather formal manner. Papa looked very pleased.

He slapped his thigh enthusiastically and said in his thick Sichuan accent:

"It looks like that match is settled!"

Papa was very conscientious. He seemed to treat the marriage of his children almost as responsibly as the major affairs of State he had handled when he was in office! Nothing made Mama and Papa happier than the happiness of their children.

After the fall of Lin Biao, his crony in Jiangxi, Cheng Shiqing, was compelled to step down. Replacing him as heads of the provincial Communist Party Committee were Bai Dongcai and Huang Zhizhen, both old cadres. Huang came to see Papa, and informed him that the Central Committee had restored Deng Xiaoping's normal Party activities. Papa had never lost his Party membership, but he had been kept under surveillance in a kind of house arrest. Now the basic rights to which all Communists are entitled were returned to him at last. A solid change, it signified the restoration of his political life.

Papa and Mama's delight was obvious from their demeanor as they chatted with Huang Zhizhen.

The Cultural Revolution Committee of Jiangxi Province notified us early in April that Feifei had been admitted to Jiangxi's College of Science and Technology, and that I would be sent to Jiangxi Medical University. Our parents' wish for us had come true. More important, this meant that Mao Zedong had not only received the letter Papa sent last year on November 8, but that he had acted upon it. This was extremely important. It showed that Mao Zedong was still paying attention to the far-away Deng Xiaoping.

Much encouraged, on April 22, Papa wrote to Wang Dongxing.

He said: "Comrade Dongxing, I haven't sent you a letter in a long time. Thanks to Chairman Mao's concern and your help, Maomao and Feifei's school problems have been solved. Maomao will be in the Medical University in Nanchang. Feifei will also be in Nanchang, studying radio mechanics at the College of Science and Technology. The schools notified us 20 days ago. We are very grateful to the Chairman and the Party for giving them such consideration!

"We are being well looked after. However my stepmother (Grandma) is going to Tianjin in three days to help my sister when she gives birth and look after the baby. Although over 70, and gradually aging, she has been working very hard in our home for several years. So we have urged her to go to Tianjin, where she will have much less to do.

"With two of the children away in school, Zhuo Lin and I will be alone, looking after our disabled son. We therefore won't be able to go to the factory for a while. (Zhuo Lin is not in very good health, either.) We would like to hire someone to do the cooking and help care for the disabled boy.

"We have made a request to the local leadership. We have heard it is difficult to find a suitable person, and that wages would be relatively high (over 30 yuan). We are waiting to see whether they can find someone. If they can't, and either Zhuo Lin or I gets sick, we won't be able to manage.

"Our oldest son, Pufang, has been here with us for nearly a year. Our observations have shown that although he has no sensation below the waist (he cannot urinate or move his bowels unaided), his ability to function is not completely gone.

"The doctors in the No. 301 Hospital were curious about this when he was there, and opened him up for a closer look. But he was moved to the Beijing Social Rescue Home before they could make a final diagnosis. We hope he can have a chance for further treatment, preferably at the No. 301 Hospital, or perhaps have another operation. It really embarrasses us to make this request of the Party."

As you can see, Papa's letters during the Cultural Revolution were mainly about "petty family affairs." He was brief and to the point. When he was in office and had to make a speech, he never wrote it out in advance. The reports he submitted were simple and succinct.

In our daily life since childhood I never saw Papa write a letter about family matters, even to Mama, his beloved wife of 30-more years. But when, during the Cultural Revolution, the family was in difficulties, when his children needed help and support, when they required medical attention, or to get into school, or to find jobs, as head of the family Papa tirelessly wrote one letter after another. He felt the children's difficulties were due to him, and he did his utmost to help them. He never asked the children to do anything for him. He bestowed on them all of his love, without expecting anything in return.

According to my estimate, the letters he wrote during the 10 years of the Cultural Revolution far outnumbered all the other letters he penned in his entire 80 years.

Concluding this letter, Papa said: "As to myself I am still awaiting instructions from you allowing me to do a few more years of work. I hope I can live out my remaining years in the north. We're not very used to the summers down here."

After several years of patient waiting, Papa made his aim plain: If possible he wanted to return to Beijing, and he wanted to get back to work.

Aunty Deng Xianqun, Papa's younger sister, was expecting a baby in September. She had written to Jiangxi asking whether Grandma could come to Tianjin and help look after the child. We had talked it over and all agreed she should go. Mama and Papa felt that Grandma had borne the heaviest burden in looking after us children in the move from Zhongnanhai to Fanghuzhai, and from Fanghuzhai to Jiangxi. Grandma saw us through thick and thin. It had been an arduous task. She needed a change of scenery, to relax, to rest. I was appointed to escort her to Tianjin.

We left Nanchang on April 25. Grandma couldn't stand being idle. The moment we got to Tianjin she immediately set to work to help Aunty with the preparations. Of course Aunty and Uncle were very solicitous. They had invited Grandma to come and take life easy. They wouldn't let her get too tired. After all those years of hard labor, Grandma was forced to "enjoy herself"!

On the return trip to Jiangxi I stopped in Beijing. My enthusiastic friend Pangpang insisted on taking me to see Uncle Wang Zhen. Famed for his outspoken fearlessness, he was known as "Whiskers Wang"! He was attacked by the radical factions during the Cultural Revolution. He wouldn't give an inch, and yelled right back at them. After the Ninth Party Congress, he transmitted verbal and written messages for many old cadres, and arranged for several of the "Black Gang" and their colleagues to return to Beijing for medical treatment.

Uncle Whiskers greeted me warmly, and insisted I stay at his house. He wanted to know all about Papa.

"Chairman Mao says your father's case is a contradiction among the people," he firmly informed me. "Tell him his question will definitely be solved. I'm going to see Premier Zhou, and I'll write letters to Chairman Mao and the Central Committee. Your Papa should come back to work!"

He urged me not to stop any place else, but return to Jiangxi immediately, and tell the family what he said.

As I left his house I walked toward Tiananmen Square. It was the May 1 holiday, Labor Day, and redolent of spring in north China. The blue sky and white clouds over the vast Square, the fluttering red flag, made my spirits soar. Six years. A full six years. Never before in those six years had I felt Beijing so beautiful. Never had the sight of Tiananmen Square so stirred and inspired me.

I hurried back to Jiangxi and told Papa what Uncle Whiskers had said. Papa smoked in silence. But I could see that he was moved.

There is a Sichuan proverb he liked to quote: "When good luck comes, no door can keep it out." For our family, 1972 was indeed a lucky year. Could our calamities really have ended and good fortune come at last? In January, Chairman Mao had said Deng Xiaoping's case was one of a contradiction among the people. In February, Papa's Communist Party activities were resumed. In April, Feifei and I were notified we could attend college. And in June, we were informed that Mama and Papa would be receiving full pay.

After Wang Dongxing received Papa's letter of April 26, he added a notation, on May 30, reading: "A letter from Comrade Deng Xiaoping requests a solution to his money and family problems. I recommend that he be given his original pay." Wang sought approval from Zhou Enlai.

On June 27, the Premier appended this endorsement: "Pay salaries to Deng and Zhuo Lin at their original rates. If his oldest son is able to be operated upon, let him come to Beijing. Have Comrade Yang Dezhong attend to this matter."

Zhou Enlai had already instructed the General Office of the Central Committee to restore original salaries starting from the month of May to

Deng Xiaoping and a few other old revolutionaries and their wives.

Life became easier for us after the regular salaries were issued again. We all knew it was not just a question of money. It meant that Papa's political question was settled. This was tremendously important.

With the help of the factory manager Luo Peng, Mama was able to hire a woman from a worker's family to help around the house and look after Pufang. It took a lot of the burden off my parents' shoulders. Her name was Miao Faxiang. We called her Aunt Miao.

Pufang had brought a wheelchair with him from Beijing. Thanks to our parents' loving care, he grew much stronger. With a little help he could get into the chair every day and wheel himself into the courtyard. There he could see the green foliage inside and outside the courtyard walls, the melons and vegetables growing in our soil, the clucking hens and chicks running after the old folks who fed them, the glistening leaves of the tong trees stirring in breeze. He could bask from head to toe in the warm sunlight. There was no place like home. Peking University, the school hospital, the hospital in Jishuitan, the No. 301 Hospital, the Beijing Social Rescue Home... were like a long nightmare that had passed.

Li Qianming, husband of aunt Deng Xianqun who was expecting a baby in Tianjin, came to Jiangxi on a trip for his academy. Qianming first traveled to Chengdu in Sichuan Province to see Aunty Deng Xianfu and her family. Xianfu told Qianming that she wanted to go to Jiangxi, too. She hadn't seen Papa, her older brother, in many years. Although they frequently exchanged letters, she wasn't sure what his situation was, and she didn't want to cause any awkwardness by a sudden visit.

So she and Qianming worked out a special plan. He would come to our house first. If Papa was alright, Qianming would phone Xianfu and say: "I agree." If he was unable to see Papa, he would say: "I disagree." It was as if they were conducting some kind of underground operation!

Aunty Xianfu gave Qianming four bottles of fine Chengdu liquor she had been saving for years. "Brother likes a drink now and then. Make sure he gets these," she instructed.

Qianming was a typical honest, good-natured husband. He carried those bottles all the way from Sichuan by boat, arriving in Jiangxi on June 23.

We were delighted to see him. Aunty Xianqun was only a teenager when China was liberated in 1949. She and Grandma moved in with us, and she grew up under Mama's "command". She and Deng Lin went to the middle school attached to Beijing Normal University. She then attended the Harbin Military Technology Academy, capital of Northeast China's Heilongjiang Province. After graduation she married classmate Li Qianming, who was assigned to the same unit as she. In all of this, Mama helped and guided her.

And so, Xianqun was especially close to my parents. She grew up in our house, and played with all of us three sisters. We played together, raised rumpuses together, all completely equal. After their marriage Qianming always followed Aunty Xianqun's "lead", for which we younger generation kids often irreverently teased them.

"Xianqun wrote that you were coming, but we heard nothing from you," Mama scolded. "We thought you had fallen into the Yangtze!"

Papa was very happy. He spoke only one sentence: "So here you are!" — and poured Qianming a glass of water.

With Grandma away, Papa was the one who "held the ladle". He marched into the kitchen, saying: "I'll make some 'jiaozi'. I know Qianming likes them."

Qianming hurried in to help. In his own home, Aunty Xianqun monopolized the cooking, Qianming had never learned how. As Papa's assistant he proved a total dud. "Not very clever, are you?" Papa muttered. Mama leaped into the breach. Qianming watched her and Papa bustling about in the summer heat. Papa sweating profusely in his old undershirt full of holes. Mama now fanning the flames of the scorching stove, now chopping vegetables and boiling water.

Qianming looked at them, and tears came to his eyes.

He finished two days of business in Nanchang and got ready to return to Tianjin. He hated to part with Mama and Papa. "You mustn't get too tired," he kept saying. "After Xianqun gives birth I'll have her and Grandma bring the baby here to Jiangxi. Xianqun will be able to give you some help."

Before he left Qianming had told us about the secret signal he had arranged with Aunty Xianfu. Papa told me to send her a telegram and say: "No need to wait for an 'I agree.' Come at once."

Xianfu was puzzled. This was not the signal she had expected. She didn't know what had happened. But she bought a railway ticket, and filled two big hampers with apples, cakes, and Sichuan beef, traveled two days on the train, and arrived in Nanchang on July 3.

I went to the railway station to meet her. We hadn't seen each other in several years. I was taller and huskier. Aunty Xianfu didn't recognize me at first. Working on the farm had toughened me. I was strong. I picked up her two heavy hampers and walked. She had trouble keeping up with me.

When we neared home, I shouted for Mama from the slope behind the house. Mama had been waiting. From an upstairs window she called: "Has she come?"

Xianfu saw Mama and Papa when we entered the courtyard. Mama was dressed in the roomy clothes Grandma had made for her. Papa was wearing a large size shirt. They were standing, all smiles, waiting at the door of the house, as formally as if welcoming a "foreign guest."

Everyone was happy to have her. Xianfu was very efficient around the house. She wanted to help Papa cook, but he wouldn't let her. He had the exclusive rights on that. He made potted meat for her, and "lion-head" meatballs, and "Italian style" noodles with beef and tomato sauce.

"When he heard you were coming he insisted on keeping for you the 20 preserved eggs the factory presented to all the workers at Dragon Boat Festival," Mama said. "And he still hasn't touched those two bottles of liquor you had Qianming bring."

"We have plenty of meat here, Xianfu," Papa assured her.

She saw that the kitchen was neatly arranged. Pots were with pots, ladles with ladles. Even the dishrags were hung in their proper places.

They wouldn't let her cook, but at least she could wash the bowls and do other odds and ends.

The next morning Mama and Papa went to work, as usual. By six a.m. they had made breakfast. Before they left, they instructed us: Don't disturb Aunty Xianfu. She's tired from the train ride. Let her sleep a little longer.

Her visit meant Mama had another companion to talk with. They spent long hours together. After an absence of six years, they had so much they wanted to ask; so much they wanted to say. Aunty Xianfu told about their relatives in Sichuan, and everything she had heard about the present situation. Mama spoke of our family's events in recent years.

Papa and Mama picked gourds and melons in the garden patch behind the house every afternoon and stewed them for Xianfu. They were good for dispelling internal heat in summer. Mama got out the candied cassia flowers she and Grandma had made, and she and Xianfu wrapped them into dumplings.

Xianfu stayed eleven days. Papa said, "It's very hot here. You'd better go and see Grandma in Tianjin."

I said to Papa, "Let's take a picture together before she leaves."

He had on an old shirt he wore while cooking, and he was damp with perspiration. If there was anything he hated it was taking pictures.

"I have no shirt to change into," he said.

We didn't care. I went upstairs, got him a tunic, made him put it on, and pulled him into the garden. Papa, Mama, Aunty Xianfu, Feifei, and I, were photographed together. Although our technique wasn't very good, and the pictures came out rather dark, still, looking at them today they bring a pang of nostalgia. It was the first picture Papa had taken in six years. He was still in Jiangxi, together with his family in his place of exile. It was a once in lifetime happening, and worth remembering.

The Central Committee General Office notified us in early October that Pufang could return to Beijing for treatment in the No. 301 Hospital. We were overjoyed, especially Mama. She longed for her son to be cured, or at least improved. On October 7 two members of the Jiangxi Revolutionary Committee and I brought Pufang to Beijing. We occupied the four soft berths of an expensive compartment, very different from the hard seat I rode on the train from northern Shaanxi to Nanchang. They even supplied mattresses and covers. Such comfort!

Our life in Jiangxi was now much easier, and we were a lot more relaxed. Although Grandma had gone to Tianjin to stay with Aunty Xianqun, and the "heavy burden" of cooking had devolved upon Papa, Pufang was now in Beijing for treatment, and there was less to do around the house. In addition to which two strong youngsters, Feifei and I, had come home, making Mama and Papa happy. The leaders and many of the workers in the factory were able to come to see us. Chen Hongxing helped us make dumplings. She and Mama chatted and laughed together.

Looking back on the first six years of the Cultural Revolution, we had never been so much at ease. Following the winding path down from the peak, was there really a way out?

28

Correcting the Extremist Errors

AFTER the Lin Biao debacle, the daily work of the Party and government was actually handled by Zhou Enlai. He carried out a series of measures aimed at rectifying the ultra-"Left" errors of the Cultural Revolution. These measures at first were supported by Mao Zedong.

They included an adjustment of wages. Zhou pointed out that all enterprises needed reform, management had to be strengthened, rules had to be restored. As a result, a general improvement became apparent. Mao approved again permitting the import of large-scale complete sets of technical equipment.

Zhou then turned his attention to the imbalance within the national economy, and the over-extension on the construction front. In spite of the many obstructions thrown in his path, he persisted. In 1972 the national economy showed some advance. The GNP in industry and agriculture rose 4.5% over the previous year.

Again in the face of strong opposition, Zhou Enlai pushed to correct the policies which had allowed the slandering of Party cadres. In April, in response to his personal instruction, *People's Daily* published an editorial castigating the attacks on veteran leaders and intellectuals, and the false accusations proliferating throughout the land. It insisted that over 90% of the Party cadres were essentially good.

That year, thanks to Zhou Enlai, well over a dozen of China's top veteran Communist leaders again appeared in public, or were released from prison, or were admitted to hospitals for treatment. Their liberation sparked the release or restoration to their posts of many more high-

and middle-ranking Communists on the Central Committee or local levels.

The deaths of two old cadres because they had been refused medical attention prompted Zhou to demand that the Ministry of Health provide old cadres with special care. He personally saw to it that 500 old comrades of vice-ministerial rank and above were given physical exams. Together, he and Ye Jianying supported the liberation of over 100 generals and the resumption of their roles as Army leaders.

A great many old comrades returned to Beijing from May Seventh Schools all over the country "for medical check-up", and took this opportunity to obtain complete exoneration. More emerged from various prisons, from "ox monster enclosures", many went back to work.

News of the rectification of the "Leftist" errors wafted like a spring breeze across the land, bringing feelings of warmth to millions. Since the eruption of the Cultural Revolution, the madness, the shocking sights, dragged everyone, willing or not, into the maelstrom. Now, after the many storms, torments, and wild twists, people were starting to come to their senses. They were starting to think, to review, to doubt.

Precisely at this time Lin Biao revealed himself, and Mao attained some degree of clarity. The Old Lord of the Sky indeed had eyes! Good fortune was emerging from disaster. Zhou Enlai's efforts to turn the situation around soothed people's hearts.

Not all the old cadres who returned to Beijing had been assigned jobs yet, nor had all had their medical check-ups. They wandered around the city looking for old comrades. Who was still alive? Who had returned? When they met, how happy they were! They deluged each other with questions, discussed the current "news", and speculated on the future of the country and the Party.

Papa was still in Jiangxi. Although there was a fundamental improvement in his position, he had heard no further news. We children had better outside contacts than before, and we were able to transmit a lot of encouraging information. Papa analyzed it coolly. His goal was clear — he wanted to return to Beijing; he wanted to be fully restored.

On August 1, 1972, he attended a meeting with all the workers of the tractor factory. They heard a report for the fourth time on the plot of Lin

Biao and his anti-Party group.

Papa wrote a letter to Mao Zedong. Two days later, on August 3, it was transmitted via the Cultural Revolution Committee of Jiangxi Province.

He said he completely supported the exposure and criticism of Lin Biao by the Central Committee. He made a simple factual examination of his own "errors," and voiced a necessary shouldering of responsibility. In conclusion he asked that he be allowed to return to work.

"In my letter to the Chairman last year in November, 1971, I already requested a return to my job," he wrote. "After committing errors I was separated from my work and all contact with society for five years, going on six. I would like, through my work, an opportunity to correct my mistakes and return to the Chairman's proletarian revolutionary line... My health is not bad. Although I am 68, I can still do some technical jobs (such as investigation and research). I can still work for the Party and the people another seven or eight years, and make up for the past to the best of my ability. I have no other requests. I beg for an order from the Chairman and the Central Committee."

Papa knew Mao was waiting to learn his attitude, including his attitude toward the criticism of Lin Biao, and toward the criticism of his own "errors". Papa believed that Mao Zedong would see his letter, but he didn't expect that Mao would act on it so quickly.

On August 14, 1972, Mao wrote the following instruction to Zhou Enlai:

"After you have read this, Premier, have Wang Dongxing print and circulate it among all comrades on the Central Committee. Comrade Deng Xiaoping committed serious mistakes, but he is different from Liu Shaoqi. (1) He was attacked in the Central Soviet days as one of the four offenders — Deng, Mao, Xie and Gu — and as leader of the so-called Mao faction. The materials against him were described in only two books: *Since the Sixth Party Congress* and *Two Lines*. (2) He has no question in his past. He never surrendered to the enemy. (3) He gave valuable support to Comrade Liu Bocheng in battle and won distinction. Moreover, after we came into the cities, he did quite a few good things, such as leading the delegation to the Moscow talks and not giving in to Soviet revisionist pressure."

In conclusion, Mao added: "I have said these things many times. I now say them again."

Zhou Enlai printed and circulated Mao's instructions the same day among members of the Central Committee.

Mao's unusual endorsement, although it did not mention putting Deng back to work, clearly manifested Mao Zedong's attitude toward him. In fact to a certain extent he spoke on Deng's behalf. Mao obviously was seriously considering making use of him again.

But the Cultural Revolution had reached a very complicated stage. It was virtually out of control. In other words, even a great man like Mao Zedong, who could "command mountains and rivers", could not do what he liked. He could not have everything his own way.

First of all, Deng was the second-ranking "largest person in authority taking the capitalist road," a man who had committed "errors" and had been overthrown. Some disposition had to be made regarding these "errors".

Second, since the fall of Lin Biao, the group headed by Jiang Qing in the Cultural Revolution Group had greatly increased its power. They would definitely resist the restoration of any old comrade such as Deng Xiaoping, and would constitute a formidable obstacle. At this time they were the only force in favor of continuing the Cultural Revolution. Mao needed their support. He could not ignore their opposition.

Third, bringing back an important political figure like Deng Xiaoping had both its advantages and its risks. To put it bluntly, would the people who had been attacked demand a condemnation of the Cultural Revolution? In such an intricate, involved situation Mao could only stir up a little momentum in the direction of using Deng Xiaoping again, while continuing to watch developments.

Lin Biao had fallen, but the political scene in China was uneasy. Although the Cultural Revolution sailed on, its course was fraught with tricky currents and dangerous shoals.

Mao Zedong gave some thought to the extreme radical aspects of the

Cultural Revolution, and permitted Zhou Enlai to ameliorate them, within limits. But Zhou's criticism of them, and the anarchistic turbulence they engendered, aroused strong dissatisfaction in the Cultural Revolution Group. Jiang Qing, Zhang Chunqiao, Yao Wenyuan and other group stalwarts openly slandered Zhou Enlai, accusing him of instigating a "revisionist resurgence." Mao took their side. His attitude basically opposed Zhou Enlai's correct stand, and put a stop to criticism of the ultra-"Left".

Mao's position was that it was all right to learn a few lessons, and correct some of the more radical measures. But he flatly refused to permit anyone to negate the extreme "Leftist" line he was enforcing. It was the last bastion of his political existence, his absolutely unshakable "principle" and stand. Unless that stand could be changed, the Cultural Revolution could not be brought to an end. The huge political farce, the huge political tragedy, would continue.

In Beijing the political tides constantly ebbed and flowed. In Jiangxi, due to the overall national situation, Deng Xiaoping's situation eased further.

Mama and Papa were a lot better off. Old comrade Huang Zhizhen, restored to his post on the Jiangxi provincial Party committee, came to see them, and increased the care they were receiving in their daily lives. The Infantry School area in which we were living frequently ran out of water, and baths were a problem. The province arranged for us to use the bathing facilities in their hostel once a week. At my parents' request our old servant Wu Hongjun and his wife were brought to Jiangxi to help us run the house. Mama and Papa's family chores were lightened considerably.

Pufang was in Beijing receiving medical treatment, but we were far from lonely. Deng Lin and the other graduates of the Central Academy of Fine Arts still had not been given their job assignments. In protest, they rebelled and simply went home. Deng Lin arrived in Jiangxi, and said she would wait here with us to be notified. The rebel factions had been very strict with students like her at the academy. Surely she deserved a good rest at home.

Deng Nan also arrived. It was a tremendous event — she was going to have a baby. What she was carrying in her belly would be our family's first grandchild. Deng Nan waddled about like a big potbellied official. She wasn't permitted to do any work, and was fed the best food. Mama busily raised a dozen hens in preparation for the post-birth First Month.

It seemed to me Deng Nan had no cause to be so proud of herself. Mama used to complain she was too willowy. Well, she had certainly expanded. It was understandable that her stomach should be big, but now she was round as a barrel everywhere. She ate enormously, saying it was for the baby, consuming only the finest. Papa watched her delightedly. Mama was a little worried.

"Don't get too fat," she warned. "You'll have trouble slimming down again."

To keep her girth in check, and not make the birth too difficult, we forced her to exercise. Every day Mama and Papa usually strolled around the courtyard, and they demanded that Deng Nan walk with them. She did, at first, reluctantly, toting her big belly. But she quit after only a few circuits.

"You're going too fast, Papa," she complained. "I can't keep up."

Deng Nan vanished from the scene. What could they do with a daughter like that?

Feifei and I had started college in Nanchang. We were Jiangxi's second batch of what were called "worker, peasant and soldier" students. Classes throughout the country had just resumed nationwide. College students were no longer admitted based on annual national college entrance exams for middle school graduates. Rather, the candidates were selected by their various factories, villages, or government units. Most of them were only of junior high, or even primary school, level. Students from factories and farms had a very difficult time. College students of primary school level were one of the inventions of the Cultural Revolution. They couldn't possibly cope with college classes, and were given special preparatory courses of six to eight months. The courses merely reviewed junior high math, science and liberal arts subjects.

At the start of the Cultural Revolution I was in the first year of senior high. Feifei was in junior high, second year. In the six years which followed he brought himself up to first or second year college level in physics through self study. Although we were both in agricultural production brigades, we never stopped studying on our own.

Our parents paid special attention to their children's education. They wanted us to study hard, to go to college, and to good ones, at that. They inculcated it in us as a clear goal. Brother Pufang, and my two sisters had all graduated from college by the time the Cultural Revolution started. Only Feifei and I had not yet gone to college.

This deeply troubled my parents. And so Papa wrote several letters to the Central Committee, requesting that Feifei and I be allowed to attend college and receive a higher education. That this request was granted was entirely due to my parents' efforts.

In those days it wasn't easy to get into college. You had to comply with many conditions in order to qualify. You had to be of good class origin, have made a good showing, and have a good relationship with the leadership. Actually, most people did everything to "get in through the back door" by using connections.

We used to laugh and say we had the biggest back door of all — Chairman Mao. Otherwise, kids like us "in need of re-education", stuck in assignments to remote agricultural brigades, wouldn't have had a chance. Now we were in college, fulfilling our parents' fondest dreams.

Feifei and I didn't really need any special review courses. They were too easy for us. We spent the time helping the other students in our classes. Feifei was relatively well behaved. But whenever I got the chance I would sneak out and go home. We are a very fond, closely knit family. We love being together. Even today, when we children are in our 50s, over a dozen family members still live in the same household with Mama.

29

Breaking the Fetters and Climbing the Jinggang Mountains

THE heat had passed in September of 1972, and winter had not yet begun. It was the best season of the year in Jiangxi. An azure sky arched above the shady tong trees in our infantry school grounds. The air was still. There was no rain. Soothing, exhilarating. A perfect time for travel.

Papa requested the Jiangxi leadership to ask the Central Committee whether it would be possible for him and Mama to go to the interior of the province and visit the Jinggang Mountains and the old liberated area of Zhangzhou. At the end of September the Central Committee indicated its approval. The Jiangxi revolutionary committee ordered that my parents be treated as the equivalent of provincial leaders. They would travel in a Volga limousine. They had only to say where they wanted to go, and the province would arrange it.

They gave detailed instructions as they prepared to leave. They were worried about pregnant Deng Nan. What if anything happened while they were away? She was going to bear our family's first grandchild! Mama reminded Deng Nan of every item she must pay attention to. She told me and Deng Lin to be sure and come home when it was time and get Deng Nan to the hospital.

"No problem," we three girls assured Mama and Papa "You just go ahead with your trip. The province has arranged everything with the hospital. When the time comes we can get a car from the province.

214

My parents and Grandma upon arriving in Jiangxi. Papa looks thinner and older after two years' house arrest in Beijing.

Where my parents, still under house arrest, lived in Jiangxi during the Cultural Revolution.

Their sitting room.

Their bedroom.

Papa broke the coal chunks and chopped the firewood kept in this backyard shed every day.

The family dining room.

This brazier was the only source of heat.

My parents worked for more than three years in the Xinjian County Tractor Factory in Jiangxi.

Papa worked as a fitter.

The red gravel path Papa trod between their residence and the factory.

Mama was happy to see me when I came from northern Shaanxi to visit them in Jiangxi after a three-year separation.

Mama and we three daughters had a reunion in Jiangxi.

My parents' hearts lightened i
1972 when the political enviror
ment improved a bit.

Mama, Grandma and their three girls in Jiangxi.

Papa became a proud grandfather in the winter of 1972.

A family photo in Jiangxi after Papa was freed from six years of virtual house arrest in February 1973.

There's nothing to worry about. You've made Deng Nan so fat, she's got plenty of strength. Giving birth will be easy. Don't worry!"

Actually, we knew it was no use talking to them. Parents never quit worrying. Didn't they know we girls were over 20 and had come through all sorts of hardships? What was so special about having a baby? Parents! They were hopeless!

In the morning of a beautiful autumn day, November 12, 1972, Mama and Papa, accompanied by Comrade Huang and a bodyguard from the provincial government, set forth in a car. Leaving the infantry school grounds, they headed south for the Jinggang Mountains.

It was their first trip in two years in Jiangxi, and six years since the start of the Cultural Revolution. It meant that their six years of restraint were over.

Papa's "question" was deemed fundamentally solved after Mao Zedong endorsed his letter on August 14, 1972. Although he was not officially "liberated", his status as "capitalist roader" was changed to that of "comrade", a change of far-reaching political significance.

He was very happy that he was allowed to travel. As he had said in his letter to Mao, he had been separated from his work, and from society, for six years. He was longing to go out and look around, to see what was happening with his own eyes.

The car rolled swiftly south over the bumpy road. The driver and the bodyguard sat up front. Mama, Papa, and Comrade Huang sat in the rear. Although it was a bit crowded, the weather was fine, and everyone was in good spirits. At noon, they stopped for lunch in Zhangshu Town in Qingjiang County. They continued on immediately after without pausing to rest, and arrived at Ji'an at four in the afternoon.

The local authorities received Papa warmly. They put him and Mama in the guesthouse where Chairman Mao had stayed in 1965. That evening Papa talked with the comrades of the local Party Committee. He asked about local conditions, and recalled old comrades in battle who had passed away.

"I haven't been back in a long time," he said. "Everything looks new to me."

The next morning, after a good night's rest, Papa and his group went on to Yongxin County. There, in 1927, at Sanwan, Mao Zedong had reorganized the Army. Moving the Party branches into the companies, he consolidated the Party's absolute leadership.

"It was an important measure," Papa said. "The Army had been badly beaten after the Autumn Uprising. It shook off its pursuers and fled here, to Sanwan. It was on the verge of collapse when Comrade Mao Zedong introduced his reforms. They were very important."

Their next stop was Maoping, where the Red Army led by Mao Zedong during the Autumn Uprising, had joined forces with the remnants of Zhu De's army which had fought in the Nanchang Uprising. Maoping became a large military encampment. The local guide told Papa and his group that Lin Biao had been claiming that the forces which had joined with Mao's were his, Lin Biao's, not Zhu De's.

"True is true, and false is false," Papa said. "Traditions must not be lost. Our Communist Party is good; it has excellent prospects. The same is true of our people, of our nation."

Papa was not only saying this to those present, he was saying it even more to himself. He was thinking not only of his own political fate and future, he was not just recalling things past. His mind was harking back, and looking ahead. For six years the nation had been in turmoil, the economy was shattered; the people were in difficulty.

The Cultural Revolution unquestionably was a mistake. But could we say that because of this mistake, because of the severe failure of Mao Zedong's policies, because certain evil persons were riding high, that our Party could not be saved? That there was no hope for our country and our people?

Looking at the situation at that time, many people must have thought it was too intricate and involved. They couldn't see any solution. But Papa was an eternal optimist. He never limited his gaze to a given thing at a given moment. He always took the long view, the historical approach. He analyzed problems in the course of their development in order to solve them.

The Party, the nation, and the people, had been deeply wounded by the Cultural Revolution. He himself had been harmed. But none of this could destroy his faith, or cause him to give up his confidence in the future. Our Party had weathered more than 50 years of storm and strife. It had a glorious history and a magnificent record. It had tens of millions of tested, dedicated members. The great masses of the people were good and staunch; they trusted our Party and loved our country. There was no reason why an arrant twist in history should shake our confidence in our future.

Papa said the Cultural Revolution was the most difficult period of his career. But he never despaired, and he certainly never lost faith.

Papa's words at Jinggang Mountains were not something he said lightly, not just a few phrases. They were the result of long consideration; they were the verbal expression of his most deeply incised creed.

As he was leaving Maoping, he said feelingly to the comrades of the Jinggang Mountains region: "Yours is a hardship area. It was very poor in the days when Chairman Mao was leading the revolution here, and it's still poor today. In the future it will be better."

On November 14, Papa and his party went to Huangyang (antelope) Crag, which has an elevation of 1,518 meters. Here, in these dangerous heights, the Red Army defeated the Kuomintang army in battle.

Although the journey was tiring, my parents were in good spirits, especially Papa. Nearly 70 years old, he marched steadily and relaxed up and down slopes, showing no signs of fatigue. The previous two years of labor had toughened him.

Someone gave him a length of bamboo to serve as a staff, and he quipped: "I've always needed a third leg. The rest of me is intact."

Noticing some wild plants by the roadside, he said: "During the Long March, the Red Army ate that stuff. It has a slight numbing effect on your mouth, but it takes the edge off your hunger and thirst."

That evening the Jinggang Mountains local government and Army leaders gave him a banquet. They were very cordial, and the guests were happy. Afterwards, a movie was shown. There wasn't much cultural fare in those days. About all that was available were the Eight Model works. The movie was a film version of one of them — "The

Red Lantern". [1]

When the character Li Yuhe appeared on the screen, Papa laughed and said: "The actor's family name is Qian. But after the Cultural Revolution started, even "money" was scorned. He could only be called Hao Liang." [2]

The party spent five days in the Jinggang Mountains, visiting old revolutionary sites. They also went to a factory which made bamboo products. Papa was very pleased. He asked detailed questions about production and sales.

On the sixth day, they drove down from the heights, and were promptly informed that Deng Nan had given birth to a little girl in the Nanchang Hospital. Still savoring the warmth of the reception they had received during their trip, they were simply delighted. The news heaped joy upon happiness. What could be better than becoming a Grandma and Grandpa of a little member of the third generation!

They were eager to get back to Nanchang and see the baby. On the 17th they went from Ciping to Taihe, where they were feasted with the famous local black-boned chicken. They also visited an agricultural machinery plant which produced rice planting machines. Papa examined them carefully, and asked a lot of questions.

"No one has found a good way of planting rice mechanically, even the Japanese," he said. "The problem is spacing the shoots evenly."

To the local cadres he said: "I also was once a secretary of a county Party committee. It's not an easy job. Mechanization of agriculture is the way to go. You must research it."

Chi Long, a veteran of the old Red Army was staying at the same hostel in Taihe. When he heard that Deng Xiaoping was there he asked to see him. Chi Long had been a leader in the Air Force before the Cultural Revolution brought him down. He had just been rehabilitated.

---

[1] Jiang Qing took over six popular modern Peking opera plays and two ballet dramas, made a few trifling changes, and claimed them as her own. In the extremist atmosphere she created in the arts, it became virtually impossible to stage any other vehicles.

[2] Qian means "money". Haoliang, the actor's given name, means "brightly glittering". The two together would have looked too crassly material for a "spiritually pure" hero, so in the cast of characters the actor was listed simply as "Hao Liang".

Papa and he had both been in the old First Front Army of the Red Army. Together they had gone through the same travails for many years. They talked and reminisced for two hours.

Pointing out the scars and wounds all over his body, Chi Long cursed the Lin Biao clique.

"That gang did whatever they pleased," Papa said. "The Cultural Revolution was a 'Leftist' movement. Bad people took advantage of it."

Regarding Mao Zedong and Zhou Enlai, he said: "The Chairman is a great man. The Premier had to eat a lot of bitterness. He protected many old cadres, including old Army comrades."

As to Lin Biao, Papa said: "Lin Biao was not without talent. But he was a hypocrite. He took advantage of Chairman Mao's prestige to issue his so-called Order Number One. It actually denigrated Chairman Mao and boosted himself." And he added: "Things will be a bit better in the Party with Lin Biao gone. But we still have a couple of bookworms making a mess."

This was the first time in six years that Papa said so much about the Cultural Revolution. He talked about Chairman Mao, and Zhou Enlai, and Lin Biao, and the "bookworms" in the Cultural Revolution Group of the Central Committee. He criticized the political figures involved in the Cultural Revolution. Papa had harbored these views for a long time, but he was a careful man not given to voicing his opinions easily. Now the political climate had changed, and he had renewed his acquaintance with old revolutionary sites and old comrades, and he spewed out everything that was on his mind.

He left Taihe with his party the next morning and went to Ji'an where he inspected a commune. They asked him what he'd like to see. "Mainly agriculture," he replied. He listened carefully to a report by the local cadres and was pleased to learn they were doing well in sideline production, and that agricultural output also was not bad. He was very interested in the pig farm run by one of the brigades, and asked many questions.

Mama and Papa made no more stops after Ji'an, but continued on to Nanchang. They arrived at 6:30 in the evening and, without pausing to freshen up, went directly to the hospital. They were told that Deng Nan and the baby had already gone home. The hospital said mother and child were doing fine. Happy, Mama and Papa wasted no more time but hurried home. You can imagine — nearly 70 before he became a grandfather for the first time. Of course Papa was eager!

Mama and Papa reached home around eight. Without stopping for a bite to eat, the moment they entered the door, they rushed upstairs to see their little granddaughter.

Deng Nan offered the child in her bosom to her parents. They each held and adored the baby in turn. Wrapped in her infant's blanket, the mite kept her eyes tightly closed, and wrinkled her little nose, her cheeks a bright red, murmuring as if very displeased. The soft, gentle noises delighted her audience.

Papa said: "In our family it doesn't matter whether she's the baby of a daughter or of a son. She's my granddaughter, and I'm her grandpa!" [1]

The arrival of this tiny member added considerable color to our family life. She was a well-behaved little lady. She ate and she slept. When she awakened she lay quietly examining her small hands. She didn't cry and she didn't fuss. We were all enchanted.

But she was also a priceless treasure. The slightest change in the atmosphere brought everyone running. Babies of course have their "calls of nature". Whenever that happened the whole family went into "emergency alarm," carrying paper, and basins, and baby talcum powder, all milling around in circles.

"Who will bring some hot water?" Mama would yell. And the new grandpa would grab the thermos bottle and cry, in his Sichuan accent: "I'm coming, I'm coming!"

That little darling threw us all into complete chaos!

Choosing a name for her was a big event. The Deng family sat down in solemn conference. We consulted books and dictionaries and produced

---

[1] The old tradition was to call a baby born to a daughter an "outside grandchild", and the grandfather an "outside grandpa", in keeping with feudal male chauvinism. Only a son could continue the family line.

a long list of names. Each proposed a favorite, only to be opposed by a counter-favorite. Mama grew impatient.

"When we were choosing names for you girls, I was the one who decided. Papa never objected," she complained. "You have too many suggestions. What a nuisance!"

Finally, I said: "She loves to sleep so much. Let's call her 'Mianmian' ('Sleepy')!"

This time no one objected, and so we gave her the nickname Little Mianmian, with her formal name as Deng Mian. We all knew this was a pun on *dong mian* meaning winter sleep, since the baby was born at a time when her grandfather was in political hibernation.

Mama doted on her little granddaughter. She was not nearly so excessive to her daughters. In anticipation of the traditional month's recuperation after birth, she had raised 14 fat hens to help restore Deng Nan's strength. But noting that Deng Nan was quite fat enough, Mama changed her strategy, and gave her three and a half. Eggs were limited to one a day. Deng Nan grumbled.

"When Grandma left she said I should have 10 chickens during the month, and five eggs per day. But you only gave me three chickens, and just as soup, at that, while the rest of you finish off the meat. It's not fair!"

Mama didn't care anything about "fairness". She wouldn't let Deng Nan go over quota even if she was ravenous. "We have to break with the wrong old customs," Mama insisted. "We should consume only the necessary amount of nourishment, and that's all. We must do things scientifically."

In our family the principle of science versus gluttony was one of the major topics of debate.

After Papa returned from the Jinggang Mountains, the General Office of the Central Committee of the Communist Party advised the Jiangxi authorities that Deng Xiaoping and his wife were allowed to travel and visit without restriction. Their status could also be raised.

This was extremely important to my parents. They had seen many things in the Jinggang Mountains, had many new impressions, had encountered much that was thought-provoking. Papa decided to go to southern Jiangxi again, and visit the old Central Soviet Area.

30

Old Places Revisited

MAMA and Papa set out for southern Jiangxi on December 5, 1972.

The previous trip was his first to that region, particularly the Jinggang Mountains. He had always wanted to see the old revolutionary bases there. This time he wanted to visit the former Central Soviet Area, which he knew well. He had worked and fought there, had endured the first upheavals in his political life.

The Party, then following the Wang Ming line, accused him of implementing a "Right erroneous line" and of being "leader of the Mao faction", which Mao Zedong referred to in his recent endorsement of Papa's letter.

Today, 40 years later, to a large extent because he had been criticized for that, he was being rehabilitated. A historical coincidence? A decision of Fate? Papa didn't believe in such things. History was in constant flux. Even when there was repetition, it was always different from before.

His status raised, Papa was given two cars — a Volga and a Jeep. After lunch at Ji'an, they continued south to Ganzhou, the largest city in southern Jiangxi, arriving after nightfall. They were warmly received by the local Party and Army officials.

On December 6, they proceeded to Xingguo County. Here they also were given a cordial reception. They were put up in a house originally prepared for Chairman Mao in the national hostel, and were served the finest local dishes. Mama and Papa were very moved.

"I've wanted to visit here for many years," Papa said, "but I never had the chance."

Accompanied by the local comrades, he and Mama visited the old revolutionary sites. They were told that Xingguo was a poor county, and constantly suffered mud slides. The farmers were very hard up. Papa said nothing, but he looked concerned.

Later, at lunch, he said: "Eating your food in Xingguo today, I remember how good the people were to the Red Army. They were extremely generous. They brought out the best they had in their homes. Every comrade who has been here has the same impression. In the Central Soviet Area days, you had a population of 23,000. Many people from your county joined our Red Army. A lot of them became generals."

Attendants at the hostel noticed that my parents had two suitcases. One of them had some changes of the clothes. The other was filled with books.

Mama laughed. "We love reading. These books are Comrade Xiaoping's treasures."

As they were getting ready to leave on December 7, Papa said, "Well, that's one wish fulfilled."

They reached Yudu that same afternoon.

Yudu was not strange to Papa. In 1931, he and Jin Weiying, his second wife, were sent by the Central Committee, then in Shanghai, to the Central Soviet Area in Jiangxi. Papa became the secretary of the Ruijin county Party committee. Ah Jin, as she was called, became secretary of the county Party committee in Yudu. Later, when he became secretary of the Huichang central county Party committee, he frequently went to Yudu. Not long after, he was criticized by the Wang Ming "left" opportunists, and Ah Jin left him.

It was here in Yudu that the Red Army, after being defeated in the Kuomintang's fifth "encirclement and annihilation" campaign, crossed the Yudu River and set out on the 25,000 *li* Long March. Today, 40 years later, Yudu had become a county town with a population of over a hundred thousand. Time had fleeted by, the earth and sky had changed, and so had people. Only the Yudu River continued flowing endlessly north. The scene remained the same.

Papa spoke of his former wife several times. "Did you know that in Soviet times the secretary of your county Party committee was a woman?" he asked the Yudu comrades. And he added: "When I left on the Long March I had a cotton-wool quilt made in Yudu that weighed four *jin* (4.2 pounds). I carried it with me all through the journey."

Memories came flooding back. That night, in the hostel, Papa couldn't fall asleep. The people with him urged him to get some rest.

He said emotionally: "It hasn't been easy. This is my first trip back in 40 years. It may be my last."

On December 8, he arrived in Huichang. It had a special meaning for Papa. In 1932 he was appointed secretary of the county Party committee of Huichang, known as the "Big South Gate" of the Central Soviet Area. Here he had convened a very successful meeting on work among the masses, in direct confrontation with radical forces within the Party.

Here too, because of his opposition to the "left" adventurism of the Wang Ming line, he had been labeled a representative of the "Right deviationists." Along with three other Communists — including Mao Zedong's brother Mao Zetan, he had been criticized and removed from his post. It was his first political setback. He was less than 30 years old at the time.

His memories of Huichang, therefore, were both pleasant and unpleasant.

In the compound of what had been the office of the Soviet government, he saw a large shady banyan tree. "It's the only tree left here," he sighed. "I used to read books and newspapers beneath its branches."

At Zhoutian, visiting a salt mine, he said: "We suffered badly from lack of salt in Soviet days." He also reminisced about how they made gunpowder.

When he visited Huichang, Papa attended a local commodity exchange fair. He was very interested, and asked all manner of questions about the production and sale of agricultural products and the farmers' income.

He left Huichang at 2:00 pm in the afternoon the same day, visiting an old residence of Mao Zedong en route. "Chairman Mao was being cold-shouldered then," Papa said. "He was under attack."

The next stop was Ruijin. "You're our old county Party secretary," the local comrades said. "Welcome!"

These simple words warmed Papa's heart. Forty years ago the Central Committee in Shanghai had sent him to the Jiangxi Soviet Area, where he served as First Secretary of the Ruijin county Party committee. He had strong emotional ties to Ruijin. He found the old revolutionary base much the same. It looked very familiar.

He visited an old Central Soviet base at Shazhou Dyke on December 9, then walked another kilometer to where the Red Army's Central Military Commission had been. He knew this section well. He didn't need any guides here. He led everyone over a small hill to the former Political Headquarters of the Central Military Commission. It had been located in a bamboo grove in a small hamlet. Papa had then been the editor of the *Red Star* newspaper and, in that hamlet, had edited and printed the paper.

Papa observed some farmers drying sliced sweet potatoes in the sun. He walked over and chatted with them.

In Ruijin on December 10, he visited a lathe factory, a telephone wire factory, and a sugar mill. After listening to an introductory report, Papa asked to see the sugar mill. He was told there were two roads leading to it, but that the shorter one was not in good shape.

"Why must we take the long road? What's wrong with the short one?" Papa demanded. "China's revolutionary path has been tortuous, not straight. Let's go!" He refused to let anyone support him. "I don't need any help," he said. "I'm still good for another 20 years."

Mama laughed. "What makes you think so?"

"I'm only 69," Papa said doggedly. "I can last 20 years more. No doubt about it."

He meant exactly what he said. Although pushing 70, he considered himself to be in excellent health and spirits. He believed he could work and contribute. The Party and the nation were at a critical juncture. Papa was determined to devote his life and hot blood to the service of the Party, the country, and the people.

What he saw in Ruijin cheered him immeasurably. After several years of morose silence, he became absolutely talkative. In the alcohol section of sugar mill, he asked: "What do you use this for?"

The man began to explain how alcohol was employed in making sugar. "It has another use you haven't mentioned," Papa interrupted. "It also can be used as motor vehicle fuel."

Animatedly, he continued: "You wouldn't necessarily remember this. In Yan'an we used it in all our vehicles."

He saw workers packaging sugar with their bare hands. He asked why the process wasn't mechanized. His escort said if they didn't do it by hand, a lot of people would be thrown out of work.

"That's not the way to look at it," Papa said severely. "They could be put on half work, half study. Your mill should arrange a reasonable program. That's the only way to improve your workers' ability and modernize the factory."

Coming out of the workshops, he and his party strolled the streets. Several people recognized him. Papa was pleased. In the evening, the authorities gave him a report on local conditions.

"It's much better now than it was in the past," Papa said. "We've done a lot since Liberation, and accomplished a good deal. But we're at least 40 years behind the countries in the West. We've got to work hard."

Papa was saying this as much to himself as to the cadres of Ruijin. The backwardness of the old Soviet Area in southern Jiangxi made a deep impression on him. He knew that this condition was not limited to this region. He felt we had to make enormous efforts. Otherwise, we'd be letting down not just the people of the old Soviet Area, but the people of the whole country.

After three days, Papa left Ruijin with some reluctance. He said to the local cadres: "Ruijin has made a big contribution to the Chinese revolution. You should open a revolutionary museum."

On December 11, Papa and his group went to Ningdu. At the Huangpo Commune he asked about the number of members, the size of the tillable area, average income, mechanization, and the extent of electric lighting. Aside from the nostalgia of this trip to southern Jiangxi, Papa's main focus was on production and living conditions. On the visit to Jinggang Mountains he had spoken fairly cautiously. This time he clearly was investigating and analyzing problems.

He knew now that his "question" was fundamentally solved, political rehabilitation was already within sight. And when that happened, no matter what he would be working on, he would have to understand the current situation. This trip to southern Jiangxi was a golden opportunity to investigate, and so he probed carefully wherever he went. He needed factual information to back up whatever he would be doing.

Papa also visited the former site of the Jiangxi Provincial Party Committee. "Li Fuchun was Party secretary then," he said. "I was appointed head of the propaganda department. But I was dismissed before I could take office."

Papa displayed no emotion. History is history. You cannot change it, and you cannot bury it.

He left Ningdu on December 12 and arrived in Guangchang that same afternoon. "I've wanted to come here for a long time," he said to the local cadres. "We had the duty to defend Guangchang, but we never actually came here. This time I've got my wish."

The next day, on the way back to Nanchang, during a stop for a rest in Nanfeng, famous for its oranges, he asked about their harvests. Mama bought a few bushels of "honey oranges" to take back for the children.

At noon they arrived at Wuzhou. Papa visited a textile mill, a medicine factory, and a factory that manufactured gauges.

"Don't just keep making military equipment," he said to the head of the factory. "Make things for civilian use as well."

He examined everything with great interest, clambering all over the place.

In the evening the local authorities invited him to dinner, and served the famous Maotai liquor. Papa knew that the son and daughter-in-law of his old comrade Wang Ruofei lived in Wuzhou and he asked his hosts to invite them. The son was away, but Jiujiu, his wife, came. Wang had died in a plane crash in 1946, but the Cultural Revolution radicals continued to slander him and persecute his family.

Papa asked Jiujiu whether they were having any difficulties. She said the Jiangxi winters were cold, and they didn't have enough charcoal for their braziers — the common source of heat in that region. Papa told the local authorities to give them more charcoal. His old comrade was long since gone, but at least he could do a little something for his descendants.

He and his party left Wuzhou for Nanchang on the morning of December 15. Jiujiu and the local leaders saw them off to the Wuzhou county line. There they were met by waiting Nanchang cadres. Their Wuzhou hosts and Jiujiu reluctantly said goodbye.

31

Farewell, Infantry School

M AMA and Papa spent 10 days on their second trip to southern Jiangxi. After their long, dusty journey, they finally returned to Nanchang. They were happy to see the family again, especially the little granddaughter. Mama told us how touched Papa was by the warm reception they had received from the local cadres. Wherever they went they were given only the best, Mama said. Even the bedding was always new.

Not long after, Grandma and my young aunt Deng Xianqun came from Tianjin with Dingding, Xianqun's three-month old baby son. My uncle Zhang Zhongren, who was married to Papa's second sister, showed up from Sichuan.

I took advantage of my school being closed for the winter vacation to accompany Big Sister Deng Lin to Beijing. I wanted to see my boyfriend's parents who had returned to Beijing after having been released from the "Monsters Enclosure" of their May Seventh Cadre School. Deng Lin went to meet a boy she was being introduced to through the intervention of Pufang, and also to visit her future in-laws.

Back in our home in Jiangxi, originally, aside from my parents, Deng Nan, Feifei, and little granddaughter Mianmian, there was also our helper Old Wu and his wife — a total of seven. But now Grandma, Aunty Xianqun, her husband and the baby had arrived from Tianjin — that was another four. Our small house in the Infantry School grounds was "crammed to the rafters". Every room, from top to bottom, was occupied.

Aunty Xianqun and sister Deng Nan were famous in our family for their loud voices. You could hear them even when you were far from the house. As to the two little grandchildren there was a difference of only two months between them. But Dingding was a large sturdy boy. Compared to him, poor Mianmian looked tiny.

Although Papa wasn't a bad cook, he couldn't compare with Grandma. Now that she was back, we had delicious food. Our small dining table was crowded at every meal. Aunty Xianqun and Deng Nan had put on a lot of weight after giving birth. They both ate heartily, the excuse being that they needed to replenish their nourishment. Mama kept a tight rein on Deng Nan. She wouldn't let her eat or drink too much. Mama forbade her to get any fatter. Grandma was very lenient. She allowed Aunty Xianqun to indulge freely. Deng Nan felt this was unfair. She grumbled and complained all the time.

Zhang Zhongren was an honest fellow, an archives curator who did his job and didn't say much. In our house he had Papa, another man, to talk with. Unfortunately, neither of them liked to speak. That wasn't strange. In our family, the "girls" did most of the talking. Nobody else had a chance. As Grandma said in her cute Sichuan accent, "Our Deng family women are really tough."

And that applied to our aunts, as well. Those two uncles of mine "followed" my aunts into our Deng family circle, and they were more than a little henpecked. But "where there is oppression there is revolt", and sometimes my uncles complained. Whenever that happened, all the women in the family crashed down on them in a chorus of "criticism".

They did have one straw to clutch at — the combined sympathy of Mama and Papa who, as family elders, always intervened in the interests of harmony.

There was rarely any quiet in our home. We were noisy, we shouted. How a serious, reserved person like Papa could have produced a family so completely his opposite was beyond me. Mama and Papa must bear the responsibility for us children being so "uneducated". Their fault, in a word, was "leniency". Papa had the reputation of being "tough". Even the old cadres working under him are supposed to have been afraid of him. But with us children he was invariably mild.

In Jiangxi we used to hang around him and plead, "Come and play with us, Old Daddy. We're having so much fun!"

"Who's got time for all that nonsense," he would retort.

That was the extent of his scolding. Actually, we had the greatest respect for him. If he said anything in seriousness, we obeyed completely, without question.

While our family in Jiangxi was enjoying a rare heavenly serenity, Zhou Enlai, in Beijing, ignoring the many obstacles thrown up by the Cultural Revolution Group, was maneuvering brilliantly to liberate the restricted cadres.

On December 18, 1972, he sent the following letter to Ji Dengkui and Wang Dongxing:

"Last night the Chairman told me that although Comrade Tan Zhenlin made a mistake (as we now know the 'Countercurrent' at Huairentang inside Zhongnanhai was provoked by Lin Biao's deliberate attempt to overthrow a number of old comrades), he still is a good comrade. He should be allowed to return. Will you two please attend to it? He fell and had a fracture in Guilin. Ask Comrade Wei Guoqing to ensure that he recovers well."

And Zhou Enlai added: "Comrade Deng Xiaoping and his wife are asking for some work to do. Please give this your consideration. The Chairman has mentioned it several times."

The wife of the former Minister of Railways, Liu Jianzhang, wrote a letter to Chairman Mao protesting that her husband, though innocent, had been thrown into jail and tortured. Mao endorsed the letter, also on December 18, with this notation: "Attention, Mr. Premier. Who approved these fascist methods of investigation? They must be eliminated."

Mao's comment gave further support to Zhou Enlai's efforts to liberate the old cadres.

Dark clouds covered the skies as 1972 drew to an end, but a glimmer of light shone through.

With the advent of 1973 the situation was still complicated. Mao Zedong continued his fanatic adherence to the Cultural Revolution. At the same time he backed Zhou Enlai's overall control of national affairs and his cadre liberation program. Mao was dissatisfied with Zhou, but he couldn't do without him. He felt some of Zhou's views were far from his own. Yet he was entirely dependent on him for rectification of the Party, the government and the Army, and even of foreign relations. Whether for open or behind the scenes affairs, Zhou Enlai's loyalty and unrelenting activities were essential.

At this critical moment Zhou was stricken by terminal cancer. It was as if a torrential rain suddenly deluged an already leaking house in the middle of the night. To Mao's mind the Cultural Revolution had to go on, and someone had to handle the daily conduct of national concerns. Under these circumstances Mao Zedong decided to let Deng Xiaoping return to work as quickly as possible.

One day in January, Bai Dongcai, Secretary of the Jiangxi Provincial Party Committee, called on Papa and notified him that the Central Committee had ordered him back to Beijing. We all were overjoyed. We had guessed that his "question" would soon be solved, but we hadn't thought it would happen so quickly, and that he would be directed to return to Beijing immediately.

We were very pleased, and naturally so was Papa. He kept his happiness within him. Papa never showed alarm when trouble struck, or exulted over good fortune.

But we could sense his joy. More than six years had passed since he was overthrown by the Cultural Revolution. Hadn't he been waiting every minute for this day? The slanders, the incredible hardships, the torments he endured inside and out of Zhongnanhai, his tireless efforts for the members of his family and his own political fate....

In those years he strove to keep himself physically fit, to toughen his spirit, to absorb the warmth and outlook of the workers with whom he daily labored. He bathed in cold water in winter. In summer he sweated at his factory job. At home he built the fires in the stove, cooked the food, chopped wood, planted vegetables, and diligently performed his duties as a husband and a father.

Even in the most difficult times he closely observed the world's changing winds, the rise and fall of the political tides, the nation's economic status, and the livelihood of the people.

Papa was no fatalist. No matter how things were going, he remained calm. His individual situation never made him depressed, or pessimistic, or disappointed. He was confident that truth would conquer slanders; that justice would prevail over evil. He believed in our Party, our nation, and our people. Now, the long-awaited day had come. He was ready. He would go back to Beijing and by his faith and loyalty demonstrate his grateful dedication.

Returning to Beijing meant Mama and Papa would be leaving Jiangxi. Although they were happy to be going, they felt a little sad to part with this place where they had lived more than three years.

"There's no rush," Papa said. "We can go after the Spring Festival." He wanted to celebrate one last Spring Festival in our small house in the Infantry School grounds in Jiangxi.

Spring Festival in 1973 fell on February 3. Our whole family celebrated China's traditional holiday joyously together. After it had passed Papa was still in high spirits. He wanted to take a trip to Jingdezhen, China's famous pottery center. The Jiangxi provincial government arranged it. On the sixth day of the lunar new year, that is, February 8, Mama and Papa, accompanied by Uncle Zhang Zhongren, set out for northern Jiangxi.

Not far from Nanchang, the car crossed into Jinxian County, where the General Office of the Central Committee had its May Seventh Cadre School. Papa thought of Wang Ruilin, who had become his secretary in 1952 at the age of 20. Wang was now doing physical labor here. Wang had been with him till the Cultural Revolution erupted,

"I have no other business in Jinxian," Papa said to the bodyguard who was accompanying him, "but I would like to see my secretary Wang Ruilin."

The bodyguard said he was afraid they would have to ask permission from the General Office in Beijing.

They reached Jingdezhen the same day, and were put up at the hostel of the Municipal Party Committee.

"Jingdezhen is very famous," Papa said to the leader who received them. "I heard about it when I was still in primary school. I want to take a good look around."

Papa and his party visited several of the larger factories and exhibition halls. At the folk pottery factory a worker recognized him, and shouted: "Deng Xiaoping!" The workshop bubbled with excitement.

Papa inspected the Guangming Factory in the afternoon on February 10. He followed the entire production process, asking detailed questions. He also wanted to know about the workers' pay, and their living conditions.

As he was leaving, just as he got into his vehicle, suddenly, as if by signal, workers from all the workshops came pouring out and surrounded the car. One of them started to applaud, and soon they all were clapping enthusiastically. Papa immediately got out of his car and waved to the crowd, deeply moved. After a long time, the sound of the workers' applause still ringing in their ears, Papa and his party got into their cars and left the factory.

The Jingdezhen cadres told Papa that Cheng Shiqing, a lieutenant of Lin Biao, coordinating with Lin's scheme to seize power, dreamed up a ridiculous idea. He tried to convert the famous pottery plant into an army amphibious vehicle factory. Today, in response to an order from Premier Zhou Enlai, Jingdezhen was again making pottery, including such items as porcelain Bodhisattva and laughing Maitreya statuettes, condemned by the fanatics as "feudal, bourgeois and revisionist".

Mama bought some crockery to take home to the children in Nanchang. The factory cadres urged her to buy things that were of a bit better quality.

"Don't get the wrong idea because we worked in the Central Committee," Mama said. "We're just a simple family."

The city government comrades were extremely cordial. They gave Mama and Papa four beautiful porcelain vases. My parents were touched.

Papa said: "Jingdezhen is world famous not only for its pottery but for its creative workers. Creative labor will change the world."

He and Mama took the vases to Nanchang, and then brought them to

Beijing, where they are still cherished possessions.

On the way back from Jingdezhen, Papa received word that the Central Committee had approved a meeting with Wang Ruilin. He and his party went directly to Jinxian County, reaching the May Seventh Cadre School around noon. Waiting at the gate was Li Shuhuai, assistant principal. Li formerly had been Deputy Chief of the Central Committee Guards Bureau. Before the Cultural Revolution our family knew him well. We hadn't seen him for years.

"We're happy to have you here, old commander," he said to Papa with deep feeling.

Papa, too, was glad. "I've come to see Wang Ruilin," he said.

"Of course," said Li. "I'll send someone for him immediately."

Wang was out working in the fields. He was startled when he was told, "Your old chief wants to see you." He climbed into the jeep that had been sent to fetch him, and went quickly to the visitors' hostel. On meeting the old superior he hadn't seen in several years he was assailed by mixed emotions. It was a reunion after what had seemed a complete disaster.

Wang Ruilin was thin, his face blackened by the sun, his feet and legs muddy. Mama and Papa were shocked. They had come specially to see Wang. They hadn't expected that the youthful, spirited young fellow they remembered would have lost the bloom of youth, and become so weather-beaten and dry.

Papa was a silent person. He said very little even to people working constantly at his side. But he was deeply emotional. He had strong feelings for a young secretary like Wang Ruilin. While not exactly the same as his love for his own flesh and blood, it was very similar.

They all had lunch together, and Papa said to Li Shuhuai: "I'd like to take Wang Ruilin to stay with me at Nanchang for a couple of days."

Li promptly agreed, and Wang returned with Papa to our small house in the Infantry School grounds, Wang saw Grandma and the rest of us again. It had been years. Everyone wanted to know all about him. We sighed over his story, much of which was sad and tragic.

After two days with us, Wang returned to his "school" in Jinxian. We saw him to the gate of our front yard, reluctant to part. But we all felt confident that in the not too distant future we would meet again.

Papa's three trips in Jiangxi were important to him. He had been restricted, confined. While we children had been able to keep him a little informed, it was all indirect. Now that he was able to see and hear for himself, he had a much better idea of what was going on.

In the more than six years since the start of the Cultural Revolution, huge changes had taken place in people and in things. Papa was a seasoned statesman. He had sensed a great deal, had given matters a lot of thought, and already had reached some conclusions. Walking round and round in our small compound with firm quick steps, as usual he said nothing. But he was thoughtful, confident, and full of hope. Six years of political torment, three years of working with his hands, had strengthened him in mind and body, had given him thorough mental preparation. He was like a ship with sails unfurled. As soon as the wind rose, he would set forth and travel far, full speed ahead.

After Spring Festival we started packing to return to Beijing.

If there's anything we learned during the Cultural Revolution, first of all it was to pack and move. We moved here, and moved there. We got to be quite good at it. Whenever the order came down we quickly got our things together, clothes, bedding, and odds and ends. Books were our most precious possessions. They had to be put in crates. And, of course, all the kitchen utensils. We had to take them, too, otherwise we'd have nothing to cook with when we got to Beijing.

Uncle Zhang Zhongren was a born hard worker. This time the hero had found his battleground. He became our family's pillar of strength.

Although in effect virtually "liberated", at home Papa was still the same. Whatever work there was to be done, he did it.

Mama and Grandma were our highest ranking generals. Those two old ladies did indeed have an air about them of "supreme commanders". They had us running around in circles. But though they kept us busy, there was no confusion.

Only the 10 chickens couldn't be packed. What could we do with them? Grandma had an idea. Kill them all and cook them into home-made salted chicken. We'd get at least one good meal out of them on the train.

We were going. We would be leaving Jiangxi, the Infantry School, and the workers at the Xinjian county tractor factory. Papa sent Mama, on behalf of himself and our whole family, to call on them. Mama bought some candies and sweets and presented them to the families we had been closest to.

The workers were very happy when they heard that Old Deng and Old Zhuo would be able to return to Beijing. But they had grown very close to them in their three years together, and hated to see them go.

"Lieutenant" Tao was not at home when Mama called, and early the next morning he came to our house with several workers. When they saw a truck standing outside the compound, they said: "It looks like they're going to leave right away!" and hurried into the yard. Mama and Papa invited them to the upstairs sitting room, and offered them fruit and sweets which Mama ordered brought down from the already loaded truck.

Tao had had the most contact with Mama and Papa during their three years in the factory. "Lao Deng, Lao Zhuo, we hear you're leaving," he said. "We've come to see you off."

"Thank you. We've been a burden to everyone," Papa said courteously in an emotion charged voice "We're going back to Beijing. Yesterday, I asked Zhuo Lin to call on you and express our gratitude."

All talking at once, Tao and the workers said: "If you get a chance to come to Jiangxi again, you must visit our factory!"

"We will, we will," Mama and Papa assured them. "You workers and cadres are fine people. We won't forget you."

On February 20, 1973, my parents and the rest of us went by car from Nanchang to Yingtan. The next day the Fuzhou-Beijing train made a special stop of several minutes for us at the Shangrao railway station. Leaders of the regional Party committee came on board for a final goodbye.

The engine emitted a great cloud of steam, the whistle blew, the big wheels began to roll. The Jiangxi farewell-wishers quickly faded into the distance. The black mountain ridges, the undulating red hills, the endlessly eastward flowing rivers, gradually vanished from view.

Our smoothly jouncing train entered Zhejiang Province. The attendants were extremely solicitous to our family party of 10. At meals, they even served us with rare bottles of Maotai liquor. Unknown to us, the head of the Special Shipments Bureau of the Ministry of Railways and the chief of Public Security Bureau were also on the train, looking after us personally. The few other passengers in our sleeping car got off at Hangzhou, and no new ones were allowed on. It was reserved for us alone.

Hurrying northward, our train crossed the fertile plains of Zhejiang, the broad coastal areas. We were no longer breathing the warm southern air, but the early spring atmosphere of North China, shivering slightly in the lingering chill of the dying winter.

32

Summer, and Back at Work

SLOWLY, on February 22, 1973, the train pulled into Platform One of the Beijing Railway Station. A few vehicles from the General Office of the Central Committee were lined up on the platform, waiting. I was there with He Ping. We watched the train drawing closer, closer. We were very excited. At last, it stopped.

Papa, smiling, was the first to emerge. He shook hands with the people who had come to greet him. One by one the rest of the family stepped down from the car, young and old, one and all, everyone talking and fussing over luggage. At last, all were seated in vehicles, and the procession moved off.

From the railway station we drove along Chang'an Avenue. We saw the Xinhua Gate of Zhongnanhai, and gazed respectfully at the red national flag fluttering on the tall flagpole in the cold winter air. We were back in Beijing. It was not a dream; it was positive, absolute reality.

Near Mashenmiao (Horse Spirit Temple) in the western suburbs we came to a place called Huayuancun (Flower Garden Village). We entered a large estate, through which a road ran north. On one side were three two-story gray buildings. They were brand new, and had been built for "leaders" newly emerged in the Cultural Revolution.

We were given rooms in the last building on the eastern side. It contained two apartments, each large enough to house an entire family. They were new and very spacious. We were delighted. They were of much better quality than our little house in Jiangxi, and very modern.

We all set to work moving in and putting our things in order.

That evening Wang Dongxing, head of the General Office of the Central Committee, came to see us. Papa thanked him for looking after us these past few years. "I was only doing what Chairman Mao wished," Wang said.

Papa was concerned about his old comrades and their families. A few days later, he sent Mama to see Marshal Luo Ronghuan's wife, Lin Yueqin. Papa had a long-standing relationship with Luo, and Mama and Lin Yueqin were good friends. Luo died during the 1960s, but the Lin Biao gang had smeared Lin Yueqin as part of a so-called "Widows' Clique". Fortunately, the persecution seemed to have passed, and Mama was glad to see that her friend was relatively safe.

Papa called on Li Fuchun and his wife Cai Chang. They had gone with Papa in the 1920s to a work-study program in France. There they joined the Chinese Communist Party together, and began revolutionary work together. Papa considered them his Big Brother and Big Sister. He was deeply attached to them both.

He hadn't seen them in a few years, and they had grown old and ill. Li, attacked as being part of the "February Countercurrent", had been restrained for several years. His health had deteriorated. Cai Chang was nearly blind, though fairly well in general. They and my folks had all had a hard time. It was a joy just to be able to see one another again.

My parents made a special trip to the No. 301 Hospital to see Marshal Chen Yi's widow Zhang Qian. All through the war years, and in office after Liberation, Papa and "Old Commander" Chen Yi had been on warm personal terms. Before the Cultural Revolution our two families were neighbors. Their house was right behind ours.

Because Chen Yi fought boldly against Lin Biao and the reactionary Cultural Revolution Group they labeled him a member of the "February Countercurrent", and criticized and mistreated him. He died of cancer in 1972.

His wife Zhang Qian, severely depressed, also developed cancer. She had a slight remission, but her spirits were low. Listening to her bitterly assail Lin Biao and the cruel Cultural Revolution Group, seemed to bring the image of the outgoing "Old Commander" back before my parents' eyes. They were very saddened.

Chen had only one daughter, Shanshan. Still quite young, she was keeping her sick mother company in the hospital. The child had recently lost her father and now would probably lose her mother. Papa's heart ached.

"I watched Shanshan grow up," he said. "From now on, she's also my daughter." He felt this was the least he could do for his old companion-in-arms.

As we began a new life after returning to Beijing, we heard the news that Premier Zhou Enlai, in Zhongnanhai, was diagnosed as having cancer.

He had strained himself to the limit in the six years of the Cultural Revolution, overseeing all the work of the Party, the government and the military, while at the same time waging a ceaseless battle against the forces of the Cultural Revolution Group. They had overthrown most of the good cadres, and he had to handle all of the country's highly complicated affairs, large and small, almost single-handed. China couldn't do without him; Mao Zedong couldn't do without him. Yet precisely at this time his illness grew worse. He passed a lot of blood in his stool, and he needed an operation.

The Premier needed an operation, and he needed rest. But what could the nation do, what would happen to the work? Zhou Enlai was stressed. He was in a hurry to put many old cadres back to work. He submitted a list of over 300 names to the Organization Department. He was in a hurry to restore his old comrade Deng Xiaoping. He knew that Deng could be of enormous help, and could take much of the burden off his shoulders. Deng was back in Beijing. The Premier had to find a way to restore him officially.

From the end of February through the beginning of March, Zhou Enlai, though ill, convened a series of meetings of the Politburo to discuss Deng Xiaoping. Zhou proposed that Deng's organizational activities within the Party be restored, as well as his position of Vice-Premier of the State Council. Jiang Qing and Zhang Chunqiao and the other heads of the Cultural Revolution Group of course didn't agree, and did everything they could to prevent it. The infighting was intense. But Mao Zedong had decided Deng should return, and although Jiang Qing's gang was dissatisfied, they couldn't prevent it.

Zhou wrote a report to Mao on March 9 relating what had transpired, adding that the Politburo requested the Central Committee to make a formal decision, to be transmitted to the Party committees of every county and army regiment, and relayed by them to their members and to the general public. Zhou told Mao that Deng had returned to Beijing.

Mao Zedong immediately appended the endorsement: "I agree." Zhou instructed Wang Dongxing to send all pertinent documents to Deng Xiaoping for examination and comment. The Central Committee issued its decision the same day.

Zhou was greatly relieved. He requested a two-week sick leave, and recommended that the daily work of the Central Committee be entrusted to Ye Jianying.

Although Papa had returned to Beijing, he didn't know anything about these matters that had such an important bearing on his future. His political acuteness told him that his restoration was near, but he hadn't anticipated it would come so quickly. In fact, one day before Mao's approval, on March 9, he wrote a letter to Wang Dongxing requesting that daughter Deng Lin be transferred to Beijing so as to be near her future husband who was working in the Metallurgy Institute. Wang approved the next day.

He sent over the documents on Papa's restoration. The whole family was very pleased.

Shortly thereafter, Premier Zhou dispatched his wife Deng Yingchao to visit Mama and Papa. She was a few months older than Papa, and my parents called her Big Sister. The relationship was deeper than what the appellation usually implied. She and Papa had done underground work in Shanghai from the end of the 20s to the start of the 30s. Zhou Enlai was with them. They risked their lives operating in the underground Party Central Committee. Members of the same small Party group, they lived in the same building, in one flat above the other.

Zhou Enlai and Deng Yingchao witnessed 24-year-old Deng Xiaoping's first love affair, and his marriage with Zhang Xiyuan. They saw the bliss of the young revolutionary couple, they shared Papa's grief when Zhang Xiyuan died in childbirth. They called Deng Xiaoping Young Brother.

Zhou Enlai and Deng Yingchao were truly older brother and sister to Papa. They went through thick and thin together for several decades, then they were separated for nearly seven years. Big Sister's visit should have been a happy occasion, but Zhou Enlai had asked her to tell them about the seriousness of his condition. Papa had not known that Zhou was in the grip of an advanced cancer.

At 10 o 'clock in the evening of March 28, Premier Zhou Enlai, Vice-Premier Li Xiannian, and Jiang Qing met with Deng Xiaoping. It was his first official work discussion since returning. It was also the first time in seven years that he saw Zhou Enlai. They met together many times after that. His closeness to Zhou Enlai would later be the cause of political turmoil for Deng Xiaoping.

On the 29th Mao convened a meeting of the Politburo in the famous library of his residence. Before it started, Mao received Zhou and Deng privately. Papa hadn't seen Mao since September 1966. At this present meeting, Mao proposed that the Politburo pass a resolution that Deng should officially participate in the day-to-day affairs of the State Council, take part in foreign affairs as Vice-Premier; and sit in on and join all discussions of the Politburo regarding matters of major importance.

After this Deng Xiaoping resumed his office of Vice-Premier under the State Council.

In the 50s when the first and second lines of the central government were set up, Deng Xiaoping was considered a possible inheritor of the Party's highest leadership position. That had been Mao Zedong's decision. The overthrow of Liu Shaoqi and Deng Xiaoping at the start of the Cultural Revolution had also been Mao's decision. It was Mao who decided to permit Deng to retain his Party membership. It was Mao who allowed him to return.

Mao was pleased to see him again. He had always appreciated Deng, always bore him in mind. Now, first of all, he wanted to watch his performance. At the same time, Mao clearly harbored high expectations of him. Mao gave Deng considerable support in his duties. After Zhou Enlai went into the hospital, Deng was called upon to be present whenever the Chairman received foreign guests. For the next three years, whether for reasons of official duties or diplomatic activities, Deng entered Mao Zedong's library on many occasions, until he was again overthrown.

Mama and Papa went to see Zhou Enlai, who was undergoing treatment in the sanitarium in Yuquanshan (Jade Spring Hills) in the western outskirts of Beijing, on April 9, at five in the afternoon. Deng Yingchao, the Premier's wife, was staying with him.

It was a wrench for Papa to see how thin Zhou was. Recalling the meeting years later, he said: "I was unable to speak." What was there to say? No words could describe the storms and bitterness they had recently endured.

Zhou was happy to see Papa. A serious person, he didn't readily reveal his views. Still less, did he openly pass judgment on individuals. But talking to Deng Xiaoping, his most trusted comrade, he told things he had concealed in his heart for years.

He said: "Zhang Chunqiao is a traitor. But the Chairman won't let us investigate him." Turning to Mama, he warned: "Zhuo Lin, don't repeat any of this."

To Mama and Papa he seriously said: "Xiaoping's health must be preserved. Select one of the two doctors in the Wu family to look after him." Brothers Wu Jieping and Wu Weiran were both famous doctors.

Zhou reminded Papa he would be confronting many dangerous political situations in his work. Zhou wanted him to be physically fit, and choose the people around him carefully.

Severely ill himself, Zhou was concerned about Papa because he trusted him, because he pinned all of his hopes upon him.

Nearly seven years had gone by. Much had changed between heaven and earth, and in the life of every individual. You could talk about it forever. And you could not, in a few sentences, discuss all the work waiting to be done in the Party and in the government. Zhou and Papa talked a long time, right up till dusk gathered. They went in to dinner, still continuing their conversation.

The verdant groves of Jade Spring Hills fell silent. Beneath the quiet waters of the azure lake the fish sank to the bottom. Around, all was still, as if nothing wanted to interrupt the important words coming from the two friends who had known each other so long.

On April 12, 1973, Premier Zhou, though ill, gave a banquet in the Great Hall of the People in honor of Cambodia's Head of State, Prince Norodon Sihanouk, and his wife. They had just returned from their country's liberated areas. Those attending the banquet observed that as the leaders and guests entered the hall they were accompanied by a short man who looked very familiar. It was Deng Xiaoping, who had been purged as the Second Biggest Capitalist Roader inside the Party!

The foreign correspondents were particularly excited. They slipped out before the meal was over and rushed to the nearby Tel and Tel Building to tell the world the important news: Deng Xiaoping was back! The next day the story was carried in many of Hong Kong's and Taiwan's papers and periodicals. Deng's return quickly became a hot topic for foreign commentators on the "China question". One of them described Deng Xiaoping as the "unsinkable little man."

At the banquet, he was quiet and relaxed. Time seemed to have made him more solid, healthier. He showed no signs of wear or aging.

He found many new faces when he resumed work as Vice-Premier in the State Council. Eight members had been overthrown. Two had died. Lin Biao had self-destructed. Four had been so severely persecuted they could not resume their former jobs. Even the chief secretary had been purged.

Only Premier Zhou Enlai and Vice-Premier Li Xiannian were at work. The huge country was beset by problems, its economy was in trouble, and its social order was chaotic. It was being called upon to "grasp revolution" and "push production". You can imagine the difficulties and the pressure. The State Council had not only to handle the economy and foreign affairs; it was also responsible for education, science, culture, and health. There were a thousand details to be dealt with.

The State Council therefore established a production leadership committee in which Yu Qiuli and Gu Mu assisted Zhou Enlai and Li Xiannian supervised economic matters. The measure was born of necessity. Even so, Zhou still had to cope with everything night and day, until exhaustion wore him out and he went into a final decline.

With the advent of the Cultural Revolution in 1966 the growing national economy slid sharply downward, then began a slow uneven recovery. In 1969, thanks to the efforts of the State Council under Zhou Enlai, in factories where work had stopped, production halted, and the economy demolished, there was a substantial restoration. Industrial production took a turn for the better, and the economy improved.

In 1970 and 1971 Mao Zedong wrongly analyzed the international situation. He believed a new world war was about to erupt, and created an atmosphere of emergency in the economic leadership. Higher targets were set, everything was speeded up, basic production was over-extended. There were "four breakthroughs" — in the number of people employed, the wages expended, the grain distributed, and the currency issued.

It caused enormous difficulties. Fortunately, with great effort, Zhou Enlai was able to ameliorate the situation somewhat. In 1972, industrial and agricultural output was higher than the previous year.

Now, in 1973, Zhou Enlai was on temporary sick leave. The burden of all the work of the State Council, especially economic matters, fell on the shoulders of Deng Xiaoping and Li Xiannian. Despite the efforts of the Premier, the damage done by the Cultural Revolution left the economy in a dangerous state. Three of the "breakthroughs" — in the number employed, the wages expended, and grain distributed — were still being implemented. A lot more had to be done to rectify the situation.

Beijing was like a strange place to Deng Xiaoping, on first returning. He was required to learn to make distinctions and become familiarized with how to perform his duties and how to handle relationships with a variety of persons. He buried himself in his work, generally performing in low key.

What concerned him most was the medical treatment of Zhou Enlai. Zhou's wife, Deng Yingchao, had the utmost faith in Deng Xiaoping. Zhou sent her to see Mama and Papa in our home in Flower Garden Village on June 9. She told them it was difficult to be optimistic about the Premier's condition.

They all were very depressed. As Zhou Enlai's assistant, Papa bore the primary responsibility. He had to give Zhou Enlai a strong arm, to stand by him at this critical juncture.

33

The 10th Party National Congress Continues the Line of the Cultural Revolution

T HE Ninth National Congress of the Chinese Communist Party had been convened in April 1969. It claimed two "achievements". The first was the passage of an amendment to the Party Constitution confirming the extreme "Leftist" line of the Great Proletarian Cultural Revolution. The second was the affirmation of the political status of a large number of powerful members of the Cultural Revolution Group, specifically naming Lin Biao as the official successor to Mao Zedong.

Mao had believed that on the basis of this "Congress of unity and victory" the great historic task of the Cultural Revolution could be gloriously concluded. He was taken completely by surprise by the many events that followed. He never dreamed that Lin Biao would turn traitor and perish in a plane crash. In only four short years since the Ninth Party Congress, of the 21 persons elected to the Politburo, seven turned out to be leaders and activists in Lin Biao's counter-revolutionary clique. Only 13 members remained in the Politburo, leaving it one-third short of a quorum, and unable to function normally.

The position of Mao's successor stood vacant. People were becoming skeptical about the Ninth Party Congress, and the Cultural Revolution. Under such circumstances, Mao felt it imperative to call another Party Congress ahead of time to deal with the numerous "fall-outs" caused by

Lin Biao's defection.

In preparation for the 10th Party National Congress, the Central Committee met in Beijing from the 20 to the 31 of May 1973. It summoned Hua Guofeng from Hunan, Wang Hongwen from Shanghai, and Wu De, who was then First Secretary of Beijing Municipal Party Committee, and appointed them observers of the Central Committee and participants in its work. It directed Zhang Chunqiao and Yao Wenyuan to draft the main political report of the forthcoming Congress, and made Wang Hongwen responsible for drawing up amendments to the Party Constitution.

One positive result of the meeting was the liberation, in keeping with the wishes of Mao Zedong, of more than a dozen old cadres.

Deng Xiaoping took part in his capacity of Vice-Premier of the State Council. Zhou Enlai stated emphatically that the Central Committee document restoring Deng Xiaoping to office was of major significance. With this, the majority of comrades attending were satisfied.

After three months of intensive preparations, the 10th Party National Congress finally convened from August 24 to 28.

There were three items on the agenda: The Political Report by Zhou Enlai, representing the Central Committee; the report by Wang Hongwen, also on behalf of the Central Committee, regarding amendments to the Party Constitution; the election of a new Central Committee.

The 10th Party National Congress approved the Political Report drafted by Zhang Chunqiao and edited by Mao Zedong, and approved the new Constitution. The report confirmed without reservation Mao's "Leftist" line. Other than excising the appointment of Lin Biao as Mao's successor, the 10th Congress was essentially the same as the 9th. There was little change in its organizational line, but it permitted still more opportunist followers of the Cultural Revolution Group and other radicals to enter the Central Committee. The only cheering note was that some of the old comrades overthrown by the Cultural Revolution Group were restored to the Central Committee. These included Deng Xiaoping, Tan Zhenlin, Wang Zhen and several other old revolutionaries.

The first meeting of the new Central Committee convened on August 30.

Mao Zedong was chosen Chairman of the Party.

Named Vice-Chairmen were Zhou Enlai, Wang Hongwen, Kang Sheng, Ye Jianying and Li Desheng.

In the various committees and sub-committees, although a certain number of old comrades were selected, many more members of Jiang Qing's Cultural Revolution Group were added. These included Wang Hongwen, leader of Shanghai's biggest rebel faction, and the scheming Kang Sheng, both chosen as Vice Chairmen of the Party. Zhang Chunqiao, head of the Cultural Revolution Group's brain trust, became a member of the Politburo's Standing Committee. The entire Central Committee and all of its divisions were split, in effect, into two big camps — the old comrades, represented by Zhou Enlai, and the forces of the Cultural Revolution Group, headed by Jiang Qing.

The most startling of these changes was Wang Hongwen. Originally a factory security functionary, when the Cultural Revolution started he rose, with the support of Jiang Qing, Zhang Chunqiao, and Yao Wenyuan, to become the head of Shanghai's largest rebel faction. Single-handed, he engineered a huge, bloody factional battle in which scores of people were killed and injured. Then, like a nouveau riche, he went "respectable", and transformed himself into the leader of the city's Cultural Revolution Committee.

Lin Biao was gone, but the question of a successor remained unsolved. Mao's mood was complicated. Making a choice was difficult. Not making a choice was worse. Mao finally settled on a compromise. He elevated a young man to a position of highest leadership, but did not designate him as his successor. Mao could use him and observe him at the same time.

He chose Wang Hongwen. He felt that since Wang had a worker, peasant and soldier background, and had been selected from a Cultural Revolution Committee position, he could be relied on to support his Cultural Revolution line.

To Mao, this was especially important. Mao himself later said, in his life he had two major accomplishments: First, he defeated Chiang Kai-shek and the Japanese invaders, and entered Beijing; and second, he

251

launched the Great Proletarian Cultural Revolution. The excellence of the latter, in his mind, definitely could not be denied. It would be a symbol of his very essence, the hallmark of his place in history. His successor had to be someone loyal both to him and his Cultural Revolution line.

Mao therefore chose Wang Hongwen — a man of no talent or virtue, an upstart from the ranks of rebel rioters, and catapulted him into the position of highest leadership in the Central Committee of the Communist Party, making him a Central Committee Vice Chairman, second in rank only to Zhou Enlai. As further confirmation of these honors, Mao directed that Wang Hongwen, as representative of the Central Committee at the 10th Party National Congress, deliver the speech on the amendments to the Party Charter.

And so, the anointed monkey vaulted into heaven in a single leap.

Wang's advance greatly strengthened Jiang Qing's clique. Within the Central Committee Wang Hongwen, Jiang Qing, Zhang Chunqiao and Yao Wenyuan now constituted the infamous Gang of Four.

After the 10th Party National Congress ended, Ye Jianying proposed to Mao Zedong that Deng Xiaoping take part in the Politburo, while continuing to head the armed forces. Mao said this could be considered.

The Congress had met, the matter of Lin Biao had been concluded, the Party Constitution had been amended, necessary appointments had been made, but Mao was still uneasy. The Lin Biao case had been a terrible blow, and had caused many repercussions. First, there was the question of a successor. He had raised Wang Hongwen in rank, but had not formally designated him as his successor. He had restored Deng Xiaoping to office, but Deng was a man who had been purged in the Cultural Revolution. To what extent could he be utilized? More time was needed to observe him.

An even more difficult problem was how to evaluate the Cultural Revolution. With the demise of Lin Biao, the question had become of the utmost importance.

To support the Cultural Revolution line meant supporting struggle, it meant criticizing any so-called "Rightist" thought which did not conform to Mao's "Leftist" ideas. In addition to criticizing Lin Biao, Mao now called for criticism of the 2,000 year old Confucian philosophy. A new nationwide campaign came into being — "Criticize Lin and Confucius".

The Cultural Revolution Group quickly added fuel to the flames. In October Jiang Qing went to Tsinghua University and stirred up an "Oppose a Rightist Restoration" tempest among the educators. The spring breeze of correcting "Leftist" methods and liberating old cadres, which had just begun was replaced by an autumn gale of vicious new criticisms.

Papa, in the State Council, was immersed in daily routine, to which foreign affairs work was added and meetings with foreign diplomats.

September 29, 1973 was the first anniversary of the normalization of diplomatic relations between China and Japan. In his capacity of Vice-Premier, Deng Xiaoping attended a reception hosted by the Japanese Ambassador. The ambassador was surprised to see a man who had been purged looking so fit. He kept Papa's signature in the Visitors Book as a precious historic momento.

In October, Papa inspected the Wuhan Steel Mill. He was very impressed by a new blast furnace, which Premier Zhou Enlai had agreed to import. This advanced equipment and the enthusiasm of the workers excited him. "Good," he exclaimed. "We'll be able to turn out 10 million tons of steel."

Canadian Prime Minister Pierre Elliott Trudeau visited China from October 10 to 14. As Vice-Premier, Papa accompanied him on a trip to Guilin. After seeing him off when he left China, Papa went to Hunan and visited Chairman Mao's old home in Shaoshan.

In spite of the unfair treatment and hardships he had endured during the Cultural Revolution, Papa still respected Mao Zedong. It was not a light or blind respect, but a heartfelt emotion, analytical and sober. In the 1930s because he had held the same convictions as Mao, he was labeled a "leader of the Mao faction". Papa had always fought under Mao Zedong's command during the long years of revolutionary warfare. He had the highest regard for Mao's intelligence and nobility of spirit.

During the period of construction Mao appointed him General Secretary of the Party. Papa was a loyal and strong supporter of Mao all through decades of the revolution. He and the old comrades of his generation stood with Mao, stirred by his courage and moved by his greatness.

But in Mao's later years they began to have some differences with him, both in understanding and approach, on how socialism should be built in China. Finally, because he had suffered as a result of Mao's "Leftist" line, and particularly because of Mao's huge error of initiating a Cultural Revolution, Papa's opposition became more visible and firm. He decided to do his utmost to bring about a rectification of that error. His respect and admiration for Mao as a leader and man never faltered, but they were tempered now by caution with regard to Mao's methods.

"I wanted to come here in 1965 and 1966," Papa said during his visit to Mao's old home in Shaoshan, Hunan, "but I couldn't get away." He looked at a photo of Mao's younger brother Mao Zetan. "He was good comrade," Papa said. He and Mao Zetan had both been attacked under the "Leftist" line in the early 1930s. Mao Zetan died in battle. He was only 29.

Papa looked at a picture of Mao Zemin, another brother of Mao Zedong. "I knew him," Papa said, "and his wife, as well. He was killed in 1943."

Mao's family had lost six members to the revolution. People visiting Shaoshan were very moved. The words "Mao Zedong" stood not only for the successes and failures of a single individual, they represented the entire path of China's Communist Party, of China's revolutionary cause and construction. A glorious path, strewn with tortuous difficulties.

Papa was busy with foreign affairs in the State Council. Something unexpected happened in November 1973.

It originated in 1971, when Mao decided to restore Sino-US relations. In July, after Zhou Enlai met secretly with Henry Kissinger, national security advisor to America's president Richard Nixon, it was announced that Nixon would visit China in 1972. America had persistently maintained an anti-China policy ever since the establishment of the People's Republic in 1949, and supported Chiang Kai-shek in Taiwan.

Nixon came in February 1972, reviving dialogues, which had been ruptured for 22 years. This world-shaking event was a triumph for Mao's far-sighted diplomatic strategy. It was also a fulsome manifestation of the diplomatic arts and experience of Zhou Enlai. The seamless coordination between the two men created a new milestone in the history of Chinese diplomacy.

In November 1973, Kissinger again came and conferred with Zhou Enlai. Negotiations were difficult, and stretched into the wee hours. They rested briefly, and resumed the talks early the following morning. Zhou saw Kissinger off at the airport. He then went to Mao's residence to report, but the Chairman had already retired.

Mao later berated Zhou for not having reported to him immediately. He alleged the talks had been handled "badly", and angrily demanded that Zhou summon the Politburo and submit to criticism.

Zhou had passed a lot of blood in his stool and was about to enter the hospital when Kissinger came, but he continued the difficult negotiations all through the night. Actually, they were quite successful, and Mao had been pleased. Zhou's "oversight" was trivial, but Mao's orders had to be obeyed. Zhou, sick as he was, called the meeting.

Jiang Qing and Zhang Chunqiao were delighted with what they saw as an opportunity to overthrow Zhou, and they slandered him with full venom. The lady screeched that it was the "eleventh line struggle, the worst since the Lin Biao plot." She said it showed Zhou "can't wait" to replace Mao. Zhou could only grit his teeth and listen.

Mao himself didn't attend the meeting, but was told by his secretaries what was transpiring. "Has Deng Xiaoping spoken yet?" he asked. Mao wanted to know what his attitude was.

Papa had just return to work. He was still only an observer, not a member, of the Politburo. He remained silent until after nearly everyone else had spoken. Since Mao had demanded that every participant criticize Zhou Enlai, he offered a few mild words. Instead he concentrated on an analysis of the international situation. He talked of the complicated relations between China and the United States, between China and the Soviet Union, between the U.S. and the Soviet Union. He said it was wrong to judge based on a single set of negotiations, or on a single statement. It was essential to view the situation as a whole.

As to the possibility of war, he said, none of the three nations was prepared. Certainly neither the U.S. nor the Soviet Union was prepared. But even if war broke out, China had no reason to be afraid. With only rice and rifles we beat the Japanese invaders. Today, with rice and rifles, we can win again.

Papa spoke for a long time. His discussion of the international situation far exceeded the original narrow limitations of simply criticizing Zhou Enlai.

Mao was happy when he heard about Papa's speech. "I knew he was a good speaker," Mao said. "He didn't need any help from me."

He wanted to send for Papa immediately, but it was already too late at night. It was plain he was watching Papa closely, and was considering him for an important post.

On December 9, 1973, after receiving foreign visitors, Mao Zedong talked with Zhou Enlai and Wang Hongwen about the criticism meeting. He said it "went well, very well." Then he criticized Jiang Qing.

"There were two mistaken statements made," Mao said. "One was about an 'eleventh line struggle.' That's wrong. There's no such thing. The other was that Premier Zhou 'can't wait.' The fact is she's the one who can't wait!"

That was how the "criticizing Zhou" fiasco ended. Mao was dissatisfied with Zhou, but couldn't do without him. He felt Zhou's approach was different from his own, that it was too "rightist". He wanted to criticize Zhou, but he certainly didn't want to overthrow him. Jiang Qing and her clique tried to take advantage of the situation. The result was they were the ones who were criticized, and their hopes were dashed.

34

Into the Military Commission and the Politburo

T EN months passed since Papa returned to Beijing in February 1973, and resumed his post as Vice-Premier of the State Council.

In that period our family went through a complete change. Deng Lin was assigned to the painting section of the Beijing Art Academy, and she married Wu Jianchang, a researcher in the Institute of Metallurgy. That meant all three daughters were now married. Mama and Papa were very pleased. Pufang continued being treated in the No. 301 Hospital. Deng Nan was assigned to the Automation Research Institute of the Chinese Academy of Sciences. Feifei and I were transferred to schools in Beijing — I to the clinical medicine department of Beijing Medical College, Feifei to the Physics Department of Peking University.

Papa had his old secretary Wang Ruilin transferred back from the May Seventh Cadre School in Jiangxi. He also sent for his old bodyguard Zhang Yuzhen and his orderly Deng Xingjun, as well as Old Wu, who had served as his orderly in Jiangxi. Nearly his whole former staff returned.

Our family's most precious treasure was naturally the little granddaughter Mianmian. "Now that I have a granddaughter," Papa joked to us children, "you don't matter much any more!" We couldn't accept that.

Thanks to this fourth generation addition, Grandma rose in rank to Great-Grandmother. Hovering over Mianmian, she complained: "The child is a bit too small." Her old aphorism had been: "To make a baby strong, keep it slightly hungry, and a little cold." Meaning you should never over-feed an infant, or swaddle it too warmly.

But now, perhaps old age made her forgetful of her sensible rule. At mealtime she stuffed Mianmian to the brim. The poor tyke grew round as a ball, with rings of fat circling her little wrists.

Mama, ever scientific, said infants need calcium. She put Mianmian in a wicker baby carriage, and let her get plenty of sunshine every day out in the courtyard. By the end of the summer Mianmian had a dark tan. Mama also shaved her head, so that her hair would grow healthy and strong. She converted the tender delicate little girl into a dusky, shiny-pated desperado!

We had been living in half a building in Huayuancun. With our population explosion it was soon too small. We were given a temporary addition next-door to accommodate those of us who came home on weekends. But then, when Papa became a Vice-Premier again, we were given the whole building.

When Li Jingquan was liberated, he moved into the building in front of ours. He had a large family, and we became well acquainted. The kids all played together, and were in and out of each other's homes. It was a lively compound. Originally, the buildings in Huayuancun were meant for "new leaders" of the Cultural Revolution. But, before that could happen, the formerly overthrown old cadres moved in. It was pretty funny.

In December 1973, after a period of observation, Mao Zedong made up his mind. He increased the importance of Deng Xiaoping.

From December 12 to 22, he called a series of meetings of the Politburo. Learning from the lesson of Lin Biao, and determined to put the armed forces under the absolute leadership of the Communist Party, Mao proposed that the commanders of the eight greater military regions rotate their posts at intervals. He also proposed that Deng be made a member of the Central Military Commission, and a member of the Politburo.

He said on December 12 that he and Comrade Ye Jianying had invited Comrade Deng Xiaoping to join the Military Commission.

"As to whether he should also be a member of the Politburo," Mao said, "that can be raised at the next session of the Central Committee." And Mao added: "Before, the Politburo didn't discuss politics, and the Military Commission didn't discuss military matters, or political matters, either. That has to change."

"We're now inviting a new military adviser," Mao said on December 14. "His name is Deng Xiaoping. Issue a notice that he will be a member of the Politburo and the Military Commission. The Politburo has overall control — the Party, the government, the armed forces, the citizens, the students — east, west, north, south, and central. I feel it should add a General Secretary. Maybe you (indicating Deng) don't like that title. Let's call you Chief of Staff."

Mao met on December 15 in his library with members of the Politburo and the commanders of the eight greater military regions.

"Today, we have invited a Chief of Staff," he said, indicating Deng. "He scares some people, but he is quite competent. His record is 70 percent on the plus side. I've invited you veteran commanders back to your posts, and I'm not the only one who's asked you. The same with you Politburo members."

Turning to Deng Xiaoping, Mao said: "Everyone's a little afraid of you. Let me offer a few words of advice: Be soft on the outside and steel within. Hide a needle inside your cotton wool. Have an affable exterior, and a steel mill interior. Gradually correct your shortcomings."

Zhou Enlai, convening the Politburo on December 18, related what Mao Zedong had said about rotating the posts of the commanders. The Politburo approved Mao's proposal, and appointed Deng Xiaoping to the Politburo and to the Central Military Commission.

On the 21st Mao attended a discussion in the Military Commission. After praising Zhu De as a "Red Commander-in-Chief", he spoke of other generals.

"The attack on Comrade He Long was wrong," he said. "I must bear responsibility. The verdict must be reversed. It's bad that He Long is gone. The cases against Yang (Chengwu), Xu (Lijin) and Fu (Chongbi) also must be overturned. They were all Lin Biao's doing. I listened to his one-sided versions and made mistakes. Xiaoping says he disapproved of the sudden attack on Luo Ruiqing in Shanghai. I agree. It also came of listening to Lin Biao."

On December 22, Zhou Enlai drafted the documents concerning Deng Xiaoping's appointment to the Politburo and the Military Commission. On the same day the rotation of the eight commanders was also announced.

No one was surprised by Papa's appointment to the Politburo. He had been a vice-premier in the State Council before the Cultural Revolution. But he had no previous military post. Why did Mao want him to control both political and military affairs? A new political situation had been created: The State Council would be headed by Zhou Enlai and Deng Xiaoping; the armed forces would be under Ye Jianying and Deng Xiaoping. This provided, in effect, powerful support to the old cadres headed by Zhou Enlai.

Wang Hongwen had risen under Mao's sponsorship, but he was still a newcomer. He had no way to intervene in Party, government, or military organizations, to say nothing of exercising any real power. These were areas where Deng was indeed strong.

What was Mao trying to do? December 26, 1973 would be his 80th birthday. After Lin Biao's defection, Mao had fallen very ill. His health had considerably declined. He wanted to arrange for what would happen after his death. It was going to be difficult, no matter how he prepared.

He divided his power: he placed Wang Hongwen, who would continue his "revolutionary line", in charge of Party affairs. He gave the practical workings of the government and the armed forces to Deng Xiaoping. But for the sake of "stability" he didn't grant full authority in any aspect to any single individual. In the highest Communist Party organs, he inserted Deng Xiaoping and other old cadres to counter the forces of the Cultural Revolution Group. To the government and armed forces he added Wang Hongwen and Zhang Chunqiao to counter the strength of the old cadres. Mao felt in this way the scales would be balanced.

He had given the matter long and painful thought. But it was an absurd, impractical arrangement, impossible to effectuate. Mao was too self-assured. He believed his plan would bring the Cultural Revolution to a peaceful conclusion after his death. His carefully crafted political scale, however, didn't wait till after his death — it flew out of kilter while he was still alive before his very eyes.

No matter how we appraise the situation today, the fact remains that at the end of 1973 Mao not only recalled Deng Xiaoping but gave him a much more important position with greatly increased power. He hoped that Deng would take over when Zhou Enlai could no longer function. Someone had to be able to operate the machinery of a great nation.

The Cultural Revolution had been raging for more than seven years. Mao created a new political set-up which he hoped would bring it to an early end. He had enough of turmoil.

After seven tumultuous years, people everywhere were longing for peace, and Mao was beginning to feel the same. But "though the tree wants quiet, the wind won't let it be". The disturbances of the Cultural Revolution could not be easily quelled. To its proponents anarchy was the foundation of their existence. Particularly now, after the death of Lin Biao, when they felt their opportunity to seize power had come, how could they permit the old cadres they had overthrown return to office? Jiang Qing and her gang wanted to get rid of them, but they had to eliminate Zhou first. They launched an "Oppose Lin and Confucius" campaign. Actually, their real target was neither Lin Biao nor Confucius. It was Zhou Enlai. [1]

Winter of 1973 was a busy time for Jiang Qing and her gang. In December she and Wang Hongwen wrote a letter to Mao Zedong requesting permission to distribute their materials on the "Oppose Lin and Confucius" campaign. Mao approved, and they disseminated them throughout China on January 18, 1974.

---

[1] Confucian precepts, as practiced in China, advocated strengthening the old established order. Mao wanted to revitalize Chinese society by "revolutionary" methods. Jiang Qing and her Gang of Four dragged Mao's approach to fanatic extremes, aiming to use these as a means of ultimately taking power. Zhou Enlai, while favoring reform, supported moderation and opposed radicalism. Since he was too respected to be attacked openly, the Gang smeared him by innuendo by targeting all moderates, whom they called "Confucianists."

On January 24 and 25, at Spring Festival time, without first obtaining the consent of the Central Committee, they held a mass rally of 20,000 people to push the campaign. Two of their big generals, Chi Qun and Xie Jingyi, gave inflammatory speeches extravagantly praising Jiang Qing, and wildly slandering the leaders of the State Council and the Central Military Commission. Jiang Qing and Yao Wenyuan took the opportunity to interject snide remarks about Zhou Enlai and Ye Jianying, both of whom were present.

After these meetings Jiang Qing, in her own name, wrote to several military units, and sent them material. She also dispatched men to try to provoke seizures of power. She used similar tactics to stir up "criticisms" within the State Council. She had no position in either of these organizations, but hoped to worm her way into the government and the armed forces and create a row, under cover of which she could attack Zhou Enlai and seize power.

Zhou Enlai and Ye Jianying fought back. On January 31, 1974, Zhou convened the Politburo. With the support of Ye Jianying and Deng Xiaoping he took steps against political instigation within the armed forces. In April, because national production levels had been falling, the State Council forbade the formation of factional organizations and the distribution of inflammatory material.

Ye Jianying had angrily walked out of the mass rally to "Criticize Lin and Confucius", and delivered a copy of Xie Jingyi's speech to Mao Zedong.

Mao felt that Jiang Qing and her cohorts had gone too far. If the situation continued, it would spread — something Mao definitely did not want. The Jiang Qing gang had to be reined in.

In a letter to Ye Jianying on February 15, Mao wrote: "The metaphysicists are running wild. They're utterly one-sided. Xie's speech was flawed. It should not be distributed. Criticisms should be raised in the Politburo. Documents which can be printed for distribution should be issued in the name of the Central Committee, not in the name of an individual, and certainly not in my name. I have never submitted any material."

Mao turned down a nationwide distribution of audio tapes which Jiang Qing had prepared of the January 25 mass rally.

Jiang Qing asked to see Mao Zedong. On March 20, he sent her a letter which said: "It's better if we don't meet. I talked with you for years in the past, but many of the things (I recommended) you didn't do. What's the use of seeing each other? Although there are books on Marxism, and my own writings, you don't study them. I'm ill, 81. Why aren't you sympathetic? You have power. After I die, what will you do with it? Big matters you don't discuss, yet you constantly send people to me about trivialities. Please think it over."

Obviously, Jiang Qing severely upset Mao. Even more, she worried him. His feelings toward her were complicated. In the early years of their marriage, he would not permit her to interfere in political affairs. But after the Cultural Revolution started, Mao made use of her. He was well aware of her irascible character. But she was, after all, his wife. No matter how dissatisfied he was, no matter how critical, Mao remained protective of, and even slightly reliant on Jiang Qing. He could refuse to see her, scold her, restrict her, but his feelings toward the members of his family, including Jiang Qing, his affection for and trust of them, were unmatched by anything he may have felt for others.

These feelings, in his final years, intensified.

35

The Storm over the Special Session
of the United Nations

IF they had any sensitivity Jiang Qing's gang would have pulled back their swords after having been criticized by Mao. But the criticism didn't worry them. Mao was on his last legs, they thought, he couldn't do without the Cultural Revolution Group warriors. Not only didn't they subside, but in March, 1974, they launched another attack.

After China regained her lawful seat in the United Nations, our government decided to send a delegation to attend the Sixth Special Session of the UN General Assembly. Zhou Enlai was too ill, and Mao proposed that Deng Xiaoping lead the delegation. Before the Cultural Revolution Deng had on several occasions represented the Chinese Communist Party and government in discussions and disputes with the Soviet Union and other Communist countries — he had diplomatic experience. Moreover, at such an important international conference it was necessary to have a representative who in the future would play an important role on China's political stage. Mao saw Deng Xiaoping as the person who would replace the ailing Zhou Enlai as the principal in China's foreign affairs.

Jiang Qing was extremely displeased. Deng Xiaoping's continuous rise infuriated her. She felt it insupportable to allow him such prominence in an international arena like the UN.

Zhou Enlai, at a Politburo meeting at the end of March, relayed a proposal by China's Ministry of Foreign Affairs, in keeping with Mao's wishes, that Deng head the Chinese delegation to the forthcoming UN special session. Jiang Qing hypocritically objected on the grounds of "personal security", and claimed that Deng, moreover, was "too busy with domestic matters". On March 24, Zhou officially approved the Foreign Ministry proposal, and formally notified Mao and the members of the Politburo then present in Beijing. Jiang Qing demanded that the Foreign Ministry withdraw its proposal.

Mao dispatched this message to Zhou Enlai: "Sending Deng Xiaoping to the UN is my idea. If all the comrades in the Politburo disagree, forget it."

Zhou replied: "Chairman Mao's suggestion is fully supported." He reported this to other members of the Politburo, and insisted that Wang Hongwen transmit Mao Zedong's recommendation to Jiang Qing, Zhang Chunqiao and Yao Wenyuan.

On March 26, the Politburo unanimously agreed that Deng Xiaoping should lead the Chinese delegation to the United Nations. Only Jiang Qing raised a fuss. Zhou Enlai sent a report of the Politburo meeting to Mao Zedong.

"Comrade Deng Xiaoping is my choice to go abroad," Mao wrote angrily to Jiang Qing on March 27. "Don't you oppose me. Be careful, Jiang Qing. Don't go against my proposal."

That same night Jiang Qing, fearful of Mao's ire, indicated agreement with Deng leading the delegation.

Zhou then wrote to Mao Zedong: "Everyone agreed with Chairman Mao's proposal that Comrade Deng Xiaoping participate in the special session of the UN. As of today, he has cut down on his duties here and has started preparations to go abroad. Full measures are being taken for his safety. We are organizing an impressive send-off when the delegation leaves Beijing on April 6."

The battle ended in victory for Zhou Enlai and Deng Xiaoping, and defeat for Jiang Qing. For the previous seven years of the Cultural Revolution Zhou had fought the powerful Cultural Revolution Group of Lin Biao and Jiang Qing, alone. He did everything in his power to keep the nation's economy from collapse, to end the anarchy, to rescue the old comrades who had been purged. For the sake of the overall situation, he swallowed insults, unjust criticisms, and slanders. His spirits were glum, his health poor. He knew his days were numbered.

With Mao's help he managed to restore a large number of high-ranking leaders, including Deng Xiaoping, to office. Now, he was no longer isolated in the Central Committee, in the State Council, in the Military Commission. He had Ye Jianying, Deng Xiaoping, and Li Xiannian, fighting with him, shoulder to shoulder. Zhou Enlai was giving his last breath to battle the forces of evil.

He knew that even if he went down, his comrades-in-arms would carry on. The country, the people, the Party had been through too much. The madness had to be brought to an end. Zhou's attitude was: "If I don't plunge into the bitter sea, who will? If I won't go through hell, who will?"

Zhou was preparing a huge send-off for Deng Xiaoping, but not only because Deng Xiaoping was going abroad. It was to celebrate Deng's ability to defeat slanders and wrongs, to mark the triumphant departure of "a hero setting forth".

Mao decided to support Zhou Enlai and Deng Xiaoping because he wanted to end, "gloriously", the Great Proletarian Cultural Revolution, to stop the rebellions, the anarchy, the turmoil. He wanted to hear no more of the absurd pronouncements of Jiang Qing and her gang. They had no choice, in the face of Mao's castigation, but to lessen their frenzy, at least temporarily. For a while, a more temperate political breeze blew.

Vice-Foreign Minister Qiao Guanhua and Deng concentrated on preparing China's address at the UN Conference. Deng insisted that it elucidate Mao's thesis that the international community was divided into three worlds — the first of two superpowers, the second of developed countries and the third of developing nations. He and the Foreign Ministry experts worked tirelessly on the draft.

Papa said the speech must state the following: "China is not a tyrant, or a superpower. If the day should ever come when China changes color and becomes a super power, and tyrannizes the world, and oppresses people, and invades and exploits others, then the people of the world should label China social-imperialist. They should expose her, oppose her, and together with the Chinese people, overthrow her."

After the Politburo approved the draft, it was sent to Mao Zedong. On it, Mao wrote the words: "Good. Approved."

Zhou Enlai made detailed preparations for Deng Xiaoping's journey. He met with responsible leaders of the Foreign Ministry and the Civil Air Administration of China (CAAC) and discussed safety during the send-off ceremony and the flight.

"Comrade Deng Xiaoping will represent the People's Republic of China at the United Nations," he reminded them. "We must clear the way for the successful accomplishment of his mission."

He had CAAC make two test flights, in the two directions along the east and the west routes, to ensure their safety. At that time our country was in a state of high alert, and closed to the outside world. Zhou Enlai approved a measure permitting CAAC to apply for a special international flight route for this very special mission.

Deng Xiaoping and his delegation left on April 6, 1974 for New York and the United Nations. Zhou Enlai, though ill, took part, with thousands of others, in an imposing send-off. The firm handclasp between the haggard premier and the sturdy Deng Xiaoping to a large extent bespoke their confidence.

On April 10, 1974, Vice-Premier of the State Council of the People's Republic of China, Deng Xiaoping, addressed the Sixth Special Session of the United Nations. To an intently listening audience he articulated the "Three Worlds" thesis of Mao Zedong and the principles of China's foreign policy. His speech won unusually long-lasting applause. The promise that China would never become a tyrant evoked a particularly enthusiastic welcome from the Third World countries. The global media wrote reams of copy and commentary about Deng Xiaoping's speech, and about Deng himself. Several said the short-statured Chinese standing at the podium of the United Nations was not only a symbol of New China — he was the "best representative" Premier Zhou Enlai could ever have had.

During the session Deng Xiaoping met many foreign leaders,

including US Secretary of State, Henry Kissinger. On April 14, in New York's Waldorf Astoria Hotel, they discussed questions of common interest. This was their first meeting. They met several more times in the 15 years which followed, and became true friends of mutual regard.

His participation in the UN confirmed Deng's important position in international political affairs. His name, from then on, attracted wide attention in the diplomatic arena.

In keeping with the planned route, the Chinese delegation flew by Air France from New York to Paris, and from there, by CAAC, to home.

While in Paris, Papa stayed in the Chinese Embassy. He usually got up about six and walked around the grounds. He loved the coffee he used to drink in the small bistros when he was a student in a work-study program 50 years before, and he asked the Embassy to send someone out to buy some for him every morning. The Embassy was very conscientious about Papa's safety. They told Sun Shaoyu, a member of the Embassy's Communist Party Committee, to do the buying. That meant Sun also had to get up at six, and carry two empty thermos flasks to put the coffee in. Pouring the coffee cup by cup into the flasks took some time. The proprietor of the bistro laughed.

"Is your guest a battalion major, or the colonel of a regiment?"

One morning, when the coffee arrived, Vice-Foreign Minister Qiao Guanhua, who had accompanied Deng from Beijing, was still asleep. The kitchen was ready to serve breakfast. "Don't wait for him," Papa said. The whole delegation filed in, and took their places at the table.

Papa asked the Embassy to help him find a place where he and Zhou Enlai had conducted secret Chinese Communist Party activities in the 20's. A few young Chinese Communists had lived in a little room in an unobtrusive hotel in a small area called Plaza Italien. Always in danger of detection and arrest by the French gendarmes, led by Zhou Enlai they enthusiastically pursued their efforts to "save China and the Chinese people". Papa never imagined, when he left France to avoid arrest, and went to study in the Soviet Union, that 48 years later he would return as a leader of New China.

The Embassy car in which Papa was riding circled around the Plaza Italien twice. For security reasons he wasn't permitted to get out. They couldn't find the small hotel. It must have been torn down. Looking through the car window, Papa sighed.

"Everything's changed. The Premier, Fuchun and I use to meet and have coffee in a little bistro near here all the time."

When he was getting ready to leave France, Ambassador Zeng Tao asked him whether there was anything he would like to bring home.

"Croissants and cheese," Papa said.

"Easy," said the ambassador. He sent out for two hundred croissants and a large variety of cheese.

After returning to Beijing, Papa personally divided and had them delivered to Zhou Enlai, Deng Yingchao, Li Fuchun, Nie Rongzhen, Cai Chang, and other comrades who had been in the work-study program and had done revolutionary work with him in Paris.

The night before they left Paris the delegation to the UN had gathered in the main hall of the Embassy, in high spirits over the mission's success. Only Papa, sitting alone on a sofa, was silent and morose.

"We're going back to nasty battle," he said. His mind was already on China's internal situation, on the savage political struggle.

The day he and his delegation were due to return, on April 19, Zhou Enlai sent a message to Mao Zedong: "Comrade Xiaoping and his delegation will arrive in Beijing this afternoon at 5:30 pm. The reception will be as impressive as the send-off."

In spite of his illness, Zhou again went to the airport to welcome Deng Xiaoping, happy and proud of his old comrade-in-arms for the victorious accomplishment of his mission.

36

An Ugly Battle

P APA took over a great deal of foreign affairs work from Zhou Enlai. Because he accompanied Zhou at Mao's receptions of foreign dignitaries, he had many opportunities to meet with Mao Zedong.

Mao received Prime Minister Zulfikar Ali Bhutto of Pakistan on May 11, 1974. Present were Zhou Enlai, Wang Hongwen and Deng Xiaoping.

The same at the reception on May 18 of Archbishop Makaries, President of Cyprus ... and at the reception of Edward Heath, former British Prime Minister on May 25.

Obviously, Mao wanted the newly risen Wang Hongwen, and the just returned-to-office Deng Xiaoping to join in his foreign affairs activities. This would develop Wang Hongwen, who had no diplomatic experience, and at the same time give Mao a chance to observe Deng Xiaoping directly. He hoped the two would comprise a new operating unit.

In the year since his return from Jiangxi Papa assumed many of Zhou Enlai's duties in the State Council and in foreign affairs. He had several clashes with Jiang Qing and her Cultural Revolution gang. But Mao supported him, and he was able to stick to his guns.

The State Planning Commission gave a report on industrial production on June 18. From June 26 to July 12 the State Council called a preparatory meeting on the mechanization of agriculture. On July 1, the Central Committee issued a call to "grasp revolution and promote production".

After having kept an eye on Deng Xiaoping for a year, Mao Zedong was in general satisfied. He felt his choice of Deng was correct.

Zhou Enlai's illness grew steadily worse. At 3:00 in the afternoon on May 27, Zhou's wife Deng Yingchao, Deng Xiaoping and three other Central Committee leaders, conferred with the medical team responsible for Zhou's treatment about his condition.

On June 1, Zhou said farewell to the courtyard house which had been his home in Zhongnanhai for 25 years and moved into PLA 305 Hospital. There he spent the last 18 months of his life. It was the most painful, tragic but courageous period of his long revolutionary career.

Everyone was miserable, but Jiang Qing and her gang were delighted. They had tried in vain to overthrow Zhou Enlai. Now they increased their slanderous assaults. Jiang Qing said, in an innuendo clearly aimed at Zhou, that there was "a big modern Confucianist inside the Party."

On June 23, in a village near Tianjin, while boasting madly about herself, she viciously attacked Zhou Enlai. Mao had criticized her not long before, and she had quieted down for a while. But now she burst forth again. Mao was very angry.

He called a meeting of the Politburo on July 17 in his library. He spoke to her directly before the assembled gathering.

"Comrade Jiang Qing, pay attention," he said. "People are critical of you, but don't want to tell you to your face, so you don't know. You're running two operations — a steel mill and a label factory. You pin labels on people whenever you please. That's bad. Get rid of both operations." (The "steel mill" symbolized political persecution.)

Mao turned to the others and said: "She doesn't represent me. She represents only herself. There are two sides to her. One is good, the other is not so good."

To Zhang Chunqiao, Yao Wenyuan, and Wang Hongwen, Mao said: "In a word, she represents herself. She's part of the Shanghai clique. Be very careful. Don't go forming a four-person faction!"

If anyone else had been criticized by Mao so severely, he/she surely would have had to step down. But Jiang Qing was not only Mao's wife; she was a "flag-bearer" in the Cultural Revolution. Mao criticized her, but she knew he wouldn't purge her. Her fate was inextricably tied to

Mao's Cultural Revolution. She therefore continued to act with assurance.

In April, we added another member to our family's fourth generation. Big Sister Deng Lin gave birth to a little boy, Mengmeng. It wasn't easy for him to come into the world. Deng Lin's health was not good, and the baby was born prematurely. He weighed only 3 *jin* 2 *liang*, (3.5 lbs.) and barely knew how to breathe.

Mama took him to the famous gynecologist Lin Qiaozhi in the Capital Hospital (Peking Union Medical College Hospital). Dr. Lin examined him carefully. "There's nothing wrong with this baby," she said, but she prescribed keeping him in an incubator for a month.

Looking at her grandson, Mama said: "This mite was born before he was ripe. He looks like a little 'meng ya' (sprout). We'll call him Mengmeng."

A month latter, when Deng Lin brought him home, he was still very skinny. His legs were no thicker than an adult's thumbs. We sisters who had no children of our own were afraid to hold him.

Then Grandma took over. She taught Deng Lin how to bottle-feed the baby, how to change his diapers, how to bathe him. In summer mornings, if it was a nice day, she would put Mengmeng in a wicker baby carriage and push him out on the balcony to get some sun.

Papa was overjoyed with the new grandson. He got up early every day, and, the first thing in the morning, went to see the baby and play with its little hands. He was inordinately proud of his two grandchildren. He reveled in his multi-generation family.

"It's children that give a family life," he liked to say.

Papa was 70 on August 22, 1974. The family threw a party in Huayuancun to celebrate his birthday. Pufang got leave from the hospital to come home. All the relatives in Beijing came. There was just enough room for everyone around the big table. It was a lively gathering. We all rose and drank to Papa's health. Even two-year-old Mianmian, with her round shining pate, bounced unsteadily over to her grandfather to clink cups and kiss him on both cheeks. Papa glowed with joy.

Later, we posed for a family group picture. Before the Cultural Revolution we took one almost every year, but this was our first in the eight years since it began. Compared with the 1965 photo we all had changed a lot. Papa disliked taking pictures. But on his 70th birthday, surrounded by children and grandchildren, he smiled broadly.

He was truly busy that first year after his return to Beijing. Not only did he have to understand the new situation and adjust to it, and do a good job in the State Council — he had to battle endlessly with the Cultural Revolution fanatics.

Papa had no qualms or hesitations. He simply worked. He didn't crave power; he didn't want position. Still less did he seek private peace and tranquility. All his life he worked for the people, regardless of what came before or lay ahead. When something had to be done, he did it.

He was 70. He knew his days of service were limited, and he treasured every minute. He wanted to devote the full measure of his remaining energies to dispelling the many hardships and disasters of the nation and the people.

The blood count in Zhou Enlai's urine increased in early August. His illness kept recurring. The cancer was spreading. The news saddened Papa profoundly. There was nothing else he could do, except work harder and take more of a load off Zhou's shoulders.

In the State Council, together with Li Xiannian, Papa had to deal with innumerable complicated financial matters and engineering problems, to ponder how to increase national production and restore normal working conditions, while devoting an enormous amount of time to receiving foreign guests and solving all sorts of diplomatic questions. In conjunction with Ye Jianying, he also helped bring order to the many complications left in military affairs by Lin Biao's downfall.

There was so much to do and so few people to do it. It was difficult, and the pressure was intense. Ye Jianying was busy, Deng Xiaoping was busy, Li Xiannian was busy. Even the ailing Zhou Enlai dragged himself through receiving foreign guests, through coping with affairs of state.

In September, in response to Zhou's suggestion, and approved by Mao Zedong, the Central Committee announced the formal clearing of the name of Marshal He Long. He had been insulted and tormented to death during the Cultural Revolution.

On September 30, at a meeting in the Great Hall of the People celebrating the 25th anniversary of the founding of the People's Republic, a gaunt Zhou Enlai read the congratulatory address on behalf of Mao Zedong, the Chinese Communist Party and the Chinese government.

By then, everyone knew how ill he was. Very moved, they responded with thunderous applause, their respect and concern for him overflowing. It was to be the last time he would convoke a national anniversary celebration meeting.

His condition grew worse. Mao had already entrusted the daily work of the Central Committee to Wang Hongwen. Someone was urgently needed to replace Zhou Enlai in handling the daily work of the State Council. On October 4, Mao, who was then in Wuhan, instructed his secretary to telephone Wang Hongwen and direct him to notify Zhou Enlai to appoint Deng Xiaoping First Vice-Premier of the State Council.

Wang Hongwen did not immediately comply. That evening, he went first to report to Jiang Qing. She was surprised and very disappointed. Deng Xiaoping's return to office, his rapid rise, his expanding powers, the press coverage of his frequent reception of foreign guests — as a result of which he saw Mao often — all this severely rankled in the hearts of the Jiang Qing gang.

It looked very much as if Mao had decided that Deng should take over from Zhou. A bad omen for the Gang of Four. But Mao had made the decision personally. It had to be announced. Wang Hongwen stalled as long as he could, then two days later, reported Mao's order to the Politburo and Zhou Enlai.

Zhou was very happy. He conferred with Deng Xiaoping on October 6. He pinned his hopes on Deng, and entrusted him with all of his unfinished affairs.

37

The Struggle for a New Cabinet at the Fourth National People's Congress

To carry out the decisions of the Ninth Communist Party Congress and continue the policies enunciated at the 10th, Mao Zedong decided to convoke the Fourth National People's Congress (NPC).

This was another important move. Party congresses complete the arrangement and organization of the central units within the Communist Party.

The National People's Congresses, in accordance with the State Constitution, organize the national government administration, and appoint government executives. Mao thought, through these two bodies, to wrap up the Cultural Revolution.

"It has already lasted eight years," he said. "Now it's time to restore peace. In the whole Party, in the whole Army, we must have harmony."

Mao felt to preserve the fruits of the Cultural Revolution positions and ranks in the Party, the government, and the army had to be settled. Unity had to be restored. He was already 80. His health was visibly declining. He used to jokingly recite the folk aphorism: "At 73, at 84, if death doesn't come calling, you knock at his door!" He had to consider what would happen after he was gone.

Government posts were of crucial importance to Jiang Qing and her gang. They had already taken high ground within the Party. Wang

275

Hongwen was a Vice-Chairman, Zhang Chunqiao was a member of the Standing Committee of the Politburo. Jiang Qing and Yao Wenyuan were both in the Politburo, too.

As big satraps in the Cultural Revolution Group, their ambition knew no bounds. They wanted power within the government and the army, as well, and they thought the Fourth National People's Congress would be their chance to get it. If they were strong inside the Party, the government and the army, when the day came that Mao was no longer around, they could control the whole country. They were avid to form a new "cabinet" composed of their own members.

In the evening of October 6, Jiang Qing called on Zhou Enlai and offered proposals to be made at the NPC, including a recommendation for the Chief of Staff of the PLA.

Zhou Enlai and Deng Xiaoping were the main obstacles to the gang's dream of expanding their power into the government, and they stopped at nothing to bring them down. Jiang Qing seized upon the so-called "Fengqing Steamer" incident to embroil both the State Council, under Zhou Enlai's leadership, and the Politburo.

There wasn't much to the whole thing. The "Fengqing", a steamer built in China, returned from a long successful test cruise. The State Council and Ministry of Communications decided to expand the fleet of this type of vessel, and bought a few abroad, since China at that time didn't have any more domestically produced. Jiang Qing immediately clamored this was "treachery", alleging that behind the Ministry of Communications there was "someone in the Central Committee".

Jiang Qing, Zhang Chunqiao, Wang Hongwen, and Yao Wenyuan ranted that the Ministry of Communications "fawned on foreigners", that it had a "comprador mentality". They said those who refused to support their attacks were "suppressing criticism" of a "reactionary political incident".

At a meeting of the Politburo in the evening of October 17, Jiang Qing insisted that members immediately express their opinions of this "treachery", saying it was essential to expose the "comprador" who was behind it.

What is your attitude? she asked Deng Xiaoping.

Deng replied coolly that he had read the documents concerned, and would examine them further. Jiang Qing demanded that he say what he thought of "slavish adulation of foreigners". Deng couldn't take any more.

"We're all equal here in the Politburo," he retorted angrily. "You have no right to take that attitude! Is that how to attain cooperation? Forcing people to agree with your ideas?"

The haughty, overbearing Jiang Qing was used to getting her own way. Deng's open rebuff came as a shock. She began shouting and screaming. Deng stood up.

"The matter hasn't been fully examined, and you're issuing condemnations," he said coldly. "It's impossible to go on with this meeting."

He walked out. Zhang Chunqiao sneered: "Deng Xiaoping is acting up again."

That night Jiang Qing met secretly with Zhang Chunqiao, Yao Wenyuan and Wang Hongwen at her residence in Number 17 Diaoyutai (Fishing Terrace). She said: "The reason Deng Xiaoping argued so loudly is because he's dissatisfied with the Cultural Revolution, because he opposes it."

Zhang Chunqiao said: "It probably has to do with the Fourth NPC and the nomination of a Chief of Staff. It's a general outburst."

Wang Hongwen said: "Deng Xiaoping dislikes the Cultural Revolution. He's angry about it. He doesn't support new developments."

Yao Wenyuan wrote in his diary: "There's been a sudden change in the struggle! At the conclusion of yesterday's meeting Comrade Deng Xiaoping stood up and cursed Comrade Jiang Qing...."

They conferred until midnight, and agreed to utilize the clash. After carefully rehearsing what he should say, they decided to send Wang Hongwen to Changsha to complain to Mao Zedong.

The next day, October 18, without notifying the Politburo, Wang Hongwen flew to Changsha. He protested to Mao Zedong about Zhou Enlai and Deng Xiaoping.

"I've come without telling the Politburo, or the Premier," Wang said. "The four of us talked till midnight, and agreed to send me while Premier Zhou is still in the hospital. I've come at great risk. Comrade Deng Xiaoping and Comrade Jiang Qing quarreled bitterly at the Politburo meeting. Deng must be in a bad temper over choosing a Chief of Staff."

Wang added a few more drops of poison. "Although the Premier is ill in the hospital," he said, "he's very active. He sends for people at night and talks with them until very late. Visitors go almost every day. Among his most frequent callers are Deng Xiaoping, Ye Jianying and Li Xiannian. It surely has to do with the appointments to be made at the Fourth NPC."

Wang took the opportunity to commend Zhang Chunqiao for his ability, and Yao Wenyuan for his scholarship, reserving his most lavish praise for Jiang Qing.

His aim was to persuade Mao to let the four of them choose their own members for the new State Council. As he later admitted at his trial: "I wanted to vilify Deng before Mao so badly he wouldn't be able to work any more, and certainly not as Vice-Premier."

Mao's political acuteness was finely tuned. After listening to Wang Hongwen's long speech he said: "If you disagree with people you should talk with them directly. This way is no good. Learn to get along with Comrade Xiaoping. He has a strong political sense; he's a fighter."

"Go back," Mao urged. "Talk more with the Premier and Comrade Jianying. Don't stick with Jiang Qing. Be wary of her."

Jiang Qing and her gang had assumed that Mao had raised Wang Hongwen to a high rank because he was considering him for his successor. They were sure Wang was the ideal person to make the complaint. They never expected that Mao, with just a few words, would brusquely send him back. Not only had the mission failed, but they had provided Mao with food for thought. That meant the Fourth NPC meeting was sure to be stormy.

The impatient Jiang Qing, before she learned of Wang's fiasco, decided to strike while the iron was hot. Both in the morning and the evening of

October 18 she summoned Wang Hairong and Tang Wensheng to her residence in Diaoyutai to talk about the "Fengqing Steamer" incident.

Because Mao's health was poor, for a long time it was difficult to get to see him. Even Jiang Qing had to ask for permission first, and then she was frequently refused. She therefore tried to reach him through these two young women. Wang Hairong, vice-minister of Foreign Affairs, was related to Mao. Tang Wensheng was the daughter of the famous diplomat Tang Mingzhao. She had grown up in the United States, and was an excellent translator. The two often interpreted for Mao when he received foreign visitors. He held them in high regard. Jiang Qing hoped to use them as a transmission line of her complaints against Zhou Enlai and Deng Xiaoping.

Jiang Qing gave them an exaggerated account of what had happened between her and Deng Xiaoping in the Politburo meeting, claiming he had brought it to an end by walking out. She said the leaders in the State Council were always plotting, that the Premier, in the hospital, instead of concentrating receiving medical treatment, was very busy with other things. She said Deng, the Premier, and Marshal Ye Jianying stuck close together. The Premier was the power behind the scenes.

Zhang Chunqiao, who was also present, said to the two young women that the nation's finances and foreign trade were in the red as a result of the "fawning on foreigners" by the leaders of the State Council. He said that Deng Xiaoping's attitude toward the "Fengqing Steamer" incident was equivalent to that of persons who had fomented the "February Countercurrent".

Jiang Qing, Zhang Chunqiao and Yao Wenyuan urged the girls to "report" this to Mao Zedong.

The whole thing sounded fishy to them. The next day, October 19, they went to the hospital and told everything to Zhou Enlai. He had already been given a full account by Hua Guofeng, Ji Dengkui, Li Xiannian and Deng Xiaoping of what had happened at the Politburo meeting, and with regard to the "Fengqing Steamer" incident.

Zhou said, as he understood it, the situation was not as Jiang Qing described, in fact she and her gang were trying to discredit Deng

Xiaoping. They had done this several times before, and Deng had suffered in silence.

Wang Hairong and Tang Wensheng now had the matter straight.

On October 20, in Changsha, Mao Zedong received the Danish Prime Minister Poul Hartling. Deng Xiaoping accompanied the foreign guest to Changsha and took part in the reception.

After it ended, Wang Hairong and Tang Wensheng told Mao the story, as Zhou had recommended. Mao was incensed.

"The 'Fengqing Steamer' was a small question, and Xiannian had already settled it," he said angrily. "Why did Jiang Qing raise such a fuss!"

He told the two young women when they returned Beijing to say to Zhou Enlai and Wang Hongwen: "The Premier is still the Premier. Zhou and Wang Hongwen are responsible, together, for preparing for the Fourth NPC and the assignment of posts."

Mao was pleased that Deng had stood up to Jiang Qing. He recommended that Deng be made the First Vice-Premier, the Vice-Chairman of the Military Commission, and General Chief of Staff. He instructed Wang Hairong and Tang Wensheng to tell Wang Hongwen, Zhang Chunqiao and Yao Wenyuan not to tail after Jiang Qing and be always carping.

Zhou Enlai was stirred by Mao's message, and immediately set to work. He was well aware of his own declining health, and that his old comrades-in-arms were engaged in a life-and-death struggle with Jiang Qing. There was not a moment to lose.

He had a series of long conversations with Ye Jianying, Li Xiannian, and Wang Hongwen. He called three groups of Politburo members then in Beijing to meetings in the hospital, transmitted Mao's instructions, and wound up the "Fengqing Steamer" incident. He also found time to talk with Wang Hairong and Tang Wensheng.

On November 6, he wrote a letter to Mao reporting on the preparations for the Fourth NPC. He said: "The names of the delegates, the draft Constitution, and the speech on the work of the government, will all be completed by the November 11.... Around the end of the month a list of proposed appointees should also be ready.... I enthusiastically support your proposal that Deng Xiaoping be appointed First Vice-Premier and General Chief of Staff."

Mao wrote on the letter: "Approved."

The same day Zhou dispatched Wang and Tang back to Changsha to report to Mao on the condition of his health, and other matters. He spoke, the next day, with Li Xiannian who had just returned from Changsha, where he had accompanied a foreign visitor received by Mao. That evening, Zhou talked with Wang and Tang, who had then returned to Beijing. They told him Mao had again criticized Jiang Qing. On November 8, Zhou met with Li Xiannian and Ji Dengkui. On November 9 he talked with Wang Hongwen.

Deng Xiaoping, about to accompany the President of Yemen to Changsha to call on Mao Zedong, visited Zhou Enlai in the hospital. The two had a long talk.

After Mao finished receiving his guest on November 12, Deng told him about his confrontation with Jiang Qing in the Politburo the month before.

"She tries to force her views on others," Mao said. "I dislike that. You're showing some steel. Good!"

"I really couldn't take any more. This isn't the first time she's come at me," Deng said.

"I approve!"

"She's attacked me seven or eight times in the Politburo."

"Forcing her ideas on people. I don't like it." Mao pointed to Wang Hairong and Tang Wensheng, who were also present. "Neither do they."

"It seems to me there's not enough democracy in the Politburo," Deng said. "I intend to go to see her. I'll meet toughness with toughness."

"Very good."

"As to what my jobs will be, you have already spoken, and that should be the end of it. But aren't you piling too much on me?"

"It can't be helped. You'll just have to cope." Mao urged Deng to carry on with his jobs, and keep up the good work.

On Deng's return to Beijing, Deng Yingchao, wife of Zhou Enlai, came and described the Premier's medical condition. Not long after, Deng went to the hospital and told Zhou about his discussion with Mao Zedong. Zhou subsequently relayed this information to Ye Jianying.

While Zhou and Deng and their comrades were busy working night and day, Jiang Qing and her gang were not idle, either. Although Mao had criticized her interference in the "Fengqing Steamer" incident, and rejected her attempts to form the new State Council, and again recommended raising Deng to higher rank, Jiang Qing persisted. Her clique had Wang Hongwen fronting for them — the man Mao had assigned to collaborate with Zhou Enlai in organizing the Fourth NPC. Wang would provide an effective voice for the creation of their own State Council.

Jiang Qing wrote to Mao on November 12, proposing several individuals for specific posts. Mao replied the same day, rejecting them.

"Don't speak out personally so much," he berated her. "Don't criticize people's articles. Don't try to form the new cabinet. You've stirred up a lot of resentment. Create more harmony." Mao added a postscript: "To know oneself is precious."

In the guise of making a self-examination, Jiang Qing wrote to Mao again on November 19. "I fuss too much over things that don't concern me," she said. "It's because I haven't had anything to do since the Ninth Party Conference. I was not given any job."

Mao replied on November 20. "Your job is to study the domestic and international situation. That's an important responsibility. I've told you this many times. Stop saying you haven't any job."

Mao's words went in one ear and out the other. Jiang Qing asked Wang Hairong and Tang Wensheng to tell Mao again the names of the persons she recommended for appointments, and added that Wang Hongwen should be named vice-chairman of the Standing Committee of the NPC, to rank second only to Zhu De and Dong Biwu.

"Jiang Qing is ambitious," Mao said to Wang and Tang when they relayed these proposals. "She'd like to make Wang Hongwen Chairman of the Standing Committee and make herself Chairman of the Communist

Party."

He instructed Wang and Tang to tell Zhou Enlai this: Ranking after Zhu De and Dong Biwu in the Standing Committee of the NPC should be Soong Ching Ling. Deng Xiaoping, Zhang Chunqiao and Li Xiannian should be Vice-Premiers of the State Council. Zhou himself should determine other appointments.

Mao Zedong and Zhou Enlai decided that Deng Xiaoping should draft the Government Report to be delivered by Zhou at the Fourth National People's Congress. Zhou insisted he would stand while speaking, though his health was very poor. If the report was long, he would never be able to finish. Deng recommended that it be limited to 5,000 characters (about 2,000 words), divided into three sections. Mao agreed. More than 10 years had passed since the Third NPC. How to encompass so many important matters in such a short review and analysis?

Deng was determined to draft not only a good speech, but one that would be a milestone in Zhou Enlai's career of over 50 years in the revolution and more than 20 years as the Premier of the People's Republic of China. He succeeded brilliantly. The Report was factual, clear and succinct. Papa looked back with emotion on Zhou's delivery before thousands of delegates to the NPC.

"I drafted that speech," he said. "We didn't go over 5,000 characters. Zhou was too weak physically. He couldn't have read it all if it was long. I saw him frequently in those days."

In anticipation of the session, Zhou kept summoning people to the hospital to confer. The huge meeting required a great deal of preparation. Numerous reports had to be written. Even more important, a list had to be drawn up of proposed members of the Standing Committee of the Fourth NPC, the State Council, and their various subordinate organizations.

Zhou devoted the feeble flames of his remaining energy to the task. On November 25, while receiving a delegation led by Dr. Henry Kissinger, he said: "Vice-Premier Deng Xiaoping and Vice-Foreign Minister Qiao Guanhua, representing the Chinese government, will conduct the negotiations with you, this time, to give me an opportunity to rest."

After Mao Zedong proposed Papa for General Chief of Staff, responsibility for his affairs was shifted from the Office of the State Council to the Office of the General Chief of Staff. Huayuancun was too far out, and getting to work was inconvenient. The Staff Office began searching for a house.

In December, we went with Mama and looked at several prospects, but nothing seemed suitable. Finally, we found a place on the northeast corner of Kuanjie (Broad Street) — an old traditional compound that had recently been renovated. An assistant head of the Staff Office examined it. He pronounced it "too shabby". Then a Deputy Chief of Staff who had just returned to office inspected it. "Too spacious," he said.

We then looked at it ourselves. The buildings were neither new nor old, and they had lots of rooms. The location was easily accessible. Precisely what we wanted. This was in the middle of the Cultural Revolution. People with different experiences had different tastes. We moved into our new home in December, and we all got busy.

It was a hollow-square compound. The courtyard in the center was empty, without a shrub or a blade of grass. When the wind blew, dust swirled everywhere. Papa loved planting trees and flowers. Our old compound in Huayuancun had been full of them. In spring we had winter jasmine, Chinese flowering crabapple and cherry; in summer, Beijing mock-orange, rose, and plantain lily; in autumn gold and white chrysanthemums; in winter pine and cypress trees.

When we moved into Kuanjie it was already winter, but the whole family immediately began planning for next spring. Our courtyard would be just like Huayuancun — the same bushes and flowers and grass. Except for a few small paths, every inch of garden would be filled with colorful vegetation.

Papa was satisfied. "I can live out my remaining years here," he said.

We were confident that the move to Kuanjie would be our last. Little did we know that in the troubled years ahead we would move again, not just once but several times.

38

The Deep Significance of the Fourth National People's Congress

THE final preparatory discussions for the Fourth National People's Congress were held in mid-December, 1974. Jiang Qing and her gang wrangled noisily over appointments to government posts. She knew it was her last chance to intervene in the formation of the new State Council. No conclusions could be reached. Finally, Zhou Enlai drew up three alternative lists of names to be submitted to Mao Zedong. Against doctor's orders, he left the hospital and flew with Wang Hongwen to Changsha.

They met with Mao three times between December 23 and 27. A fourth time Zhou talked with the Chairman alone.

"Don't be a Gang of Four," Mao warned Wang Hongwen. "You'll fall if you form a faction. Jiang Qing is ambitious; can't you see that? I can. I told her three 'Don'ts' — 'Don't be always criticizing,' 'Don't push yourself forward,' and 'Don't take part in organizing the government'."

Mao said she and her gang should criticize themselves. He directed Wang Hongwen to sit down immediately and write out a self-criticism. At the same time he said one had to see "both sides" of Jiang Qing.

As to Deng Xiaoping, Mao said: "He's strong ideologically, a man of rare talents." And he added, turning to Wang Hongwen: "Much better than you."

He reiterated his wishes regarding major government appointments.

"Xiaoping should be the First Vice-Premier," he said, "Vice-Chairman of the Central Military Commission, and General Chief of Staff."

To Zhou Enlai and Wang Hongwen, he said: "You stay here and continue talking. Let Xiaoping take charge in Beijing. That Gang of Four stuff has to stop. There are a lot of people in the Central Committee. We must have unity."

"Premier Zhou is still our Premier," he said to Zhou Enlai. "Your health is no good. After the Fourth National People's Congress you must relax and take treatment. Leave the State Council to Xiaoping."

Regarding appointments to major offices, Mao said it would be better to convoke the second session of the 10th Central Committee of the Communist Party before holding the Fourth National People's Congress. Zhou Enlai agreed, and proposed that Deng Xiaoping be appointed a Standing Committee member of the Politburo or the Vice-Chairman of the Party Central Committee. Mao promptly approved. Deng should be a Vice-Chairman of the Party Central Committee, he said, and a Standing Committee member of the Politburo.

Mao also indicated his preferences in appointees to high government posts, and recommended that Zhang Chunqiao be named Director of the General Political Department of the PLA.

December 26, 1974, was Mao's 81st birthday. On that day he and Zhou Enlai had a private discussion. Mao talked at length on two subjects of special interest to him: — "the dictatorship of the proletariat" and "preventing and opposing revisionism". All his life Mao had looked for a means to their achievement. Now in his final years, he was still searching. But could he find one? Was it not a tragedy that he should be still obsessed to the very end?

With Zhou Enlai, his companion in battle of half a century, Mao talked of how necessary it was to liberate old cadres quickly, to restore harmony, to improve the national economy. Together, they worked out a list of appointments to be submitted to the Fourth National People's Congress.

Zhou knew this was probably his last chance to talk with Mao privately. He frankly raised the question of bad spots in Jiang Qing and Zhang Chunqiao's past. Mao said he already knew they both had committed serious political errors.

Yes, he knew, but he hadn't let that interfere with their starting the Cultural Revolution. He hadn't permitted anyone to speak of their unsavory past. Still less now, when the situation had reached its present confused state, would he allow the question to be raised. Had it been anyone else with such murky pasts, they would long since have been exposed and overthrown.

There were no standards of truth in the Cultural Revolution. Political expediency prevailed. Zhou's urgings had no effect on Mao. But the talk, between the two statesmen so profoundly important in China's political arena, did indeed exercise a major influence on the coming Fourth National People's Congress and on China's political future.

Generally speaking, Mao Zedong supported Zhou Enlai and Deng Xiaoping, and sternly criticized the Jiang Qing gang. But during the Cultural Revolution the unexpected constantly happened. The talks between Zhou Enlai and Mao Zedong had a direct bearing on whether the Party and nation would live or die. Their fate hinged on one man — Mao Zedong, on just one of his ideas.

Papa's long political experience, and many years of thought, taught him that to pin the future of the Party and the nation on a single individual was a questionable and dangerous course. At the same time he was well aware that a political situation of this sort was not the product of a single day, a single era, and certainly not a single event. It had its own deep, historical, complicated roots.

China had been a feudal society for 2,000 years. It had never passed through anything remotely resembling a democratic period, but had leaped directly into modern socialism. The nation, the people and society had to undergo a multi-faceted, brand new transformation in their thinking, their theories, their concepts and even their customs. This would take time; it could not be skipped over. And a cost would have to be paid, perhaps a very painful price.

Zhou Enlai flew back to Beijing on December 27, very weary but in high spirits. Mao had finalized the arrangements for the Fourth National People's Congress, including the appointments to office. At this critical juncture Mao had once again demonstrated his intelligence and skill, and steadied the political scales in a highly volatile situation.

The Second Session of the 10th Central Committee of the Communist Party met from January 8 to 10, 1975. It discussed the agenda of the coming Fourth National People's Congress, and offered suggestions for its consideration. The session confirmed Deng Xiaoping as a member of the Politburo, vice-chairman of the Central Committee, and a member of the Standing Committee of the Politburo.

Zhou Enlai spoke at the concluding session. He said he had asked Chairman Mao for a slogan, and Mao had proposed: "Stability and unity are best." The conference adopted this as its political foundation.

Mao wanted stability, the people of the entire nation wanted stability. The Cultural Revolution had been raging for over eight years, and the people had made up their minds. Mao thought his recent painstaking arrangements could bring stability about. He didn't realize that a political situation beset by dangers on all sides could not possibly be stabilized after eight years of turmoil by the decisions of a people's congress, no matter how well-balanced or willing to compromise. To say nothing of the fact that Zhou Enlai, Ye Jianying, Deng Xiaoping and Li Xiannian, representing the old revolutionaries on one side, and Jiang Qing, Zhang Chunqiao, Wang Hongwen, and Yao Wenyuan representing the Cultural Revolution Group on the other, had congealed into open antagonists as irreconcilable as fire and water. Any unity between them was impossible.

Actually, both sides were planning, through the meetings of the Fourth National People's Congress, to strengthen their respective political positions. The Jiang Qing gang hoped to increase their power so as to be better able to seize power after Mao died. The forces of Zhou Enlai and Deng Xiaoping wanted to correct the errors of the Cultural Revolution and repair the huge losses it had engendered.

The Fourth National People's Congress formally opened on January 13, 1975. All the lights were on in the 10,000-seat auditorium of the Great Hall of the People. The air was solemn. In the first row of the presidium Zhou Enlai and the older generation of revolutionary leaders sat on the right. Wang Hongwen and Jiang Qing sat on the left, representing the Cultural Revolution group. The two clearly contending camps no longer had any thought of concealment.

Premier Zhou Enlai read the "Report of the Government". Zhang Chunqiao read a report "On Amendments to the State Constitution".

As Zhou stepped to the speaker's podium, the 2,864 deputies to the National People's Congress greeted him with warm emotional applause. His speech called for the modernization of agriculture, industry, the armed forces and science and technology before the end of the century, thus moving China into the first ranks of the world economically. His ringing exhortation on behalf of the Chinese people brought tears to the eyes of the assembled deputies. Their thunderous applause expressed their deepest respect and admiration. The NPC approved both reports, and selected persons to fill leading positions in the NPC and in the People's Government.

This NPC served an important function in China's history. Although it was not able to solve the fundamental failings of the Cultural Revolution, thanks to the strenuous efforts of Zhou Enlai and Deng Xiaoping and those under them seeking justice, it accomplished a great deal, under the circumstances. The Four Modernizations target which the NPC set reflected the will of the people and encouraged them to build a modern nation. It defined the strategy for China's long-time advance.

Although Jiang Qing's gang was able to insert their people into control of the Ministry of Culture and the Ministry of Health, because Zhou Enlai and Deng Xiaoping were now stronger in the State Council, more experienced old cadres were able to join the Council in positions of leadership, creating a base for future all-out rectification.

39

Prelude to All-out Rectification

DESPITE the Fourth National People's Congress, and Mao's desire to restore tranquility and curb the extreme methods of the Cultural Revolution, the general political line and policy supported the "Leftist" errors. The Jiang Qing gang may not have achieved their aim of seizing full national power, but they gained important areas of control within the Party, the government and the military, everywhere creating disorder. Their own ranks were split into squabbling factions. Many forged links with local gangsters. Riots broke out, and pitched armed clashes.

The economy was at a low ebb. Factories were closed; trains didn't run; output plummeted. The political atmosphere and the work improved slightly in government organizations with the restoration of some old cadres. But it was difficult to get things done. There were innumerable impediments. Within the forces of the Cultural Revolution there was no end to sharp and irreconcilable differences.

Deng Xiaoping now had more important posts and duties than before the Cultural Revolution. It was clear that the aging Mao Zedong held him in high esteem. Mao respected his ability and integrity. He hoped that Deng would never demand a reappraisal of the charges made against him during the Cultural Revolution and oppose its line, that he would not stir things up and be overthrown again. Mao hoped that, like Zhou Enlai, Deng would bolster the State machinery of the huge People's Republic of China.

Deng did indeed keep his word that he would not demand a review of the charges against him. It was not because he was seeking some hidden advantage. It was because of his unfailing faith in the Party, his deep respect for Mao personally. In considering a problem, or when looking at history, or appraising a person's merits and shortcomings, Deng Xiaoping always employed a historical perspective, a dialectical perspective, a factual perspective, viewing the matter as a whole.

His attitude remained the same even after the Cultural Revolution ended, and he summed up what he had learned. He had sought to return to work, not to gain any personal power, and certainly not to prepare for the day when he could demolish the case against him. It was because he felt he had a historical responsibility. He openly opposed the errors of the Cultural Revolution; he hated the Gang of Four and Lin Biao for their crimes against the Party, the country and the people. He went back to work to correct the errors and repair the losses.

He knew he would meet impediments and risk dangers. He hoped Mao Zedong would repent the mistakes he made during the Cultural Revolution and rectify them. At the same time, Deng was mentally prepared. He would not be surprised if Mao disagreed with him. But he would do what he had to do, regardless of personal consequences. He was already 71. Not many people had the opportunity to start a new political career at that age, and one filled with political dangers, at that.

Time sped by like an arrow. He could no longer wait. He had to act quickly and decisively. He would be thorough, go all out. That was Deng Xiaoping's style.

On January 25, a week after the conclusion of the Fourth National People's Congress, Deng, as General Chief of Staff, summoned a meeting of officers of regimental level and above at the Headquarters of the General Staff of the PLA. He said that after Lin Biao assumed leadership of the armed forces in 1959, and particularly in his final years, the military fell into severe disarray. Many of its fine traditions were lost. "I think the overwhelming majority of our army comrades are dissatisfied with the present state of affairs," he said. "It is for this reason that Comrade Mao Zedong has called for the consolidation of the army.

"In recent years, our army has been confronted with a major new problem, factionalism,..." he said. "Unless factionalism is eliminated, stability and unity cannot be achieved... We must enhance Party spirit, eliminate factionalism, heighten the sense of discipline...." He said that the Headquarters of the General Staff, the General Political Department and the General Logistics Department would be the first to be consolidated.

Deng's point was clear, his attitude firm. He would strive to correct the errors of the Cultural Revolution, and launch an all-out rectification drive.

Jiang Qing's bid to form a State Council with Cultural Revolution Group members had failed. Mao had reprimanded her. Boiling with rage, she summoned Wang Hairong and Tang Wensheng and hysterically poured invective on every member of the Politburo. She urged them, when interpreting at Mao's receptions of foreign guests, to press her point of view on him.

They told Mao about this. "There's only one person she has any respect for," he said, "and that's herself."

"What about you?" they asked.

"She doesn't respect me, either." Mao thoroughly understood Jiang Qing. He added sadly: "She'll eventually break with everyone. Right now, some people are still flattering her. After I die, she's going to make trouble."

Mao ignored her. He concentrated on supporting Deng Xiaoping and trying to restore stability. He issued three directives: study the theory of the dictatorship of the proletariat, build stability and unity, and improve the national economy. Although Mao again emphasized class struggle in these directives, he also repeated his support for the work of Zhou Enlai and Deng Xiaoping. Deng adopted the directives as slogans for his rectification campaigns.

Jiang Qing and her gang couldn't bear to watch the fruits of their eight years of efforts begin crumbling away. Mao called for stability and unity. They began drawing lines for a battle to the death. They were not concerned about production, or the economy. They didn't care whether the ordinary people lived or died. Their main concern was how to counter-attack the forces of Deng Xiaoping.

In January 1975, almost at the same time when Deng Xiaoping, the new General Chief of Staff, made his speech on the consolidation of the army, Wang Hongwen told his confidents in Shanghai in private: "What I fear the most is that the army is not in our hands...." Wang's words showed the deep hatred the Gang of Four held for Deng.

Zhou Enlai placed his hopes on Deng. But he knew the continuing struggle would be fierce. Instead of devoting himself to receiving medical treatment, he spent much of his flagging energies on supporting Deng. Zhou asked him to draw up a list of new Vice-Premiers under the State Council, and define their divisions of labor.

"If he can't do it," Zhou said, "I will."

On February 1, at a meeting of the State Council, he announced the appointments of 12 Vice-Premiers. First Vice-Premier Deng Xiaoping would be in charge of foreign affairs. While Zhou Enlai was under medical care, Deng would preside over meetings and sign important documents on Zhou's behalf.

Zhou convened a meeting of 10,000 persons from the various departments and committees of the State Council. He reminded them that Mao had appraised Deng Xiaoping as a "man of rare talents", possessed of a "strong political ideology".

"I am ill," he said. "In future meetings of this sort, Comrade Xiaoping will preside. I hope there will be a new atmosphere in the new State Council, and that the Fourth Five-Year Plan, which starts this year, will achieve, and exceed, its targets."

Deng Xiaoping also addressed the meeting.

His most important duty as head of the State Council was to improve the economy, with particular emphasis on transport, coal and steel. Under the chaotic situation then prevailing it would be a truly difficult task.

The "criticizing Lin and Confucius" drive launched by the Jiang Qing gang caused further confusion. The limited stability so painfully restored was again disrupted. In some places there were riots. The leadership in several organizations was again paralyzed. The economy dipped lower.

During the first half of 1974 several local industrial enterprises were unable to meet their targets. Many steel, chemical and military-industrial products were far fewer than planned. Problems in coal production and rail transport were extremely serious.

Because production had dropped, so did government income, but expenses increased. Gross agricultural and industrial output in 1974 crept up only 1.4 percent over 1973, with industry rising only 0.3 percent, and agriculture increasing by 4.2 percent. Steel and coal production dropped. The overall economy was in the red.

The entire national economy had to be reorganized. But how? Industry, agriculture, commerce, finance, education, science and technology... were all in trouble. It wasn't enough to solve the problems of only one enterprise in one sphere; it was necessary to solve them all. Where to start?

It had always been Deng's habit to confront complicated problems coolly, to cut to the heart of the matter. He felt the fundamental question was in the top management, in the factionalism which infected it. A resolute struggle had to be waged against those ambitious individuals within the enterprise leadership greedy for personal privilege, scheming to seize power. Criticize those who had to be criticized, transfer those who needed to be removed. Don't give an inch!

Once this was solved, all of the formerly effective rules and systems had to be restored. Without them there could be no operating structure. Only with them could normal production be guaranteed. All else was empty talk.

This was what Deng Xiaoping decided upon as the opening wedge in his drive for all-out rectification.

40

The Railway Restoration Confrontation

THE national economy was suffering from thousands of ailments, and those of the railways were among the most serious. In February 1975, the major rail hubs in Xuzhou, Nanjing and Nanchang were virtually inoperable, delaying traffic along China's four main trunk lines Tianjin-Bengbu (Jinpu), Beijing-Guangzhou (Jingguang), Lianyungang-Lanzhou (Longhai) and Zhejiang-Jiangxi (Zhe'gan). This affected other trunk lines, severely harming industrial production and, to some extent, the lives of the people in the cities.

To restore the economy, Deng Xiaoping first had to invigorate its main artery — the railway network. Deng immediately set to work in his usual incisive manner.

At the State Council meeting in mid-February, he spoke heatedly the moment he entered the room. He said the railways were a mess. They had to be cleaned up. After a general discussion, he pounded the table. "We must start rectification right now," he said.

From February 25 to March 8, he called together the Communist Party secretaries responsible for industry in every one of the nation's provinces, cities and autonomous regions. The theme of their conference was how to solve the problem of rail transport.

"The whole Party must now give serious thought to our country's overall interest. What is that interest? The Reports on the Work of the Government at the First Sessions of the Third and Fourth National

People's Congresses both envisaged a two-stage development of our economy: The first stage is to build an independent and relatively comprehensive industrial and economic system by 1980. The second will be to turn China into a powerful socialist country with modern agriculture, industry, national defence and science and technology by the end of this century, that is, within the next 25 years. The entire Party and nation must strive for the attainment of this great objective. This constitutes the overall national interest.

"Chairman Mao has said that it is necessary to make revolution, promote production and other work and ensure preparedness in the event of war. I am told that some comrades nowadays only dare to make revolution but not to promote production. They say that the former is safe but the latter dangerous. This is utterly wrong. What is the actual situation in production? Agriculture appears to be doing comparatively well, but the per-capita grain yield is only 304.5 kilograms, grain reserves are small and the income of the peasants is pretty low.

"As for industry, it deserves our serious attention. Its existing capacity is not fully utilized, and its output last year was inadequate. This is the final year of the Fourth Five-Year Plan, and if production doesn't increase, we are sure to have difficulties in carrying out the Fifth Five-Year Plan. We must foresee that possibility and earnestly address this problem.

"How can we give a boost to the economy? Analysis shows that the weak link at the moment is the railways. If the problems in railway transport are not solved, our production schedules will be disrupted and the entire plan will be nullified. So the Central Committee is determined to solve this problem....

"To solve the problems of the railways, it is essential to strengthen centralized and unified leadership....

"The decision of the Central Committee also covers the formulation of essential rules and regulations, and a strengthening of the sense of organization and discipline. The present number of railway accidents is alarming. There were 755 major ones last year, some of them extremely serious...."

Deng continued with some warmth:

"The decision of the Central Committee also includes instructions on combating factionalism. Factionalism now seriously jeopardizes our overall interest. This question must be brought before all personnel and explained to them clearly as a major issue of right and wrong. It is no use tackling specific problems unless we have first settled this general issue. Persons engaging in factional activities should be re-educated and their leaders opposed. Generally speaking, such leaders can be divided into two categories. One category consists of persons who are obsessed by factionalism, have engaged in factional activities for several years and have lost their sense of right and wrong. For them, Marxism, Mao Zedong Thought and the Communist Party have all disappeared. If they correct their mistakes, then we will let bygones be bygones, but if they refuse to mend their ways, they will be sternly dealt with.

"The second category consists of a few bad elements. They can be found in all lines of work in every province and city. They fish in troubled waters by capitalizing on factionalism and undermining socialist public order and economic construction. They take advantage of the resulting confusion to speculate and profiteer, grabbing power and money. Something must be done about such people....

"If the pros and cons are clearly explained to them (Chinese railway workers), the overwhelming majority of railway personnel will naturally give their support. So the mobilization drive in March should be thorough, with the issues made clear to everyone, including the family members of railway personnel and the peasants living along the railway lines.

"The experience gained in handling the problems in railway work will be useful to the other industrial units....

In conclusion, Deng said: "Clear-cut policies should be worked out for tackling existing problems. We should bear the overall interest of the country in mind and solve these problems without delay. How much longer can this be put off? How can we afford to delay in advancing the cause of socialism?"

Deng's speech was a manifesto against the "Leftist" errors of the

Cultural Revolution. It was a declaration of full-scale war.

The Central Committee then issued a resolution incorporating the essence of what Deng had said. Deng designated Wan Li, who had recently been restored to his post as Minister of Railways, to head the rectification. The Ministry, by telephone conference, notified all of its departments of the Central Committee resolution, and other documents. The departments, in turn, conveyed the resolution to every worker and employee of the railways, as well as the members of their families. The Central Committee and Ministry of Railways were confident of general support.

The most serious problem in the railway network, and where factionalism was at its worst, was in the Xuzhou Bureau — the major hub on the Huaihai area. Factionalism was rife, and evildoers had taken control. Damage to production and transport had been severe. In 21 months the Xuzhou Railway Bureau had not once met its quota under the national plan.

Since ancient times Xuzhou had always been of strategic importance. Attackers had to occupy it in order to win. Thirty years before, Deng Xiaoping, commanding an army of 600,000, had defeated a Kuomintang host many times its size. Today, he was again leading the forces of justice, on the same battleground he knew so well, in a showdown with the factional rebels of the Cultural Revolution.

On Deng's orders, on March 10, Wan Li, the Minister of Railways, marched into Xuzhou as the head of a work team. Wan Li convened a mass meeting of 10,000 people, and explained the message of the Central Committee resolution against factionalism. He called for a "people's war" to rectify the operation of the railways.

At the same time the Ministry sternly criticized those leaders within the Xuzhou Bureau who had been guilty of serious factional activities, and set a time limit within which they had to reform. If they failed to do so, decisive action would be taken against them. They could be fired, or transferred.

As to those who deliberately incited factional strife, such as armed clashes and work stoppages, they would be dealt with severely. Deng

Xiaoping personally endorsed the warrant for the arrest of Gu Benhua, head of Xuzhou's extreme factionalists.

A series of measures made a clean sweep. The situation was quickly turned around. With the support of the majority of the people, the Xuzhou Railway Bureau vastly improved rail shipping. By the end of April it completed its national transport quota three days ahead of schedule. The same pattern was followed in 20 different railway bureaus. Even Nanchang, the last and most difficult hold-out because it had been supported by certain elements within the provincial government, was finally resorted to normal operation by June.

The solution of the problem of the railways not only removed a major obstacle to the development of the national economy; it set up a clear and successful model for rectification in every field. It was Deng's first engagement against the errors of the Cultural Revolution since becoming acting head of the State Council. Even more, it was a declaration of war against Jiang Qing's forces of the Cultural Revolution, an initial victory in the campaign for rectification throughout the land.

Deng Xiaoping had been back in office for only a little over a year. Mao Zedong had given him high rank in the Party, the government, and the military. With the support of Zhou Enlai, Deng had plunged into rectification with banners flying, arousing in Jiang Qing and her Cultural Revolution cohorts jealousy, anger, and some fear. They saw his success as their greatest danger. They watched Deng carefully, and used every possible means to impede him. Their latest effort was an assault on what they called "empiricism."

All during the next few weeks they wrote polemics against it, and issued statements, topped by Jiang Qing's cry that it was the "accomplice of revisionism", that it was the "main enemy". Actually the furor was a veiled attack on Zhou Enlai, Ye Jianying, Deng Xiaoping and other old comrades who had long practical experience, and who were working to correct the "Leftist" excesses of the Gang of Four.

The cancer in Zhou Enlai's body spread. On March 26, a malignant tumor was removed from his abdomen. In anticipation of the operation, he examined all documents awaiting his decision, and directed that future matters be turned over to Deng Xiaoping. As soon as he was able to receive visitors again, in April, he discussed pending issues with Deng on three different occasions. Weak as he was, he again offered his encouragement and support.

Jiang Qing, in mid-April, raised the question of "empiricism" at a meeting of the Politburo, and demanded that it be discussed. Deng Xiaoping brusquely opposed her request.

Mao Zedong, who had returned to Beijing, received his old friend and comrade in arms Kim Il Sung, leader of Democratic People's Republic of Korea and its Workers' Party, on April 18. It was an emotional occasion for both of them.

"Comrade Dong Biwu is gone," Mao said, "and the Premier is ill. So are Comrades Kang Sheng and Liu Bocheng. I'm not well, either. I'm 82, this year. I haven't got much longer. We're depending on people like you."

Mao pointed at Deng Xiaoping, who was also present.

"I don't want to talk about political affairs," he said. "You can talk with him about them. His name is Deng Xiaoping. He knows how to fight wars, and he knows how to fight revisionism. The Red Guards attacked him, but now there's no problem. He was forced out of office for several years, but today he's back. We need him."

After the reception was over, Deng told Mao about Jiang Qing's assault on "empiricism". He said he disputed her allegation that it was the "main enemy" today. Mao said he agreed with Deng.

Mao knew about the battle between Deng and the old cadres versus the Jiang Qing clique, and he was observing both sides closely. Deng had successfully straightened out the railways. But the Jiang Qing gang did nothing but oppose him, without a let-up. This was completely at odds with Mao's call for peace and stability. Mao felt it was time to put a stop to Jiang Qing's raving.

A statement by him appeared in the press on April 23. It read: "What we should oppose is revisionism, which includes empiricism and a doctrinaire approach. Both are forms of revisionism. You shouldn't just stress one and neglect the other." Mao continued: "Not many people in our Party understand Marxism. Some think they do, but they don't really know much. They lecture others at the drop of a hat. That itself shows a lack of understanding of Marxism. I recommend that the Politburo discuss this matter."

The Politburo convened a meeting on April 27 at which Ye Jianying and Deng Xiaoping both spoke, sharply criticizing Jiang Qing and Zhang Chunqiao for their campaign against empiricism, and all the factional strife the Gang of Four had incited over the past few years. Because Mao Zedong had demanded it, Jiang Qing had no choice but to make a "self-criticism".

Both sides knew, however, that the dispute was by no means over. Zhou Enlai, in the hospital, was very concerned. He asked Deng, and others who had been at the meeting, for a detailed report of what had transpired.

Ye and Deng were prepared for the intense struggle to continue. Jiang Qing, smarting from her criticism, was entirely unrepentant. Both sides prepared for battle.

41
Mao Zedong Criticizes
the Gang of Four

THE Gang of Four were very distressed by Mao's criticism of Jiang Qing and the self-criticism she had been forced to make at the Politburo meeting. They talked it over and decided to have Wang Hongwen serve as their spokesman. He was new, and had been raised to prominence by Mao personally. His words surely would carry some weight. They had him write to Mao, in the form of a report on the just concluded meeting of the Politburo, and lay out their charges. Wang's letter slandered Zhou Enlai, Ye Jianying and Deng Xiaoping, claiming that they had exaggerated the situation, and that they had permitted and supported the circulation of the vilest rumors.

"They have been saying what has been inconvenient for the Premier to say aloud," Wang alleged, referring to Ye and Deng. "Their aim is to overturn the verdict of the meeting of last December."

Wang's letter annoyed Mao. He had just criticized Jiang Qing's clique for their assault on "empiricism", and now they were clamoring again. He couldn't permit this to go on. To put an end to the conflict, he would have to come forward himself. On May 3 he convened a meeting of the members of the Politburo then in Beijing, and made his position clear.

"I was wrong not to have read Chunqiao's article carefully," he said "You hate only pragmatists, but you don't hate doctrinaires. It seems to me the ones criticizing empiricism are themselves the ones who worship

302

it. They don't have much of an understanding of Marxism...Jiang Qing herself is a small worshiper of empiricism...."

Mao then directly addressed his remarks to Jiang Qing and her cohorts. "Don't be a Gang of Four, don't do it," he urged. "What's the point? Why can't you unite with the other more than 200 members of the Central Committee? Being a carping minority is no good. It never has been. Don't be so irresponsible. Be disciplined, discrete; don't insist that others accept your point of view. If you have arguments, raise them in the Politburo. Documents should only be issued in the name of the Central Committee, not in the name of an individual. I never permit documents to be issued in my name. I have never sent in any material....

"Be disciplined. The armed forces must be cautious. Members of the Central Committee should be even more cautious.... I spoke with Jiang Qing, and I spoke with Xiaoping. Wang Hongwen has asked to see me, and Jiang Qing has telephoned for an appointment. I refused to see them. If they want to come, let everyone come together....

"That's it. Sorry. That's how I am. I have nothing to add. I have only three axioms. Whether at the Ninth or the 10th Congress they would be the same: Marxism not revisionism, unity not division, and open-mindedness not conspiracy."

Mao Zedong criticized Jiang Qing and her gang, but he didn't touch on the root of their errors. While he directed them to make self-criticisms, at the same time he said: "It seems to me their error is not serious. There is no need to blow it up. Since there is a question, it should be discussed. If it can't be settled in the first half of this year, then maybe in the second. If not this year, then maybe the next. If not next year, then maybe the year after."

Mao was going on 83. Because he had cataracts on both eyes, he couldn't read. His life was nearing its end. It was unusual under such circumstance for him to call a meeting and attempt to mediate. Obviously he wanted to put an end to the turmoil, but his health wouldn't permit it. It showed that the Jiang Qing clique, although retaining a modicum of respect for Mao personally, had nothing to fear. They had no regard for anyone.

It also showed that Mao could only bring about a superficial amelioration, in no way affecting the fundamentals. This was the last time Mao Zedong summoned and appeared at the Politburo. His ailments worsened as his life drew to its final stage.

The next day, on May 4, Zhou Enlai came out of the hospital and convened a meeting of the Standing Committee of the Politburo in the Great Hall of the People to discuss the essence of Mao's speech on May 3. Wang Hongwen, Ye Jianying, Deng Xiaoping and Zhang Chunqiao attended. After the meeting Zhou supervised the drafting of a resolution calling for the study of Mao Zedong's theories and for an examination of the work of the Politburo. Zhou firmly endorsed Mao's criticism of the Jiang Qing clique.

"Those who have committed errors should criticize themselves," he said. "I agree with Comrade Deng Xiaoping's ideas. People who wish to criticize themselves should do so. They can say a little or say a lot, or say nothing at all. No one should be forced."

Zhou continued the discussions on May 8. It was agreed to call a meeting of the entire Politburo after Deng Xiaoping returned from his visit to France.

It was clear to Zhou that Mao's criticism of the Jiang Qing clique presented a rare opportunity. Although the Gang of Four might not change fundamentally, they at least would have to draw in their horns. This would provide Deng with an excellent chance to continue his push for thorough rectification. It was an occasion not to be missed.

Deng Xiaoping, Vice-Premier of the People's Republic of China, in response to the invitation of the French Republic, paid a friendly visit to that country from May 12 to 17. It was the first time since the two countries established diplomatic relations in 1964 that a Chinese leader paid a formal state visit to France.

The United States and the Soviet Union, the two superpowers, were then locked in a cold war. Between them was Europe, as a special area of contention. The nations of Europe, for historic and present practical reasons, were involved in an extremely complicated and unstable situation. All of Europe was divided into two spheres of influence of the two great powers.

Of the major countries in Western Europe, Britain was a United State's faithful follower. Germany was split into eastern and western sections. France was then the largest independent nation in Europe. After the end of World War II, under the leadership of General de Gaulle, despite a highly convoluted international situation, France managed to maintain its nationalist independent spirit, and its important position in European and world affairs. At a time when the West — the United States in particular — was hewing to its anti-communist line, France was the first country to establish diplomatic relations with New China. From then on, the two nations maintained friendly ties.

President Georges Pompidou paid China a friendly visit in 1973, and met with Chinese leaders Mao Zedong and Zhou Enlai. Relations between the leaders of the two countries became increasingly cordial from then on. The present visit by the Chinese delegation was a further evidence of the friendship between the two lands.

In an age of cold war between East and West, with the US and the Soviet Union as the two superpowers seeking to rule the world, Mao Zedong demonstrated the brilliance of his global thinking. He decided to first revive dialogues between China and the US, then restore normal relations with Japan, thereby opening a new diplomatic front, and enabling us to become a political weight on the scale of international relations which could not be ignored. Secondly, Mao determined to strengthen ties with France, allowing China to adopt a still more positive stance and play a livelier role in international politics.

Because Zhou Enlai was ill, Mao selected Deng Xiaoping to head the official Chinese delegation to France. He wanted to use this opportunity to push Deng forward on the international political stage. This was another important manifestation of Mao's wish for Deng to play an even more important role in China's future political life.

The special plane landed in France in the early morning of May 12. After an impressive welcoming ceremony, the short Chinese visitor walked upon the red carpet reserved for honored guests. Fifty years before, when he was a student in a work-study program in France he had entered the spiritual halls of revolution. French gendarmes had watched and pursued him. The young revolutionary had left France, still being hunted by the French police. Today, he had returned as a guest of the French government and had received a warm welcome.

Life has many twists and turns. Our fate is misty, unpredictable, and full of surprises.

No sooner had he again set foot on French soil again than Deng Xiaoping plunged into a whirl of diplomatic activities. The French government gave an imposing welcome to the Chinese government delegation which he led. Although Deng came as a Vice-Premier, he was afforded the full ceremonies reserved for a head of state. President Valery Giscard-d'Estaing and Prime Minister Jacques Chirac both had individual meetings with him. D'Estaing hosted a welcoming banquet and directed that he be accommodated in the Maragny.

These unusual courtesies clearly indicated that the French government considered this Chinese political figure, who had just been extricated from the grip of the Cultural Revolution fanatics, a rising star in China's political firmament.

Deng Xiaoping exchanged views with the French leaders on major international issues, and on enhancing relations between the two countries. It was agreed to increase political discussions, and further develop commercial trade.

The mission returned to China on May 17. Although the visit had lasted only five days, it was very successful. From a national point, it implemented Mao's diplomatic strategy. For Deng personally it meant that, like his attendance the previous year representing China at the UN, his mission to France confirmed his status as a world-ranking political figure.

After discussion, Mao Zedong and Zhou Enlai decided that Deng Xiaoping, in addition to heading the Politburo, should also take charge of the general work of the Central Committee. Obviously, Mao's trust and confidence in Deng had increased. It might be said that Mao to a large extent now felt that Deng was qualified to be his successor.

The Politburo, in keeping with Mao Zedong's wishes, held meetings on May 27 and June 3 to discuss what Mao had talked about in the Politburo meeting of May 3, and to "help" Jiang Qing and her coterie. Ye Jianying, Li Xiannian and Chen Xilian severely criticized the Gang of Four. Jiang Qing and Wang Hongwen, near the end of the session, had no choice but to criticize themselves. Later, they felt obliged to submit self-criticisms in writing.

Mao supported Deng and criticized Jiang Qing because he wanted to halt her wild behavior, prevent the Gang of Four from impeding "stability and unity", and provide an atmosphere in which Deng could do his work. Mao had no intention of toppling Jiang Qing. He hoped, rather, that as a result of this criticism, she would retract a bit, and Deng would be satisfied. Even more, he hoped that the tension between them would be vitiated, that they would cooperate, or at least not continue to clash.

With this in mind, Mao told Jiang Qing to go and have a talk with Deng Xiaoping. She had no choice but to get off her high horse and "respectfully" visit him at home as a gesture of her "sincerity".

When we heard she was coming to our house on Kuanjie, the whole family went into a state of high alert. Mama ordered us to stay in our rooms and not come out. If Jiang Qing asked to see the rest of the house, and we met her, we were to be very careful in what we said. Remember, one careless remark could cause a lot of trouble. It was as if we were preparing for the plague. All the windows and doors were shut. We battened down in tight preparedness.

Peeping through the curtains, we saw her arrive. She wore a hat and a long overcoat. Chest out and head high, she marched in a haughty affected manner. Papa waited in the parlor. He did not come forth to greet her. Even Mama stayed in her room. Jiang Qing entered the parlor and talked with her "antagonist" Deng Xiaoping. Their discussion was brief. Jiang Qing emerged. Papa did not see her off. That was how she came, and that was how she left. They had not argued, but had settled none of the differences between them.

As Papa later said: "Jiang Qing came to see me. Chairman Mao told her to, and she dared not refuse. Our talk didn't go well. She blew her usual trumpet. Pretty low quality stuff."

Both of them knew in advance that they differed on basics. No single talk could bring them together.

Jiang Qing seethed with hatred to the marrow of her bones after having been criticized by Mao Zedong, but on the surface she put on a show of warmth. She was a very mercurial person. Some nerve in her head must have twitched, and she came up with a new fantasy. Although she had inveighed against "restoration of the ancient", and had attacked Confucius, now she suddenly professed a love of Tang Dynasty costumes. Probably she felt Mao Zedong would soon be passing away, and then she could take over as an emperor like Wu Zetian in the Tang Dynasty (618-907). But when a woman emperor mounted the throne she needed to have ceremonial robes. And so Jiang Qing dreamed up a costume in what she considered Tang Dynasty style.

Actually it was a concoction that was neither here nor there, and very ugly. Jiang Qing thought it was beautiful. She designed it herself and wore it herself. She boasted about it, and touted it wherever she went. Since she was supposed to be demonstrating her "warmth" toward people like Deng Xiaoping, she introduced it to Mama and Li Xiannian's wife Lin Jiamei, and urged them to have a few similar ones made.

It was an awkward situation. The two ladies didn't like it at all. Mama, in particular, didn't want to go to Jiang Qing's house to take measurements and talk about choosing materials. Jiang Qing's haughty airs disgusted her. But under those special circumstances Mama had to go even though it distressed her.

She had a few "Tang style" costumes made and brought them home. We all tried them on, strutting around in the exaggerated postures of Peking Opera, and choking with laughter. The weird garments provided rare moments of merriment in tense and serious times.

During the face-to-face clashes with the Gang of Four in April and May 1975, Zhou Enlai played an active role, despite his illness. He kept tabs on what was going on through his talks with all of the principal players (before and during the meetings). On June 7 he sent a report to Mao Zedong via Wang Hairong and Tang Wensheng.

Wang Hongwen was dispatched to Shanghai to "help with the work", in keeping with Mao's intention to break up the Gang of Four. Jiang Qing submitted a written self-criticism on June 28. Zhang Chunqiao, Yao Wenyuan and Wang Hongwen also superficially admitted their mistakes. Zhou Enlai forwarded Jiang Qing's self-criticism to Mao and members of the Politburo then in Beijing, endorsing a comment of welcome. Deng Xiaoping and Ye Jianying added a note that they "agree with the Premier". Mao read the document and marked a circle, indicating his approval.

Temporarily, the imperious, conceited Jiang Qing was quelled. Forced to control herself, she did not appear in public for a considerable time.

In June, after receiving a foreign guest, Mao had a talk with Deng Xiaoping. They discussed the recent criticism of Jiang Qing in the Politburo.

"I think it was successful," Mao said. "The matter was brought into the open."

"But in the end, they denied there was a Gang of Four," said Deng. "The Politburo comrades were very angry. I urged them not to pursue it any further."

"That was right. Leave them a little ground. As long as everyone is clear about it, that's enough. I want to talk to Wang Hongwen. From what you say, his prestige is not high."

"Many comrades in the Politburo felt his final statements were not honest."

"Jiang Qing doesn't like him, either. She constantly complains to me about him. You ought to work on him," Mao said. Referring to the Gang of Four, Mao continued: "They had some merit in the past — they opposed Liu Shaoqi, they opposed Lin Biao. Now, they're no good. They oppose the Premier, and Deng Xiaoping, and Marshal Ye, and Chen Xilian. Tell Zhuang Zedong to go to Chen Xilian if he has any problems, and stay away from Wang Hongwen and Jiang Qing."

Deng said: "The wind is going to change soon in the Politburo."

"Marshal Ye recommended you for General Chief of Staff. I approved," Mao said. "'The breeze will surely bring out the fragrance of the grove,'" he quoted, reflecting his high hopes for Deng. "You must do your job well."

"I am determined to do so."

With the support of Mao Zedong and Zhou Enlai, Deng and the old revolutionary comrades won a temporary victory. Although the war was far from over, and although the coming struggles would be even more complicated and intense, the success did provide a firm foundation for Deng's efforts to effectuate a full-scale rectification.

42

All-out Rectification

WIELDING a big axe, Deng Xiaoping, backed by Mao Zedong and Zhou Enlai, continued to hew out a path to full rectification.

In April 1975, on the recommendation of Zhou Enlai and Deng Xiaoping, the Central Committee issued a decision that set free more than 300 high-ranking cadres from confinement. They were provided for and given medical treatment, and received salary arrears. A number were given work assignments.

On May 17, Mao Zedong ordered a special disposition of the cases against Red Army veterans He Cheng and Fu Lianzhang. Deng Xiaoping had forwarded to Mao a letter he received from He Cheng's daughter. On the letter, Mao wrote an endorsement: "He Cheng is innocent. Of course he must be given a new assignment. All slanderous statements against him must be expunged.... Fu Lianzhang was hounded to death. Fu must be cleared. He Cheng fortunately is still alive, but Fu is interred in the ground. What a tragedy!"

A tragedy indeed! He Cheng and Fu Lianzhang had been doctors in the old Red Army. During the years of war they saved the lives of countless revolutionary fighters, but they themselves were tortured by villains in times of peace. Truly heart-breaking! Mao Zedong's endorsement in effect commended the efforts by Zhou Enlai and Deng Xiaoping to liberate the old cadres, and thereby created better conditions for implementing Party policy. It was an important step forward.

Deng, at the same time, made considerable progress in clearing up the problems saturating the fields of culture, education, the steel industry, military industry, and the armed forces.

With the railways running again, Deng Xiaoping zeroed in on steel production. In April, after hearing a report on the serious problems bedeviling the industry, he said angrily: "To let this go on would be sheer sabotage. The time has come to straighten out steel." He proposed calling a national conference.

Between May 8 and 29, Deng presided over meetings in Beijing, summoned by the Central Committee, of Communist Party secretaries responsible for steel production in 17 provinces, municipalities and autonomous regions, plus the heads of 11 major steel mills, together with the leaders of related divisions of the State Council.

The first to speak was Minister of Railways Wan Li, who told how they rectified operations in his industry. Ye Jianying, Li Xiannian and Gu Mu also spoke. Deng Xiaoping analyzed the situation in his usual incisive manner.

In his speech, Deng pinpointed key problems confronting the iron and steel industry that must be solved.

"The main cause of our sluggish iron and steel production is the leadership, which is weak, lazy and lax. That of the Ministry of Metallurgical Industry is weak... The quality of the leading groups varies from one factory or enterprise to another. Some are lax, which is a failing related to factionalism. One of the major problems with cadres at present is that they are afraid to touch thorny issues, to touch a tiger's backside... A leading group is like a command post, and efforts to boost production, carry on scientific research or combat factionalism are all like military operations. If the command post is weak, the operations cannot be effective.... Unless the matter (the questions of the leading groups) is properly handled, it will be difficult even to begin to move, let alone to lead the masses forward..."

The next was to combat factionalism.

"The leadership must be clear-cut and firm in its opposition to factionalism. How long can we afford to wait for persons who have wrought havoc with the Party's cause to recognize their mistakes? Courage is of primary importance here. Those who cling to factionalism should be transferred to other posts, criticized or struggled against whenever necessary. We should not drag things out and wait forever. Moreover, we should call on the masses to join in the effort against factionalism... The way to deal with these people is to mobilize the masses to struggle against them, and not give an inch... We must have faith in the masses. We must bring the documents of the Central Committee directly to them so that its line is truly made known to every family, including housewives and children, and the initiative of the masses against factionalism is thus brought into play..."

Deng foresaw the complications in fighting factionalism. "I certainly don't mean to say that no one is opposed to them (measures fighting the factionalism)... Individuals who express such views do exist. But don't be afraid of them. If we take a clear-cut attitude and have correct policies, the situation will be easy to handle...

"As the experience of the railway departments and of the city of Xuzhou and other areas shows, the number of those who should be made targets of attack in the struggle against factionalism is very small... We must be determined to win in our anti-factionalist struggle...

"After the aforementioned matters have been well handled, the next step is to mobilize the masses to establish and improve essential rules and regulations... In recent years, there have really been no rules and regulations to speak of, and many problems have consequently arisen... Discipline in some factories is very lax. The personnel may or may not come to work and may or may not observe the regulations. It should be clearly stated that although previous instances of this kind may be excused, no recurrence will henceforth be tolerated... In enforcing the rules and regulations, it is better to be a bit on the strict side; otherwise, they cannot be properly established.

"In a word, there is a lot to be done to improve the production of iron and steel. In my opinion, it is most important to pay special attention to the points I have discussed."

By using Mao Zedong's exhortations — to study political theory, seek stability and unity, and improve the national economy — as weapons, Deng waged a firm struggle against the Gang of Four. Though not very long, his speech was clear and to the point.

The Central Committee made changes in the leadership of the Ministry of Metallurgical Industry, and the State Council set up a special committee for the iron and steel industry. In less than a month of restructuring, steel production showed signs of improvement. Daily output exceeded the daily average called for in the national plan. By the end of June reform of the metal industries produced initial results.

Restructuring the defense industries began in March. As with other enterprises the most serious problems stemmed from factionalism and the scramble for control among the chieftains of the rebel groups. The Office of National Defense Industry adopted a tactic of "luring the tigers down from the mountains", that is, it summoned all of these chieftains to Beijing for a meeting. Study sessions were set up. Persons with technological skills or managerial experience were put in charge of special units. Production began to improve.

At a meeting of key defense enterprises convened in April, Deng Xiaoping stressed that they must shorten their battle lines, simplify their formations, strengthen centralized control, grasp scientific research.

The Standing Committee of the Central Military Commission met in May to discuss the strategic missile research being conducted by the State Commission of Science, Technology and Industry for National Defense. It proposed that first priority be given to inter-continental missiles.

From July 20 to August 4 the Central Committee again convened a conference to discuss the restructuring of the defense industries. Ye Jianying, Deng Xiaoping and Li Xiannian all spoke. Deng addressed the meeting on August 3. He reiterated the three guidelines laid down by the Central Committee: Form a courageous leadership body; insist on quality; give devoted care to the people's livelihood. Li Xiannian, in his speech, emphasized the necessity for a responsibility system and a normal production schedule.

After this conference, thanks to united efforts, the defense industries were more orderly, and there was an overall improvement in production.

At the same time the railway, steel and defense industries were being restructured the State Council conducted a series of meetings between June 16 and August 11 on re-planning of the national economy. Leaders in all branches evolved specific measures designed to restructure the economy and speed its advance.

Several months of firm, efficient rectification in the first half of 1975 turned the economy around. In October the Central Committee published a report from the State Council. It said: "Since March industrial production and communications and transportation have improved month by month. Oil, coal, electricity, chemical fertilizer, cement, internal combustion engines, paper and paperboard, and rail shipments in May and June, reached record heights. Defense industry production was also quite good. National industrial output in the first half year achieved 43 percent of the annual target. We balanced the budget, in fact we were a little over."

In only six months, restructuring and hard work reversed the nationwide chaos and stalled industry resulting from the Cultural Revolution. Industrial production looked much better.

Clearly, the damage inflicted by the Cultural Revolution was not irreversible. Production was up, the people's livelihood was improved. If it hadn't been for the Cultural Revolution, if all ranks of society had gone all out during the previous nine years, we would have shucked off poverty and advanced toward prosperity.

Nine years earlier the economic foundations of our neighbor Japan were not much better than our own. But during the nine years of our chaotic Cultural Revolution, Japan vastly improved its economy and high technology so that it became one of the leading nations of the world, while we remained still striving to reverse our socio-economic disorder. The Cultural Revolution lost us nine years. That was much too long. The price our nation, our people, had to pay was far too high!

Nine years was like a dream, and when we awoke we found there had been a huge change in the world. Science and technology in the developed countries had taken a big step forward. Their productive capacity had improved rapidly. Their industrial power had greatly strengthened. Some formerly backward developing countries next-door had also recorded eye-opening advances. A few neighboring lands economically had already left us far behind.

How could we help being uneasy? There were people who said Deng Xiaoping was in too much of a hurry with his rectification drive. Yes, he was in a hurry. How could he be otherwise? After six years of a grueling wait he finally had been able to emerge. After difficult and dangerous struggles he at last had the authority and the means to put rectification into motion. He was already 71, and the political battles were still very risky. Many disturbing things still loomed on the horizon. Time, opportunity, were of the utmost importance. He had to make the best of them in order to pay his debt to the nation and the people. He had to grasp what might very well be his last opportunity.

He had to be firm, efficient, and thorough, with no vacillation. He knew that he would anger the forces of the Cultural Revolution, and, very likely, displease Mao Zedong as well. But he had decided on this path after years of consideration. It was the path he would have to follow, regardless of the consequences to his political future, or to his very life.

From the day the Chinese Communist Party was formed, its principle was that political power comes out of the barrel of a gun. For an all-embracing national rectification it was necessary that the army be rectified. From June 24 to July 15 the Central Military Commission met at a conference in Beijing. Attending were the leaders of all of the PLA headquarters departments, the heads of every branch of service, and the deans of the major military colleges and academies — a total of over 70 people. Discussion centered on correcting working style, compressing the size of the armed forces, revising the tables of organization, and providing for cadres in excess of quota. Ye Jianying, Deng Xiaoping, Xu Xiangqian and Nie Rongzhen spoke at the conference.

Ye sternly assailed the Gang of Four for stirring up factional discord and casting a pall over the entire country. He said Jiang Qing was scheming to get her hooks into the army and turn it upside down. "You've got to resist the gang!" he cried to the assembled audience.

Deng Xiaoping spoke on July 14. He said that due to the sabotage of the Lin Biao gang, the army had been plagued with problems that Deng summed up in five words: "bloating, laxity, conceit, extravagance and inertia."

"That is what the armed forces have to rectify," he said. "They must resolutely oppose factionalism and return to their glorious traditions."

The Military Commission, he said, had two tasks: First, to supervise the rectification. Second, to prepare against war. Tables of organization, armaments, strategy — all had to be correct. From the highest to the lowest, every leadership unit had to go through rectification. They had to earn respect, show courage.

"At present, whether the undesirable tendencies in the PLA can be overcome and whether the fine traditions of so many years can be carried forward depend mainly on how much we older comrades can do to help and guide the young and middle-aged cadres and pass on our experience to them. In my view, if we all set an example by following Comrade Mao Zedong's motto, 'unity, alertness, conscientiousness, liveliness', we will find that the problems in our army are not hard to solve, and that the line, principles and policies of the Party can be implemented effectively."

Near the end of the conference Marshal Ye had a private talk with the top generals. He relayed Mao Zedong's criticism of the Gang of Four, which, he said, Mao called the "Shanghai Mafia". Ye urged the generals to be vigilant, maintain calm in the ranks, and order in the command.

On July 15, Ye reported the results of the conference to Mao. On July 19, with Mao's approval, the Central Committee issued the conference documents and the speeches made by Ye Jianying and Deng Xiaoping. The message from the conference was warmly accepted by army commanders on every level.

After the conference, under Ye's supervision, the leadership units of all the large military contingents instituted rectification, and effectively stymied the scheme of the Gang of Four to seize power in the armed services. This was something dearly coveted by Jiang Qing and her clique, and their failure rankled deeply. The convening of the conference, and the rectification then being conducted within the army, aroused their bitter hatred. Wang Hongwen and Zhang Chunqiao sneered that the conference had "raised a lot of useless questions". As to the speeches by

Ye and Deng, they said: "Those are the documents which ought to be criticized."

Although they couldn't stop the all-out rectification Deng had inaugurated, the Gang definitely hadn't given up. An "exciting drama" was yet to come.

At the same time rectification was going on in the economic arena and the armed forces, Deng Xiaoping was pushing it in the fields of culture and education.

Starting in May, Zhou Rongxin, the Minister of Education, with the support of Zhou Enlai and Deng Xiaoping, began a rectification drive following the speeches they had made. He called meetings and held discussions with persons within and outside the ministry, solicited opinions and sought information. He focused on Lin Biao's and Jiang Qing's sabotage in the field of education, stressing that education and China's economy should be mutually responsive. He called for a revival of respect for intellectuals and educators, for a restoration of all the activities which had been so severely damaged in the field of education.

Zhou Rongxin's efforts were enthusiastically welcomed by the many educators who had been harmed by the Cultural Revolution. They replied with a flood of articles and opinions, which evoked a huge public response. Like a warm spring breeze, the rectification drive caressed the educators. During the Cultural Revolution they had been the first to come under attack.

To conduct a rectification campaign of national magnitude was a Herculean task. It needed the backing of a powerful team of political theorists. In June, Deng recommended to the Central Committee the creation of a Political Research Office under the State Council. His proposal was approved. The formation of the office was announced, with Hu Qiaomu heading an impressive team of hard-hitting political experts. They proved fully capable of firing a barrage of articles in support of the rectification that easily countered the arguments of the poison pen artists of the Gang of Four.

From its inception, the Cultural Revolution was regarded by the Gang of Four as their own special "sphere of influence". They guarded it zealously. To conduct a rectification within that sphere was particularly difficult. On July 9, Deng Xiaoping asked the Political Research Office to collect and organize material relating to culture and education. He said in addition to the policy of welcoming a wide variety of cultural forms, the Party also has a policy of free contention among all manner of philosophies and theories.

"We must avoid becoming mentally ossified," he said. "So many of the articles today are all in the same mold. Unless we observe these policies we cannot further enliven and beautify our literature and art...."

The Political Research Office assembled material on these matters and turned it over to Deng Xiaoping.

Mao Zedong was also aware of serious questions in literature and art. He talked to Deng about it in July, saying: "There aren't enough model operas. A person is castigated if he makes the slightest mistake. We lack a flourishing of culture in a wide variety of forms.... People are not allowed to express their opinions. That's no good."

On July 14, Mao wrote: "Party policy on the arts needs reform. It could take a year, or two, or three, but the range of creative works should be gradually expanded. We are short of poetry, and novels, and essays, and literary criticism. Writers should be encouraged, not bashed.... Problems in the arts are ideological. But they are nothing to worry about. If you don't let people see what is being created, how can they appraise them? ... Be circumspect when handing out punishments. Don't be too quick to dismiss people from their jobs, or lock them up. That's a sign of a weak brain."

Mao's attitude was very clear. It gave strong support to rectification in the arts.

The movement employed very different tactics from those used in other areas, such as calling meetings, arousing the masses, reshuffling cadres, restoring or creating rules and regulations. Rectification in the arts was primarily an arduous and determined struggle against the Gang of Four.

Jiang Qing, on July 18, viciously attacked a feature film about the Daqing Oilfields, which had been constructed by the workers under extremely hazardous conditions. She said it had "serious flaws", prohibited it from being shown, and vowed she would seize the "black hand behind the scenes." The director, Zhang Tianmin, sent a letter to Mao Zedong and Deng Xiaoping, protesting the statement by Jiang Qing and the clique she controlled in the Ministry of Culture, and requesting that the film be released. Deng forwarded the letter to Mao Zedong.

Mao wrote this endorsement on the letter: "There is nothing seriously wrong with the film. I propose that it be shown. We mustn't demand perfection. (Jiang Qing's) list of errors is too long and too exaggerated. It is not helpful to the Party's policy of rectification in the arts. Refer this letter to the Ministry of Culture and to the unit to which the director belongs."

Jiang Qing hotly denied responsibility. She claimed the list of errors was written by others, that it was all an attempt to smear her. "There definitely was a person, probably a bad person, behind the letter written by that young man.... Someone was forcing Chairman Mao to comment." Of course she was hinting that Deng Xiaoping was the "black hand behind the scenes."

As to the rectification drive in the arts, already in process, Jiang Qing openly bared her fangs. "People are attacking the Ministry of Culture, putting pressure on it, saying it's a big company gang," she snarled. "I'm sticking up for it. They can't scare me!"

No matter how Jiang Qing ranted and raved, the Central Committee, in the spirit of Mao Zedong's endorsements, began to revise various policies pertaining to the arts. The magazines *People's Literature* and *Poetry* resumed publication. Nie Er and Xian Xinghai's music was performed at memorial concerts. A few films Jiang Qing had labeled "poisonous weeds" were again publicly shown.

The storm over the film about the Daqing Oilfields had passed, but the struggle to rectify the arts was far from over. The next battle concerned another movie about the life of a fisherman's daughter.

After it was completed in 1975 Zhou Enlai, Zhu De and Ye Jianying each previewed it. They all liked it and recommended that it be shown. But the Ministry of Culture, manipulated by the Gang of Four, sealed all the films negatives and rushes, asserting it was a "typical comeback of the black line". Xie Tieli and Qian Jiang, the directors of the film, penned a protest to Mao Zedong. On July 29, Mao noted on their letter: "Print and distribute copies of this to all comrades in the Politburo."

Deng Xiaoping promptly summoned members of the Politburo then in Beijing and showed them the movie at a special screening in a room in the Great Hall of the People. The two directors sat between Deng Xiaoping and Li Xiannian, talking with them as the film unrolled. Gang of Four flunky Yu Huiyong, the Minister of Culture, seated nearby, watched their every move. When the screening ended, he rushed to report to Jiang Qing.

Deng Xiaoping, Li Xiannian, and other members of the Politburo could see nothing wrong with the film. The Central Committee approved its nationwide release.

Jiang Qing was furious. She brought this incident out as "evidence" when Deng later came under attack. She alleged he had supported the film, and said "This account must be settled!" She even planned to have the author of the script arrested.

Many analysts of this period say 1975 was a year of successive dramas. For that was when Deng Xiaoping, after having taken charge of the work of the Central Committee, together with his comrades, in an astonishing display of courage and vigor, swung the great axe of nationwide rectification to slash away the damage inflicted by the Cultural Revolution on China's economy, culture, education, science and the military. It was a tremendous achievement. The people saw production return to normal, political affairs stabilized, and peaceful life resumed. Rectification brought them determination, confidence, justice, and hope.

One dramatic performance succeeded another. They were vehicles of sharp conflict between good and evil, packed with constantly shifting elements. They were fine operas, excellently crafted, and beautifully sung. But how difficult it was to put them on!

43

Documents on National Rectification

Z HOU Enlai's health worsened in mid-1975. Central Committee comrades listened to a report about it by the medical committee, arranged by Deng Xiaoping, at eight o'clock in the evening of June 5.

President Ferdinand Marcos of the Philippines visited China in early June. Zhou Enlai introduced him to Deng Xiaoping. Zhou apologized, explaining that he was not well. He said Deng would represent him at all future discussions and banquets, to give him a chance to get more rest. His purpose was to let international friends know he was smoothing the way for Deng to assume a number of his functions.

A ceremony was held at the Cemetery of Revolutionary Martyrs on June 9 to inter the ashes of Marshal He Long. The Marshal had been wronged by Lin Biao and Jiang Qing during the Cultural Revolution, and brutally tormented. He died a miserable death in prison in June 1969.

Mention of He Long came up at a meeting in December 1973. Mao Zedong, who finally understood the situation, said: "I was wrong about Comrade He Long. I must bear the responsibility. The decision against him should be reversed."

In 1974 he told Deng Xiaoping that He Long's name should be cleared. Deng relayed these words to the Politburo. On September 29 the Central Committee issued a resolution restoring Marshal He Long's honored status.

Six years after the cruel death of Marshal He Long his ashes were finally laid to rest. Present at the ceremony were his old comrades-in-arms Ye Jianying, Deng Xiaoping, and Li Xiannian. They placed floral wreaths of commemoration.

The ailing Zhou Enlai arrived. As he entered the hall he called the name of He Long's widow, Xue Ming, tears streaming from his eyes. "Xue Ming," he cried in a voice that trembled, "I didn't protect him!"

After He Long died, Xue Ming had been secretly transported by the Lin Biao clique to the mountains of Guizhou, and there held under detention. Only by resorting to every possible device, was Zhou Enlai able to get her released.

"Premier," she sobbed, with tears in her eyes, "thank you for your concern for our whole family."

"Take care of your health, Uncle Zhou," Xiaoming, He Long's daughter, urged.

"I don't have much longer," Zhou told them softly.

At this, all of those present, who had been controlling themselves with difficulty, broke down and wept. Their lamentations were the bitter expressions of the accumulated grief suffered during nine years of the Cultural Revolution; they were angry indictments of the crimes of Lin Biao and Jiang Qing; they were the sternest protests against the many ultra-"Left" errors committed.

On behalf of the Central Committee, Zhou Enlai solemnly delivered the funeral address.

The convictions had to be reversed, thoroughly reversed. Otherwise, there would be no peace for the wronged spirits in the nether world, no solace for the humans on earth!

Zhou Enlai's uneasiness increased after the ceremony for He Long. He determined to devote his final energies to supporting Deng Xiaoping's arduous rectification drive. Zhou had long talks with Deng on June 27, July 4, and July 16. He knew how ugly and dangerous the situation was. He told his personal staff, after having a group photo taken with them: "This will probably be the last time we can be photographed together."

He knew how the Gang of Four hated him. They would harass him as long as he lived. Nor would they desist even after his death. They would continue to slander him and accuse him of every crime. He had no illusions about the Gang of Four. He was very concerned about the coming struggles.

Just as Zhou anticipated, Mao's criticism of the Gang of Four went in one ear and out the other. Jiang Qing's gang launched a new assault on Zhou Enlai and Deng Xiaoping. On July 12, the Shanghai newspaper *Wen Hui Bao*, in two articles used historical allegory to imply that Zhou and Deng represented the forces seeking to restore the persons who had been overthrown. It called for struggle against these "Confucianists". The *Guangming Daily*, on July 13, attacked what they called over-reliance on experience. Shanghai's *Liberation Daily* also turned out similar innuendoes. All were obviously pointed at Zhou Enlai and Deng Xiaoping, and were very belligerent.

In August, Wang Hongwen called a number of meetings at which he trumpeted: "Beware of revisionism taking over.... Prepare for guerrilla warfare... We'll fight in the streets...." He personally inspected the local militia units, and led their training exercises.

In this battle in the heartland of the Gang of Four, either the net would break, or the fish would be killed. Since peaceful means hadn't succeeded, the Gang prepared to resort to war. Wang Hongwen, who rose to power through factionalism, had merely led a couple of clashes in factional fights. For him to dream of commanding the militia in a full-scale war was preposterous.

One unpredictable struggle followed another in the clash between two clearly defined political lines. Deng Xiaoping was calm. He had no illusions, and he had no intention of compromising. The Gang of Four slanders left him unmoved. His mind was clear. His only wish was to act quickly, to seize this opportunity to bring about a rapid change.

The Communist Party Committee of Zhejiang Province discussed rectification in meetings between June 20 and August 4. Deng Xiaoping received several reports on the situation. He sent people to investigate and help. With this encouragement, the Provincial Party Committee took measures against the factional leaders. Production was restored and stability and unity improved throughout the province.

Deng addressed the participants attending the fourth session of the

Study Program for the members of the Central Committee on July 4. His topic was "Strengthen Party Leadership and Improve the Party's Style of Work".

"At present, effective Party leadership either has not yet been established or has been weakened in quite a number of localities. This problem exists at all levels," he said. "The key to the solution of this problem is to build effective leadership at the level of the provincial Party committees."

He also talked about factionalism.

"But even if the two factions which appeared at the early stage of the Cultural Revolution were likewise formed naturally, their perpetuation now would be quite a different matter," he said. "Comrade Mao Zedong has called for stability and unity. How can stability and unity be achieved if a small number of persons are allowed to continue making trouble? ...

"In order to achieve stability and unity and to develop the socialist economy, it is essential to strengthen the leadership of the Party and to spread and further develop the Party's fine style of work."

In addition to implementing measures to restore order and production in the railways, the iron and steel industry, the military, education, culture, and Party building and work-style, Deng Xiaoping in July dispatched a team under Hu Yaobang and Li Chang to the Chinese Academy of Sciences to start a rectification in the arena of science and technology.

"The crux is in building, after rectification, a strong, courageous leadership," Deng said. He instructed the team to investigate the situation in the Academy, work out a plan for future development, and submit to the Central Committee a proposed list of names for a new core of the Academy's Party Committee. Deng promised that he himself would act as a bolster for the community engaged in scientific and technological research.

He paid special attention to the correct application of Party policy toward several famous scientists. He criticized putting them into fields which were not their specialty, and inquired into their working and living conditions. Many of these scientists later made important contributions.

When the nationwide rectification reached a certain level, Deng felt it advisable to summarize its achievements. He had the State Planning Commission draft a document entitled "Speeding Up Industrial Development". Some industries had made improvement. If, on this foundation, they could improve still further, it would encourage a restoration of order in all industries, and increase production. This, in turn, would move the entire national economy a big step forward.

In a discussion about the proposal at a State Council meeting on August 18, Deng Xiaoping made several points: 1. Confirm that agriculture is the foundation of the national economy. Industry must support it and speed up its modernization. 2. Bring in new technology and equipment from other countries, expand imports and exports. In return for more exports, obtain technology and equipment of the highest quality. Speed up the reform of industrial technology and raise labor productivity. 3. Strengthen scientific research in State enterprises. 4. Bring order to the industrial management. 5. Stress product quality. 6. Restore and improve rules and regulations. 7. Enforce pay according to work, an extremely important principle in the period of socialist construction.

The State Planning Commission edited the draft in keeping with the spirit of Deng's speech, and produced a document entitled "Twenty Points in Industry". It included:

1. Political study should aim at stability and unity, and expediting production. This is not "putting all stress on the productive forces" or "placing professional work in command".

2. In rectifying our enterprises we must first improve the Party leadership. We must complete this in a year or so, and create a leadership body, which is neither weak, lazy nor lax and which takes back the power evildoers have usurped. It must be keen not bloated, strong not soppy, able to fight tough battles and not collapse at the first shove.

3. Improve enterprise management. Strictly observe the system.

Strengthen Party organization and discipline. Fight against any manifestation in violation of policy, system, plan or discipline. Responsibility for failure to achieve the State plan lies with the leadership.

4. Implement Party policy. Remove any labels wrongfully imposed on workers, technicians, and cadres. Have confidence in our technicians; give full rein to their intelligence and usefulness. Don't incorrectly transfer them. Make necessary adjustments.

5. Make a specific analysis of "rebellions" and the so-called "revolutionary" conduct indulged in during the Cultural Revolution. Support what is correct; criticize what is wrong; halt what is reactionary. Turn down anyone who, in the name of "rebellion", applies to join the Party, or become an official. Firmly resist factionalism, fight it blow for blow, don't give an inch.

6. Pay according to work. Paying the same for all jobs whether they are light or heavy, arduous or easy, and make a big contribution or small, is not conducive to production. Show concern for living conditions of workers and employees.

7. Modestly learn from advanced experience in foreign countries. Set priorities and bring in, according to plan, whatever is useful to us and which speeds up the development of our national economy.

8. Develop a large contingent of "red" and "expert" specialists, cadres, workers, and technicians needed for our socialist modernization.

Looking back on them today, Deng's speech and the "Twenty Points" were of flawless logic. But the Cultural Revolution was a time when all systems were smashed, a period of lawlessness when truth was turned upside-down and rebels usurped control. The recommended measures not only were not promoted, they were opposed. Nine years of the Cultural Revolution had brought a perversion of right and wrong, a twisting of human and moral concepts. Only by setting their jaws, by relentlessly criticizing errors without fear of "giving offense", could the reformers hope to accomplish anything.

Because Deng Xiaoping later came under repeated attack, the document was never formally circulated. But it was seen by many while being drafted, and was warmly welcomed by leaders on every level and the majority of people engaged in industry. They all longed for stability and unity, and to increase production and improve their living conditions. It therefore had a positive impact on rectification in industry.

Another important document created at that time, at Deng's urging and under his supervision, was "A Report on Several Problems Concerning Scientific and Technological Work". During a meeting on September 26, he gave it high praise. He said: "Unless our scientific research moves forward, it will act as a brake on our entire national construction."

The ranks in science and technology "have been sadly depleted," he said. "They must be built up again... A minority of people is secretly attacking them, as if they were criminals. Chen Jingrun is one of their targets."

As to scientists who had been labeled as "white" (bourgeois) experts, he said, "What about these so-called 'white experts'? As long as they are useful to the People's Republic of China they're a lot better than persons engaged in factionalism and holding others back."

Some veteran scientists had been assigned to teach subjects outside their fields of expertise. "There's a lot of that," Deng said reprovingly. "We should be encouraging the expansion of their talents. Assign a special Party secretary for them. Give them technical support groups. It all comes down to a question of the leadership. Why should we keep in the leadership units persons who are scientifically ignorant, unenthusiastic and go in for factionalism? Why can't talented, knowledgeable technologists be institute heads?

"We need to prepare the next generation. That's a matter we put to the Ministry of Education. What should be the function of college education? What sort of persons should it be producing? Some colleges are only the equivalent of middle level technical schools. Is that what we need colleges for? A crisis will probably erupt in the field of education, affecting the entire level of modernization."

Deng spoke about the status of teachers and professors. "They're forever being reviled," he said. "Is that any way to inspire their enthusiasm?"

He considered "A Report on Several Problems" very important, not only to the Chinese Academy of Sciences, but to the worlds of science and technology, education, and other fields as well. Thanks to his support, the report broke through the defenses of the Cultural Revolution, and proclaimed the principle that "science and technology are also part of the productive forces".

The position of the report was clearly divergently opposite to the ultra-"Leftism" of the Cultural Revolution. It was sent to Mao Zedong, but did not receive his approval. Nevertheless, word of the new spirit spread rapidly, and proved a great stimulus to rectification of scientific research institutes and in education, then already in progress. Like a torch in the darkness of night, it kindled hope in the hearts of the people.

For an all-out rectification to succeed, in addition to the courage to smash the fortifications of the Cultural Revolution, also needed was clear ideological guidelines. Starting in August, at Deng Xiaoping's behest, the Political Research Office of the State Council organized the drafting of a new document, edited by Deng Liqun, to be called "A General Outline of the Tasks of the Party and the Nation". It was based on three principles advocated by Mao Zedong: "Study the theory of the dictatorship of the proletariat", "stability and unity are best", and "improve the national economy". They would constitute the grand strategy for attaining the Four Modernizations.

The effect was to mark "stability and unity are best" and "improve the national economy" equally important as "class struggle" — formerly held out as the sole political duty. It was the hardest blow the Cultural Revolution crowd received in nine years.

"We respect Mao Zedong's teachings," said the General Outline. "We recognize the dialectic unity of opposites between politics and economics. We acknowledge the leadership role of politics, and at the same time know that politics provides a guarantee for the implementation of our economy. It serves the economic base.

"Some of our comrades take a metaphysical approach to politics and economics, to the relationship between revolution and production. They talk about politics, but not about economics. They talk about revolution, but not about production. The moment they hear we want to promote production and do a good job of economic construction, they say we are 'pinning everything on the productive forces', they say we are going revisionist. These accusations have no foundation in fact."

The General Outline continued: "In the years of bitter revolutionary warfare Chairman Mao attached great importance to economic construction and our material basis. Today, we have become a socialist country under the dictatorship of the proletariat. Surely we should devote every moment, and exert every effort to quickly raise our economic level and strengthen our socialist material basis."

The General Outline severely criticized the Gang of Four. It said: "These class enemies who oppose Marxism have inherited Lin Biao's mantle. They pervert our revolutionary slogans, crack them open, insert smuggled goods, mix black and white, turn the truth upside down, and confuse the thinking of some of our comrades and some of the masses. In some places, in some Party organizations, they split the ranks of the Party, the working class, the masses... They overthrow good Party cadres and advanced model personalities, seize leadership in some localities and organizations and impose on them a dictatorship of the bourgeoisie."

Quoting Lenin's comment that "The test of political education is its economic effectiveness," the General Outline then quoted from Mao Zedong, as follows: "Whether the policies of a Chinese political party and their implementation are good or bad for the Chinese people, important or trivial, ultimately depends on whether or not they are helpful to the people's productive forces, on whether they fetter or liberate these forces."

In a fatal thrust the General Outline said acidly: "In some places, in some units, where production is very poor, it is utterly fraudulent to say it is very good. Those who claim they have only to grasp revolution and production will automatically and easily improve believe childhood fables about turning stones into gold."

While the documents regarding industry and science and technology criticized the ultra-"Left" errors in those fields, the General Outline demanded a thorough rectification of the thinking of the leadership and its orientation and policy, and aimed its spearhead, from a theoretical standpoint, directly at the ultra-"Left" errors of the Gang of Four itself. From the start of the Cultural Revolution Zhang Chunqiao and Yao Wenyuan had used their control of the media to invent many absurd theories and hair-raising phrases, while stifling correct voices and slandering honest innocents.

Now, for the first time since the inception of the Cultural Revolution nine years before, people could take up their pens and present the truth. Leaders of a number of units under the State Council and a number of political theorists were able to launch an all-out political counter-offensive. Documents like the General Outline were a thunderous neighing of ten thousand stampeding horses. They were a roar of justice, a roar of hope. They were a spear into the wicked corpus of the Gang of Four. They were a declaration of uncompromising war.

44

Great Accomplishments

RECTIFICATION proceeded on all sides. There were thousands of things that had to be done. Damages to the nation over nine chaotic years were severe and diverse. There could be no hesitation in the rectification. Every effort had to be devoted to it.

In July, August and September of 1975, Deng Xiaoping was really busy.

While the three documents on rectification were being drawn up, campaigns in favor of reform were unfolding all over China, with "drums beating and cymbals clashing". The Ministry of Education convened a conference to discuss rectification in their field. They drafted an appropriate document, consulting with Deng several times during its preparation. He repeatedly reminded them that the Four Modernizations was the primary target of the Chinese Communist Party, and that education had a direct bearing on the entire modernization process.

"What happens in the next 25 years," he said, "depends on how well our education bodies develop talent....The core of the question of successors in scientific research lies in our education organizations. Now we have a crisis — people are not reading. Teachers are not being given their proper status, and the education authorities are not arousing their enthusiasm."

The draft document on education, coupled with the three documents on other sectors, formed an outline for overall rectification. Well-received by the majority of teachers and students, it provoked deep hostility in the Gang of Four.

Deng Xiaoping in August proposed a rectification of State-owned enterprises, and spoke at the meeting on key divisions of military industries. As usual, he was clear and to the point.

He said what was needed was "1. A leadership with guts, that would fight against factionalism, and establish necessary rules and regulations. 2. Putting quality first. Without a system of responsibility, quality could not be guaranteed. Arouse the enthusiasm of the professionals. Weren't they being called the 'stinking old ninth'?" [1]

Deng reminded his audience that Chairman Mao had said, "The old ninth cannot go." Which, in State enterprises, meant specifically that engineers and technicians must be treated with respect.

Also necessary was 3. Concern for the living conditions of the masses. "Just saying so won't solve it. A lot of solid work has to be done," Deng noted. "For example, iron and steel workers have a very tough job, but they don't get enough vegetables and meat. You can't guarantee their basic needs. That problem must be specifically analyzed and solved."

Deng was a very practical man. He made detailed suggestions on how to develop subsidiary occupations to improve the workers' living conditions. He talked about building pigpens. This would provide additional food for the workers and, at the same time, bring more income to neighboring farmers.

In July he sent a letter to Mao Zedong proposing that a talk he gave in 1956, called "On the Ten Major Relationships", be published. "It's extremely important," Deng wrote. It has a direct bearing on the present situation and the future, and provides theoretical guidance....I hope it can be edited quickly and publicly circulated. It will be valuable material in the nationwide study of political theory."

Mao agreed that the talk be edited, but said that public distribution should be delayed for a while.

---

[1] During the Cultural Revolution eight categories of persons were targeted for attack: landlords, rich peasants, counter-revolutionaries, rascals, "Rightists", traitors, spies, and capitalist-roaders. Intellectuals were later added as a "stinking old ninth".

In August, Deng Xiaoping added his mark of approval to that of Zhou Enlai for the 10-year plan of the State Publishing Bureau, which included the publications of Chinese and foreign language dictionaries. For nine years the Cultural Revolution had rejected culture. No books had been published on the technical aspects of culture. Now the Central Committee was proposing a rectification of the policy on the arts, a reform of the policy regarding intellectuals. Even dictionaries were coming under the scrutiny of the Central Committee and the State Council. It was truly heart-warming. The cultural realm had been sadly trampled by the Cultural Revolution. Were fresh buds really appearing on the gnarled old branches?

As part of the rectification of industry, the All-China Federation of Trade Unions convened a Ninth National Congress in September. Deng urged them to pay close attention both to production and to support services for the workers. He said they should not be deterred by smears that they were "putting production above all", or that they were "social services unions." Deng felt that with the restoration of production it was all the more important to improve the workers' living conditions and support services. They had suffered more than enough hardships in the recent years of turbulence and chaos. The turbulence must be brought to an end. Everyone should have enough food to eat, and clothes to wear. It wasn't asking very much, but it would be a tough goal to attain.

The Central Military Commission, with the approval of Mao Zedong and the Central Committee, announced on August 30 a reshuffle of the heads of all military departments. Many veteran high leaders who had been attacked and mistreated during the earlier years of the Cultural Revolution were restored to their former posts. Although Zhang Chunqiao remained as head of the General Political Department of the PLA, and the poison injected by the Lin Biao gang was still not completely expunged, overall the armed forces were returned to the leadership of the Party. Control was again in the hands of loyal Communist Party generals. With the leadership refurbished and authority stabilized, a very important foundation was set for winning decisive victories in the intense battles which lay ahead.

Deng Xiaoping had to be concerned about no end of things. In August he called a meeting of the heads of air transport, electronics and the munitions industry, plus the leaders of the Air Force, and listened to their reports. Those in military industries must put quality first, he said, especially those manufacturing equipment for the Air Force.

On the 19th, while seeing off a foreign guest at the airport, he talked about service with one of the directors. He said that people in civil aviation should know their jobs well, and strive to improve service. Also that they should be given more training.

He saw the play *Ten Thousand Rivers and Mountains* in September. He urged people in the theater to artistically present the history of the Long March. Not long after, several excellent vehicles cut through the blockade of the Jiang Qing gang and played on China's stages. Although spring had not yet come to the world of Chinese arts, Jiang Qing's stranglehold on everything in the arts was broken at last.

The Third National Games were held in Beijing from September 12 to 28. Thirty-one teams comprising over 10,000 athletes from all over the country competed. Four athletes and one team broke three world records, two for individual events and one for group events. Two athletes equaled two world records and many fine performances were turned in. After Deng Xiaoping took over the field of national sports, the majority of the cadres and persons involved firmly resisted Jiang Qing's attempts to intervene, and this meet was an obvious result. The air was festive. Zhu De, Ye Jianying, Deng Xiaoping, and other Party and government leaders all showed up at the opening and closing ceremonies.

In 1975, after Deng Xiaoping assumed management of the daily affairs of the Party and government, he instituted a nationwide rectification, with the support of most cadres and the general public. Its success was very evident. The economy, which had halted and was declining, quickly turned around and began to climb. Annual combined value for industry and agriculture rose 11.9 percent over the previous year. Grain, steel, coal, crude oil, output of electricity, investment in infrastructure construction, rail transport tonnage, and retail sales of consumer goods, all showed increases.

It was a great victory for the Party and the people against the "Leftist" errors of the Gang of Four. Not only had the dangerously weakened economy been saved. Even more important, it showed concrete results to the entire Party and public. It demonstrated the strength action could generate; it aroused hope in the people's hearts; it firmed their determination to fight the evil forces of the Gang of Four; it heightened their confidence in the future of the Party and the nation.

The Gang of Four unrelentingly continued their efforts to seize power at every level. They compiled phony "evidence" and smeared left and right.

But Mao Zedong, on the highest level, hoped the two sides would compromise and cooperate. It was a very impractical wish. A struggle to the death was going on which would determine the destiny of the nation and the welfare of the people. It left no room for manoeuver. In July, August and September of 1975, the all-out rectification campaign, and the battle between the two sides reached high tide.

The State Council convened a conference of 3,700 people on agriculture, called "Learn from the Dazhai Production Brigade". It ran from September 15 to October 19. Deng Xiaoping spoke at the opening meeting. He said it was perhaps the largest gathering of leading officials since the "Conference of Seven Thousand," in 1962.

"The modernization of agriculture is the most arduous of the Four Modernizations of agriculture, industry, the military, and science and technology," Deng said.

"Agriculture is the base. No matter how rapidly industry develops, no matter how high we raise the level of science and technology, without the impetus of agriculture the other three modernizations cannot advance. If agriculture goes badly, it probably will hold back our national construction. We call on the Party committees of every region and province to promote agricultural development. The more industrially developed areas should put more stress on agriculture, give it first priority."

Deng talked also about rectification. "We're having problems with it in several parts of the country," he continued. "Chairman Mao has said the military needs adjustment, and so do many elements of the local governments. Industry, agriculture, commerce, culture and education, the science and technology community, all require rectification. Chairman Mao has called for rectification in the arts. As a matter of fact, it's going on right now. Rectification is necessary in all aspects of our work."

Deng's speech won enthusiastic applause from his audience. This mightily displeased the Gang of Four. Jiang Qing couldn't control herself. While Deng was speaking, she threw in several sarcastic interjections. At a reception for members and cadres of the famous Dazhai Brigade, she kept making negative remarks. Although this was a conference about agriculture, she went on at great length to attack *Outlaws of the Marsh*, a famous Chinese classical novel of the Ming Dynasty (1368-1644).

"Don't think appraising *Outlaws of the Marsh* is merely a literary exercise," she said. "Comrades, it's more than that. It's not just a critique of history, it has practical application to the present. Enemies will disguise themselves and hide in our midst.

"Song Jiang went up to the mountain fortress and took over the leadership. How did he do that? Comrades, he did it by making a figurehead of the leader, Chao Gai. And how did he make him a figurehead? By bringing in big officials, generals, military experts and literati, as supporters. He brought them in and they all took leading positions in the fortress. That was his organization.

"We not only acknowledge class struggle — it is not over — we see a fierce struggle going on in our Party between two (political) lines!"

Jiang Qing's implication was plain. She talked about Song Jiang, a major protagonist in *Outlaws of the Marsh,* but she meant Deng Xiaoping. When she said Song Jiang made a figurehead of Chao Gai, another major protagonist in the classical novel, she was really claiming that Deng Xiaoping was making a figurehead of Mao Zedong. Her remarks were addressed to the cadres and people present at the meeting. Even more, they were meant for Mao's ears.

On a visit to the Dazhai Brigade, Jiang Qing, speaking to a gathering of culture and education experts, made her point plainer.

"There is a lesson for us in *Outlaws of the Marsh*," she said darkly. "Song Jiang made a figurehead of Chao Gai. Is anyone trying to make a figurehead of the Chairman today? I say there is...." And she cried grand eloquently: "There are moderates in our Party, and also Leftists. The leader of the Leftists is yours truly!"

"Recently, I transmitted a letter from Chairman Mao, in which he criticized me, to the Politburo. Without first discussing it, the Politburo published it," she complained. "I'm being cursed every day. The revisionists are cursing me. Is a true Communist afraid of being cursed? In Beijing I've fought them for more than half a year!"

Jiang Qing demanded that the conference broadcast an audiotape of her remarks and publish a written transcript.

In actuality, the conference had been a battleground in the war between Deng Xiaoping and the Gang of Four. Each side sang its own tune. The political division was very clear to the nearly 4,000 participants. Deng Xiaoping was practical and firm. Jiang Qing was hysterical and ugly. They left a deep impression on all those present. With the whole Party and the entire country earnestly demanding stability and unity, and an improvement in the national economy, people knew exactly where to stand.

Jiang Qing's demands for a broadcast and publication of her speech at the agricultural conference were transmitted to Mao Zedong. He was very angry. Time and again he had patiently explained, and advised, and criticized her, but Jiang Qing hadn't listened.

"Dog farts! Utter nonsense!" he exploded. "Don't circulate her speech, don't broadcast it, and don't publish it," he ordered.

Again Mao had supported Deng Xiaoping, again he threw water on the Gang of Four. Not only were Jiang Qing's unreasonable demands turned down, but her speech was not even broadcast in Shanxi Province, where the Dazhai Brigade was located.

The Central Committee organized a conference on agriculture, held in Beijing from September 23 to October 21. One of the subjects was a letter it had received from Chen Yonggui. He proposed that commune members' income be shares of what their brigades earned, rather than the earnings of the teams which comprised them. In the name of "averaging the wealth", he was in fact proposing an egalitarian method whereby the better teams supported the backward. At that time, the rural productive level was very low. Such an idea would have been impossible to implement.

There was a difference of opinion at the meeting. Some supported Chen Yonggui's proposal, but most were against it. Because Mao had criticized Jiang Qing's position at the Dazhai Conference, there was less opposition from the radical forces, and the meeting ran relatively smoothly. The meeting, chaired by Li Xiannian, passed a resolution not to change, temporarily, the existing system of ownership and accounting. "Leftist" interference was thereby prevented and another possible calamitous clash in the countryside averted. This squelching of the radical "Leftists" provided a guarantee of calm and steady implementation of rural economic policy.

Deng Xiaoping spoke twice — on September 27 and October 4.

"There is at present a need to put things in order in every field," he said. "Agriculture and industry must be put in order, and the policies on literature and art need to be adjusted. Adjustment, in fact, also means putting things in order. By putting things in order, we want to solve problems in rural areas, in factories, in science and technology, and in all other spheres. At Political Bureau meetings I have discussed the need for doing so in several fields, and when I reported to Comrade Mao Zedong, he gave his approval.

"The central task in putting things in order is to consolidate the Party. Once this central task — the consolidation of the Party — has been accomplished, the rest will follow.

"I always feel that there is a big problem we have to solve: How should we spread Mao Zedong Thought? Comrade Luo Ronghuan was the first to express his disapproval of Lin Biao's vulgarization of Mao Zedong Thought. He said that when we study Chairman Mao's works we must study their essence. At that time, the Secretariat of the Central Committee discussed Comrade Luo Ronghuan's views and concurred

339

with them. Lin Biao urged people to study only the 'three constantly read articles' (later, after two more were added, they became the 'five constantly read articles'). This was a way of fragmenting Mao Zedong Thought. Mao Zedong Thought is rich in content and constitutes an integral whole. How can one designate only the 'three constantly read articles' or 'five constantly read articles' as Mao Zedong Thought, while brushing aside Comrade Mao's other works? ... The problem of fragmenting Mao Zedong Thought actually remain unsolved...

"I'm afraid that the problem of how to study, propagate and implement Mao Zedong Thought systematically exists in quite a few fields. Mao Zedong Thought is closely bound up with practice in every sphere, with the principles, policies and methods in every line of work. We must study, propagate and implement it in its totality and not base our conclusions on a partial understanding or an erroneous interpretation by others."

In 1960 Deng had already voiced his opposition to a vulgarization of Mao Zedong Thought, particularly the over-simplification by Lin Biao. Now, 15 years later, when Mao stood as the absolute authority, and democracy within the Party had sunk to its lowest level, Deng again raised the question. Although this exposed him to considerable personal risk, he felt it was a matter of the utmost importance to the Party and the state that could no longer be avoided.

Deng knew that during the Cultural Revolution this was a touchy subject, a danger of unfathomable depth. But sooner or later it would have to be dealt with. To him the words "Mao Zedong Thought" represented not merely the name of the man and his lifetime, but a page in the long scroll of China's history, an era in modern China. A grasp of Mao Zedong Thought, an appraisal of Mao as an individual, was directly linked to an appraisal and ranking of China's entire modern revolutionary history, and to the future of China, the Chinese people and the Chinese Communist Party.

Deng knew it was entirely possible his comments on how Mao Zedong Thought should be studied and taught might be twisted and used against him. Mao himself might not agree. But Deng would speak out;

he had to. After six years of harassment he had finally been restored to office. But he wanted to use this opportunity to get back to work and stand for justice. He was determined to give his whole heart for the Party, for the nation, and for the people he loved so deeply. Without hesitation, with no regard for his personal future, he was long mentally prepared to give his life if need be.

45

A Critique of *Outlaws of the Marsh*, and the Last Days of Zhou Enlai

T oo many things occurred in 1975. In the history of New China, from whatever aspect, it was an unforgettable year.

Mao Zedong was nearly blind with cataracts on both eyes. He couldn't read documents; he couldn't read books. He had lost the main joy of his life. A feeling of helplessness made him irritable and miserable.

Of the comrades in the Central Committee, Zhou Enlai was the most concerned. The big question was could Mao's ailment be cured, and if so how to go about it, how to do it safely? On July 6, 1975, disregarding his own failing health, Zhou Enlai called together Ye Jianying, Deng Xiaoping, Zhang Chunqiao and Wang Dongxing, of the Standing Committee of the Politburo, with Wang Hairong and Tang Wensheng sitting in as auditors, to discuss treatment of Mao's condition. They met again on July 20 and agreed that an operation could be performed, and discussed the procedure to be followed.

Mao disliked being medically treated, and he hated operations. But since that was the only way his vision could be restored, he agreed to being operated upon, as the Politburo proposed. The 82-year-old Mao was operated on for cataracts in the evening of July 23, by a team of surgeons under the famous doctor Tang Youzhi. Zhou Enlai came out of the hospital to stand by in Mao's residence, where the operation was performed. It was done safely and successfully.

Mao was delighted that he was again able to read, with the aid of

Mama and Papa in 1974, after returning to Beijing from Jiangxi.

Mao Zedong, Zhou Enlai (right) and Wang Hongwen (left) during the 10th National Congress of the Chinese Communist Party in August, 1973.

At the ceremony welcoming Norodon Sihanouk Deng Xiaoping made his first public appearance on April 12, 1973, after returning to office. He aroused wide attention.

Deng Xiaoping and Deng Yingchao, wife of Zhou Enlai, at the Party Congress in August 1973.

An ailing Zhou Enlai sees Papa off at the airport on April 6, 1974. Deng Xiaoping led the Chinese delegation to a special session of the UN General Assembly.

Deng Xiaoping, Vice-Premier of the State Council of the People's Republic of China, speaking at the special session.

On returning to Beijing, April 19, 1974.

My parents, Deng Nan and I, in a light-hearted mood in summer of 1974.

With his little granddaughter on May 1, 1974, during the Labor Day celebration.

A family celebration in August 1974 of Papa's 70th birthday.

The first session of the Fourth National People's Congress opened in January 1975 in Beijing.

Premier Zhou Enlai presented the Government Work Report on January 13, 1975, reiterating the country's determination to realize the "four modernizations."

After returning to office in 1974, Deng Xiaoping pushed hard for overall rectifications.

In his final years, although entrusting Deng with important duties, Mao hoped he would save China's economy without opposing the Cultural Revolution.

On April 19, 1975, Premier Zhou Enlai, accompanied by Deng Xiaoping, met Kim Il Sung, general secretary of the Workers' Party of the Democratic People's Republic of Korea.

In May 1975, Chinese Vice-Premier Deng Xiaoping paid an official visit to France.

A warm welcome on May 17, 1975, at the Beijing Airport on his return to China.

The economy began to turn around in the first half of 1975 after arduous efforts.

Deng Xiaoping on a visit to Dazhai Village, Shanxi Province, in 1975. He had to battle Jiang Qing when starting rectifications in agriculture.

1975: Mao Zedong seemed content. He felt he'd finished with personnel arrangement to ensure smooth transition of the leadership.

glasses. He was in much better spirits.

Nationwide rectification moved into high gear. Mao generally approved and supported it, but he was skeptical in part, and reserved judgment on a number of issues. He did not endorse the documents drafted by the Chinese Academy of Sciences. With the new wind of rectification blowing all across the land, no one anticipated that a serious mis-step would soon occur.

It came about like this:

Although Mao's vision was better after his cataract operation, it still wasn't very good, and so he invited Miss Lu Di, a teacher in the Chinese Department of Peking University, to read to him. On August 14, she was reading from one of China's classic novels — *Outlaws of the Marsh*. Mao commented casually on two of his other favorites — *Three Kingdoms*, famous Chinese classical historical novel of the Ming Dynasty (1368-1644), and *A Dream of Red Mansions*, ancient Chinese classic of the early Qing Dynasty (1644-1911). Then Mao turned to *Outlaws*.

"The good thing about the book is that it deals with surrender," he said. "It's good negative material. It teaches people how to recognize capitulators. The outlaws were only against the corrupt officials; they didn't oppose the emperor. Except for Chao Gai (original leader of the outlaw band), all 108 surrendered. Song Jiang (who succeeded Chao as leader) gave in, he went revisionist. He changed the name of Chao's Fraternity Hall to Loyalty Hall, and had everyone accept an amnesty…

"Lu Xun's critique of *Outlaws* was correct. He said: 'It's very clear: because the outlaws didn't oppose the emperor, the moment the big imperial army came at them, they accepted an amnesty. They fought for the government against other outlaws — ones who didn't claim, as they did, to 'act in Heaven's behalf'. In the end they behaved like slaves.'"

Mao Zedong loved China's classics. He knew them by heart, and had opinions about every one of them. Hearing *Outlaws* again, it was normal enough for him to express his views. But it provoked abnormal results.

If some ordinary person had spoken, it wouldn't have made much difference. But this was no ordinary person — this was Mao Zedong, the absolute authority, and the highest pinnacle. In those days, "one sentence (by Mao) was worth more than ten thousand by others". Any offhand emotional response was treated as a "supreme directive".

People who lived in that period no doubt remember that whenever any "new directive from Chairman Mao" came down, it immediately spread throughout the land. Whether in broad daylight or late at night, people immediately took to the streets, cheering, marching, and gathering in Tiananmen Square. Many major stages of the Cultural Revolution originated in just such a fashion. New "movements" were aroused; new "struggles" erupted.

How much more so when the Gang of Four, with their "revolutionary hearts", were there to seize upon any of Mao's words or deeds, and embroider upon and use them as weapons in their "struggles".

The day Mao commented on *Outlaws of the Marsh*, Miss Lu Di wrote down what he said. Yao Wenyuan, poison pen artist of the Gang of Four, heard about it. He felt this was a golden opportunity, and immediately penned a letter to Mao Zedong.

He said: "Questions of grave significance exist regarding China's Communists, China's proletariat, the poor and lower-middle peasants, the present and future of the revolutionary masses. Will Marxism be maintained in this century and the next? Will opposition to revisionism, will Chairman Mao's revolutionary line, be maintained? We must learn from negative examples."

Yao proposed that Mao's critique of *Outlaws*, together with his, Yao's letter, be printed and issued to members of the Politburo then in Beijing, and distributed to all major newspapers and magazines in Beijing and Shanghai, and that critical articles be organized and circulated.

Mao appended a simple endorsement on Yao's letter: "Agree."

The criticism of *Outlaws* thus became an important political matter. The Central Committee issued Mao's critique. Yao Wenyuan saw to it that *Red Flag*, the Communist Party official magazine, carried a short editorial on August 28. Near the end of the month Jiang Qing summoned her flunky Yu Huiyong, the Minister of Culture, and lectured him on the subject's importance.

"The Chairman's analysis of *Outlaws* is realistic," she said. "The crux is making a figurehead of Chao Gai. Today, there are people in the Politburo who would like to make a figurehead of the Chairman."

The *People's Daily*, the Party newspaper, on August 31, reprinted the *Red Flag* editorial, and carried an anonymous article, entitled "Appraising *Outlaws*". After it was published, the Gang of Four whipped up a campaign across the nation to "criticize the surrender faction". Their objective was plain. [1]

On September 4, *People's Daily* published Mao's critique of *Outlaws*, and added an editorial about it which said analyzing *Outlaws* was part of another major battle on China's political-ideological front. At once, criticisms proliferated everywhere, their spearheads pointed openly at Zhou Enlai, Deng Xiaoping and other Party and government officials.

Zhou and Deng were well aware of this. Zhou said on September 15: "They (the Gang of Four) really go too far. It's very clear who they are aiming at in their criticism of *Outlaws*, and the 'surrender faction'."

During a series of meetings with provincial Party secretaries in September and October, Deng said: "What's this analysis of *Outlaws* all about? The Chairman spent three months re-reading the 71-chapter edition, and then offered his analysis. Someone tried to capitalize on this analysis and make an issue of it."

Zhou Enlai's pain from his cancer was severe in August 1975. Deng and other leaders called on him several times. Even Jiang Qing went to see him. Zhou knew his time was limited. Fighting for his life, he used every moment to do final battle with the Gang of Four.

---

[1] Jiang Qing and her Gang of Four hated Zhou Enlai and Deng Xiaoping for staunchly opposing their fanatical persecution of veteran revolutionaries in the name of implementing Mao Zedong's revolutionary line. When Mao sarcastically criticized the Song Dynasty outlaws in the classic novel *Outlaws of the Marsh* for surrendering to the emperor in exchange for an amnesty, the Gang, by innuendo tried to draw a parallel between them and Zhou and Deng, alleging that they, too, had gone over to the enemy — in this case, capitalism and revisionism.

Aside from the fact that this was untrue, as a literary analogy it was also quite inept. The Song Dynasty outlaws were loyal subjects of the feudal establishment, and never had any intention of opposing it. They claimed only that they were being maligned by corrupt ministers.

In that crucial period Deng Xiaoping's heart was closely linked with Zhou Enlai's. When Zhou went into the operating room on August 7, his loyal comrade Deng Xiaoping was there in the hospital, waiting. On September 17, Zhou talked with him. Deng Yingchao, Zhou's wife, called on Deng at home in the morning of September 19 and told him about Zhou's medical condition. It was not encouraging.

Ilie Verdet, who headed a Romanian party and government delegation, paid a visit to Zhou Enlai in the hospital on September 7.

"I've already received an invitation from Marx (in Heaven)," Zhou told him. "Never mind. No one can go against the laws of nature."

He said after more than half a century under the tutelage of Mao Zedong Thought, the Chinese Communist Party had developed many talented, competent leaders.

"I'm ill, unable to work any more," he went on. "Comrade Deng Xiaoping has taken over my duties in the State Council. He's very efficient. You can trust him implicitly. Comrade Deng Xiaoping will continue to carry out our Party's internal and external policies. He is in full charge."

This was the last time in Zhou's glorious diplomatic career that he met with a foreign visitor.

In the afternoon of September 20, the doctors readied Zhou Enlai for a major operation. Deng Xiaoping, Zhang Chunqiao, Li Xiannian, Wang Dongxing and Deng Yingchao waited in the hospital. Before he went into the operating theater Zhou asked that a written record of a speech he delivered on June 23, 1972, called "On Kuomintang's (in Taiwan) Rumors and Slanders About the So-called 'Wuhao Incident'", be brought to him.

On it with shaking hand he signed his name and the words: "Prior to entering the operating room, September 20, 1975."

The Gang of Four schemed against Zhou Enlai and slandered him as a "traitor". He knew he was approaching the end of his life, and that the Gang of Four, who hated him to the marrow of their bones, would not let him rest even after death.

Zhou wanted evidence recorded in black and white that he was a crystal-pure, loyal Communist, to refute the Gang's slanders. How tragic that a man who had devoted his every drop of blood to the service of the Party, the country and the people, should be reduced, in the final hours of his life, to defending his purity and dedication by such a method!

As he was being wheeled into the operating room, Zhou Enlai asked: "Is Comrade Xiaoping here?"

Deng went quickly to his side and leaned over him. With an effort, Zhou lifted his arm and grasped Deng's hand in his own. "You did very well this year." Zhou forced out the words loudly. "Much better than I!"

The cart began to move. "I'm true to the Party, I'm true to the people!" Zhou shouted.

That tragic, angry cry moved everyone present who had the slightest inkling of the real situation.

The operation lasted five hours. Zhou's powerful determination again won through. But the surgery revealed that the cancer had spread to every part of his body. The doctors announced it was incurable.

With a heavy heart, Deng Xiaoping instructed the medical team to do everything possible to diminish the pain and extend Zhou's life. It was the only thing he could do for the comrade-in-arms he loved like an older brother.

Sixteen years later, on September 29, 1991, Deng was very moved to see a documentary film about Zhou Enlai. Watching the scenes showing him and the members of the Standing Committee of the Politburo waiting in the hospital, he remembered the words Zhou shouted as he was going into the operating room.

"He was speaking from his heart," Papa said, "and he wanted the Gang of Four to hear, as well."

Zhou went through six major and eight minor operations. His condition deteriorated rapidly in September, as the cancer continued to spread. Wracked by pain, he showed no outward sign. His will was indomitable. Zhou Enlai faced death calmly. He gave final orders as a fearless dialectic materialist.

"Don't keep my ashes after I die. Fertilize the fields with them, feed them to the fish."

He said to his doctors: "Not much can be done to cure cancer these days. After I die, I want you to do a thorough autopsy and analysis of my body. I will be happy if I can make a small contribution to our country's medical knowledge."

He left instructions that his funeral be simple, not more elaborate than that of any member of the Central Committee, absolutely nothing special. He and his mate of a lifetime, Deng Yingchao, had years before agreed that their ashes should be scattered over the rivers and mountains of the vast motherland.

Near the end, Zhou's only concerns were the future of the Party and the country, the madness of the Gang of Four, and that truth had not yet prevailed over falsehood. The signs were ominous — the situation was deteriorating, his battle comrades were in great danger. Zhou was very worried.

On the 11, 12 and 17 of October he talked with Deng Xiaoping, Li Xiannian, Wang Dongxing, Ji Dengkui, and Wu De, who came to see him. On November 2, he spoke privately with Deng Xiaoping, on November 3, with Wang Hairong and Tang Wensheng.

When no one came, medical staff observed that he lay quietly, looking upward, as if he wanted to penetrate the ceiling and gaze at the fathomless firmament. At times he lapsed into a deep silence, at times he shook his head slightly and sighed....

46

Wicked Persons First Accuse

U_P to September 1975, Mao Zedong still supported the rectification drive launched by Deng Xiaoping. He still thought of him as successor to Zhou Enlai, and as one of those who would hold the political reins after his own death. On September 24, Mao received Le Duan, First Secretary of the Central Committee of the Vietnamese Labor Party.

Mao said: "Today the poorest country isn't yours, it's ours. We have a population of 800 million. We're having a leadership crisis. The Premier is in bad health. He's had four operations in one year. Very dangerous. Kang Sheng's health is bad. Ye Jianying is also not well. I'm 82. I'm sick, too."

He pointed at Deng Xiaoping, who was also present. "He's the only sturdy conscript among us."

From those remarks, it is apparent that Mao had some understanding of the situation. One, that China could then be considered one of the poorest nations under the sky. Two, that China was suffering from a leadership crisis. And three, that Deng was a "sturdy conscript" — meaning that Mao still pinned considerable hope on Deng Xiaoping.

Although Deng's handling of the rectification didn't meet entirely with his approval, Mao viewed the overall picture. He recognized the problems confronting the Party and the government, and acknowledged that someone had to lead the rectification. As long as the rectification didn't go "too far", he could accept it. The rectification also demonstrated Deng's effectiveness. Mao appreciated his courage, his appeal, and his ability.

Under those circumstances, although the Gang of Four kept throwing up obstacles to the rectification, Mao maintained a policy of restraining the Gang of Four and supporting Deng Xiaoping.

But Mao's attitude began to change, and this led to earth-shaking consequences.

On August 13 and October 13, Liu Bing, the deputy secretary of the Party committee of Tsinghua University, wrote letters to Mao Zedong revealing that behavior by two other deputy secretaries, Chi Qun and Xie Jingyi, was in violation of Party principles, that they were bullies of the Gang of Four, and that one of them was spreading lies because he hadn't been elevated into the Central Committee and made a government minister. The letters, strictly in accordance with fact, had been relayed to Mao by Deng Xiaoping.

Mao made no response to the letters, but they certainly displeased him. He knew that although the accused two had "shortcomings", they were ranking generals of the Gang of Four. In relaying the letters Deng had shown his opposition to them and his support of Liu Bing. This didn't suit Mao's purposes. Although it seemed a small matter, shortly thereafter it fused an explosive situation.

After the Lin Biao debacle of 1971, Mao had fallen very ill. He never fully recovered. The state of his health constantly fluctuated. In 1975 he was already 82, and growing feeble. Because leadership posts were then lifetime appointments, and all authority over the Party, the government, and the military was concentrated in a single individual, the destiny of the nation rested in the hands of Mao Zedong, a man in declining health.

His health became worse in the latter half of 1975. It was difficult for him to walk and speak. At his own suggestion, Mao Yuanxin acted as his liaison with the Politburo. The Lin Biao affair had proven to him it wasn't safe to entrust power to any one person. In the Politburo he let different political forces mutually contend. On a personal level he trusted only his own intimates. The older he grew, the more serious this mental condition became.

Mao Yuanxin was the only son of Mao Zedong's younger brother Mao Zemin, who had died a hero's death before Liberation. When the

Cultural Revolution erupted, Yuanxin was a student in the Institute of Military Engineering in Harbin, in Northeast China's Heilongjiang Province. He became the prominent head of a rebel faction, and rose quickly to leadership positions in the Revolutionary Committee of Liaoning Province, and in the Greater Shenyang Military Area.

Before the Cultural Revolution he was not particularly friendly with Jiang Qing. But now, because they had need of each other, their relationship grew very close. Under the tutelage of the Gang of Four, Yuanxin was soon a proud general thundering and storming all over the province of Liaoning. Mao Zedong's appointment of him as his liaison immediately converted him into a core figure in the central political authority. As Mao's nephew he not only was the transmitter of Mao's words, that is, his liaison, he also was one of the few persons who had access to Mao Zedong and had opportunities to converse with him.

Deng Xiaoping knew all about this, and kept a wary eye out. In a letter to Mao Zedong on October 31, he wrote: "I need to talk with you and receive your instructions on a number of things. Any time tomorrow afternoon or evening (November 1) would be fine. Please notify me if satisfactory."

Mao sent for him in the evening of November 1. He criticized Deng for having relayed Liu Bing's letter. Deng asked him for his appraisal of the orientation of the Central Committee and of government policy. Mao said: "They are correct."

The Gang of Four was very stimulated by Mao's appointment of Mao Yuanxin as his liaison. Most of the leaders in the Central Committee had difficulty in getting to see Mao in his old age. Even his wife, Jiang Qing, rarely had the chance. It was hard for the Gang to get to Mao with their "complaints". But now that they had one of their own people at his side, they were able to whisper directly into Mao's ear. It was a boon beyond their fondest dreams. They happily set to concocting means to hasten Zhou Enlai and Deng Xiaoping to their graves.

Mao Yuanxin, in his capacity as "the emperor's closest minister", was quite willing to serve as the tool of the Gang of Four. Of course, his motive was not entirely selfless. His ambitions and greed for power were greatly heightened by his vault into the heart of the Central Committee. He wanted political status. After Mao' death, he thought, Jiang Qing would become the "woman emperor", and he would share in the political spoils. The day for Mao Yuanxin's "honorable mission" had arrived.

He reported to Mao Zedong the morning of November 2. "During my work in the province this year," he said, "I became aware of a tendency regarding the Cultural Revolution."

First, how to view the Cultural Revolution. To see it as a whole, or only certain aspects? To say it is 30 percent failure and 70 percent successful? Or 70 percent wrong and 30 percent right? Do we confirm it, or condemn it?

Second, concerning the attitude toward the criticism of Lin Biao and Confucius. Should we view the main stream, or only the tributaries? Today, some people will say a few grudging words of commendation in public, but secretly they are full of complaints. They say nothing favorable about the campaign.

Third, should we continue to criticize the Liu Shaoqi and Lin Biao lines? Today, hardly anyone talks much about criticizing the Liu Shaoqi line....

Mao Yuanxin rambled earnestly on. There is a tendency against the Cultural Revolution, fiercer than the one in 1972 against the ultra-"Left" and the Cultural Revolution, he said. As to Deng Xiaoping's attitude toward Mao Zedong's Three Directives, he doesn't say much about the directive stressing class struggle; he just talks about the Three Directives generally.... I disagree. Class struggle and line struggle are the main issues. Deng concentrates everything on improving production.... Mao Yuanxin denied the improvements attained in industry, agriculture, finance, education and culture after preliminary rectification.

"What we should do is further implement the Party's policy on cadres and, at the same time, educate them," he proposed to Mao Zedong. "They need to have the right attitude. They should thank the masses for helping and teaching them. I'm worried about the Central Committee. I'm afraid some of them will want to go back to the way things were before."

Mao Yuanxin piled on the provocations. "When some comrades get together they always discuss the bad side of the Cultural Revolution," he said to Mao Zedong. "They complain. Some treat it as a disaster. I've been paying close attention to the speeches of Comrade Xiaoping. I sense a question. He rarely mentions the accomplishments of the Cultural Revolution. He rarely criticizes Liu Shaoqi's revisionist line. This year I haven't once heard him talk about how to study theory, or criticize *Outlaws of the Marsh*, or criticize revisionism...."

When Mao Zedong showed him the letter from Liu Bing of Tsinghua University exposing Chi Qun and Xie Jingyi, Mao Yuanxin sprang to their defense. He said essentially they had been firm in implementing Mao Zedong's revolutionary line in education. "Seven out of ten" were good....

Mao was attracted by Yuanxin's "report" because it focused on Mao Zedong's most vital concerns. Namely, how to judge the Cultural Revolution, and whether there were people seeking to call it to account. If anyone dared to question the Cultural Revolution, Mao definitely would not stand idly by.

He indicated his agreement with Mao Yuanxin. "There currently are two attitudes," Mao Zedong said. "One is dissatisfaction with the Cultural Revolution. The other is a desire to call it to account. The thinking of some comrades, particularly the old comrades, is still back in the era of our bourgeois democratic revolution. They don't understand the socialist revolution. They resist it, or even oppose it."

Mao continued. "The situation at Tsinghua University is not isolated. It reflects the present struggle between the two lines. Liu Bing's letter accuses Chi Qun and Xiao Xie. As I see it, his motivation is not pure. He wants to overthrow them. Actually, the spearhead is directed against me." And Mao added, "Xiaoping favors Liu Bing."

He was very angry. After all that time and careful planning, there were still a great many people who were dissatisfied with the Cultural Revolution and wanted to reverse its judgments. Mao would never permit it. To him, a person's attitude toward the Cultural Revolution indicated whether he was for or against Mao himself. Mao would devote every effort to defending this movement he considered of such great significance.

Yet, at the same time, Mao remained cool. Naturally, he would criticize anyone who opposed the Cultural Revolution. But there was no escaping the fact that he was old. He hadn't the spirit to again smash the political balance he had so carefully maintained. He no longer had the spirit or the will to organize again a large-scale political structure. Mao Yuanxin complained that the main obstacle was Deng Xiaoping. Mao Zedong intended to criticize Deng, but he had no intention of overthrowing him again.

To Mao Yuanxin he said: "Get hold of Deng Xiaoping, and Wang Dongxing, and Chen Xilian, and talk to them without mincing any words, and also Li Xiannian, Ji Dengkui, and Hua Guofeng. Say I want them to come here. Tell them what I think, frankly and openly. I have already talked with Xiaoping, twice. Last night I spoke to him again."

Mao hesitated a moment, then said: "First call a meeting with Xiaoping, Xilian and Dongxing. Tell them all the things we discussed. Then come here."

He was straining hard to convey Mao Yuanxin's ideas to them clearly. At the same time, to make the items more palatable, he made a point of not summoning any of the Gang of Four. Mao knew of the conflict between Deng and the Gang. He was afraid the presence of any of its leaders would disrupt the discussion. If only Deng and his colleagues could accept Mao Yuanxin's ideas it would be a blessing of the greatest good fortune!

That was what Mao Zedong wished. What happened was exactly the opposite. The reason was simple. Mao Yuanxin never intended simply to "offer a few proposals". His aim was, with the backing of the Gang of Four, to create and provoke an incident. Deng Xiaoping and his comrades were well aware of Mao Yuanxin's insidious scheme. What Mao Yuanxin would say was not true, and touched on matters of policy. A man of Deng's probity would never give an inch. A battle was sure to follow.

In keeping with Mao Zedong's instructions, Mao Yuanxin on

November 2, in his capacity as "liaison", called Politburo members Deng Xiaoping, Chen Xilian, and Wang Dongxing together for a meeting. Emboldened by Mao Zedong's support, he openly expressed his opinions.

Deng sat quietly smoking, as he listened. He replied without the slightest hesitation, speaking in a calm, temperate tone.

"You should give the matter some more thought," Deng said. "According to you, the Central Committee has been carrying out an entirely revisionist line, it has abandoned Chairman Mao's line in every area. The Central Committee is headed by Chairman Mao. I don't think you can say it has been carrying out a revisionist line."

Deng made a detailed review of his main work and statements since taking charge of Central Committee operations. "What kind of line have we implemented in the past three months? That's something that can be discussed. The responsibility is mine. Has the national situation improved, or has it become worse? Comrade Yuanxin has his own opinion on that. The facts can show whether things are better or worse."

He concluded with a simple statement. "Last night, November 1st, I asked the Chairman what he thought of the orientation and policy of our work in this recent period. He said they were correct."

On November 4, Mao Yuanxin reported to Mao Zedong about his "argument" with Deng Xiaoping during their meeting on November 2. Deng had stiffly rejected his "opinions".

Mao was very disappointed. "Continue to hold meetings," he told Mao Yuanxin, "only enlarge their scope a little. Also invite Li Xiannian, Ji Dengkui, Hua Guofeng, and Zhang Chunqiao. The eight of you can discuss the matter first."

Somewhat heatedly, Mao insisted on confirming the Cultural Revolution. "The general consensus," he said, "is that the Cultural Revolution has been 70 percent right, and 30 percent wrong. It made two mistakes: Calling for down with everything, and causing all-out internal warfare." He wanted the eight people to discuss the struggle between the two lines, and concentrate on the Cultural Revolution, using his analysis to sum it up.

At an enlarged session of the Party committee of Tsinghua

University, on November 3, Wu De, First Party Secretary of the Beijing Municipality, quoted what Mao had said at the end of October: "Tsinghua University's Liu Bing and others sent me a letter accusing Chi Qun and Xiao Xie. I feel their intention is to have them overthrown. Actually, it is directed against me." Further, Mao had said: "I'm right here in Beijing. Why didn't they send it to me directly, instead of asking Xiaoping to relay it? Xiaoping is prejudiced in favor of Liu Bing. The Tsinghua question is not an isolated one. It is a reflection of the struggle between the two lines."

Mao had clearly voiced a definitive conclusion. The Tsinghua University Party Committee convened an enlarged session on November 12 of 1,700 people to study and discuss Mao's statement. A meeting of the entire school gathered on November 18 to criticize Liu Bing. Even Zhou Rongxin, the Minister of Education, and his colleagues were attacked for "rejecting the revolution in education, and repudiating the judgments of the Cultural Revolution."

After this meeting, posters went up in Tsinghua and Peking universities openly targeting Liu Bing and Zhou Rongxin. Beijing, and other provinces and municipalities were ordered to organize visits of their cadres and masses to the two schools to read the posters. The text of the posters was quickly transmitted all over the country, and many schools then held similar meetings.

The Gang of Four was behind all this. Their ultimate aim, however, was not to criticize Liu Bing and Zhou Rongxin, but to overthrow Deng Xiaoping.

With Zhang Chunqiao participating as one of the eight persons designated by Mao Zedong, you can imagine what the atmosphere of their meeting was like. When it finished, Mao Yuanxin reported back to Chairman Mao.

"The overall feeling about the Cultural Revolution is that it is essentially correct, with some failings," Mao said. "Now, we should analyze its inadequacies. Opinions won't necessarily be the same." He had hoped criticism and persuasion during the meeting of the eight would bring about some unity of understanding.

Mao Yuanxin said: "I think we reached a preliminary consensus, which improved unity. Through discussion, and unity, we will be able to do our jobs well. Isn't that the idea?"

"Right," Mao said. "Don't tell Jiang Qing about this," he cautioned. "Don't say anything."

He was hoping a unity of understanding would calm things down and support the structure and environment of "unity and stability" he was trying to maintain. He didn't want Jiang Qing and her cohorts coming in and raising a rumpus.

Perhaps Mao was being too simple. Perhaps he didn't know Mao Yuanxin had already joined Jiang Qing's crew. The meeting was something Mao Yuanxin had engineered, and Zhang Chunqiao had taken part in it. How could Jiang Qing not know? Probably Mao Zedong was using this method to warn Mao Yuanxin not to get too close to Jiang Qing.

47
Difficult Days

OUR family moved again in October 1975. Our home on Kuanjie was at a crossroads. It was very difficult for visitors to get in and out. After Papa took over the general affairs of the Central Committee, people were constantly coming to consult. Our courtyard was very small. There was no room to park. People like Politburo members had to leave their cars on the main street. It was not convenient, and not safe. The General Office of Central Committee arranged for Papa and Mama to move to 17 Dongjiaominxiang Street.

Built in the early 50s, it contained four buildings in a courtyard running from south to north. You might say we were fated to live there. In 1952, when we first arrived from Sichuan, we were assigned Building Three. Before moving, Papa first went to visit Marshal Luo Ronghuan. Luo was in very bad health, and his house was damp.

Papa said: "This place is no good for you. You can have the house the Central Committee gave me." He arranged for Marshal Luo to live in Dongjiaominxiang. We settled in Zhongnanhai.

At the start of the Cultural Revolution the Dongjiaominxiang compound was occupied by the families of Marshal Luo Ronghuan, Marshal He Long, Chief Procurator Zhang Dingcheng, and one other. As the frenzy progressed, Marshal Luo's widow and their children were driven out. When He Long came under attack, Premier Zhou Enlai hid him and his wife in his own house in Zhongnanhai. Later, Lin Biao had him imprisoned, and his children were forced to evacuate.

No. 17 Dongjiaominxiang was left empty. No one lived there. When

Zhou Enlai became ill, the Central Committee had it repaired and refurbished, intending to give it to him to recuperate in. But he never took up residence, and all the four buildings in the large compound remained empty.

Mama and Papa moved into what had been He Long's house, then shifted over to the place that had been readied for Zhou Enlai. They considered the move only temporary, and took none of the younger family members with them. But then they felt lonely, and brought in Mianmian and Mengmeng, the two grandchildren. These were followed by us three daughters, me, Deng Lin and Deng Nan, and our spouses. The Deng family loved lots of noise and activity!

But that left us with not enough bedrooms. We had over a dozen people. We converted what had originally been offices into living quarters. My husband He Ping and I used the room intended for a library next to the parlor. Having been deprived of his library, Papa put his desk and a chair in what had been an enclosed porch on the south side of the building. He said the light was good there, it was airy, and he could see the children running around the yard. It was an ideal "office".

Since returning to Beijing in 1973, we moved from Huayuancun to Kuanjie to Dongjiaominxiang — three times within two years. It was really wild.

The festive air was quickly supplanted by a new political atmosphere. The meeting of eight people Mao Zedong had directed Mao Yuanxin to convene presaged the coming of a political storm. A somber quiet settled on our household. Papa was very busy with duties in the Central Committee and the State Council. In addition, he frequently had to receive foreign dignitaries. In October, he met with an emissary of the Japanese premier, the chairman of the Yugoslav Administrative Committee, the US Secretary of State, and the Prime Minister of the Federal Republic of Germany. At public functions he appeared spirited and smiling. But when he came home, we often saw him sitting in his chair alone in the enclosed porch, his eyes closed, his brows knit in a frown.

Though he said nothing to any of us, we knew from past experience an unpredictable danger was likely to happen. Outwardly, he showed no signs of disturbance. He kept to his usual schedule. He rose at the same time, had his meals, read official documents, retired in the evening, read for a while in bed, and went to sleep. But, as his family members, we remained alert to change.

One night Papa accompanied Mao Zedong when he was receiving a foreign guest, and he returned home late. He looked very tired. Mama gave him a sleeping pill, and he went to bed. After he fell asleep, we hung up his clothes. In one of his pockets we found a slip of paper. On it, in very large script, were Mao Zedong's characters! We knew Mao was having difficulty in speaking, and that he sometimes dotted down a few words to make himself clear. But we never expected to actually see one of his memos. Screwing up our courage, we read the note in the dim light of a lamp. Mama, Deng Nan, and I examined it carefully. The characters, written large, were shaky, lopsided, and disconnected. Some were completely illegible. Probably, they were simply additions to something Mao was saying. We couldn't make head or tail of them, no matter how we tried.

Actually, we weren't particularly interested in Mao's handwriting. What we were hoping was to find some hint of Papa's political situation. Papa had always been strict. We were breaking the rules by reading anything in his possession. Keeping very quiet, we put the note back in his pocket. Had it not been for the unusual circumstances we would never have dared to go so far.

Although we knew Papa was being criticized, we wouldn't ask him about it. First of all, he wouldn't have told us. Secondly, we didn't want to upset him. All we could do at this time was to give him even more care and warmth, and try to ease his unhappiness. We kept him company, and let the kids play more nearby. If he fell silent and closed his eyes we moved them swiftly away. We spoke more quietly, or simply sat with him in silence. Our family's usual noisy laughter was now unnaturally stilled. At night a single lamp burned in the darkened enclosed porch. Papa sat there, alone, often for a long, long time.

People continued to come and go at our house on 17 Dongjiaominxiang Street. Only they were different persons than before, and their purposes were different.

Vice-Premiers Li Xiannian and Ji Dengkui, and Hu Qiaomu were frequent callers. They came to talk about work. Deng Yingchao also often came to discuss the Premier's illness. Wang Hairong and Tang Wensheng came even more frequently, to speak privately with Papa. Because they were present when Chairman Mao received foreign visitors, and had an opportunity to talk with him, they were in an important position. Mao was not well. It was more difficult than ever to get to see him, even for high leaders in the Central Committee. And so the best way to get word to him was through them. They could speak to him after the foreign visitor had gone. Jiang Qing several times asked them to convey a message to Mao. But they both disliked her, and had nothing in common with her precious Gang of Four.

They respected Zhou Enlai and Deng Xiaoping, who trusted them both. Seriously ill, Zhou frequently sent for them. He spoke about their work in foreign affairs, and more often about the importance of resisting the Gang of Four. For the same reasons, they often came to our home. Papa sometimes sent for them. He would ask them to convey a message to Mao, or to get his opinion on something. They were extremely useful in enabling Papa to maintain a line of communications with Mao Zedong.

After Mao Yuanxin complained and Papa came under attack, it was more difficult for Wang and Tang. But they still called to our house often and talked with Papa's secretary Wang Ruilin for hours. Like us, they had a sense of foreboding about the way things were developing. When the new "criticize Deng" campaign started, Wang Hairong and Tang Wensheng were our last visitors.

We had one very unusual caller at number 17 — Mao Yuanxin. Mao Zedong knew he was critical of Papa, but told him to call on Papa and speak frankly. When we heard he was coming we knew it couldn't be for anything good. We all went strictly on our guard.

Mao Yuanxin arrived; the image of a pompous newly appointed high official. Papa was waiting for him in the parlor, silently smoking. After the visitor was seated, the discussion began.

He Ping and I lived in the adjoining room, which originally had been a library. It was separated from the parlor only by wooden bookshelves. Fairly loud voices were clearly audible. That day, Deng Nan was with me, and we could hear snatches of the conversation going on in the parlor.

The talk between Papa and Mao Yuanxin went badly. When Mao left, Papa did not see him out. Reserved, relaxed, undisturbed by Mao Yuanxin's "complaint" against him, he had no intention of abandoning his grand strategy of national rectification. His mind had been made up from the time he returned to Beijing and resumed office. The Gang of Four raised a rumpus. He didn't waver. Mao Yuanxin came to fuss. Papa didn't stir. Although the situation was now more complex, he stood firm. Nine years of storm and strife had strengthened his conviction, steeled his resolve.

On a visit to Hu Qiaomu to discuss work, Papa said he had been criticized for having relayed Liu Bing's letter to Mao Zedong. Hu said he didn't believe that was the reason, more likely it was because of the way he was conducting an all-out rectification. Mao had been critical from the start. And now the difference in their appraisal of the situation had become increasingly clear. There was a deeper political reason behind Mao's criticism of Deng, said Hu. This brewing storm was not likely to subside.

About this time, Wang Hongwen, whom Mao had dispatched to Shanghai to "help with the work", returned to Beijing. Deng, who had taken over Wang's job of handling the daily affairs of the Central Committee, proposed to Mao in a letter on November 15 that he give the job back. The evening of the same day, Mao endorsed a reply: "Let Comrade Xiaoping continue for the time being. We can consider this again later."

It was obvious that Mao would not use Wang's return to get Deng to step down and restore power to Wang Hongwen. Mao was dissatisfied with Deng, but he didn't like the Gang of Four. If Deng couldn't do a good job, a replacement would have to be found. But who? Mao was considering, but he hadn't decided. His mental state was complicated.

Not long after, things took a sudden turn for the worse.

Kang Sheng, who was already hopelessly ill, told Mao that Deng Xiaoping "wants to overturn the verdicts of the Cultural Revolution". Adding this to Deng's uncompromising stance in recent meetings, Mao decided it was no longer a simple question of "unifying thinking" and "strengthening unity" where Deng was concerned, but rather a matter of someone who wanted to repudiate the Cultural Revolution. Mao was determined to nail down an affirmation of the Cultural Revolution before he died. No negative appraisals would be permitted.

The Politburo convened a meeting on November 20, 1975, to specially discuss the current appraisals of the Cultural Revolution. Mao Zedong hoped in this way to reach a unity of understanding. He proposed that Deng Xiaoping conduct a meeting that would enable the Central Committee to issue a "resolution" proclaiming that the Cultural Revolution was "seventy percent successful and (only) thirty percent a failure". If Deng Xiaoping would support such a resolution it would stop the mouths of those who held similar negative views. It would also give Deng a chance to change his stance.

Mao indeed treated Deng with the "utmost benevolence". While recognizing Deng's ability and probity, he was exasperated by his attitude toward the Cultural Revolution. Mao was very fond of Deng, but he hoped he would be able to compromise, and accede to this — Mao's final aspiration.

But Mao was too old, too weary. The atmosphere of "stability and unity" he had put forward after long consideration had fizzled out. He hadn't the energy to try anything new. Unfortunately, Deng Xiaoping's stubbornness matched his own. Deng would never give ground on a matter of principle. He refused to accept Mao's proposal. As an excuse he said he had been divorced from public affairs for six years during the nine years of the Cultural Revolution. As an "outsider" he didn't "understand" it, and so it would be "inappropriate" for him to draft the resolution.

The fact was he could not bring himself to affirm anything so repugnant to him.

His refusal led Mao to decide to call for a "criticize Deng" campaign.

In the final stage of his political existence, Mao was determined to defend the Cultural Revolution. He would tolerate no contrary opinions; he would permit no one to reverse its verdicts. This was his final, uncompromising stand.

On November 24, the Central Committee, on Mao's instructions, convened what was later called a "Reminder Meeting". Attending were all of the Politburo members then in Beijing, and responsible comrades in the Party, government, and armed forces — at total of more than 130. It was chaired by Deng Xiaoping, who was then still in charge of the work of the Central Committee. He addressed the opening session.

"All of the Politburo members now in Beijing are here today," he said. "More than 100 others are also attending. I will first read the main points for discussion, drawn up by the Politburo and approved by Mao Zedong.

"They are the following:

"1) The letter by Liu Bing, deputy secretary of the Party Committee of Tsinghua University, and others, slanders Chi Qun and Xie Jingyi. It was actually directed against Chairman Mao. In keeping with the Chairman's instruction, the Tsinghua Party Committee has already conducted a full debate on Comrade Liu Bing's letter, and the debate has now been extended to include the entire student and faculty bodies.

"2) Chairman Mao has pointed out the purpose of the letter was to 'overthrow Chi Qun and Xie Jingyi, and in fact was aimed at me'. Chairman Mao's instruction is very important. The Tsinghua University question is not an isolated one. It is a reflection of the struggle between the two classes, the two roads, the two lines. It is a Rightist wind seeking to blow down the verdicts. There are some who are displeased with the Cultural Revolution, who want to settle accounts with it, to reverse the judgments. It is essential that we, through argument and discussion, clarify our thinking, and tighten unity among our comrades.

"3) Chairman Mao has directed that we call these matters to the attention of some comrades to help them avoid making any new errors."

Deng then offered what he called a "few small points of clarification." Firstly, regarding what Mao referred to as the "three correct attitudes" that is, correct attitudes toward the Cultural Revolution, toward the masses, and toward oneself.

Secondly, Deng continued, "When Chairman Mao says we must consider class struggle fundamental, he is simply reiterating the Party's basic line. It is not correct to say Chairman Mao's Three Directives are fundamental. Class struggle is fundamental. The other two are goals."

Third, "We should have a correct approach to new developments. We should affirm and support them, and not indulge in a lot of nit-picking. People in education, and in all the various professions and occupations for that matter, should pay particular attention to this."

Fourth, "The old, the middle aged and the young should work together, particularly with regard to the young cadres. Don't beat them to death for any little mistake."

Finally, "The big debate in Tsinghua University will soon extend all over the country, or certainly to the education and cultural fields, at a minimum."

By his transmission of Mao's "main points", plus the "clarifications", Deng was, in effect, notifying the old comrades of the criticism Mao had directed against him. Mao had two purposes in calling for the convening of this meeting. He wanted to compel Deng to criticize himself, and to clearly notify the old comrades of Mao's attitude. He wanted to get them to turn their minds around and not make any more "mistakes."

On November 26, the "Reminder" was sent to the leaders of every Party, government, and military organization in the land, with a demand that they discuss it, and report the outcome of their discussions to the Central Committee.

As a result, a new campaign was commenced to "oppose the Right-deviationist attempts to reverse the judgments." It quickly spread nationwide. The all-out rectification that had been going on for nine months came to a halt. The scope of the campaign deepened and broadened — from criticizing Deng Xiaoping without mentioning his name to attacking him directly.

Their dream of "criticizing Deng" realized at last, the Gang of Four was ecstatically happy. Already, in October, Wang Hongwen had conferred several times with the leaders of the Shanghai revolutionary committee and with Liu Qingtang of the Ministry of Culture.

"Pay close attention to what's happening in Tsinghua and Peking universities," he instructed these adherents of the Gang of Four. "It's something big. Consider your tactics. Gird your loins and get ready for battle."

Subsequently, he summoned Shanghai's main Gang of Four hatchet men to Beijing and infused them with his insidious slanders. "Deng Xiaoping is the head of the landlords' revanchist militias," he hissed. "Hua Guofeng, Ye Jianying and Li Xiannian are his lieutenants."

To Deng, none of this was unexpected. He knew when he decided upon a nationwide rectification and took an uncompromising stand he would again be criticized and purged. He was mentally prepared for it, and unafraid. He said: "Old cadres should face up coolly to being knocked down again. We should do our jobs well. Even if we're overthrown, we will have made a contribution."

When he was being criticized, in addition to his regular work in the Central Committee and the State Council, what concerned him most was the illness of Zhou Enlai and the medical treatment he was being receiving. He went to see him frequently and did his utmost to ensure that he was being given the best of care.

He and other Central Committee leaders in the afternoon of October 16 heard a report in the Great Hall of the People on Zhou's health. In the afternoon of October 17 he discussed the treatment with Zhou's wife Deng Yingchao. He spoke with her again at his home on the 4th of November. At 9:30 in the evening of November 11 he and other Central Committee leaders listened to another report on Zhou's condition by the medical team in charge. At 10:30 on the night of the 16th, together with Wang Hongwen, Zhang Chunqiao, Li Xiannian and Wang Dongxing, he listened to another report by the medical team. At three in the afternoon of November 27 he and other Central Committee leaders again heard a report by the medical team.

The renewed attack on the so-called "Rightists" angered and worried Zhou Enlai. Deng Xiaoping visited him in the hospital on December 8. Wang Dongxing, Wang Hongwen, Li Xiannian, Chen Yonggui, Wang

Hairong and Tang Wensheng also went, separately, the same day.

In his talk with Wang Hongwen, the Premier reminded him of what Mao Zedong had warned in Changsha in 1974: "Jiang Qing is ambitious." Lying ill in bed, that was all Zhou could do for his old comrade-in-arms Deng Xiaoping. He was very concerned by the heat of the attack, and whether Deng could withstand it. He sent for him and asked: "Will you change your position?"

"Never," Deng replied.

Zhou was happy. "Now I can relax," he said.

These two old veterans were both speaking from the heart. They shared a political belief that scorned any consideration of personal glory, or even life itself. It was a very important discussion. Papa recalled it many times more than 10 years later. Many times he told us children about it.

The Politburo held a series of meetings criticizing Deng Xiaoping in December 1975. They were very intense. The Gang of Four poured a frenzy of invective on Deng Xiaoping and the broad rectification campaign he had led. It was crazy. The meetings criticizing Deng Xiaoping were chaired by none other than Deng Xiaoping! The whole thing was a charade. As Papa later recalled: "Actually, all I did was to say 'The meeting is opened,' at the start, and 'The meeting is concluded,' at the finish." He sat in silence throughout the entire proceedings, and never said a word.

He made a "self-criticism" at a meeting of the Politburo on December 20. As an indication of what he thought of it, he spoke without any formal notes. But we do have a copy of the minutes of the meeting. Deng Xiaoping said the following:

"First, let me thank the Chairman for his teachings, and thank you comrades for your help. My recognition of my faults has been gradual. Regarding my thinking, for a time prior to the No. 9 Document, I observed that production had stagnated in a considerable number of industries. There were a lot of accidents and, in many places, severe factional strife. I really was quite worried. During February and March rail shipment had a lot of problems, which influenced many aspects of national production. So I proposed dealing with the railways first. In addition to stressing unity in managerial structure, I particularly emphasized arousing the masses, criticizing bourgeois factionalism, and moving swiftly to straighten things out. We focused on the handful of leaders of factional fights, and firmly put them in isolation.

"After we solved the problem in Xuzhou, the picture in all our railways quickly improved. It seemed to me our method had been very effective. We hit only a small area, but had a big educational response, and very quickly. Since using our experience with the Jiangsu railways we solved other kinds of problems in the province fairly rapidly, I thought why not also use the same method elsewhere? So I applied it in the steel industry, in the mechanized divisions, in certain areas and provinces, even in rectifying the Chinese Academy of Sciences.

"Before our meeting here today, I had already come to the conclusion that our method was correct. And so I was surprised and a bit resentful when some comrades criticized it."

In his "self-criticism" Deng talked about his attitude toward factionalism, industrial production, cultural and educational organizations, harmony between the old, the middle-aged and the young, new phenomena, and especially with regard to the Cultural Revolution. He said the main, and most fundamental, reason for making a self-criticism was his attitude toward the Cultural Revolution. It was due, he said, not because he had been isolated and cut off from work for eight years, but because he had failed to understand it.

What he was saying, in effect, was that the methods he used in the all-out rectification were correct, and that he was surprised and resentful of the criticism directed against him. He said candidly that his "error" was not due to having been isolated for eight years, but to his attitude toward the Cultural Revolution. His "self-criticism" stated his thinking and understanding plainly, without any reservations.

After the meeting Deng Xiaoping sent a letter to Mao Zedong, and included in it a copy of his "self-criticism". He wrote: "Chairman, at the meeting this evening (the 20th) I spoke examining my errors. I enclose the speech for your perusal. Of course, this is only preliminary. I hope to have an opportunity to receive your teaching directly. The time, naturally, can be at your convenience."

Deng was no longer able to see Mao. He was hoping, by sending this "self-criticism", to indicate his desire to speak with him directly.

Mao made no notation on Deng's letter and speech. But the meetings to criticize and "help" him continued.

In December, 1975 the notorious figure in the Cultural Revolution Kang Sheng died.

Kang Sheng was a very unusual individual in the history of the Chinese Communist Party. Born to an aristocratic Shandong family, he joined the Party quite young. He had a deep knowledge of Chinese culture, and knew all the ancient treatises and histories. After receiving a "correct" Marxist education in the Soviet Union, he became one of Party's "theorists". His interests were broad. An expert on antiques, a lover of Peking opera, he had an excellent memory for faces and names. Everyone in the Party, regardless of rank, hailed him as "Master" Kang.

Amiable on the surface, he was a very complicated and devious personality. He was completely different from what he appeared. His soul was deep. He knew every aspect of the hidden twists and turns of the struggle inside the Party. Kang Sheng pretended to be a weakly convalescent, but the moment a political breeze stirred the grass, his ferocity immediately surfaced.

His relationship with Jiang Qing was long standing. Jiang Qing's mother had been a servant in his family household. His relationship with Mao Zedong was also special. He had been able to find and bring back to China two of Mao's sons who had been wandering abroad.

During the "Rectification" in Yan'an, Kang Sheng capitalized on Mao's trust to harm a great number of people. Later, he realized he was on shaky ground. He crept into a cocoon of alleged illness to gain time for a metamorphosis. With the advent of the Cultural Revolution he felt his moment had come. Girding himself in full battle array, he became an advisor to the Cultural Revolution Group, and went on to rise to the rank of member of the Standing Committee of the Politburo and Vice Chairman of the Chinese Communist Party. He gave full vent to his viciousness during the Cultural Revolution. Naming names and conducting investigations, he ruined many an innocent.

Although he and the Gang of Four were originally in close harmony, they became fierce enemies in squabbles over power. When our family returned to Beijing in 1973, my parents went to visit him in Diaoyutai (Fishing Pavilion), and took me along. He was lying in bed, very ill, just skin and bones. The moment he opened his mouth he began swearing at Jiang Qing and Zhang Chunqiao, seething with rage. If it were someone else reviling the Gang of Four, there naturally would be nothing strange about it, but coming from Kang Sheng, it sounded odd. We had just returned to Beijing and were not familiar with the situation. We couldn't make head or tail of what was driving him. By then Kang Sheng and the Gang of Four were implacable foes.

His character hadn't changed when he was dying at the end of 1975. He was still as two-faced as ever. Summoning Wang Hairong and Tang Wensheng, he urged them to tell Mao Zedong that he, Kang Sheng, had never betrayed the Party, but that he had proof of the treachery of Jiang Qing and Zhang Chunqiao. He said he already knew when they were in Yan'an, but he hadn't told Mao and the Central Committee. He also wanted to upset Mao Zedong, as Mao Yuanxin had done, with a claim that Deng Xiaoping intended to "reverse the judgments" of the "Cultural Revolution." At death's door, he used his last breath to puff up flames of discord.

Kang Sheng died of illness on December 16, 1975, another leading actor gone from the Cultural Revolution stage. One performer followed another, many stars in many different roles. In Kang Sheng's brief glittering run in the political theater as a villain and clown, he managed to do irreparable damage to our country, our people and our Party.

370

48

Tragic Misery

THE winter of 1975 was really cold! Strong winds blew from early December. Bicycle riders wore thick padded tunics and trousers, topped by padded hats with earflaps down and tied beneath the chin. Even with padded gloves hands were quickly frozen purple and stiff.

It was cold at year's end, and people's hearts were even colder.

Economically, it had been the best year of the nine years of the Cultural Revolution. Industry and agriculture combined had climbed 11.9 percent higher than the previous year, with agriculture up 4.6 percent, and industry 15.1. Grain, steel, coal, oil, and electricity brought large increases in tax revenue. Thanks to the all-out rectification, production had revived, order was restored, and factionalism was curbed. Confidence among the cadres and the masses improved considerably, and it was a generally gratifying situation.

But it didn't last long. When the wild "oppose the Right-deviationist attempts to reverse the judgments" movement sprang up, it denied all the successes the nine-month rectification had achieved, and brought it to a halt. China's economy plunged to a new low.

The most tragic blow was to people's hearts. The good results of the rectification had just become visible, hopes had just been raised, when again the country was immersed in uneasiness and confusion.

But this was not the lunatic early stage of the Cultural Revolution. After nine years of political strife the Chinese people had become more mature. They were not so easily duped. A sudden shift in the political situation, a new criticism drive, this time evoked not blindness and excitement, but a big question mark.

1975, with its ups and downs, with its mystifying "criticize Deng" environment, had drifted to a close. 1976 was a new year, and Deng was compelled to write a new "self-criticism".

There was no relaxation of the pressure on him. On January 3, just two days after the advent of the New Year, Deng Xiaoping was required to make a second "self-criticism" (or, what might be called a "supplemental criticism") before the Politburo. Perhaps because the first one had been so informal, this one had to be submitted in writing. Deng had already said whatever he wanted to say, he had already made his attitude plain. The content of his new "self-criticism" was essentially the same. The only difference being that he added a clause that he had not previously asked approval by Chairman Mao or reported to the Politburo his position regarding the "three directives as the foundation".

He then wrote the following letter to Mao Zedong: "After a preliminary criticism before the Politburo, Comrade Mao Yuanxin relayed to me your important instructions. First, six comrades, and then at two meetings, comrades strictly analyzed my errors, and helped me realize that my self-criticism had been inadequate. The meetings criticizing me must continue. But I hope I can have a chance to express my recognition of my faults to you personally, and receive your teaching. Naturally, it would be at your convenience."

Deng again had asked for direct talks.

Mao Zedong did not receive him. After reading Deng's second "self-criticism", on January 14, Mao issued an order regarding it and the previous one of December 20, 1975.

"Print and submit to Politburo for discussion". Obviously, Mao was displeased. Continuing "discussion" meant continuing criticism of Deng Xiaoping.

In the gloomy political atmosphere, Zhou Enlai's life steadily ebbed away. The Premier lay in bed, listening, as daily news reports were read to him. He was very concerned with the political strife going on. He struggled to withstand the torment of his terminal illness, tightly grasping the nurse's hand when the pain was too great, striving to conceal the agony. Zhou tried to speak with the visitors who came to see him, but he was too weak, and could only utter a few words.

His condition took a turn for the worse in mid-December, when Beijing was enveloped in a frigid winter. He constantly lapsed into unconsciousness. To ease his pain, the doctors kept him heavily sedated, as they fought to preserve his life.

Near the end Deng Xiaoping came twice to the hospital to see his old comrade and friend. Zhou also spoke with Ye Jianying. He instructed him to weigh political tactics carefully — under no circumstances should power be allowed to fall into the hands of the Gang of Four.

At times, Zhou and his loving wife and companion in battle for over 50 years, Deng Yingchao, softly sang *The Internationale* together, as a sign of their mutual devotion and support.

From the day he went into the hospital on June 1, 1973 until January 8, 1976, Zhou Enlai underwent more than 10 operations, large and small. He continued to work, reading papers, endorsing documents. Zhou held 161 discussions with leaders of the Central Committee, talked 55 times with other Central Committee officials, and received 63 foreign guests. While battling with the Grim Reaper, Zhou Enlai never relaxed his selfless devotion to duty.

Deng Xiaoping, all during the period he was being criticized, continued to do his utmost for his old companion in battle, the man he knew thoroughly and respected since his youth. At seven o'clock in the morning of December 20, Zhou requested that Luo Qingchang be sent for, to talk about Taiwan. The hospital phoned Deng and asked what to do.

"The Premier is so ill," Deng said. "Let him see anybody he wants."

On December 22 at 1:30 pm in the afternoon, he and other Central Committee leaders listened to an urgent report by the team in charge of Zhou Enlai's medical treatment. Deng was called out of bed after midnight on the 28 — Zhou was being given emergency treatment. Deng and five leaders of the Central Committee rushed to the hospital and stayed with Deng Yingchao, who was at Zhou's bedside. At 2:10 in the morning, Zhou was again snatched back from the jaws of death.

Despondency cloaked the arrival of 1976.

Zhou's last operation took place at dawn on January 5. Deng Xiaoping, Li Xiannian and Wang Dongxing were there, waiting. That afternoon and evening Ye Jianying and other members of the Politburo then in Beijing were informed of Zhou's condition. They came to the hospital, one after another. On January 7, at 11:00 at night, Zhou began slipping away.

On January 8, 1976, at 9:67 am, Zhou Enlai, great son of the Chinese people, loyal Communist, superb leader of the Chinese Communist Party and Chinese government, left us forever. He was 78.

Zhou Enlai was dead! The tragic news shocked the world.

The blow broke open the floodgates of the hearts of the people. Tears gushed from their eyes. They couldn't believe it. Their beloved Premier was gone. How could he have departed in such misery and pain? Exhaustion had struck him down; exhaustion had destroyed him. Anger at those despicable criminals had killed him! Sorrow wrung the hearts of the Chinese people. But their minds were very clear. While they wept at the loss of Zhou Enlai, a founder of the country, national fury rose in their breasts.

Zhou's death pushed aside the meetings criticizing Deng Xiaoping. Deng was nominally still in charge of the Central Committee's general affairs. With heavy heart he assumed full responsibility for the funeral arrangements. He wrote immediately to Mao Zedong requesting that a formal announcement of Zhou's passing and the names of the members of the funeral committee be broadcast at once. On January 9, Mao endorsed his approval.

Heads of state of many countries requested permission to attend the funeral, but Mao decided against it. However, at Deng's request, and with Mao's consent, Deng accepted a formal condolence call from the Albanian ambassador. Qiao Guanhua received the ambassador from Japan, and Han Nianlong received the Sri Lanka ambassador.

A funeral committee was announced on January 9. It was composed of 107 members headed by Mao Zedong, Wang Hongwen, Deng Xiaoping and Zhu De. At Tian'anmen, Xinhuamen, the Working People's Cultural

Palace, and the Ministry of Foreign Affairs, flags flew at half-mast. The five-star blood-red banners rippled in the icy breeze against a backdrop of white clouds and blue sky.

Heads of Party and government and 10,000 mourners, on January 10 and 11, gathered at the Beijing Hospital to pay their last respects to Zhou Enlai, who was lying in state. Venerable old Marshal Zhu De walked with heavy steps to the bier of his veteran friend and raised his right hand in a final salute. Deng Xiaoping, Soong Ching Ling and Li Xiannian also sorrowfully bid Zhou Enlai farewell.

Thousands of mourners crowded to the hospital's entrance. Many, brushing hot tears from their eyes, hoped for a last look at their beloved Premier, for a last chance to manifest their respect and sorrow.

"Zhou Enlai" became synonymous with greatness, with undying national spirit. He lived for the liberation of the people and the nation, battling tirelessly for China's construction. He died as the proud representative of their hearts and souls. His tragic death stirred up a truly significant tidal wave, a glorious people's revolt.

Only the Gang of Four members were happy over the passing of Zhou Enlai. All of their efforts had not been able to bring him down. Now that he was gone; a great obstacle had been removed. Naturally they were pleased. On January 7, when Zhou was dying, Jiang Qing was quite unconcerned, and concentrated on wildly attacking Deng Xiaoping. At a meeting of the Politburo, she accused him of wanting to reverse the verdicts of the Cultural Revolution all across the land. She said he was urging old cadres not to fear being overthrown again, to stake their lives on their views.

Yao Wenyuan, on January 9, forbade *People's Daily* from carrying articles memorializing Zhou Enlai. In the six days following Zhou's death it published only two news items about him.

Everyone who went to Zhou Enlai's bier to bid farewell looked sad and stricken. Jiang Qing didn't even remove her hat. During the moment of silence ceremony, she kept gazing all around. Her disgusting performance was seen by millions of indignant viewers on a nationwide television broadcast.

On the day of national mourning, the Gang of Four issued an order forbidding anyone to wear black armbands or send floral wreaths, or set up memorial halls, or hold memorial services, or hang up pictures of Zhou Enlai. They even ordered every unit and organization to check on whether their members had hung pictures of Zhou Enlai in their homes and draped them with black bunting.

Prominent lieutenant of the Gang of Four, Yu Huiyong, Minister of Culture, insisted that theatrical companies perform as usual, and directed his security divisions to investigate anyone who phoned in a protest.

The actions of the Gang of Four were in obvious sharp contrast to the misery of the general public. Their attempts to suppress the people's sorrow aroused furious resentment. They prohibited wearing black armbands; people simply put them on under their overcoats. They prohibited memorial services; people gathered in silent reverence before flags at half-mast beneath the broad blue skies.

Dr. Lin Qiaozhi, famous gynecologist at the PUMC Hospital, had the utmost respect for Zhou Enlai. When hospital inspectors made a round of the rooms they found a portrait of Zhou hanging in her office. They took it down. The 70 year old doctor wept angry tears. The moment they left, she put it up again.

The people's love for Zhou Enlai was deeply etched in their hearts. You couldn't tear it away; you couldn't move it away. Their dislike for the Gang of Four turned into utter hatred.

On January 11, the body of Zhou Enlai was to be brought to the Revolutionary Martyrs Cemetery for cremation. The people heard, and the people came — from every part of the city, from miles around, from every corner of their native land. Braving the winter winds they stood in silence on both sides of the long Chang'an Avenue to watch the funeral cortege roll by, paying their respects, seeing off their dear Premier to his final resting place.

Slowly the hearse drove by. Hot tears flowed from the people's eyes; watchers were choked with sobs, completely bereft. Zhou Enlai had died in sorrow and pain. But his spirit, hearing the heart-felt cries, would surely be comforted, be proud of the people and fully confident in them.

Over 10,000 people from every walk of life, from January 12 to 14, gathered at the Working People's Cultural Palace to conduct memorial services. Many more, in defiance of the restrictions of the Gang of Four, held their own remembrance meetings. Many wore black armbands and carried white flowers to the Monument to the People's Heroes standing in Tian'anmen Square. In a few days it was covered with garlands. Weeping people draped the pines lining the Square with wreathes of white flowers they had woven themselves. Layer upon layer fell like snowflakes on the eternal pines.

There were memorial services in Beijing, Shanghai, Tianjin, Guangzhou, Wuhan, Xi'an, Nanjing, Chongqing, in every city, large and small, and they kept growing larger. The ordinary people of China thus silently mourned their beloved Premier Zhou, thus manifested their worry over the future of the Party and the country. Still further, they demonstrated their rage against the Gang of Four.

The Politburo at a meeting approved the wording of a speech to be read at a formal national memorial service. Mao endorsed it. The question was who should read it. Although Deng Xiaoping had been criticized, he had not been removed from office. Nominally, he was still in charge of the work of the Central Committee, and should be the one to read the speech.

Zhang Chunqiao opposed. He proposed Ye Jianying, instead. Marshal Ye saw through this gambit of the Gang of Four to denigrate Deng. He insisted that Deng be the speaker, and defeated their scheme.

The day before the memorial service Yao Wenyuan arranged that an article appear on the front page of the *People's Daily* entitled "A Great Debate Will Bring a Great Change". Its aim was to focus on "rejecting the Rightist attempt to reverse the judgments of the Cultural Revolution", and vitiate the people's bitter sorrow over the death of Zhou Enlai. On January 13, he sent three directives in a row to the head of the Xinhua News Agency. Such as: "Don't let the memorial services elbow out the regular news on grasping revolution and promoting production," and "You have published too many cables of condolence in the last few days, too many at one time." He directed that in future they all be put on the back pages.

Irreconcilable battle positions between the people and the Gang of Four were being clearly drawn.

Deng Xiaoping was busy with carrying out what Zhou Enlai had requested be performed after his death. In a letter to the members of the Politburo on January 14, Deng wrote: "Comrade Dongxing has discussed with Older Sister Deng where the ashes should be scattered. They learned there was no longer any water on Yuquan (Jade Springs) Mountain, and decided to have them strewn from a light plane over China's rivers and mountains instead. Older Sister Deng will carry the ashes to the airfield. Someone else will do the scattering. This is better than the original plan for a definite location. Please approve. Comrade Dongxing has already made the necessary preparations."

Fourteen members of the Politburo endorsed their agreement on the letter. Deng was glad he had been able to take what might be his last opportunity to perform a specific service for Zhou Enlai, his close comrade-in-arms.

An impressive memorial service for Zhou Enlai was held in the Great Hall of the People on January 15. His portrait was hung at one end of the auditorium. The red banner of the Chinese Communist Party draped the casket containing his ashes. Those attending stood in sorrowful silence. Deng Xiaoping, Vice-Chairman of the Central Committee of the Chinese Communist Party, Vice-Premier of the State Council, and deputy chairman of the Central Military Commission, read the memorial address as their representative. He praised Zhou's glorious record, his splendid contributions to the revolution and national construction, his fine spirit and character.

"Comrade Zhou Enlai was true to the Party and the people," Deng said. "He carried out Chairman Mao's proletarian revolutionary line. For the liberation of the Chinese people, for the victory of the communist cause, he battled valiantly, humbly serving the people, selflessly giving his all. He fought for the cause of communism all his life, he steadfastly stood with the revolution all his life. He was a model for our entire Party, our whole Army, for all of our people."

Deng was expressing what was in the hearts of Zhou Enlai's loyal friends, and all of the people of China. For half a century he and Zhou had known each other intimately, and fought side by side. The address was his last salute; it represented also his solemn pledge on behalf of China's masses to uphold justice and truth. Deng Xiaoping praised Zhou Enlai's glorious life, his embodiment of China excellent spiritual qualities.

The memorial meeting concluded with everyone present bowing solemnly, in turn, three times before the portrait of Zhou Enlai. Later, in accordance with Zhou's wishes, his ashes were scattered over the waters and hills of the country he loved so well.

Zhou Enlai, a great Chinese of the 20th century, added luster to his times and honor to his land. He will live forever in the hearts of the people!

49

"Criticize Deng, Oppose the Right-deviationist Attempts to Reverse the Judgments"

T HE reading of the memorial address for Zhou Enlai on January 15, 1976 was the last time Deng Xiaoping was seen on the nation's television screens. A new, larger scale drive to "Criticize Deng, Oppose the Right-deviationist Attempts to Reverse the Judgments" followed next.

Mao had directed the Politburo to "discuss" Deng's two previous "self-criticisms". It had been postponed because of the death of Zhou Enlai. But after the memorial services, the "criticize Deng" flames immediately flared up again. The Politburo met on January 20, and began the "discussion".

Deng was mentally prepared to be overthrown once more. He knew Mao wanted the criticism to continue, and that it would surely intensify. He hadn't wavered when Mao sent Mao Yuanxin to urge conciliation, and he had no intention of giving in now.

Just as he anticipated, the Gang of Four launched a feverish attack at the Politburo meeting. They demanded to know why he had requested to speak to Mao. Deng calmly replied that in addition to reporting his recognition of his errors, he wanted to talk about his duties.

"I feel my request was reasonable," he said. "That is still my wish."

Not to talk about class struggle, he said, was his "old failing". (In other words, he still didn't agree that class struggle was the fundamental problem.)

"If you consider this an error," he said, "then my fundamental stand is in error, and all of my work is being done wrong."

No wonder the Gang of Four were angry. This was no "self-criticism". In fact, Deng had taken the opportunity to restate his position.

As to their claim that in previous self-criticisms he had sought to reverse the judgments of the Cultural Revolution, he said: "I have looked my statements over, and I stand completely by what I said."

To the Politburo he asserted: "I am not a suitable person to be responsible for important duties."

Actually, he was asking to be relieved. He had done three self-criticisms. He knew Mao would not be pleased with them. The Gang of Four would not let him rest. Being overthrown again was just a question of time. Since he couldn't effectively continue his duties, the best thing to do was to request to step down.

Enraged by Deng's stubbornness, the Gang fired a fusillade of assaults. Because of his well-known deafness he couldn't hear, and didn't want to hear, their raucous persiflage. He said nothing more, and sat quietly, taking occasional sips from his mug of tea. As a result of all the liquid he imbibed, he had to leave the smoke-filled hall frequently for trips to the men's room. The dictatorial Gang of Four accused him of finding an excuse to escape listening to criticism.

Later the same night, although it was very late, Deng took up his pen. In the light of the lamp on his office desk, he wrote a letter to Mao Zedong which said:

"Chairman: After my self-criticisms of December 20 and January 3, you directed the Politburo to discuss them. The comrades demanded to know why I had requested to see you. I enclose a brief copy of my reply for your examination. I had requested twice to see you, Chairman, because I wished, in addition to reporting on my errors and requesting your correction, to talk about my duties. I hesitated to raise this question at a time when I was undergoing criticism. I was afraid if I did, I might be thought trying to avoid reproach. If I didn't, some might say it was because I hated to give up power. After careful consideration, I decided it would be better to raise the matter. To delay any longer would affect the work of the Central Committee, and add to my errors. I therefore, Chairman, beg that you approve my request to be relieved of my duties as head of the daily work of the Central Committee. I am not an appropriate person to handle important duties. It would be wrong of me not to ask. I am entirely at the disposition of the Chairman and the Central Committee."

Deng Xiaoping signed his name and affixed the date: "January 20, night."

The next day, Mao heard a report from Mao Yuanxin on what transpired during the Politburo meeting on January 20.

Regarding Deng Xiaoping, Mao Zedong said: "It's still a contradiction among the people. If he's guided well, it needn't become a hostile one, as it was with Liu Shaoqi and Lin Biao. Deng is different. He's willing to criticize himself. Those two absolutely refused."

Mao Yuanxin said Deng had requested a chance to tell Mao personally about his mistakes and seek Mao's guidance. He also wanted to discuss his work.

"We can talk about Xiaoping's work later," Mao said. "My idea is that his duties be reduced, but not completely. You mustn't crush him with a single blow."

"You mean let him 'learn from past mistakes'? That we should 'treat the patient and cure the illness'?"

"Right."

Obviously, Deng Xiaoping could no longer remain in charge of the general affairs of the Central Government. But who should replace him? Mao Yuanxin told Mao that three vice-premiers — Hua Guofeng, Ji Dengkui and Chen Xilian, had requested Mao to designate a responsible comrade to assume overall command of the State Council, and said they would do the practical work.

"Let Hua Guofeng take over," Mao said. "He himself says his political level isn't very high, so Xiaoping can handle foreign affairs."

The Gang of Four naturally had been delighted when Mao criticized Deng Xiaoping. But they were very disappointed when they learned about Mao Yuanxin's conversation with Mao. Why was he still treating Deng's case as a contradiction among the people? And saying he shouldn't be crushed with a single blow? And putting him in charge of foreign affairs? Why was he treating Deng so tenderly? According to the rules of the Cultural Revolution Group, a person like Deng Xiaoping, who was clearly opposed to the Cultural Revolution, should have been overthrown long ago.

But it appeared Mao had no intention of letting that happen. Mao was a hard person to figure out!

Another thing displeased the Gang of Four. Their original idea was, after knocking out Deng Xiaoping, to have Wang Hongwen resume control over the general affairs of the Central Government, with Zhang Chunqiao running the State Council. To their surprise, Mao put Hua Guofeng in charge of both. The haughty Jiang Qing had never even considered him. The fruits of victory, which the Gang of Four thought were so near at hand, had been snatched away by Hua Guofeng.

Mao's decision was a great blow to the Gang of Four. They hadn't come even close to attaining their goal. But they refused to quit. They felt the vast land and everything under the sky in China, after Mao's death, should belong to them.

The Gang of Four busily continued their campaign to oust Deng with a variety of petty slanders and backbiting. Nor did they spare other old revolutionary veterans. On February 2, 1976, the Party Central Committee issued that year's first official announcement. It said the Politburo, in accordance with Mao Zedong's proposal, had approved the appointment of Hua Guofeng as Acting Premier of the State Council. Also on Mao's recommendation, it approved placing Comrade Chen Xilian in charge of the Central Military Commission, when Comrade Ye Jianying was ill.

One year before, in 1975, the Central Committee had appointed Deng Xiaoping Vice-Chairman of the Central Military Commission of the Chinese Communist Party and General Chief of Staff of the People's Liberation Army. Only a year later, everything was turned upside down. Not only was Deng Xiaoping removed from his jobs in the Party and State Council, even Ye Jianying was declared "ill", and no longer allowed to function in the Military Commission

In addition to Deng, Ye was another important person thought likely to reject the Cultural Revolution. These changes of status were clearly a result of Mao's determination to defend it. Yet, at the same time, Mao remained coolly objective. He did not give the Gang of Four any real authority in either the government or the military.

They were very upset. Zhang Chunqiao had held high hopes for changes in personnel. Unable to suppress his bitter disappointment, he pinned a nasty article, sneering that the new appointees had "come on quick and strong, and would go just as fast." He was reviling not only Deng Xiaoping and Ye Jianying, but Hua Guofeng as well. Deep in the hearts of the Gang of Four was still another sentiment they dared not voice — namely, a hatred for Mao Zedong.

While Deng nominally had not been removed from his Party, government, and military posts, actually he was unable to perform any duties. He attended Politburo meetings if he was notified. If not, he stayed away. He felt much better at home with his children and grandchildren than having to look at the mad faces of the Gang of Four.

Mao Zedong's health took a severe turn for the worse in February 1976. At the end of the month, American president Nixon visited China. As Nixon later wrote in his book *Leaders* (pp. 239): "When I returned to China in 1976, Mao's condition had deteriorated considerably. His speech sounded like a series of monosyllabic grunts and groans. But his mind remained quick and incisive. He understood everything I said, but when he tried to answer, the words just would not come out. If he thought the translator had not understood him, he would impatiently grab a note pad and write out his comments. It was painful to see him in this condition. Whatever one may think of him, no one can deny that he was a fighter to the end."

At this time of political crisis, China's future and fate still depended on Mao Zedong. He was extremely weak. Anything could befall him at any moment. For the Chinese Party, for Mao himself, the situation was a misfortune.

The Central Committee, on March 3, requested and received permission from Mao to issue "Important Instructions of Mao Zedong", which had been compiled by Mao Yuanxin, in the form of Central Committee documents to provide guidance in the campaign to "criticize Deng and oppose the Right-deviationist attempts to reverse the judgments".

The "Instructions" included the following quotations:

"Is there class struggle in a socialist society? Just because we seek unity and stability doesn't mean we don't need class struggle. Class struggle is fundamental, the rest is incidental. What is the Cultural Revolution? It is class struggle. The ones who say they can't see any clear conflicts between the classes, are themselves representatives of the bourgeoisie. Some comrades, particularly old comrades whose thinking is still mired in the bourgeois democratic revolution period, do not understand the socialist revolution. They resist it; even oppose it. They have two attitudes toward the Cultural Revolution. One, they are displeased. Two, they want to call it to account. You want to wage a socialist revolution but you don't know where the bourgeoisie are? They are in the Communist Party. They are persons in authority inside the Party who are taking the capitalist road. And they are still doing it. In general we can say the Cultural Revolution has been essentially correct, with some shortcomings. Now we want to examine the reasons for those shortcomings. Seventy percent successful, thirty percent errors, though not everyone agrees with this appraisal.

"There were two mistakes made in the Cultural Revolution: 1) Down with everyone. 2) All-out civil war. In the first, some deserved to be overthrown, such as the Liu Shaoqi and the Lin Biao cliques. Some should not have been attacked, such as many old comrades. They may have made some mistakes. Criticizing them should have been enough. China has been free of war for more than 10 years. It's all been internal strife. People have seized guns, though most of them have been issued. A bit of fighting helps steel people. That fellow Xiaoping doesn't put much stock in class struggle, He's always been like that. For him it's a matter of 'black cat, white cat,' he doesn't care whether it's imperialism or Marxism. Xiaoping's case is an internal one among the people. If he's guided well it may not turn hostile, as it did with Liu Shaoqi and Lin

Biao.... He should be criticized. But don't strike him down with a single blow."

Mao's main purpose was to define the Cultural Revolution he himself had launched, to appraise it, to give it a political summation that future generations would be unable to dispute. In his final months he demanded the criticism of Deng and an "oppose the Right-deviationist attempts to reverse the judgments" campaign precisely to prevent a repudiation of the Cultural Revolution, which he considered the second major accomplishment of his political career. He had won many glories and victories in his more than 80 years, scores of epochal achievements.

Unfortunately, he grew more and more stubborn in his late period, more and more confused. He marred a lifetime of huge accomplishments with a huge error — the Cultural Revolution. It must be counted as one of the two major events in his political lifetime. Not only was it Mao's personal tragedy, it was a political tragedy of the utmost magnitude in the history of China's revolution and in the modern history of China.

The same day the Central Committee issued the "Instructions", it issued the remarks Mao made in his speeches regarding criticism of Deng and the "attempts of the Rightists to reverse the judgments", and ordered that all heads of county and above, and all regimental commanders and above, study them. A formal, large-scale movement to criticize Deng had begun within the entire Party.

The Gang of Four's long awaited moment had arrived at last. Zhang Chunqiao, at a meeting in February, assailed Deng Xiaoping as a "monopoly bourgeoisie", a "comprador capitalist", who practiced "revisionism internally and surrender externally".

Jiang Qing, on her own initiative called a meeting on March 2 of the leaders of 12 provinces and autonomous regions and made a long speech. "Deng Xiaoping is the general manager of a rumor factory," she grated. "He is a Marshal of the counter-revolution...a big traitor...a bourgeois comprador.... Let us join forces against the enemy, against Deng Xiaoping!"

Carried away by her own oratory, Jiang Qing revealed her ambitions. "Someone wrote a letter to Lin Biao saying that I was another Wu Zetian, another Empress Dowager Lü," she cried. "I don't deserve the honor. Empress Dowager Lü was an uncrowned empress. Actual power was in her hands. Slandering Empress Dowager Lü, slandering me, is really intended to slander the Chairman."

Jiang Qing's hysterical ranting irritated Mao Zedong. "She meddles in too many things," he said. But the lady, riding the crest of her wave, was undeterred.

The Gang of Four continued their attacks. They were determined to destroy Deng Xiaoping. They saw to it that every major newspaper and periodical carried articles condemning Deng and his "attempts to reverse the judgments", and negating the national rectification he had led. The articles castigated his political positions, and the alleged heresies of leaders in the arts, education, and science. They called for the criticism of all "unrepentant capitalist roaders following a revisionist line".

Jiang Qing concocted a new slogan: "The old cadres are a democratic clique, the democratic clique is capitalist roaders." She wanted to knock down again the only recently "liberated" veteran leaders.

As a result of the renewal of the Gang's attacks, the calm that had been achieved in 1975 through the rectification, and the improvement in the economy, were both shattered. Many efficient measures were discarded. Leaders of brawling factions who had been removed were re-instated. The flames of factional struggle were again ignited. Social order in many localities deteriorated. Industrial enterprises were unable to attain their targets. Some factories stopped production; many could not meet their payrolls. Several railway hubs were again paralyzed. There were shipping jams, pile-ups of merchandise. Trains ran late. All over China was great confusion, and a wild profusion of criticisms.

A number of Central Committee leaders who had supported the rectification initiated by Deng were removed from their jobs, and again subjected to criticism. Among them were Wan Li, Hu Yaobang and Hu Qiaomu. Zhou Rongxin, the minister of education, was so harassed by daily savage interrogations that he died during a nasty session on April 12.

People of China, after nearly 10 years of the misery of the Cultural

Revolution, when will you be able to walk out of the miasma, when will you be able to see the blue sky again!

50

The Great April 5 Movement

Although Mao Zedong had declared that Deng Xiaoping's case was a contradiction among the people, Papa was mentally prepared for the situation to become worse. Having accompanied him during his nearly 10 years of "steeling" in the Cultural Revolution, our family, like him, were "veterans". We understood what he was up against, and we were quite ready for him to be overthrown again.

In March 1976, Papa decided we should leave 17 Dongjiaominxiang and move back to our home on Kuanjie Avenue. We did a lot of moving during the Cultural Revolution. To Tea Kettle Lane after being driven out of Zhongnanhai, from Beijing to Jiangxi, from Jiangxi back to Beijing, from Huayuancun to Kuanjie, and then to Dongjiaominxiang. Now we were again returning to Kuanjie.

Politics ruled during the Cultural Revolution, it affected even your moving. Each time we moved it was either because we sensed a worsening in the political atmosphere, or because we thought it was getting better. Our political experience told us when to move. We were moving to Kuanjie because the prognosis of the whole family was that a vicious political battle would soon be upon us.

People were uneasy about the revival of attacks on Deng Xiaoping. Rumors started floating through the streets and lanes of Beijing, in large cities and small, all over China. The Gang of Four hastily tried to track them down, because most of them were about Jiang Qing. That she had been a third-rate movie actress in Shanghai in the 1930s.... That she had led a dissolute life.... That she had capitulated to the Kuomintang.... True

389

or false, as long as the stories were about Jiang Qing, people believed them and passed them on. They flew on winged feet.

The ordinary people talked about Jiang Qing not because she intrigued or amused them, but because it was their only means, in that dark oppressive political climate, of giving vent to their hatred and contempt for her and the Gang of Four.

Their misery over the passing of Zhou Enlai still tormented them. Now, the wild attacks exacerbated their overly sensitive spirits.

All over China the Gang of Four picked up the tempo of slanders against Deng Xiaoping. Newspapers and periodicals carried a flood of articles orchestrated by them, or which they themselves wrote, reviling him as a revisionist, compradore capitalist, fascist, unrepentant capitalist roader... for daring to question whether class struggle was the foundation of all phenomena.

Nor did other moderates escape their venom. Zhou Enlai was accused of "restoring capitalism" because he had opposed "Leftist" excesses in 1972. According to Jiang Qing: "Seventy-five percent of the old cadres inevitably follow the capitalist road." The *Guangming Daily* even took a swipe at Hua Guofeng. Flunky Minister of Culture Yu Huiyong called for artistic creations attacking the "capitalist roaders"....

Jiang Qing claimed that ever since Deng had resumed office the Gang had been kept in a cage. Now they were out, she said, now they could speak. They wanted revenge; they wanted to spew out all the bile that was in their bellies. Beneath the pitiless spotlights the Gang were like actors performing lunatic roles. Their mad words and villainous behavior exposed them before all the people of China.

The sparks of the people's anger ignited in February and March. On February 23 a poster appeared in East China's Fujian Province listing the crimes of the Gang of Four. A Fuzhou University professor, in a February 26 poster, excoriated Lin Biao and the Gang of Four. Posters appeared on the streets of Wuhan, capital of Central China's Hubei Province, on March 2, bearing titles like "Carry out the will of Premier Zhou and implement the Four Modernizations". Seven young workers put up a poster in Guiyang, Southwest China's Guizhou Province, on

March 9. It was entitled: "A few ideas about the present situation and our new responsibilities". Over 200 persons in the Wuhan Boiler Plant met on March 26 and openly criticized Jiang Qing and Zhang Chunqiao. In other parts of the country there was a proliferation of anti-Gang posters, slogans, and pamphlets.

The broad masses, by their practical deeds, boldly launched a tit-for-tat battle against the Gang of Four.

On March 3, the Shanghai newspaper *Wen Hui Bao* published an article commemorating Lei Feng, and cut from it a laudatory comment the recently deceased Premier Zhou Enlai had made. On March 25, the same paper published an article attacking by thinly veiled allusion not only Deng Xiaoping, but Zhou Enlai, as well.

Like a rock cast in a pool, the article stirred up huge ripples. People were furious. From all over the country protesters bombarded *Wen Hui Bao* with letters and telegrams and phone calls. "How dare you smear Premier Zhou?" one demanded. "Who does *Wen Hui Bao* belong to?" cried another. "The whole nation is waiting for *Wen Hui Bao* to tell the truth!"

The grief of the people had turned to strength, their wrath forged into action.

The day of the Pure Brightness, the traditional day in April when the Chinese people remember loved ones who have passed away and pray for them and tidy their graves, was fast approaching. In 1976 they paid particular reverence to their adored Premier Zhou Enlai.

When he died the Gang of Four had prohibited them from holding memorial ceremonies. But their love for him was buried deep in their hearts, and they had started preparing services long before the Pure Brightness Day.

Children of a Beijing primary school, on March 19, laid a wreath to their "Good Premier Zhou Enlai" at the Monument to the People's Heroes in Tiananmen Square. It marked the opening salvo of an historic people's battle against the Gang of Four.

People in Nanjing marched on March 24 to Yuhuatai, where the Kuomintang had executed scores of revolutionaries during the civil war.

They laid wreaths, and held a large meeting commemorating Zhou Enlai and excoriating the Gang of Four. On March 28, Nanjing University students, bearing a large portrait of Zhou Enlai and a big floral wreath, held a huge demonstration opposing the Gang of Four. Slogans against the Gang went up in every street and lane in Nanjing on March 29. In indelible paint on trains going all over the country angry Nanjing students scrawled: "Dig out the dirty backers behind *Wen Hui Bao!*" "Down with anyone who opposes Premier Zhou!" On March 31, workers and staff of the Nanjing Automotive Plant erected an enormous eye-catching slogan on the busiest street in the center of the city: "Down with the ambitious schemer Zhang Chunqiao!"

Wang Hongwen retorted heatedly. "The Nanjing activities are directed against the Central Committee," he cried, "The posters are trying to create public opinion for reversing the judgments."

The Politburo met on April 1 and discussed the memorial activities being held in Nanjing and many other places. It issued a declaration reading: "In the last few days posters and slogans have appeared in Nanjing opposing leading comrades in the Central Committee. These are political acts aimed at splitting the Central Committee led by Chairman Mao, and diverting attention away from criticizing Deng Xiaoping." It demanded immediate effective measures to suppress the protesters, and an investigation to find "the ones behind the scenes" and "those creating rumors."

The bluster and threats of the Gang of Four failed to frighten the people. More and more places held memorial services, and they grew larger in size. At the end of March and the beginning of April crowds took to the streets in mass demonstrations in defiance of the Gang of Four and held memorial services for Zhou Enlai in Hangzhou, Zhengzhou, Xi'an, Taiyuan and Fuzhou.

After the Beijing primary school children presented their wreath on March 19, citizens of the capital city began coming to Tiananmen Square in droves and congregating at the Monument to the People's Heroes. They brought floral wreaths and baskets, and tied white paper flowers on the boughs of the pines and cypress surrounding the Square.

The numbers who came to commemorate Zhou Enlai increased daily. Long lines formed on the east and west ends of the broad Chang'an Avenue, and stretched from both sides of Qianmen Gate all the way to the Square. White flowers smothered the short pine hedges, and rose in layers to the branches of the tall cypress trees. It was as if everything had been blanketed by a great snowfall, ever deeper, ever higher. The people had made those floral wreaths with their own hands. Piled like wrathful clouds at the foot of the Monument, they seemed to lift it high into the heavens.

Twenty-nine members of the Beijing Federation of Trade Unions, on March 30, were the first to post an expression of mourning for Zhou Enlai on the Monument. A flood of slogans, posters, and verses followed in the succeeding days, on the Monument and all over the Square:

"Beloved Premier, come back, we think of you day and night!"

"You fought for a new China in life, your ashes fertilize the land in death!"

"Fiends howl with glee at the tragic demise, we weep and the demons laugh! Shedding tears for the hero, grimly we pull our sword from the scabbard!"

Expressions of grief for the Premier and hatred for the Gang of Four poured into the Square. They were quoted in every street and lane, in every school and factory. Emotions rose to fever pitch. Beijing became a city that never slept.

The Gang of Four was frightened. Obviously, the situation was very serious. They used every means to suppress it. On April 2, in the name of the Central Committee, they ordered Beijing's police and militia to put a stop to the memorial activities, and sent plainclothes men to arrest the participants. At the same time Yao Wenyuan issued a "proclamation" alleging: "The Pure Brightness Day is a devils' holiday," and "Sending floral wreaths is a backward tradition." He prohibited the people from going to the Square to mourn the Premier.

But their resentment was already a smoldering volcano. No person, no force, could stop it. Their thunderous outcry, from mourning Zhou Enlai, had expanded to denouncing the Gang of Four. They were not just targeting any single individual or event. Their thrust was now clearly directed that great calamity — the Cultural Revolution.

No person in Beijing could have remained unmoved, and that certainly included Papa and all the members of our family. The people's mourning for Zhou Enlai echoed the sorrow in our hearts. Their denunciations of the Gang of Four were completely in accord with our own. Some hung little bottles on the pines surrounding the Square. The term for "little bottles" is "xiao ping" in Mandarin. Although the ideographs are different from the " Xiao Ping" in "Deng Xiaoping", they are pronounced the same, and were an obvious pun intended to mean Papa.

Everyone who went to Tiananmen Square brought floral wreaths, wrote verses, copied the verses of others, or simply savor the moving atmosphere.

Only our family was unable to go. The Gang of Four was claiming that Deng Xiaoping had engineered the whole thing. If one of us was caught at the Square the Gang would seize upon this as "proof". Papa ordered us to stay away, and not give the Gang any excuses. We reluctantly agreed. We could only peddle past on our bicycles along Chang'an Avenue and glimpse the stirring scene from a distance.

Everyone knew that although this huge public protest was not backed by Deng Xiaoping, he was, in every sense, the spirit behind it. It was he who boldly hewed open a nationwide reconstruction with striking results. His militant confrontation with the Gang of Four showed the people the way forward, gave them hope, heightened their courage to do battle with the evil clique.

Deng Xiaoping was well aware that he would very likely be overthrown again. But, he knew, too, that this would be the supreme catalyst, awakening the Chinese people and bringing them to a new point of departure. He was convinced that regardless of his own political fate, justice and truth would prevail. The surging crowds in Tiananmen Square, their angry cries, clearly demonstrated to him China's future and aspirations.

As Deng Xiaoping's family, we were very conscious of the moving scenes in the Square, and we longed to go there. We knew the political situation had reached a critical point, and Papa's second overthrow was imminent. But after nearly 10 years of the Cultural Revolution, of enduring with Papa stormy winds and rain, we had learned how to meet tumultuous political change. In the recent three years since returning to Beijing, Papa's statesman-like brave behavior had particularly convinced us. We were proud of his fearlessness and determination, of his dedication to the nation and the people. Papa had chosen a selfless, uncompromising road. From the bottom of our hearts we were glad to travel with him.

Although we couldn't go to the Square, we were stirred by every bit of news, every song and poem, that wafted to us. The hearts of Deng Xiaoping's family beat as one with the hearts of the people crowding Tiananmen Square.

The nation's mourning for Zhou Enlai reached a high tide on Pure Brightness Day, which fell on April 4 in 1976. The number converging on Tiananmen exceeded two million. Emotions ran unprecedentedly strong. People knew the Gang of Four had sent undercover police to infiltrate, to watch, and take pictures, but they were undeterred.

They continued to bring floral wreaths, festoon the cypress trees with paper flowers, put up their verses. Some protesters posted mourning lines they had written in their own blood. Some argued openly in favor of Deng Xiaoping. Some openly criticized Jiang Qing. Some emotionally sang the *Internationale*. Some climbed the lamp posts fringing the Square and yelled denunciations of the Gang of Four. Waves of shouted protest slogans rose in waves from all over the Square.

The two-million strong demonstration in front of Tiananmen, plus the memorial and protest ceremonies taking place in many parts of the country, together composed a stirring, powerful, righteous paean.

51

The "Two Resolutions" and Deng's Second Overthrow

T HE demonstrations at Tiananmen Square greatly alarmed the Gang of Four. They could not stand idly by in the face of a mass outcry aimed directly at them. Shaken, they had to find some way to suppress it.

In a small three-story gray building in the southeast corner of the Square, on April 2, they established a so-called "unified command post" for units of militia, police, and garrison troops, and mustered some 3,000 of them, to be held in reserve. That same afternoon, the "command post" worked out a plan of action.

At dawn, at 4:40 in the morning of April 3, the self-appointed special commander Wang Hongwen went personally to Tiananmen Square with a few cohorts to inspect. Fearful of being discovered, they sneaked around in the darkness, using flashlights to illuminate some of the floral wreaths and memorial tributes near the Monument. At the sight of the mountain-high piles of wreaths and the angry verses and denunciations, Wang Hongwen exploded. He telephoned his cronies in the Public Security Bureau and ordered them to send men immediately to photograph the "reactionary verses" for use as evidence in future "prosecutions".

Unable to control himself, he also phoned the *People's Daily*, and said: "The activities around the Monument to the People's Heroes are counter-revolutionary in nature!"

On his instructions, the Ministry of Public Security dispatched plainclothes personnel to the Square to take pictures. They also began making arrests. By 10:00 in the evening 26 persons had been detained. The opening curtain of the suppression had risen.

A meeting of the Politburo was convened by Hua Guofeng in the evening of April 4. Ye Jianying and Li Xiannian were not summoned because of "illness". The meeting, under the manipulation of Jiang Qing and her clique, passed a resolution decreeing that the memorial activities at the Square were "counter-revolutionary" and the result of "long preparation by Deng Xiaoping".

Mao Yuanxin submitted a written report of the meeting and its resolution to Mao Zedong. It said: "This counter-revolutionary attack was planned and organized.... Last year Deng Xiaoping said the criticism of Lin Biao and Confucius was actually aimed at Premier Zhou Enlai.... (This year) he is again using the Premier as an excuse, claiming that attacking a reversal of the judgments is also an attack on the Premier."

Mao Zedong marked a circle on the report indicating it had been read.

Full suppression started on April 5. Between 1:00 and 2:00 in the morning floral wreaths in the Square were trampled and carted away. There had been great layers of them. It took over 200 trucks to remove them all. Fifty-seven people in the Square were searched, seven were arrested. At 5:00 in the morning Wang Hongwen came to the "command post" to take charge of the suppression.

The sky lightened. As the sun rose, more and more people came to the Square. They saw that the floral wreaths had been trampled and taken away, and they were furious. Ignoring the prohibition, they brought more wreaths. There were men on duty where streets meet the Square, who set up "dissuasion points". But they couldn't intimidate anyone. People pushed through with new floral wreaths. On the one hand, citizens were bringing wreaths, on the other, men were trying to stop them. Tiananmen Square had become a vast area of confrontation.

That night, at 6:30, high frequency loud speakers at the Square broadcast the voice of Wu De, First Secretary of the Beijing Party Committee. He called the activities at Tiananmen Square "counter-revolutionary", and asked the crowds to leave immediately. At 9:30 pm,

10,000 militia and 3,000 police entered the Square, surrounded the persons remaining, and viciously beat them with clubs. Thirty-eight people were arrested and thrown into prison.

April 5, 1976, was a tragic day in the history of the People's Republic. The darkness of that long night of terror could not conceal the bloody crimes of the Gang of Four.

After hearing reports on the "Tiananmen Incident", a portion of the Politburo, just after midnight on April 6, designated it as "thoroughly counter-revolutionary". Mao Yuanxin, at 3:00 in the morning, reported the Politburo discussions to Mao Zedong.

At 11:00, the Chairman issued a commendation: "Bold fighting spirit. Good, good, good."

The Square, so recently the scene of fierce struggle, was quiet and chill. There were scattered bloodstains at the foot of the Monument.

Around 9:00 that morning, when the sun was already high, a few scores of workers carried into the Square a huge floral wreath they themselves had made. Grimly, they placed it on the north side of the Monument. At 6:00 in the evening, several dozen trucks arrived, filled with militia. Only 100 or so people still remained in the vicinity of the Monument in the quiet dusk, reluctant to leave. The single great floral wreath, braced by the chill breeze of early spring, stood proudly alone. By 7:00 pm, the Square was under martial law. The last of the protesters had been expelled.

Mao Yuanxin, on April 7, at 8:05 in the morning, relayed to Mao Zedong a "first-hand report" by Yao Wenyuan on the events at Tiananmen, and told the Chairman how the matter was being handled. The report called the people's memorial services for Zhou Enlai and the events at the Square "counter-revolutionary". It said they "had openly supported Deng Xiaoping, madly pointed their spearhead at the great leader Mao Zedong, and had attempted to split the Central Committee headed by Chairman Mao, and divert the main thrust away from criticizing Deng and his attempts to reverse the judgments."

The feeble Mao, after listening for more than an hour, issued the following directives: "Remove Deng from all posts, but retain his Party membership, so as to keep his future behavior under observation.... The capital, Tiananmen,...they were handled well. The situation has changed, it was right to drive them out!" And "Let Hua Guofeng be Premier." Mao proposed that Hua also be appointed Vice-Chairman of the Communist Party, and agreed that Yao Wenyuan's report be publicly circulated.

The Gang of Four gave themselves a banquet in the Great Hall of the People at noon on April 7 to celebrate their "victory". Jiang Qing was beside herself with joy. "We've won," she chortled. "Congratulations!" Drunk, Zhang Chunqiao grated: "Those guys with their reactionary verses wanted to make Deng Xiaoping another (Imre) Nagy, the head of the Hungarian counter-revolution!"

In the afternoon, in the Jiangxi Room of the Great Hall of the People, the Politburo met to discuss Chairman Mao's latest directives on the "Tiananmen Incident".

The Gang wildly accused Deng Xiaoping of being the behind-the-scenes mastermind. They said he rode to the Square in a car and personally took command. Jiang Qing and Zhang Chunqiao said everyone should be prepared for a possible attack on and seizure of Deng by the "masses".

Hua Guofeng, who was chairing the meeting, said Deng Xiaoping should be asked whether it was true that he drove to the Square and directed the activities. The Gang would have preferred to ignore this suggestion, but Hua had just been put in charge of the work of the Central Committee, and they had to listen to him, like it or not.

No one wanted to accept the responsibility of questioning Deng Xiaoping, least of all, Jiang Qing. Finally, she said: "Let Wang Dongxing go."

Wang was worried by her and Zhang Chunqiao's hint that Deng Xiaoping might be raided. At the start of the Cultural Revolution, the Cultural Revolution Group, which she controlled, had organized "the masses" to seize Peng Zhen and subject him to struggle sessions. Now, would they stage a seizure of Deng Xiaoping in the name of "the masses'?

Wang felt on such an important matter he had better ask Mao Zedong. He left the Hall and, instead of calling on Deng Xiaoping, he had his driver take him directly to nearby Zhongnanhai.

He informed Mao about the emergency meeting of the Politburo, then in session, and the discussion of the "Tiananmen Incident" and Deng Xiaoping.

Wang told Mao that Deng might be raided. Mao said that mustn't happen; he mustn't be seized. He asked Wang whether he had any way to deal with it. Wang suggested that Deng move back to the house on Dongjiaominxiang. Mao approved.

Wang immediately notified the Central Guards Bureau to prepare the house for occupancy. He told the staff officer the reason, and they formulated a security plan. Wang Dongxing sent word to Deng's secretary to tell Deng he wanted to speak to him. Guards Bureau would send an ordinary car to bring him to where Wang Dongxing would be waiting.

After the "Tiananmen Incident", Papa and the whole family knew that his most fateful day was fast approaching. Although prepared for the worst, we were not afraid. At 3:00 pm on April 7, a telephone call notified Papa's secretary that a Guards Bureau car would be coming to take him to talk with Wang Dongxing. His secretary and bodyguard would not be allowed to accompany him.

Not only were we not scared, we behaved very calmly.

Shortly after 3:00 pm, the car arrived. The whole family, young and old, mothers carrying children, saw Papa off. Deng Nan, a fast thinker, slipped a pack of cards into a pocket of Papa's jacket. We walked with him out of the house, across the courtyard, to the front gate. We watched him placidly get into the car, saw it leave the gate and drive off.

Only after the big gray gates were closed, did tears well to our eyes. Maybe this was our last farewell. The stubborn anger with which we had been consumed gave way to an infinite sadness. Deng Lin could not suppress her sobs.

"What are you bawling about?" I snapped. "This is not the time to cry!"

At about 5:00 pm, the Central Guards sent a car to fetch Mama. We were very worried when Papa left because we didn't know where he was going, and what was happening. Now Mama would be able to join him. That surely would be a great solace to him. They could keep each other company, and deal with any difficulties together. But whether this was a good sign or a bad, no one could say.

With tears in our eyes we helped Mama pack, urging her to take as much as possible, for Papa and herself. At least they wouldn't be cold, in a poor environment.

After she left, we worried about them. We thought one of us should stay with them and look after them. We all talked it over. Everyone wanted to go. But Deng Lin and Deng Nan had babies to take care of. I volunteered. I discussed it with He Ping. It would be good for Mama and Papa if I were with them. Of course if things went wrong, maybe none of us would be able to return. He Ping supported me. I made up my mind — I would go even if it meant crossing a mountain of knives and a sea of flames.

I wrote a letter to Wang Dongxing, stating my urgent request. But orders came down from above, and they refused me. We were very dejected, and it increased our worries about Mama and Papa. Where were they? What sort of place were they in? Were they being "struggled" against? Heavy gloom weighted our hearts.

Night was falling. Soon darkness would envelop the land, a darkness so black that even the stars would be invisible.

Deng Xiaoping met Wang Dongxing at Dongjiaominxiang. Wang told him what was going on, and formally asked him whether he had gone in a car to Tiananmen to command the operations. Deng said he had gone in a car to the Beijing Hotel to have a haircut, and hadn't taken "command" of anything. Wang sent for my mother, Zhuo Lin. After she arrived, Wang told Papa there were people who might want to raid him. Don't go out, he said. If you want to take a walk, do it inside the courtyard.

Wang returned to Zhongnanhai, and reported to Mao Zedong.

By then it was evening. The Politburo had already passed Mao's "Two Directives" and received his approval. Its meeting continued after dinner. Jiang Qing asked Wang Dongxing what Deng had said. Was it true that he had gone in a car to Tiananmen and taken command? Wang said all he did was to go to the Beijing Hotel for a haircut. Zhang Chunqiao was not satisfied. He demanded that Wang submit a written report of his conversation with Deng Xiaoping.

"We asked you people to go, and you wouldn't do it. I'm not going to write any report," Wang retorted hotly. "Don't ask me to go again. The next time you question him yourselves!"

He hadn't told anyone that, with Mao's agreement, he was concealing Deng in Dongjiaominxiang. Later, on several occasions in meetings of the Politburo, Jiang Qing complained that no one knew where Deng had gone; people had looked for him at his house on Kuanjie, but he was never home. Clearly, the Gang of Four were planning to stage a raid on Deng Xiaoping.

At 8:00 pm of April 7, the Central People's Radio Station broadcast to the whole nation the "Two Resolutions" passed by the Politburo. The first proclaimed the appointment of Hua Guofeng as Vice-Chairman of the Central Committee of the Chinese Communist Party, and Premier of the State Council. The second stated that: "The Politburo has discussed the counter-revolutionary incident at Tiananmen Square and Deng Xiaoping's recent actions, and believes that the nature of Deng's question has become a hostile contradiction. In keeping with the recommendation of great leader Mao Zedong, the Politburo has unanimously decided to remove Deng from all posts, in and outside the Party, but to allow him to retain his Party membership, so as to keep his future behavior under observation."

The *People's Daily*, and every major newspaper in the land, on April 8, published in full on the front page, the Central Committee's decisions, and an article entitled: "The Counter-revolutionary Political Incident at Tiananmen Square".

The people's rally at Tiananmen Square, so laudatory yet so tragic, was crushed. The nationwide activities mourning Premier Zhou Enlai were crushed. Deng Xiaoping, who had brought new hope to the people of China, and his comrades in battle, was again overthrown. The Gang of Four and their flunkys ran amok, and instituted a White Terror above and below.

But the just flames in the hearts of the people were already enkindled. They could not be extinguished. On April 7, as soon as the "Two Resolutions" were broadcast, a cadre in the Central Broadcast Bureau took up his brush pen and wrote these slogans: "Jiang, Zhang and Yao, attackers of Premier Zhou, will not die a natural death!" and "Down with Jiang Qing, Yao Wenyuan, and Zhang Chunqiao!"

An army deputy battalion commander in the Beijing Garrison posted a denunciation of Jiang Qing and Zhang Chunqiao on a white poplar outside the camp. It called them false Marxists, and said, "We cherish Vice-Premier Deng Xiaoping". It called on everyone to "learn from the heroes at Tiananmen Square!"

Big slogans went up at Beijing Second Foreign Languages Institute: "Battle anyone who attacks Premier Zhou!" "Down with the reactionaries Zhang, Jiang and Yao!"

The newspapers and periodicals which published the "Two Resolutions" were flooded with telegrams and phone calls protesting their distortion of the events at Tiananmen. They expressed mourning for Zhou Enlai and support for Deng Xiaoping, and castigated the Gang of Four.

On the surface the Gang of Four had won, and the people's resistance had been crushed. But a moment of euphoria was not final victory. Examining the matter closely, the Gang of Four had to recognize that many hidden, and still more complex, problems remained.

First of all, when the Tiananmen Incident ended, Mao Zedong, after considerable thought, formally designated Hua Guofeng his successor. The Gang of Four had busily used every trick, with the result that they had only been "cutting clothes for another groom." The Gang was extremely dissatisfied.

Second, although their longtime enemy Deng Xiaoping had been removed from office, to their amazement Mao, in a clear show of affection, let him retain his Party membership, depending, moreover, on his "future behavior"! Another twinge in the heart for the Gang of Four.

Third, true, the mass demonstrations at Tiananmen had been quelled, but more demonstrations were constantly being staged in other parts of the country. Things were far from stable. It was much too early for the Gang of Four to claim victory.

Mao was obviously nearing the end of his days. The Gang knew they had to move quickly. They had to increase their attacks on Deng, they had to continue their suppression, and, still more important, they had to hasten a seizure of power. Once power was in their hands, neither Deng, nor Hua Guofeng, nor resistance activities, would be anything to worry about.

They pushed "criticizing" Deng nationwide on a still larger scale. Their controlled press ran a whole series of anti-Deng articles. In Beijing they engineered a big mass rally. They diligently sought the directors and participants in the "Tiananmen Incident". They probed for those who spread "rumors". They checked on all manners of "counter-revolutionary" activities. Every move was investigated. Everyone had to account for himself. Terror gripped the entire land.

Adherents of the Gang in Beijing's Public Security Bureau, by June 17 had collected 583 poems and memorial statements, in addition to pictures of 180,000 more of the same, plus photographs taken at the Square, which they had forced participants to hand over. The Gang selected from these some 600 items and compiled them into a volume of "evidence", to which they added "important material" of their own, bringing the total to 1,980 items, and presented them in so-called "trials" of 388 persons they arrested. This did not include the countless number of individuals who were isolated, questioned and harangued. There were tens of thousands in Beijing alone.

In spite of the harassment, most people were not deterred. By whatever means they could muster, they continued memorializing Zhou Enlai, shunning criticisms of Deng, rejecting "investigation", and opposing the savagery of Gang of Four. Beneath the broad mantle of terror enveloping the nation, flames of stubborn resistance burned bright.

52

Fearlessly Confronting the Waves

Papa and Mama were again confined to 17 Dongjiaominxiang. But this time the restraint was both protective and political in nature.

On April 8, the day following the broadcast of the "Two Resolutions," Papa wrote a letter care of Wang Dongxing stating his position to the Central Committee and Mao Zedong: He supported the appointment of Hua Guofeng as Vice-Chairman of the Chinese Communist Party and Premier of the State Council, and was thankful for the retention of his Party membership.

Papa truly supported with all his heart Mao's decision to appoint Hua Guofeng his successor instead of handing power over to the Gang of Four. To have done so would have placed the Party and the nation in terrible jeopardy. The vast majority of the people would have been plunged into even more severe difficulties. With his health rapidly waning, for Mao to have been able to reach so sober a decision was indeed a stroke of good fortune in a period of manifold misfortune.

Mao had preserved Deng's Party membership when he was overthrown the first time in the Cultural Revolution. Now, the second time, Mao did it again. His attitude toward Deng was very complicated. Before the Cultural Revolution Mao had considered him a potential successor. And also for a time after the Cultural Revolution started. Mao appreciated Deng, and placed high hopes in him.

But Deng's opinion of the Cultural Revolution was diametrically opposed to Mao's. Mao was disappointed, angered, hurt, and saddened. After Deng was restored to office, the nationwide rectification he instituted was a rebuttal of the Cultural Revolution. Mao criticized him, but did not seek to have him overthrown again. He thought Deng was a man who "could admit his mistakes", and would change his mind.

To Mao's surprise Deng's attitude was more stubborn than ever. And just at that time the Tiananmen incident erupted. Mao decided to have Deng again removed from office. Yet he still protected him from the evil daggers of the Gang of Four, and let him keep his Party membership. Perhaps Mao knew his own "final departure" was very near, and so he used this special method to save Deng Xiaoping. His over eight decades of life, and over half a century of political experience, must have told him that China after he was gone would not be a peaceful land, that it would be torn by political strife, that Hua Guofeng and the Gang of Four would clash. How it would turn out, no one could say.

Perhaps, and this is only perhaps, an unknowable perhaps, a perhaps Mao would not live to see, perhaps that was why Mao decided to preserve Deng Xiaoping's Party membership. Deng's very special character, his powerful political vitality, would not be sunk by the turmoil. Perhaps at that time, under those particular circumstances, history would give Deng the opportunity to intensify the blaze of his unquenchable political flame....

Mao's decision to preserve Deng's Party membership was a positive, though not decisive, factor in later determining whether he could again be restored to office.

Papa was probably a little surprised. He had been through many changes during the Cultural Revolution, but he had been extremely unyielding. Papa understood Mao very well. The entire process of using him, supporting him, then criticizing him, and finally agreeing to his being overthrown again — was typical of Mao's convoluted, troubled personality, and reflected his disappointment, despite his many efforts, at being unable to bring Papa around to his way of thinking. Papa knew if only he had been a bit more flexible, Mao would again have kept him in office.

But with China at such a dangerous juncture, how could he abandon the chance to halt the anarchy, how could he surrender principle for the sake of his personal advantage? Without hesitation, he chose the more risky course. Although he had been overthrown again, although he had been bombarded with criticisms, his heart was steady, his mind at ease. He had done everything he ought to do. He had received the support and approval of the people. His conscience was clear.

Back in the familiar surroundings of 17 Dongjiaominxiang, and cut off from news of their children, Mama and Papa became more mutually dependent as they once more began a life in captivity. At first they did their own house cleaning, washed their own clothes, and did the cooking themselves. Teng Hesong, the security guard, helped with the shopping. A few days later, Teng got permission to contact Li, our old cook. Li came every day and made lunch and dinner. Still later, at the request of Mama and Papa, the Security Bureau arranged for Deng Zhiqing, a relative who had been serving as nursemaid for the babies, to move over and help keep the place clean. Her company gave the place a more family air.

Teng had been on several missions with Papa in the past. He knew our family well, and was particularly fond of Papa. In addition to being in charge of security, he did all sorts of errands for Papa and Mama. They completely trusted him. He even helped with the delivery of letters to the Central Committee.

Papa placidly kept to his accustomed daily schedule, in spite of the boring environment. They couldn't escape the critical clamor against Deng Xiaoping, which grew noisier by the day. The newspapers, the radio broadcasts, were full of it. But Papa remained unruffled and undisturbed.

The rest of the family, still at Kuanjie, were not allowed to leave the house. No one even went to work, or to school. We set up our own "study group". The Secretariat of the General Office sent two people to conduct it. In addition to our family members, at Kuanjie we also had Papa's secretary, a security man, Papa's driver, and his former orderly. We were supposed to join together every day in "study and criticism" sessions.

The first "lesson" was to "expose" Papa, and to reveal whether any of us went to the Square at the time of the "Tiananmen Incident". The purpose of this was obvious — to prove that Deng Xiaoping was the behind-the-scenes manipulator and exercised his "command" through his children.

We all vehemently denied it. We said not only didn't any of us children go, but Papa had specifically ordered the whole family to stay away. The rest of the family and the staff were equally firm. We knew it was important not to give the inquisitors the least opening. After they finished questioning us they dropped their probe, but continued running our daily "study" sessions.

During the 10 years of the Cultural Revolution everything was class struggle. Study and criticism, day after day, year in and year out. We became experienced veterans of political "movements", talented in mouthing the terms "study" and "criticism". The Cultural Revolution was supposed to have "tempered" people. Well, all that criticizing certainly "tempered" us till we were razor-sharp!

Papa had been overthrown again, and we were fully prepared to tough it out. In our "study and criticism" sessions, we just went through the motions. This one had to go to the bathroom. That one thought she heard the baby crying, and had to look. Another said it was getting late, and she had to prepare lunch. Everyone found a reason to escape.

We had some amusing moments, too. Once, it was Zhang Baozhong's turn to speak. He was our security guard. Adopting a serious manner, he first drank some hot water, cleared his throat a couple of times, then launched into his "criticism". The more he spoke, the thirstier he became, and the more water he drank, the more times he had to get up and walked to the middle of the room to refill it, because he still hadn't reached the end of his rambling dissertation.

He Ping, who had been sitting beside him, noticed a thread of Zhang's woolen underwear sticking out from the top of the back of his pants. He Ping stealthily nipped it and held on. With Zhang's frequent trips to the thermos placed in the middle of the room, the thread grew longer and longer, until it trailed behind Zhang like a woolly tail. Every one of us, except Zhang, could see it.

We burst out laughing, shattering the atmosphere of what was supposed to be a serious study session, laughing till our sides ached. It was impossible to continue a solemn "criticism" of Deng Xiaoping amid such hilarity. The laughter gave vent to our resentment, to our contempt, for the study sessions imposed upon us. They ended about 10 days later.

Eggs were in short supply at that time, they were difficult to buy. But we had a two-year-old and a four-year-old baby in our household. How could we get along without eggs? One day Papa's secretary Wang Ruilin called us privately into his office, and handed us a cardboard shoe box. It was heavy. When we took it back to our room we found it was full of eggs. Wang saw that the children had no eggs, and he gave us the whole ration that had been issued to himself and his staff for their evening meals.

The two little grandchildren were the family's main concern. Papa had been overthrown. We grown-ups were all right, and we were sticking with him. What happened to us didn't matter, but there were the two grandchildren. If we ran into trouble what would become of them? It made our hearts ache to see those lively, innocent babes. Deng Lin and Deng Nan sometimes said: "A family like ours shouldn't have any babies!"

They talked it over and decided, if things got worse, to send the babies to relatives in the country. We grown-ups could fend for ourselves, but the grandchildren had to be saved, come what may. In those evil times we sons and daughters of Deng Xiaoping could be arrested at any time.

We knew from experience that we soon would be driven out of Kuanjie, and began packing even before the study sessions were over. Sure enough, a person in charge came from the Central Committee's General Office and told us we had to move. "Move where?" we asked him. "To your office, to your school," he said nastily. "We don't care!"

"Forged" in the Cultural Revolution, we didn't scare easily. They got tough, we got tougher. "We've kids here, and an old grandmother," we shouted. "Our work units never gave us any housing. It's not so easy for us to move. You have to give us a place to stay, in a courtyard, big enough for our whole family. Otherwise we won't leave. Just try and move us out. You'll have to tie up every one of us!"

In 1967 when we were chased out of Zhongnanhai, there were just a few of us. We girls were only teenagers and students then, but we still didn't let them move us any way they wanted. Now we were nearly a dozen people, and several were big and strong. We had plenty of experience with "campaigns". They'd have their work cut out if they tried to move us!

Our family had been scattered by the winds during the Cultural Revolution; it suffered bitter hardships. Now they wanted to drive us out again. We were depressed, and angry. We argued with the General Office man, yelling at him from inside the house to the outside, from the rear yard to the front yard, all the way to the entrance gate. The three of us, Deng Lin, Deng Nan and me, shouting and weeping, loudly objected. The PLA guards at the entrance watched us sympathetically. The General Office man couldn't do a thing with us. He left muttering.

Although we had won a temporary victory, we knew, sooner or later, we would have to move. We began getting our things together that same night. Sure enough, the moment our study session ended we were notified a small courtyard had been found for us in Yuqun Lane, behind the National Art Museum. We were ordered to move within three days.

Three days, not bad. The last time we were expelled we had only two hours in which to get out. Three days were enough. We were experienced movers. Everyone pitched in, and we started packing. With all of us so busy, who could look after the little ones? Fortunately, our young nephew Chubby had come to Beijing to recuperate from an illness, and was staying with us. We put him in charge of the kids.

He was only 16, just a big kid himself, a simple, honest boy who didn't talk much. But he surprised us all. He sat with the two youngsters in a big wicker chair in the garden, and told them stories from morning till night. They listened, enchanted, good as gold. We asked him where he got so many stories. "I don't know many," he admitted, "so I just made them up."

It was a great help, having him take care of the children. We were enormously busy, packing. It was much more difficult than the last few times we moved. Papa and Mama weren't with us, but we had from little babies to an old grandma to look after, a total of almost a dozen people. This time we had to move everything. Nothing was to be left behind. We asked permission to take some of the furniture that came with the house, but we were refused. Again we raised a fuss, and finally we were allowed to take a couple of wooden beds, plus a few old pieces that our family had used since the 50's.

Moving day arrived. We were too busy to eat or sleep, and were occupied every minute of the day. Late at night, we finally remembered Chubby and the two tykes. He was still telling them stories. Four-year-old Mianmian couldn't keep her eyes open. Two-year-old Mengmeng was fast asleep in the wicker chair. When we carried them into the house we found they were so begrimed from playing all day in the garden they looked like a couple of coal balls.

We managed to get everything neatly on the truck. After it rolled away, we stood in the courtyard for a final look. We had lived here for two years. When we first came the courtyard was bare. Now it was full of greenery and flowers. The roses we had planted were in bloom; all the plants were flourishing. "How beautiful," we said. "Let's take them with us."

We dug up the bushes and put them on a handcart used for delivering coal. Roses, peonies, amaryllis — we hauled them all the way to our new home in Yuqun Lane. We had to make several trips, but nobody minded.

. The house we had been provided with was in a very small courtyard. An old Red Army veteran lived in the rear. It consisted of a northern wing and an eastern wing, of three rooms each. Still, it was much grander than the two-room place we had in Fanghuzhai after being expelled from Zhongnanhai in 1967.

We laid out our furniture, made the beds, and put the kitchen utensils, pots and pans and bowls, in place. The house was now, as you would say in Beijing dialect, "completely furnished". And we even had the flower bushes we had so painstakingly moved from Kuanjie!

Feifei went to work with the vigor he had acquired in the farming brigade. His big hoe soon converted the small barren yard into a well-turned flower garden. His sweat mingled with the water with which he sprinkled the soil. He chanted a little jingle as he swung his hoe: "Enrich the family and be a hero, stay in poverty and be a dud!" He had picked up the tune from some disapproved movie, never expecting to apply it to a "handkerchief-sized" plot in Yuqun Lane. The flowers that spread their fragrance in that little garden were a joy to behold.

We moved all too many times during the Cultural Revolution, shifting from place to place like gypsies. Yuqun Lane was another stop on the long political road whose end we could not envision. It was late at night when we finally settled in our new home. We all wondered: "Mama. Papa, where are you?"

We returned to our respective jobs and schools. They all were "criticizing Deng" and investigating the "Tiananmen Incident". Work and classes had halted. Beijing was where the "Tiananmen Incident" had occurred, and the atmosphere was particularly tense on every level.

But in spite of the pressure, most people were clearly opposed. In a number of places the leaders merely kept up appearances. They said a few words at meetings, and conducted superficial investigations. In our workplaces and schools we were happy to discover that most people were very cordial. Even some we barely knew came up and greeted us. As sons and daughters of Deng Xiaoping we were prime targets for "investigation". But both leaders and masses spontaneously gathered round to protect us. Some mornings when I came to school I would find on my desk written messages of sympathy and support.

For persons to behave so boldly in that tightly-lidded political pressure cooker moved us deeply. We were very proud of our Chinese people.

He Ping had remained with us through it all. As our family's son-in-law, he endured the same hardships days as the rest of us. He had not visited his parents since the Tiananmen Incident. But he was concerned about them, and rode his bike back to see them.

My father-in-law and mother-in-law had been sent to a school in Jiangxi for cadres of the Ministry of Health. They returned to Beijing in

1972, and lived in a hostel provided by the State Council. A vice-minister in the Ministry of Health, my father-in-law had been labeled a "capitalist roader". Although he had returned to Beijing he still had not been given a new assignment. Neither had my mother-in-law. She was a veteran cadre of the old Red Army. Father-in-law also had been in the Red Army, doing medical work. He didn't talk much, but he was a very righteous person. When he stood up against the radicals in the Cultural Revolution, they nearly fractured his spine.

Like many of the old cadres he had been overthrown, struggled against, sent down to a cadre school, compelled to take part in "reform through labor", and at last allowed to return to Beijing. The experience only toughened his spirit. He and my mother-in-law had been very worried by the repercussions from the Tiananmen Incident. Not because of their son He Ping, but because of their in-laws, Deng Xiaoping and his family. They had no news of our family after the "Two Resolutions" were promulgated, and were so concerned they slept badly.

When He Ping appeared they clutched him and demanded a detailed account. He told them Mama and Papa had been taken away, and not been heard from since. Tears came to their eyes.

Father-in-law said to He Ping: "You needn't stay long. Go back quickly and bring Feifei here." He Ping hurried to our new home and got Feifei, and me. We went together on our bicycles.

After I married He Ping a strong affection had sprung up between me and my in-laws. Seeing them again, gray-haired and very upset, I felt a twinge in my heart. I held back my tears with an effort, and forced a smile. I knew how worried they were. I didn't want to make them feel any worse.

My father-in-law addressed the three of us. "Pingping, Maomao, Feifei, listen to me," he said in a serious voice. "I have three sons. Pingping and Maomao are married, which means I have given this son to the Deng family. Pingping, you needn't worry about us. Stick with the Dengs. Live, if you live, with the Deng Family. Die, if you die, with the Deng family."

Tears ran from his eyes. "They are in danger. There's no telling what

413

the Gang of Four will do. They might kill you all. The Dengs' have two sons. One has been crippled, only Feifei is intact. I want to hide him in our old home in Hubei. We must save this son of the Deng family."

We all wept aloud. Feifei appreciated my father-in-law's good intentions, but how could he abandon our family at a time like this?

"Thank you, uncle," he said, "but I can't go. I must stay together with our family." Father-in-law was sincere, but Feifei was firm.

We got on our bikes and slowly rode away. Looking back we saw the elderly couple still standing on the steps in front of their building, gazing after us. Their gray hair shone softly in the fading sunlight.

53

Heaven Angered, the People Enraged

At 17 Dongjiaominxiang Mama and Papa had each other for company, but they still missed the family. Before they knew it, the end of April was drawing near, and on April 30 little grandson Mengmeng would be two. They remembered the day he was born. He weighed just 1.7 kilograms (3.71b). He was so tiny only the most meticulous care enabled him to grow. That made him particularly precious. Now, he was going to be two. They really missed him!

They felt they had to give him something. They sent out for a few things, and Mama wrote a note.

The gifts arrived just when we were worrying because we hadn't heard anything from our parents in a long time. We were very moved. The note said: "Tomorrow is Mengmeng's birthday. Here is some fruit and candy and a couple of little bottles for him to play with. He can share the things with sister Mianmian, and give a big apple to Little Chubby. Grandma"

We wept at the sight of Mama's familiar handwriting. News at last! That they were able to send the note and the gifts proved that, although under restraint, they still had some freedom and were not being mistreated. We were so happy we couldn't eat or sleep.

Their grandparents' love was more precious than gold to the little children. They played delightedly with the two little bottles, unaware they came from a doting Grandmother and Grandfather whose freedom was limited.

In Dongjiaominxiang, Mama's eyes began troubling her again. Sparks had injured her corneas when she watched a fireworks display years before. She asked Teng, the security guard, to get her some eye drops. The pharmacy in the No. 301 Hospital said Deng Xiaoping was no longer in office; they couldn't supply him or his wife with any medicine. It took a special letter from the assistant superintendent of the hospital before the pharmacy would comply.

But the drops didn't work. In fact Mama's eyes became worse. They examined her at the No. 301 Hospital. The eye doctor told her she had a viral infection, and needed to stay in the hospital for treatment. Mama didn't want to leave Papa alone, but the doctor said if she didn't receive treatment immediately she probably would go blind. And so, on May 11, Mama moved into the surgery division of the No. 301 Hospital.

The biggest political storms never ruffled Papa's calm, but he found loneliness hard to bear. He was accustomed to the warmth and noisiness of our large household. If he read the newspapers they were full of "criticize Deng" articles, and phrases like "capitalist roaders are still on the road" and "Deng Xiaoping was behind the Tiananmen Incident". If he listened to the radio, the broadcasts were the same. He had nothing to read. All he could do was pace the room.

Luckily, Deng Nan had slipped a pack of cards into his pocket when he left Kuanjie Avenue, and he was able to play solitaire. He used those cards until the edges turned white. They were his sole relief from boredom.

The "Tiananmen Incident" and its repercussions definitely were not good news to the seriously ailing Mao Zedong. His worries intensified. On April 30, Mao received the visiting prime minister of New Zealand. Hua Guofeng, also present, remained behind after the meeting and reported on major national conditions.

With a palsied hand, Mao wrote three sentences on a sheet of paper and handed it to Hua Guofeng. The first sentence said: "Take it easy, don't be impatient." The second said: "Keep to the old formula." The third said: "With you in charge, I feel at ease."

In spite of his severe illness, Mao was mentally sharp. He knew the Gang of Four was very displeased with his appointment of Hua Guofeng as his successor, and surely would make trouble after his death. He wanted his wish clearly set forth in black and white. China's shaky family fortunes must be placed in the hands of Hua Guofeng.

Deng Xiaoping had been overthrown. The Gang of Four was unreliable. That left only Hua Guofeng. Mao knew he was an honest man, who had worked in Mao's birthplace, Hunan. He was the last person Mao could entrust.

Hua Guofeng relayed Mao's words to the Politburo.

Mao received Lee Kuan Yew, Singapore's Prime Minister, on May 12, and Premier Zulfikar Ali Bhutto of Pakistan, on May 17. On TV, Mao looked haggard, he moved with difficulty, his face expressionless. Soon after the meetings, the Chinese government announced Mao Zedong would make no more appearances at diplomatic functions. Mao had entered the final stage of his existence.

Treating Mama at the No. 301 Hospital were two women ophthalmologists. She frequently had difficulty with her eyes in the past. They had examined her before, and had become good friends. There was nothing remarkable about that. But they continued being cordial even though Papa was now under a cloud. What was more, they brought Mama up to date on all the latest news. They expressed disapproval of the "criticize Deng" furor, and hatred for the Gang of Four. They were very worried about the country's future.

Although Mama lived in an ordinary room, she had it to herself. She wasn't lonely because the two doctors called on her frequently. One day they told her privately they heard Chairman Mao was in a critical state. The Central Committee had sent out a notification.

Mama became very upset. Papa was alone in Dongjiaominxiang. He couldn't know anything about it. How could she get word to him? Fortunately, Teng, the security guard, came to see her. She quickly wrote a note and asked Teng to deliver it. The note said: "Under no circumstances must you leave your present residence, no matter who asks you. I will come out of the hospital as quickly as possible." She hoped that although Papa still wouldn't know what was happening, at least he would be more vigilant.

When Papa read the note, he guessed that Mama had heard some important news in the hospital. She had urged him not to leave, but he couldn't remain by himself. He wouldn't be safe unless he could get together with the family. On June 10 he wrote to Chairman Mao and the Central Committee, care of Wang Dongxing. He said that Zhuo Lin was in the hospital, that he was alone, and would like to be reunited with his family. Security guard Teng delivered it.

Wang recommended that Papa be more specific. Then he could take action better if Mao approved. Papa amended his request. Several days passed with no reply. Mao had gone through two crises. They had to wait until Mao was a trifle better before the request could be presented to him. When Deng Xiaoping's letter finally reached him, Mao could only say, verbally: "This can be approved." The letter was endorsed by every member of the Politburo.

Mama's eyes were essentially cured after 50 days in the hospital. She didn't want to stay another minute. At her request, she was released on June 30. She hurried to Dongjiaominxiang, and was relieved to find Papa as usual. They were notified that, with Mao Zedong's approval, they and the family would be allowed to move back to Kuanjie Avenue. The old couple were overjoyed, and couldn't wait to go.

Those of us in Yuqun Lane were also informed. We were amazed. We had only been there a little more than a month, and now we could return. Best of all, Mama and Papa would also be going back. What a relief. Despite the cries of "down with Deng Xiaoping" and "criticize Deng Xiaoping", the whole family was to be together again. It was a victory.

We quickly packed. It was something of a wrench to leave the small lane. Although we had been there only a short time, it had given us shelter. We cleaned the place spic and span. The rose bushes we had moved over were now in full bloom. With a last look at the small courtyard, we locked the gate and left Yuqun Lane.

We were happy to return to Kuanjie Avenue, but the place had obviously deteriorated somewhat in the short time we were away. An overthrown Deng Xiaoping could not enjoy the same status as before.

The carpets were gone, as well as the living room sofas, and Papa's desk and chair, even his desk lamp. The house seemed empty.

I think we felt worst about those holes in the garden left by the rose bushes we had uprooted. Without carpets, the floors would be easier to keep clean. Furniture we could always manage. A few simple wooden beds — we had our own quilts and bedding anyway.

We swept the floors, and washed the windows sparkling bright, and put the courtyard back in order. Luckily, we found an easy chair that had "escaped the net". We put it in the empty living room, and placed a small tea table beside it, for Papa to use.

We were all excited, as if we were preparing for a festive holiday. But after we had everything ready, there was no news of Mama and Papa. We waited uneasily. Had anything gone wrong?

Just as they were about to move back to Kuanjie Avenue, Marshal Zhu De, one of the founders of the People's Republic of China, had died on July 6, 1976. He was 90. 1976 was a tragic year for China. Zhou Enlai had passed away at the beginning of the year, and now Zhu De — both of whom had made enormous contributions to the liberation of the people and the construction of the country. Everyone was worried. To whom could China's future be entrusted?

Mama and Papa's return was delayed because of the death of Zhu De, but on July 19 they at last rejoined the family at Kuanjie Avenue. The house was at a busy intersection, and the Security Guards Division of the Central Committee didn't move them from Dongjiaominxiang until 11:00 at night, when the streets were relatively deserted.

They were home; we were all together again! It was a dream come true. They were reunited not only with their children, but with their adorable grandchildren as well. Unfortunately, Mengmeng had fallen and scraped the bridge of his nose. The wound was covered by a big white gauze patch, and he looked all the world like a comic character in a Peking opera. The grandparents' hearts were sore, but they couldn't help laughing.

Returning to Kuanjie Avenue didn't mean the end of Papa's restraint. He was still under virtual house arrest. With nothing to do he looked for at least a little physical exercise. Noticing that the grass in the courtyard was tangled and overgrown, he got a big scissors and went to work. He did it squatting down. Papa was 71, and Mama thought cutting in that position for a long time would be too much of a strain. She brought him a little bench to sit on. That was better, but he still sweated profusely, cutting grass in the hot summer sun. His sole upper garment was an underwear top that was full of holes. It soon was drenched. That was Papa's way of keeping fit.

To Papa, one of the great advantages of coming home was that he had books to read. The problem was we had only ceiling lights, which were too dim to read by. We decided to make him a desk lamp, and a floor lamp as well. Wu Jianchang, husband of my big sister Deng Lin, was handy with tools. This was a chance for the "hero to wield his weapons". Wu drew a number of sketches until a "final blueprint" was agreed upon. The actual crafting was to be done by him and me.

We sawed a big board into three circular plates, large, medium and small, and bonded them together with strong fish glue. That was the base of our floor lamp. On it, according to Wu's design, we set a 10-centimeter-high wooden cylinder, which I decorated with a pretty design, to serve as a support. Wu drilled a hole through the support and the base, and glued the two firmly together. We then painted them with several coats of white paint. In the hole, we inserted a long narrow steel pipe. Our lamp was nearly ready. With wire we shaped a frame for a big lampshade. Deng Lin cut up one of Mama's old skirts and made panels which she sewed on to the frame, adding a ruffled border. We ran a wire through the pipe to a socket and switch and a bulb. We turned the lamp on.

It glowed prettily, a very professional job, the result of family wisdom and endeavor! In the evening, Papa sat beside it in his easy chair, reading, while his grandchildren gamboled at his feet. A picture of family life, a warm and pleasant island in a sea of turbulent waves.

Papa was unable to leave the house, and his hair grew long. He Ping cut it for him. He had learned how when he was in college. Although he wasn't as good as a professional barber, he wasn't bad. He Ping was happy to display this sign of son-in-law devotion.

"How many people are there who can cut an old gentleman's hair?" he crowed vaingloriously. "It takes a real expert!" He did Mama's and Grandma's hair as well. They weren't going out to any formal parties, so it didn't matter.

Papa's toenails were my job. They gave him trouble, and needed special care. When he was criticized in 1975, I wondered who could treat them if he was overthrown. I watched, in anticipation, whenever the pedicurist came to the house, and gradually accumulated some of his scissors and scalpels. Now the time had come for me to show my skill. It's a tricky job, and I wasn't very good at it. I frequently nicked Papa's toes and made them bleed.

Papa never scolded me, but He Ping gave me the devil. I admitted my technique was poor, and said: "You're right. I'll practice on you!" Thereafter, He Ping's poor feet were the victims of my lacerations.

It was a rare pleasure for the whole family to be together again, but our world was far from idyllic. The Gang of Four whipped up wave after wave of "criticize Deng and oppose the Right-deviationist attempts to reverse the judgments". They pushed wide-scale searches for an alleged instigator and participant behind the scenes in the Tiananmen Incident.

Although the majority of the cadres and masses resisted, some units had to yield to heavy pressure by adherents of the Gang of Four. Deng Nan worked for the semi-conductor research division of the Chinese Academy of Sciences. Flunkies of the Gang in the Academy, in addition to attacking Hu Yaobang, stuck their black hands into the semi-conductor research division. They hoped, through Deng Xiaoping's daughter Deng Nan, to find evidence that he was the mastermind behind the Tiananmen Incident.

The criticisms were fierce, the investigations severe. The rank and file sympathized with Deng Nan. Although they dared not be seen talking with her, they made their feelings plain. Occasionally someone would whisper to her the latest news. As the anti-Deng campaign intensified, the research division became a focal point for attacks by the Gang of Four. During one meeting, an adherent said: "Today there are people hiding in the shadows." Obviously, he was referring to Deng Nan.

The Gang organized a work team comprised of eight or nine people from the Public Security Ministry and the Chinese Academy of Sciences, and sent them into the research division to investigate. They seized a man who worked in the same office as Deng Nan. A rumor was afloat that Deng Nan was next. You can imagine how she felt. During the day, she was ready to be grabbed. In the evening when she came home, she spent as much time with Papa and the old folks as possible. She urged us young people to look after little Mianmian if she was arrested.

"Disasters never come singly," the old saw goes. We liked to scoff at it, but it's often so. As if the calamitous upheavals caused by the Gang of Four weren't enough, on July 28, 1976, nature struck the Tangshan area in North China's Hebei Province with a devastating earthquake.

I had seen He Ping off at the Beijing Railway Station in the evening of July 27. He was on an assignment to Liaoyang in the Northeast. It was after midnight by the time I got to bed. I had just fallen asleep when I was wrenched awake by a violent shaking and a huge noise. I sat up drowsily, and then I realized — it was an earthquake!

At 3:42 in the morning of July 28 an earthquake of 7.8 degrees on the Richter scale had hit Tangshan. Beijing, only about 200 kilometers away, was also badly shaken.

I ran out to the porch, yelling: "Earthquake! Earthquake!" There was a boom! I whirled around. A big piece of the ceiling had fallen in the porch. I thought of Grandma. I rushed to her room. The ground, the whole room, was swaying. Grandma was clinging to a table, unable to stand erect, unable to move. I grabbed her, and supported her outside.

By then Deng Lin and Deng Nan had come. We looked at each other.

"Papa! Mama!" we cried.

Ordinarily, for safety's sake, they locked their bedroom door before retiring. We couldn't get it open. Frantically, we found a big stick and burst the lock. They had both taken sedatives and were fast asleep. We awakened them and helped them walk unsteadily outside.

The ground and sky were moving. A deep terrifying roar welled from the bowels of the earth. We had just brought the old folks to safety when Deng Lin suddenly cried: "The children!"

In the excitement we had completely forgotten them. We ran to their room and carried them out — still sleeping soundly. Three generations, nearly a dozen people, all together in the courtyard. A narrow escape. If the house had collapsed the kids would have been finished.

The tremors continued. Our Kuanjie Avenue residence was an open square compound of old single-story buildings. From outside the compound wall everything looked normal, but inside there was a lot of rubble. The corner of one of the buildings had collapsed. Those structures were decidedly unsafe. We moved some chairs out for the old folks and the children.

The sky in the east was starting to turn light. The ancient city of Beijing, strewn with rubble, wrapped in fear, greeted a new day.

Heavy dark clouds blocked out Beijing's usual morning sunshine. After this great disaster, the hearts of heaven and men were equally depressed. No one dared to return to his or her homes. We took a few bamboo poles that had been used for a gourd trellis, and a large sheet of plastic, and erected a canopy for the old folks and children to sit under.

It began to rain, harder and harder, until it was absolutely pouring. The plastic sheet was unable to sustain its burden of rainwater, and the flimsy canopy collapsed. We had no choice but to go back into the house. The whole family sat on the porch near the door, ready for a quick dash outside if the earthquake struck again.

I thought of He Ping's parents after things quieted down a bit. Two small grandchildren lived with them. Had they been hurt by the earthquake? I took Feifei and Little Chubby, both able to do hard work if needed, and we set out on our bikes.

The streets and lanes of Beijing were jammed with local residents. Some of the men were stripped to the waist, or wore only briefs. Grown-ups were shouting, children weeping. The whole city was frightened, confused. Most homes were in antiquated traditional quadrangle courtyards. Many of the older buildings had been damaged. Fearful of aftershocks, everyone lived outside. People were busy carrying out chairs and beds, and building campsites. They were very upset.

We've been hassled to distraction by the "Tiananmen Incident", and "criticize Deng", and "pursuing suspects", they thought, and now the Old Lord of the Sky hits us with an earthquake! How are we ordinary people going to survive?

We got to the complex of apartment houses where He Ping's parents lived. There, too, no one dared remain indoors. Every inch of space in the surrounding gardens was crammed with people. Very flurried, they also were moving furniture outside. I found my mother-in-law sitting alone in front of the entrance to her apartment house, holding her two small grandchildren in her arms.

Tears welled to my eyes. With Feifei and Little Chubby I rigged up a shelter between two trees, and put a bed beneath for the old lady and the kids to rest on. On the way I had heard that yesterday, when the earthquake struck, two trains passing Tangshan had been overturned. There had been many casualties. I was very worried. He Ping's train had been passing Tangshan just about that time! Telephone and telegraph lines had been snapped. Rumors were rife. It was maddening. There was no way of making contact. We could only wait.

Three days later, communications were finally restored. A telegram arrived from He Ping, in Liaoyang in Northeast China. Our tensely suspended hearts were able to come down to earth.

Slowly the news filtered through. It was shocking and painful. The powerful earthquake had leveled the city of Tangshan with its population of one million, and had inflicted severe damage on both Beijing and Tianjin. 240,000 people had been killed, countless more had been injured. For this terrible natural disaster to strike on top of the man-made torments inflicted by the Gang of Four was almost too much to bear.

The Central Committee of the Communist Party, the State Council, and the People's Liberation Army, with Hua Guofeng taking charge, immediately organized relief efforts. From all sides, rescue teams, medical units, and construction gangs rushed to the disaster area. Huge amounts of supplies poured in. The stricken victims bore up staunchly under the loss of their dear ones and the destruction of their property. Rising from the rubble, they plunged bravely into the battle for restoration. Their courage was a lofty monument standing high on

China's vast land.

Meanwhile, the Gang of Four ignored the misery of the people. "So what if Tangshan was wiped out?" they sneered. They attacked the Central Committee and the State Council for "using the disaster as an excuse for not criticizing Deng". Jiang Qing called the Central Committee and the local leaders of Hebei Province "panic-stricken capitalist roaders". Under pressure from the Gang of Four, China refused all aid offered by foreign countries.

People's Daily, on August 11, in an editorial sponsored by Yao Wenyuan, proclaimed: "Leaders of the opportunist line within the Party are seeking to take advantage of the temporary difficulties caused by the earthquake to deviate from the revolutionary orientation and restore capitalism". The thrust was clearly aimed against Hua Guofeng and Central Committee leaders directing the rescue work.

Jiang Qing issued more "criticize Deng" material. She labeled the three documents he had issued while in office regarding rectifications in government and Party, in industry, and in science and technology, "three poisonous weeds". She demanded that they be criticized nationwide.

The general public angrily rebuffed her. The sinister schemes of the Gang of Four had been thoroughly exposed. Their attempts at "criticism" were broadly resisted by the majority of the people and cadres.

People used to say, "When Heaven is angry there is Hell on earth." But history has proven that man's destiny is determined not by Heaven, but by man.

54

Mao Zedong, a Great Man, Passes

Pᴇʀsᴏɴs who had been Mao Zedong's attendants wrote this recollection:

"The earthquake struck Tangshan on July 28. It was 3:42 in the morning. The shocks were also felt in Beijing. The Chairman had suffered a severe heart attack in June, but was somewhat better in July. With all the medical equipment, his bedroom was too small. The doctors and nurses could barely turn around. We moved him and his large bed into his library, where he sometimes had received visitors.

"His mind was still clear. He knew an earthquake had happened. Though he couldn't speak, he gesticulated as if urging us not to be alarmed. We were asleep when the shocks hit. We ran to the library. He was lying there in bed. Four of us held a large sheet above him, each of us holding one corner, to ward off anything that might fall from the ceiling.

"When it was daylight, with the doctors' permission, we moved the Chairman to an earthquake-proof room nearby. News of the disaster immediately began appearing in the press. Lying in bed, the Chairman read every word. The last time he was so ill, he lost his hearing and he couldn't see. We used to read documents to him. Then he had an eye operation, and could read a little if he wore glasses. His hearing was still very weak. He read a report on the earthquake, marked a circle on it and gave his approval that Hua Guofeng go to the disaster area and supervise relief."

In August, the Central Committee issued three emergency bulletins to major leaders regarding Mao's dangerous state. On August 28, Mao Zedong's daughter Li Min obtained permission from the Standing Committee of the Politburo of the Party Central Committee to see her father. Mao opened his eyes with an effort and saw her standing beside him. He squeezed her hand, then closed his eyes, but did not speak.

His condition worsened on September 2. On September 8, Mao Zedong was dying.

Our family knew nothing about this. Like all the other residents of Beijing after the earthquake we were busy every day with the details of food and shelter.

It rained hard the day of the earthquake, and our plastic sheet shelter collapsed. We stayed in the house on the porch during the day, but it wasn't safe after dark. Where could all dozen of us go? We talked it over and worked out a plan: In the living room we set three parallel rows of long narrow tables, and placed across them the wooden platforms which had supported the mattresses of our beds. We put the mattresses on the floor beneath, together with bedding and pillows.

Great! Not only did it look nice, it conformed completely to the rules for safety precautions against earthquakes. Even if the beams and ceiling fell, we'd be all right. We ran a wire and a desk lamp underneath, so that we could read. We also made a roster for each of us to take turns on duty at night. Someone would give the alarm if there was another quake.

Organized, planned and secure, our new life began. At night, we all moved from the garden into the house. Adults and children crept under the tables. The kids loved it. They laughed and called to each other. It was like "playing house". They were very excited. We grown-ups liked it, too. Our makeshift beds were comfortable and cozy.

But "every brilliant scheme has its flaws". We thought we had taken everything into consideration, but we forgot one thing: The shelter was built low. Getting in and out was no problem for us young people. But Mama and Papa and Grandma were old. They had difficulties — especially Papa. He was going on 72, and his back and his legs were stiff. We tried to think of a solution, but we couldn't come up with anything suitable.

Late at night when everyone was in the shelter, all was finally still, except for a few faint snores, perhaps from those who had worked too hard during the day. The person on duty, with an ear cocked for any unusual noises, sat reading in the light of a small desk lamp. It was very silent, strangely peaceful after the turmoil of the disaster.

But three days of this form of existence, we concluded it wouldn't do. The problem was Papa. He had the typical old man's enlarged prostate gland, which meant he had to get up several times during the night to urinate. The shelter was low and bending was difficult. That wasn't so bad, but he sometimes bumped his head. Worried, we decided to move back outside.

At first we placed the beds in the garden, and rigged mosquito netting frames over them, topped by plastic sheets. But the sheets were too thin and light. Any wind blew them open, or blew them away. We were kept busy patching the frames. Luckily, the General Office sent us two big tarpaulins used on army trucks. We immediately went into conference on how to utilize them. Everyone was full of ideas. Finally, we boiled them down to a scheme for a new anti-earthquake shelter.

We grouped the beds together inside a large square, and sank posts in each of the four corners. In the center we erected a tall thick pole supporting the big tarpaulins. Plastic sheets attached to the posts formed sides to keep out the rain. We were prepared for any eventuality. On each bed we built a frame and mosquito netting. Every improvement inspired another. We set up light bulbs in the big shelter, and brought in our television set. Papa was able to read his books. Mama and Grandma could fan themselves and chat inside their mosquito nets. The kids could play, while we grown-ups watched TV, or played cards or mahjong.

It was more like being in a children's summer camp than in an earthquake shelter. Probably it was just the sort of quarters Gengis Khan and his "Heavenly Cavalry" used when they swarmed by tens of thousands across Asia. We were better off. He didn't have television!

The General Office sent us an army tent. We set it up, also in the garden, but nobody wanted to live in it. In the heat of summer the temperature inside climbed to 40 degrees C. Hot and stuffy, it couldn't compare with our airy, lively, big shelter.

Papa was 72 on August 22. He had been overthrown, and there had just been an earthquake. Perhaps we shouldn't have been much in the mood to celebrate. But Papa had been born in the year of the Dragon, and this year was a Dragon year. Such a rare coincidence of cycles shouldn't be missed. Besides, we felt the more troubled the times, the more we ought to celebrate Papa's birthday — and celebrate it joyously.

To demonstrate how well we young people had been "tempered" in the Cultural Revolution, we wouldn't let Grandma make the meal. We three sisters took over in the kitchen. We drew up a formal menu of the best that was available, and submitted it for the family's approval. There were no objections. We donned our aprons and set to work. Deng Lin made the cold dishes, Deng Nan sliced the ingredients, and I did the cooking.

We were busy all morning. Finally, the rice was hot, the dishes were ready, the soup was steaming. Proudly, we laid everything out on the large round dining table.

"Not bad," Papa complimented us.

"What good filial daughters," Mama said.

Grandma sniffed. "The questions is: Does it taste good?"

All dozen of us wished Papa a happy 72nd birthday.

Others could "criticize" and shout "down with..." The earth could shake and tremble. We remained cool. Optimism, cheerfulness in the face of difficulties, has always been our family's most outstanding trait, the one we have been proudest of.

Because our home on Kuanjie Avenue had a courtyard we were not overly crowded after the earthquake. But life was much harder for most Beijing residents. The streets and lanes were jammed. Beds had been moved out into the streets. Some people had rigged plastic shelters atop the wooden beds. They were roasting during the day beneath the blazing summer sun. At night they were very crowded, with many persons sleeping on a single wooden bed. They had to take turns lying down, or just sitting there.

Food supplies were very tight. Both adults and children were lucky if they had enough to eat. People slept badly and ate poorly. Many became ill from the heat, but it was hard to get medical treatment.

We couldn't find eggs or milk for the two small grandchildren, though we went searching. A couple of friends of He Ping and me made a special trip into the country and bought us a few kilos of eggs. We thanked them profusely. They said, "Your old Papa gave us charcoal when we were freezing that winter down in Jiangxi!" At the sight of the eggs, our whole family was all smiles.

In my in-laws' family my mother-in-law ruled the roost. They lived outside after the earthquake in a shelter. My father-in-law was an honest fellow, but very stubborn. He said: "Naturally, I'm not moving." He refused to leave the second floor apartment. Their oldest son, a doctor, had gone to Tangshan with a medical relief team. Their second son was working in the Northeast. My mother-in-law was very upset. She begged me and He Ping to try and persuade the old man. But though we pleaded till our lips cracked, he wouldn't budge.

Fortunately, there were no large aftershocks. Beijing had many fearless people like my father-in-law. Some were paralyzed with fright; some were completely unruffled. Some scrambled to stake out an area for themselves, some gave everything for the sake of others. There were all sorts.

The bulk of the population really suffered after the big earthquake in the summer of 1976. The only good that came of it was that everyone was very busy coping with the disaster. The government offices, the schools, the factories had to forget about their "study" or "criticize Deng" sessions.

The upsetting summer days gradually passed. In September, the weather was somewhat cooler. There were no new tremors. People were more relaxed. They went back to their homes during the day. Only at night did they still live out of doors, just to be on the safe side.

Starting at noon on September 9, radio stations announced repeatedly: "There will be a special broadcast this afternoon at 4:00." News in our family was hardly up to the minute. Besides, the Gang of Four was forever issuing "special bulletins", so we didn't pay much attention.

At about 4:00 pm, some children still hadn't finished their nap. Papa was sitting in the living room, reading. The house was quiet. I was out in the courtyard. Suddenly, far off, I heard the sound of music. It was a funeral dirge! I ran into the house and told Mama and Papa. We turned on the radio. There it was. Mao Zedong was dead.

Mao Zedong, Chairman of the Central Committee of the Chinese Communist Party, founder and leader of the People's Republic of China, had closed his eyes and left this world forever 10 minutes after midnight, on September 9, 1976.

The people's first reaction was shock. Mao was gone. What was China going to do? Under his leadership the revolutionary war had been victorious, China was building socialism, the revolution was continuing. What could China do, without Mao? For 26 years the Chinese people had shouted: "Long live Chairman Mao!" They loved him, venerated him, boundlessly trusted him.

Suddenly, he was gone. What could China do? When Mao was here, in good times and in bad, whether right or wrong, we could always rely on him. Now, he was here no longer. Who could we depend on? Zhou Enlai had died, Zhu De had died, Deng Xiaoping had been overthrown, Hua Guofeng was still being groomed as successor. And the Gang of Four was blindly and savagely striking in every direction. What would China's future be? Who should be given authority over the nation, the Party, the military? In this extremely complicated political drama, could Hua Guofeng play the leading role? Would the Gang of Four peacefully relinquish power?

These worries and doubts knocked all personal consideration out of our heads.

The funeral dirge echoed, China's red flags hung at half mast. In cities and villages, all over the land, in every place, in every organization, the people conducted memorial services; they cherished the memory of Mao Zedong, China's great man of the 20th century.

Mao was gone. A huge split immediately appeared in the political structure he had carefully fostered during his lifetime.

When he was slipping into his final decline, the Gang of Four intensified their schemes to seize power. They tightened links with adherents all over the country, stepped up criticism of so-called "old and new capitalist roaders", vowing they would grab them on every level.

In July and August, Wang Hongwen, in Shanghai, warned that there was "revisionism in the Central Committee", and urged the Gang's followers to "prepare to take the hills and wage guerrilla warfare." He called for the formation of a "second armed force", utilizing the arms and ammunition in Shanghai's arsenals. In August, 70,000 rifles, 300 artillery pieces, and 10 million rounds of ammunition were issued to the city's militia units.

Jiang Qing hurriedly organized the publication of historical material stating that after Liu Bang, the first emperor of the Han Dynasty (206 BC-AD 220), died, his empress, Empress Lu, "got rid of all the remaining kings and dukes." Jiang Qing couldn't wait to become China's "woman emperor". Instead of staying by Mao's side as a dutiful wife when he was dying, Jiang Qing ran all over the place. Now the Xinhua Printing Press, now Tsinghua University, now Peking University. She had the media carry news of her visiting Beijing's residents "on behalf of Mao Zedong".

On a trip to a farm community outside of Tianjin, on August 28, Jiang Qing called Deng Xiaoping the "manager of a rumor factory," and gave a shameless discourse on "matriarchal society."

"The men must give way," she ranted, "and let the women take over. With the development of the means of production, women comrades will be the custodians of the country."

"Women can also be emperors," she said. "There will be female emperors even under communism."

She put on another mad show during an "inspection visit" to an army unit on August 30. Dressed in a slightly worn uniform, she carried a dispatch case casually slung across one shoulder, with a white cloth attached to the strap, in the manner of a veteran army scout. As she swaggered before the troops, she boldly announced: "When the Chairman is gone, I will be the imperial sovereign."

On September 2 and September 3, when Mao was sinking fast, Jiang

Qing went to Dazhai, in North China's Shanxi Province, although she knew Mao disapproved of her going, and continued babbling about "women emperors". She had no feelings for Mao, at all. Only after an urgent telegram from the Central Committee, did she finally return to Beijing in the evening of September 5, but not until she had first played a few more games of cards.

She spent little time with Mao in Beijing. Again she went to the Xinhua Printing Press, where she gave another dissertation. She said: "When the First Emperor of the Qin Dynasty went traveling, he came upon a jade plaque which predicted: 'This year the imperial dragon will die.'" Jiang Qing was insane with the desire to become female emperor. She hoped that Mao would die soon.

When she did go to the hospital, she made a great nuisance of herself. Over the doctors' protests she insisted on giving Mao back rubs, and exercising his arms and legs. On September 8, Mao's last day on earth, Jiang Qing went to the Xinhua Printing Press again and made another speech. In defiance of doctors' orders, she had kept pulling Mao about on his sickbed, searching everywhere for a will.

On September 16, 1976, two days before the memorial service for Mao Zedong, the Gang of Four placed an editorial in the *People's Daily*, the *Red Flag* magazine, and *Liberation Army Daily*, entitled "Chairman Mao Will Live Forever in Our Hearts". They falsified what they claimed were Mao's "final wishes". In his instructions to Hua Guofeng, on April 30, 1976, Mao had said "Take it easy, don't be impatient; keep to the old formula; and with you in charge, I feel at ease." The Gang changed this phrase to "continue with the present methods," — meaning treating everything in terms of endless hostile class struggle. As the most fervid proponents of the so-called Cultural Revolution against "class enemies", the Gang hoped to qualify as Mao's "most orthodox" successors.

A solemn memorial service was held for Mao Zedong on September 18. Jiang Qing was dressed in black, and wore a widow's black veil, but her face showed no emotion. Zhang Chunqiao and Yao Wenyuan looked somber and sinister. Wang Hongwen craned his long neck to stare at Hua Guofeng, who was mournfully reading the memorial address. The people of China, watching the live television broadcast, saw with hateful clarity the ugly visage of the Gang of Four.

The next day, the Gang requested an emergency meeting of the Politburo. At the meeting, Jiang Qing demanded that all of Mao's documents and papers be turned over to her and Mao Yuanxin, as custodians. She raged for four or five hours, knowing she was putting Hua Guofeng in a difficult position.

In Shanghai, in response to the Gang's orders, militia headquarters conducted a "battle exercise", in preparation for an armed uprising. On September 21, Zhang Chunqiao, in Beijing, on hearing that arms had been issued in Shanghai, told his flunkies: "Keep a close eye on the trend toward class struggle." A Wang Hongwen's adherent in Shanghai sent a telegram on September 23, warning: "Class struggle is not over. The bourgeois elements inside the Party refuse to accept their defeat. They surely will put Deng Xiaoping forward again."

Zhang Chunqiao, on September 27, warned the Gang's followers in Shanghai: "Beware of the Central Committee going revisionist." On September 28, he sent word to them: "Shanghai is about to face a big test. There will be war!" On September 29, the Gang rioted in a meeting of the Politburo from late at night till early the following morning. They insisted that Mao Yuanxin, whose duties as "special liaison" to Mao Zedong had ended, remain in Beijing, and not return to Liaoning. Jiang Qing wept and ranted.

She spoke at Tsinghua University on October 1, and said there were people who wanted to rehabilitate Deng Xiaoping — meaning Hua Guofeng, representing the Central Committee. She also squalled that Deng should be "expelled from the Party."

Wang Hongwen, on October 2, had an "official photograph" taken, in preparation for having it posted everywhere after he took office. On October 3, he spoke in Pinggu County, on the outskirts of Beijing. "What should you do if the Central Committee goes revisionist?" he asked. "Overthrow it, of course!" The spearhead was openly pointing at Hua Guofeng.

The Gang was plotting to send tanks into Beijing at a moment's notice. Wang Hongwen set up a special "Duty Room" in Zhongnanhai. Usurping the name of the Central Committee General Office, he notified Party units throughout the land to clear all important matters with him and his ilk directly. He also orchestrated "loyalty pledges" and "urges to assumption of command" to be sent to Jiang Qing from places like Tsinghua University, Peking University and the Xinhua News Agency. One such missive urged that Jiang Qing be made chairman of the Central Committee and chairman of the Military Commission.

The lady herself had formal garments tailored in Tianjin, in readiness for "mounting the throne". A rumor circulated by the Gang of Four alerted everyone to be prepared for "very joyous news" on October 8, 9, and 10.

Mao Zedong was gone for less than a month, but the political edifice he had painstakingly constructed was already crumbling. The Gang of Four believed the critical moment for the seizure of power they had so long hungered for had arrived at last.

55
Thoroughly Smash the Gang of Four

Hua Guofeng and the other leaders of the Central Committee were well aware of the Gang of Four's eagerness to seize power, particularly after the ugly performance of Jiang Qing.

A number of the old comrades realized that after Mao died the Party and the nation were confronted with an extremely dangerous situation. Old revolutionaries such as Chen Yun, Deng Yingchao, Xu Xiangqian, Nie Rongzhen, and Wang Zhen, were very worried. Although they were out of the main stream, they used every means to keep abreast of developments and exchange news. Each of them sought out Ye Jianying.

Ye Jianying was a veteran marshal and one of the founders of the People's Liberation Army since its inception at the Nanchang Uprising in 1927. After the fall of Lin Biao, Mao Zedong gave Ye Jianying command of China's armed forces. Thanks to Ye's painstaking efforts, a large number of high military officers of probity and competence were returned to their positions of leadership, thereby putting the military again under the command of the Party. This was an important contribution to stabilizing the country in times of danger.

When Deng Xiaoping was restored to office, Ye proposed that he be made Vice-Chairman of the Central Military Commission, and gave strong support to his nationwide rectification drive. Then, Deng was again overthrown, and Ye's control of the Central Military Commission was terminated due to his alleged "illness."

But although Ye ostensibly was "inactive", he was deeply respected by Chen Xilian, the general handling the day-to-day affairs of the

436

Commission. Real control remained in the hands of Ye Jianying. Moreover, Ye was still Vice-Chairman of the Party's Central Committee, a member of the Standing Committee of the Politburo, Vice-Chairman of the Central Military Commission, and Minister of Defense. He took part in meetings of the Politburo and its standing committee.

And so, when old comrades were upset about national affairs, Ye Jianying naturally was the person they went to. One by one they called on him — Chen Yun, Nie Rongzhen, Wang Zhen, and many other high-ranking leaders. Ye was acutely aware of how dangerous the situation was. He knew that only a battle to the death could defeat the Gang of Four.

Ye's responsibility was unavoidable. But he needed the support of the country's present leader, Hua Guofeng. He went to Hua and said bluntly: "They refuse to quit. They can't wait to seize power. The Chairman is gone. It's up to you to fight them!"

Hua Guofeng was moved by Ye's words. The situation was tense. The Gang of Four had twice openly revealed their ambitions in Politburo meetings. Hua didn't reply immediately. He knew he would have to take a stand against the Gang of Four. But he had assumed office only recently, and had neither Ye's political experience nor his confidence. He needed more time to consider.

Hua's attitude was important in the battle against the Gang of Four. But there was another person who would also be a major player. That was Politburo member and Director of the Central Committee General Office — Wang Dongxing. Veteran of the old Red Army and the Long March, Wang headed the Central Security Bureau. He had been loyal to Mao Zedong and despised the Gang of Four. Ye went to see him in Zhongnanhai and talked frankly.

"I will do whatever you and Hua say," Wang responded. He advised Ye to limit operations to a small number of people, and maintain absolute secrecy.

On September 21, Hua Guofeng conferred with Li Xiannian. "It looks like a clash with them is unavoidable," he said. He requested Li to speak to Ye Jianying on his behalf, and urge him to work out a specific plan.

Now that Hua had made his position clear, Ye Jianying was able to concentrate on the details. Use legal process? There was no time. A military strike? That wouldn't do either. Ye talked it over with Hua Guofeng and Wang Dongxing, and they decided upon a simple ruse. A meeting of the Standing Committee of the Politburo would be called to discuss the preparation for Volume Five of the *Selected Works of Mao Zedong*. Yao Wenyuan would be invited to participate. At the meeting he, and Wang Hongwen and Zhang Chunqiao would be arrested. Jiang Qing would be attended to elsewhere. The date was set for October 6.

It would be a very tricky operation. To avoid being spied on by Wang Hongwen and to keep the Gang of Four in the dark, Ye Jianying moved several times in the intervening days. He also gave certain instructions to the military establishment.

October 6. The meeting was set for eight pm. Ye Jianying and Hua Guofeng arrived at Huairentang an hour ahead of time. Wang Dongxing and his Security Bureau people were already waiting in the reception hall. Ye and Hua entered the meeting room, sat down together on a sofa, and talked quietly.

A large clock was ticking. Minute by minute the time grew nearer. It was nearly eight. The first of the Gang of Four to arrive was Wang Hongwen. He could see there had been a change as soon as he came into the hall. At once he went into the brawler's stance he had used so frequently in Shanghai, punching and kicking and flailing wildly. He was no match for the security men, who quickly subdued him. They pulled him into the meeting room. He saw Ye Jianying and Hua Guofeng sitting together. Like a mad beast he plunged toward them. The security men pressed him to the floor. Hua Guofeng pronounced charges against him.

"I never thought it would come so soon!" Wang shouted resentfully.

Zhang Chunqiao was the next. In the reception hall he was told his bodyguard could not go with him into the meeting room. Zhang sensed something was wrong. "What's going on?" he kept asking. The moment he entered the meeting room, Hua Guofeng addressed him sternly:

"Zhang Chunqiao, listen to this: In collusion with Jiang Qing and

Wang Hongwen, you opposed the Party, opposed socialism, and committed unforgivable crimes!" Hua ordered that Zhang immediately be placed in isolation, pending further investigation.

The Gang's "Grand Advisor" and "Font of Wisdom" went to pieces. His legs trembled as guards led him away.

Yao Wenyuan arrived late. There was no need to use an "ox-slaughtering cleaver" on this "tender chicken of a scribe". A deputy chief of the Central Security Bureau announced the charges to him in a side room. At which point this poison pen scoundrel of the Gang of Four keeled over in a faint. He had to be supported in order to be escorted out.

That left only Jiang Qing. She was wearing silk pajamas in her residence at 201 in Zhongnanhai, reading a document and idly watching an imported video film at the same time. When security people entered her bedroom, at first she didn't understand.

"What are you doing here?" she shouted.

They read the charges. She was confused.

"Why? Why?" she kept asking.

Only when the security people urged politely: "Let's go someplace else," did she calm down sufficiently to leave the house, still very irate, escorted by two female guards.

The last to be apprehended was Mao Yuanxin, who had been closely involved in the Gang of Four's scheme to seize power. Li Lianqing, Mao Zedong's old bodyguard, was sent to do the job. Mao Yuanxin was living temporarily in a small compound in Zhongnanhai. Li read him the decision of the Central Committee. This "crown prince" of the Gang of Four and self-professed "liaison" with Mao Zedong offered no resistance, though he was found, when searched, to be carrying a pistol.

From the Cultural Revolution of May, 1966 to October, 1976, the Gang of Four ran amok for a full 10 years. They were crushed cleanly and utterly in the space of one hour without a gun fired or a single bullet wasted. Hua Guofeng and Ye Jianying also dispatched troops to take over the Central People's Radio Station, the Xinhua News Agency, and other media organizations long controlled by the Gang of Four.

Members of the Politburo then in Beijing were ordered to go at once to Ye Jianying's residence in the Western Hills for an emergency meeting of the Politburo. At 10 o'clock in the evening of October 6, hand-in-hand, a smiling Hua Guofeng and Ye Jianying entered the meeting room and told the gathering how the Gang had been smashed.

Their words stirred a frenzy of excitement, punctuated by delighted applause. In an exultant mood, the Politburo session lasted all night. It passed several important resolutions: That Hua Guofeng be Chairman of the Communist Party Central Committee, and Chairman of the Central Military Commission; that, starting October 7, meetings be held at every level throughout the land to inform the nation of the destruction of the Gang of Four.

The actual news spread much faster than its official filtering down from level to level. The Gang of Four had been arrested! In that lovely golden autumn the glad tidings echoed far and wide.

We on Kuanjie Avenue were very isolated. Even as the planning and capture of the Gang was unfolding, we were still brooding over their increasingly obvious intention to seize power. If they succeeded, it would spell disaster not only for Papa and our entire family — heads would roll all over China. We weren't nearly so worried when Papa was first "criticized", or even when he was overthrown a second time after the Tiananmen Incident.

But when Mao Zedong died, the situation entered a new critical period. Our trepidation increased day by day. Papa's gloom deepened. Obviously, many things were on his mind. Mao's death had caused a big split in the Politburo. The internal struggle could only intensify. No one could foretell the result. Looming on the horizon for the Party and the nation was the worst possible scenario. Papa, an "overthrown" person with no freedom of action, was quite helpless. All he could do was watch, and wait.

On October 7, the day after the smashing of the Gang of Four, an old Army friend of He Ping's father came hurrying to his house with the good news. He Ping's parents phoned He Ping at his workplace. They told him to go to Kuanjie Avenue immediately, and inform us. He Ping practically flew over on his bike. He ran into the house, yelling, "Come here, come here, quick!" He was streaming perspiration.

We knew something was up. Because we were wary of planted listening devices, whenever we wanted to talk about anything important we would all go into the bathroom and turn the taps in the tub on full force to drown out the sound. So there we were — Papa, Mama, Deng Lin, Deng Nan, and me. We shut the door and opened the taps wide. We crowded around He Ping and listened to him tell about the destruction of the Gang of Four.

Papa was pretty deaf, and with the water rushing into the tub, he couldn't hear clearly. The news had to be repeated. The Gang of Four was down! Was it true? We couldn't believe it! We three sisters were jumping for joy, and our hearts leaped with us, pounding so hard we could hear them! Shock, doubt, tension, exultation, joy and anger, sorrow and happiness, all suffused us.

Papa was very excited. The cigarette in his hand trembled slightly. With the water roaring in the background, we asked questions, spoke, discussed, softly cheered, and cursed lightheartedly. It was as if no words could adequately express the emotion and joy that was in our hearts.

On October 10, after obtaining confirmation, Papa wrote a letter for Wang Dongxing to transmit to Hua Guofeng and the Central Committee, expressing his support to the resolute and courageous action the Party Central Committee took to smash the Gang of Four.

Papa concluded with words he had never uttered before: "Like all the people of China, let me hail this splendid victory, and cheer it from the bottom of my heart: Hurrah! Hurrah! Hurrah!"

Hurrah! Hurrah! Hurrah!

China and the Chinese people were born again.

It was a victory for the Party, a victory for the people.

Hurrah! Hurrah! Hurrah!

The Party Central Committee formally announced the smashing of the Gang of Four on October 16, 1976.

On October 21, one and half million people took to the streets of Beijing. They came from their homes, their offices, their schools, their factories, their farms, and massed at Tiananmen Square and the adjacent Chang'an Avenue in a huge joyous parade.

We all went. It was a glorious sunny autumn day. Amid the crowds, we laughed and sang and shouted slogans. Ping! Someone shot off the first cracker. The marchers cheered. Cymbals clashed, drums pounded, more firecrackers exploded, more cheers went up. The people had won back their freedom, their liberation.

Because He Ping was tall, his office let him set off their crackers. He carried two large army knapsacks full of "double-kickers". Each was attached to a launcher, which he held high above his head when he ignited the fuse. He lit one after another. Although he wore heavy work gloves, by the end of the parade he had a very swollen hand. Despite several washings, He Ping smelled of gunpowder for days.

The celebration was duplicated in all of China's 29 provinces, municipalities and autonomous regions. Released from the 10-year oppressive Cultural Revolution, the people rejoiced. Many grog shops sold out.

October is the month of succulent crabs and golden chrysanthemums. Famous painter Huang Yongyu did a subtle picture which he entitled "Grabbing Crabs". He presented it to Ye Jianying — the illustrious marshal who had engineered the arrest of the Gang of Four. Catching crabs and eating crabs at once became a nationwide pastime. People who bought them always asked for "three males and one female". It was a sarcastic quip reflecting their hatred of the Gang of Four.

Ten years of the Cultural Revolution had brought unprecedented disaster to China: Political chaos, social turmoil, sabotage of production, hardships in daily life, and the economy on the brink of collapse. Thousands of cadres overthrown or slandered, countless individuals in every walk of life hurt in innumerable ways.

From the start of the Cultural Revolution to October 1966, in less than half a year 397,000 persons labeled "ox demons and venomous spirits" were expelled from the cities into the countryside. In just over 40 days between late August and the end of September 1966, 85,000 people were forced to leave Beijing and return to their places of origin, 1,772 were killed, and 33,000 had their homes raided, in Beijing alone. From 1967 to 1971, prisons in the outskirts of Beijing held over 500 high-ranking cadres, among whom 34 were tortured to death, more than 20 were crippled, and over 60 were driven insane.

Political, economic, scientific, cultural and educational units were severely damaged. Attacks, slanders, criticisms, struggle sessions were everywhere. Many of the fine moral qualities which emerged after the establishment of the People's Republic were badly sullied. Intellectual development was caged; political quality was suppressed. In the name of "revolution", "class struggles" went on without end, to the great detriment of the people's minds and bodies.

The Cultural Revolution was an artificially created and artificially enforced movement. It caused a tremendous catastrophe in Chinese history. Whether from the theoretical or the practical viewpoint, it was a dreadful error. During its 10 years, it committed one mistake after another. The only accidental "good" that came of it was that it served to educate the Chinese people, to awaken them. And it dug its own grave.

The Chinese people, after 10 years of bitter suffering, by their righteousness and courage defeated wrong and began to seek again the shining path to truth and hope.

56

A Splendid Restoration

THE Gang of Four had been smashed. The disastrous Cultural Revolution had ended. But the people of China had to conquer many difficulties before they could stand erect again, free of the restraints on thinking, free of economic hardship. Much painful searching had to be done before they could break the hobbles keeping them from taking the true road.

No immediate change was visible in Papa's political future. The Central Committee was still in the course of "criticizing Deng". There was no re-assessment of the "Tiananmen Incident". The "two whatevers" was still the current credo, namely: "We firmly support whatever decisions Chairman Mao made. We eternally follow whatever instructions Chairman Mao gave." Although the Gang of Four had been demolished and the Cultural Revolution had terminated, the long-lasting "Leftist" influences could not vanish overnight.

Mao Zedong unquestionably was a great man, the representative of the new era following the establishment of the People's Republic, a man already worshipped as a deity. Among many, fidelity to Mao Zedong was the prime criterion. Such a mindset had not been created by the decision of any single individual, but by lengthy special historical circumstances. In such an atmosphere, it was unrealistic to expect a re-evaluation of the Tiananmen Incident, and a restoration to office of Deng Xiaoping. A period of time was needed which could not be skipped over.

Our family was still on Kuanjie Avenue. Since "criticize Deng" had not been terminated, Papa remained under virtual house arrest. In October, the weather began turning cold, and we dismantled the earthquake shelter in the courtyard. There had been no new tremors, but people were not entirely free from fears. We continued to take safety measures after moving back into the house. Like many Beijing residents, we erected board platforms above our beds.

People were enthused over the downfall of the Gang of Four, and were impatient with the discordant "criticize Deng" echoes. They were concerned about him, and wanted him returned to office. The matter was a subject of heated discussion in the streets and lanes. But it was a slow process because of the "two whatevers" and the continuing "criticize Deng" campaign.

Papa's prostate gland became infected on December 4, causing severe urinary retention. Doctors sent to our home from the No. 301 Hospital performed a temporary urethral catheterization. They left medicines to be taken orally and by injection. I was in med school, and knew how to give injections. Deng Nan wanted to help, and learned how to give injections too. But she didn't have the nerve to practice on her own father. Deng Lin said to her: "I'm not afraid of it hurting. You can practice on me."

The injections we gave Papa helped a bit, but his condition kept getting worse. Everyone was very worried. Finally, at our request, he was admitted to the No. 301 Hospital at 11:00 at night, on December 10.

The hospital had made careful preparations. Papa was given the whole fifth floor of the newly refurbished south building. Because he was still in political isolation, the hospital had to keep him from outside contact. A guard was stationed in the corridor, and the rear stairway was locked.

At first, only Grandma and Deng Nan and little Mianmian were allowed to move in to keep him company. But when we saw how cordial the head of the hospital and the doctors and nurses were, the rest of us moved in as well. It was a whole floor, and there were plenty of empty rooms. We really relaxed. We brought in an electric stove and did our own cooking. It was like setting up house for the entire family.

Dr. Wu Jieping, one of China's leading urologists, held conferences on December 12 and 13 regarding Papa's condition, and decided to operate.

By then, two months had passed since the destruction of the Gang of Four. The call for the restoration of Deng Xiaoping was becoming louder. Many old comrades were working for it actively. Ye Jianying was particularly diligent. The public pressure was irresistible. It was only a question of when, and what form it would take.

The Central Committee passed a resolution on December 14 restoring Deng's right to read classified documents. The first batch was delivered to him at the hospital. It included a Central Committee document entitled: "Material number one regarding the crimes of Wang, Zhang, Jiang, and Yao."

After he finished reading it, Papa put the document aside and said: "There's no need for 'material number two' or 'three.' There's more than enough evidence here to convict them."

Papa was not the only one to feel that way. The whole country was looking forward to bringing those heinous criminals to trial before the tribunal of people's justice.

Hua Guofeng and Wang Dongxing, on December 16, approved the hospital's decision to operate on Deng Xiaoping. On December 24 a partial prostatectomy was performed in the No. 301 Hospital. It went without a hitch. Thereafter, Papa recovered very quickly.

His stay in the hospital was supposed to be secret, but the secrecy was hard to maintain. People speculated about the lights seen burning on the fifth floor of the south building every night. Who could it be? It wasn't long before the news slipped out. It was Deng Xiaoping.

Ordinarily the fifth floor of the south building was guarded, and the door from the corridor was locked. Many people wanted to see Deng Xiaoping, but they couldn't get in. Later, someone figured it out. The door was opened when the medical personnel came out at noon to have their lunch. That was the chance to get in.

The first to barge in was old general Yu Qiuli, who had lost an arm in battle. "Who says I can't see him?" he snapped, waving the remaining limb. "I'm going in!"

Papa was delighted to see his old comrade. We all sat around, talking in high spirits about anything and everything, particularly the Gang of Four.

"Uncle Yu," we young people joked, "we heard that at a meeting when the smashing of the Gang of Four was announced everyone applauded except you. Is that true?"

"You kids are the limit, teasing me," Yu chuckled. "Who ever heard of a one-armed man applauding? But that didn't stop me. I beat one hand on the table!" He roared with laughter, in which we all joined.

As he was leaving he said to Papa: "We're looking forward to you coming out, Comrade Xiaoping."

News of Yu breaking through the barrier quickly spread. Many other old comrades followed in quick succession. All expressed an eagerness for Deng Xiaoping to return to work.

Papa had recovered, and was able to leave the hospital. But our house on Kuanjie Avenue was still in poor shape because of the earthquake, and was not ready for occupancy. Several military comrades, who were also patients in the No. 301 Hospital, dropped by. As the news spread, visitors to the fifth floor of the south building came and went in a steady stream.

Our family spent the New Year Day 1977 there. On February 3, after 55 days in the hospital, Papa was discharged as cured.

Marshal Ye Jianying had arranged new quarters for us. We moved to a residential area for members of the Military Commission in the Western Hills, outside Beijing. Ours was house number 25, formerly occupied by Wang Hongwen. Needless to say, it was quite a place. It even had a special hall for watching movies. The new aristocrats of the Gang of Four really knew how to live it up.

Our house was on the summit of a hill. Following the driveway down, below us was number 15, the residence of Marshal Ye. One evening as we were having dinner, Toutou, the Marshal's youngest son, drove up and told us softly he had been instructed to invite the "old master" of our family to come and visit the "old master" of his family. Papa immediately rose to comply.

Toutou's car was parked outside our gate. Papa got in the rear. I sat up front with Toutou. By some miracle he delivered us safely to Number 15. As Papa was entering Ye's front gate we could see the Marshal, supported by a couple of people, coming to greet Deng Xiaoping.

"Old brother!" Papa loudly hailed him, and hurried forward.

The two warmly clasped hands. For several minutes neither was able to speak. Finally, supporting each other, they walked into the house. They talked together a long, long time.

Papa wrote a letter to the Central Committee on April 10, criticizing the "two whatevers" concept. He said for generations to come we must accurately and comprehensively use Mao Zedong Thought to lead our Party, our Army and our people, and thereby victoriously advance the cause of the Party and socialism, and the cause of the international communist movement. He raised the question of how Mao Zedong Thought should be comprehensively understood.

The Central Committee published Deng Xiaoping's letter on May 3, and expressed agreement with it.

In a conversation with two Central Committee comrades on May 24, Deng said plainly he felt the "two whatevers" concept does not accord with Marxism. He said:

"We cannot mechanically apply what Comrade Mao Zedong said about a particular question to another question, what he said in a particular place to another place, what he said at a particular time to another time, or what he said under particular circumstances to other circumstances.

"This is an important theoretical question, a question of whether or not we are adhering to historical materialism. Neither Marx nor Engels put forward any 'whatever' doctrine, nor did Lenin or Stalin, nor did Comrade Mao Zedong himself.

"When we say we should hold high the banner of Mao Zedong Thought, we mean precisely that we should study and apply Mao Zedong Thought as an ideological system."

Certain individuals in the Central Committee demanded that Papa write a self-criticism, and admit that the Tiananmen Incident was "counter-revolutionary". He flatly refused.

"If this principle (two whatevers) were correct, there could be no justification for my rehabilitation," he said. "Nor could there be any for the statement that the activities of the masses at Tiananmen Square in 1976 were reasonable."

In response to the efforts of old comrades like Ye Jianying, Chen Yun, Li Xiannian, and Wang Zhen, in response to the resolute demands of the people of the entire nation, nine months after the fall of the Gang of Four, in July, 1977, Deng Xiaoping was finally restored to office.

It was what the people wanted, it had a vital bearing on the destiny of China, it was a glorious restoration.

57

In Conclusion

T HE 10-year Cultural Revolution had ended. The massive calamity of 20th century China is now only a distant memory. But although more than 20 years have gone by, anyone who experienced it still has sharp recollections. Times pass, never to return, but the scars on people's hearts are not irradicable.

The Cultural Revolution occupies a very special page in China's history, and deserves careful study. It swelled into an extremely wrong massive eruption, highly complicated, erratic, an objective development that could not be halted. It left not only a residue of pain, but also valuable object lessons. Without them our country and our people, and especially our Party, could not have easily emerged from the miasma of confusion and reached the painful decision to adopt reforms. We might have traveled a much longer road.

People say Deng Xiaoping was able to launch a new stage of reform and opening-up because of the lessons the country, the people, the Party, and he himself learned during the Cultural Revolution. They all had witnessed the manifest differences between the true and the false, and observed many phenomena not visible before. Deng Xiaoping began to realize we must shunt off the shackles on our thinking, and to wonder how to open a completely new socialist road.

Down in Jiangxi the locals dubbed that small red gravel path Papa had trod the "Deng Xiaoping Path", as a symbol of his thinking. All his life Deng gave much thought to China's history, her present-day

Braving the chilly winds a million people lined both sides of the long Chang'an Avenue in January 1976, silently watching the funeral cortege of Zhou Enlai roll by, paying their respects to their good Premier on the way to his final resting place.

Deng Xiaoping delivered the funeral oration at the national memorial meeting, on January 15, 1976.

People blanketed the trees at Tiananmen Square with white mourning flowers, in March and April, 1976.

In the first week of April, 1976, a million people gathered in the Square to commemorate Zhou Enlai.

A wave of public condemnation arose against the Gang of Four.

After Deng Xiaoping was purged again, Mao Zedong selected Hua Guofeng to take charge of the daily work of the Party and government.

My parents and Ye Jianying. Marshal Ye cleverly and courageously headed the arrests of the Gang of Four.

The Cultural Revolution was over and Papa had returned to office. Deng Xiaoping and his family reunited.

realities, her future. It was a pattern that persisted during the more than 70 years of his political career.

Both before and after, and particularly during, the Cultural Revolution, Deng Xiaoping pondered the theories and the realities. Finally, he settled upon a new objective — to find a correct road. Once restored to office, he and his colleagues led the Chinese people forward in a new search. It was not easy, but they succeeded.

If one were to ask what did Deng Xiaoping learn from the Cultural Revolution, I would say the main things are the following:

First. When summing up the Cultural Revolution, one cannot talk only of one particular individual's successes and failures. You must start from the viewpoint of historical materialism, determine the facts and sum up the lessons with the aim of continuing forward. After the Cultural Revolution ended, Deng focused on the large historical signposts, utilizing the past to usher in the future.

Mao Zedong was a great man who committed grievous errors in his late years. Deng Xiaoping made a responsible appraisal of Mao as an integral whole. At that time, two attitudes were current. One, influenced by traditional long-standing concepts, stubbornly clung to regarding Mao as a deity. The other, while able to break free of the old fetters, negated him completely. Deng neither calculated old scores, nor concerned himself with personal grudges, but concentrated on the main things, on the political aspects in the light of historical materialism.

The history of any country, of any race, is always a continuing process, although it has its ups and downs, its glories and its shames. It cannot be basically changed at the will of any individual, nor can anyone halt its unfolding. We sum up history; we appraise historical figures, for the sake of the present, and even more, for the sake of the future. Under the supervision of Deng Xiaoping, our Party adopted "Resolution on Certain Questions in the History of Our Party Since the Founding of the People's Republic of China". It summarized our history fully, objectively, and accurately. It enabled us to discard our heavy prejudices, rid ourselves of the blinders on our thinking, and provided an ideological basis for our

Party and our people to enter a new stage in a new spiritual aura.

Second. Before, and especially during, the Cultural Revolution, many flaws became apparent in our political structure. For over 2,000 years China had been a feudal, autocratic monarchy. Although Dr. Sun Yat-sen led a bourgeois-democratic revolution in 1911, it ended in failure, and was quickly followed by chaotic battles among warlords and individual dictatorships. Right up to the establishment of the People's Republic, China never experienced modern democracy in the true sense of the word.

When China started a new era, therefore, the Party and the government were unable to fully develop democratic, systematized institutions based on the rule of law. Under adverse domestic and international pressures, errors appeared and worsened. Democracy within the Party eroded by the day. Arbitrary decisions by, and worship of, an individual rose to an extreme, resulting in a whole series of still more serious errors.

After the Cultural Revolution ended, Deng Xiaoping and his colleagues, in addition to restructuring the economy, placed great stress on a reform of the political system within the Party and the government. This included ending lifetime appointments for top-ranking leaders, establishing a system of democratic centralism within the Party, strengthening the National People's Congress, improving the State Constitution and the whole national legal system, thus bringing China's laws and systems in line with generally accepted norms.

It was only then we could say that China entered the modern age. Only then was China able to create a Chinese-style socialist democracy in keeping with modern historical developments and the specific conditions of Chinese society.

Third. While continuing to promote ideological and political preparation, Deng Xiaoping boldly pushed economic restructuring. Mao Zedong was the eternal revolutionary. He sought a realm of endless revolutionary spirit. While pursuing his ideal, he gradually became divorced from reality. In considering the relationship between the productive forces and the relations of production, he stressed endless reform and adjustment within the relations of production, but to a large extent failed to examine the productive forces.

On the one hand he took the concept of classes and class struggle, germane during the war years, and applied it wholesale to the construction period after Liberation, seriously distorting the relations of production. On the other hand, he misinterpreted the productive forces, severely impeding their development.

The economic structural reforms instituted after the Cultural Revolution were in harmony with the productive forces and relations of production. As the relations of production were being put in order and adjusted, and the productive forces were being freshly appraised, it was determined that economic construction was the core of the primary stage of socialism.

The condition precedent to economic restructuring was the sober affirmation that China was only at the primary stage of socialism. Our production level was low; our science and technology had stagnated. An improvement in the people's livelihood was hampered by an antiquated economic system. Our reform had to be bold but gradual, we had to swing a big ax yet be meticulously careful, seize every opportunity yet cautiously feel our way, push constantly forward but keep an eye cocked for changes in the weather.

After 20 years of economic structural reform, China has finally found her rightful road in history, her rightful place in a rapidly advancing world.

I haven't the ability to tell of what happened after the Cultural Revolution, particularly the developments and changes China has experienced during the reform and opening-up period. What I can say is that Deng Xiaoping was a seeker after truth all his life. That he was loyal to and trusted the Party. That he had long revolutionary experience, and was tempered in the Cultural Revolution. That all of these, together, provided a firm foundation in the new period for his outstanding contributions to his beloved country and people. He strove for rapid growth for the country and prosperity for the people. To him, the country and the people stood above all. His sole criterion was whether a thing was good for China's socialist development, whether it enhanced her strength, whether it improved the livelihood of the people.

It was this which won him the public's recognition and support. It was why so many threw themselves into China's reform and opening-up. The reason was complicated, yet simple — the people wanted these changes, they suited China's conditions. Without the support of the people, no one could have inaugurated them.

Originally, on Papa's 95th birthday, I had been intending only to write a short piece commemorating his experiences during the Cultural Revolution. I never expected it would come out so long. The Cultural Revolution was too complicated a stage in history, and Papa was too important a figure in history. There really was no way to write about them briefly.

In writing about Papa during the Cultural Revolution I wrote about our entire family at the same time. They gave me enormous support. I had them look over my every word. They checked me for accuracy, helped me remember details, avoid mistakes, compare drafts. My 83-year-old mother was the most meticulous. She went through everything with a fine-toothed comb.

If I was able to reflect even a bit of the experiences of Papa and the family during the Cultural Revolution it was entirely thanks to Mama and my sisters and brothers — Deng Lin, Deng Pufang, Deng Nan, and Deng Zhifang (Feifei), and to my husband He Ping. Without their help, I could never have done it.

Looking back, it's inconceivable to me that Papa is already gone three years. Time flies like an arrow. I've been writing for exactly half a year. I can still hear Papa's voice, see his smiling face. In my dreams I am often walking beside him. I can't believe he has left us. He is still with us, sitting together with the family, listening to us speak, watching us smile, silently savoring the utmost warmth and joy available to man.

We miss you, Papa.

November 15, 1999, Beijing

454

Glossary

An Ziwen (1909-1980) — Veteran member of the Chinese Communist Party and former head of the Organization Department of the CPC Central Committee. He was purged during the Cultural Revolution and later rehabilitated.

August 1st Nanchang Uprising (1927) — Led by Zhou Enlai, Zhu De and other revolutionaries, the August 1st Nanchang Uprising marked the beginning of the Communist Party of China to independently lead the armed revolution. August 1st is recognized as the Army Day.

Bai Dongcai (1916-) — Veteran member of the Chinese Communist Party, was Secretary of the Jiangxi Provincial Party Committee in the later years of the Cultural Revolution.

Bo Yibo (1908-) — Veteran member of the Chinese Communist Party, former alternate member of the Politburo and Vice-Premier of the State Council. He was severely persecuted during the Cultural Revolution. In September 1982, he was elected to the Central Advisory Commission at the 12th Party National Congress and at the commission's First Plenary Session, he became its Vice-Chairman.

Cai Chang (1900-1990) — Veteran member of the Chinese Communist Party. She went to France on a work-study program in winter 1919, joined the Chinese Socialist Youth League together with Deng Xiaoping in 1922, and became a member of the Chinese Communist Party in 1923. She was chairwoman of the All-China Women's Federation before the Cultural Revolution.

Chen Boda (1904-1989) — Former alternate member of the Politburo, director of the Political Research Office of the CPC Central Committee and Mao Zedong's secretary. During the Cultural Revolution, he was head of the Cultural Revolution Group, seeking theoretical basis for the Lin Biao and Jiang Qing cliques. He was later sentenced to 18 years' imprisonment for his participation in their criminal activities.

Chen Changfeng — Vice-director of the Revolutionary Committee of Jiangxi Province during the Cultural Revolution. He was Mao Zedong's bodyguard during the Long March (1934-1935).

Chen Duxiu (1879-1942) — One of the founders of the Chinese Communist Party and its principal leader during the first six years. He carried out wrong political and military strategies that caused the failure of the First Revolutionary Civil War (1924-1927).

Chen Jingrun (1933-1996) — A researcher at the Institute of Mathematics of the Chinese Academy of Sciences. His study of Goldbach Conjecture in the field of analytic theory of numbers won esteem among international mathematicians. His research results have been termed Chen's Theorem.

Chen Xilian (1915-) — Former Commander of the Greater Shenyang Military Area of the PLA. During the Cultural Revolution, he was a member of the Politburo, member of the Standing Committee of the CPC Central Military Commission. He became a member of the Central Advisory Commission in 1982.

Chen Yi (1901-1972) — Marshal of the People's Republic of China, member of the Politburo and Vice-Premier of the State Council. Severely persecuted during the Cultural Revolution, he died in 1972.

Chen Yonggui (1914-1986) — A member of the Politburo of the CPC Central Committee and Vice-Premier of the State Council in charge of agriculture in 1975. Before the Cultural Revolution, he was secretary of Party Branch of Dazhai Production Brigade, Xiyang County, North China's Shanxi Province. He rose to national fame for his leadership in turning the rocky hills surrounding the village into terraced farm fields.

Chen Yun (1905-1995) — Former member of the Secretariat of the CPC Central Committee, Vice-Premier of the Government Administration Council and concurrently the head of the Central Financial and Economic Committee, and Vice-Premier of the State Council. In 1956, at the First Plenary Session of the Eighth Central Committee of the CPC, he was elected member of the Politburo of the Central Committee, member of its Standing Committee, and Vice-Chairman of the Central Committee. He was purged during the Cultural Revolution. In 1987, at the Third Plenary Session of the Eleventh Central Committee of the CPC, he was elected member of the Standing Committee of the Politburo, Vice-Chairman of the Central Committee, and First Secretary of the Central Commission for Discipline Inspection. In 1987, he served as Chairman of the Central Advisory Commission.

Cheng Shiqing (1918-) — Director of the Revolutionary Committee of Jiangxi Province in the early days of the Cultural Revolution.

Chi Qun (1932-) — Secretary of the Party Committee of Tsinghua University and Director of the Tsinghua University Revolutionary Committee during the Cultural Revolution.

Deng, Mao, Xie and Gu — Deng (Xiaoping), Mao (Zetan) — Mao Zedong's brother, Xie (Weijun) and Gu (Bo), all holding political and military positions in the Central Soviet Area in the early 1930s, were wrongly accused of committing errors, persecuted and stripped of their jobs by the then CPC Central Committee.

Deng Yingchao (1904-1992) — Veteran member of the Chinese

Communist Party and former Vice-Chairwoman of the All-China Women's Federation. After the Cultural Revolution, she became Chairwoman of the National Committee of the Chinese People's Political Consultative Conference.

Dong Biwu (1886-1975) — Veteran member of the Chinese Communist Party. Before the Cultural Revolution, he was Vice-President of the People's Republic of China.

Empress Dowager Lü (241-180 BC) — Wife of Liu Bang, founder of the Han Dynasty (206 BC-AD 220). She became the empress when Liu Bang was enthroned as the first Han Dynasty emperor.

Feng Yuxiang (1882-1948) — A patriotic general of the Kuomintang army. Deng Xiaoping worked as political commissar of Feng's army in 1927.

Fu Lianzhang (1894-1968) — Veteran member of the Chinese Communist Party and former Vice-Minister of Public Health and Vice-Director General of the Health Division of the PLA's General Logistics Department. He was hounded to death during the Cultural Revolution.

Gu Mu (1914-) — Former Minister of the State Construction Commission. He was criticized in the early years of the Cultural Revolution and became Vice-Premier of the State Council in 1975. After the Cultural Revolution, he became Vice-Chairman of the National Committee of the Chinese People's Political Consultative Conference.

Guan Feng (1918-) — A member of the Cultural Revolution Group with Wang Li and Qi Benyu.

Han Nianlong (1910-2000) — Vice-Minister of Foreign Affairs during the Cultural Revolution. He was a member of the Central Advisory Commission in the 1980s.

He Cheng (1902-1992) — Former President of the Military Academy of Medicine of the PLA.

He Long (1896-1969) — Former member of the Politburo of the CPC Central Committee, Vice-Chairman of its Military Commission and Vice-Premier of the State Council. He was hounded to death by the Lin Biao and Jiang Qing counter-revolutionary cliques. The Central Committee decided in September 1974 to posthumously restore his good name. His complete rehabilitation was announced in October 1982.

Hu Qiaomu (1912-1992) — Mao Zedong's secretary and former alternate member of the Secretariat of the CPC Central Committee. He was purged during the Cultural Revolution. In 1980, he became a member of the Secretariat of the CPC Central Committee, and President of the Chinese Academy of Social Sciences.

Hu Yaobang (1915-1989) — Former member of the Politburo of the CPC Central Committee and head of its Publicity Department after the Third Plenary Session of the 11th Central Committee held in December 1978. He was elected a member of the Standing Committee of the Politburo of the Central Committee and General Secretary of the Central Committee at the Fifth Plenary Session of the 11th Central Committee in February 1980, and became General Secretary of the Central Committee at the Sixth Plenary Session of the 11th Central Committee in June 1981.

Hua Guofeng (1921-) — First Vice-Chairman of the CPC Central Committee and Premier of the State Council in April 1976. In October the same year, the Politburo of the Central Committee took drastic measures to defeat the Gang of Four. Afterwards, he served as Chairman of the Central Committee, Chairman of the Central Military Commission, and Premier of the State Council. Because Hua stuck to the "two whatevers" principle and continued to affirm the wrong theories, policies and slogans of the Cultural Revolution, the 11th CPC Central Committee, at its Sixth Plenary Session in June 1981, unanimously agreed that he should resign as Chairman of the Central Committee and of the Central Military Commission.

Huang Yongsheng (1910-1983) — Chief of the General Staff of the PLA in late 1960s and a member of Lin Biao's clique. He was sentenced to 18 years' imprisonment after the Cultural Revolution.

Huang Zhizhen (1920-1993) — Veteran member of the Chinese Communist Party, he was first purged but later restored to his post during the Cultural Revolution.

Imre Nagy (1895?-1958) — Former Hungarian statesman who led the coup in Hungary in 1956.

Ji Dengkui (1923-1988) — Alternate member of the Politburo of the Ninth CPC Central Committee (1969-1973) and Secretary of the Henan Provincial Party Committee.

Ji Xianlin (1911-) — Professor of Peking University and a famous scholar.

Jiang Qing (1914-1991) — Mao Zedong's wife. Nominal chief of the Division of Cinema, Publicity Department of the CPC Central Committee, she never worked claiming illness. During the Cultural Revolution, she organized and led the counter-revolutionary clique known as the Gang of Four. In January 1981, she was sentenced to death, deferred for two years. In January 1983, her sentence was reduced to life imprisonment. She died of illness in 1991.

Kang Sheng (1898-1975) — Former alternate member of the Politburo and member of the Secretariat of the Central Committee of the Chinese Communist Party. During the Cultural Revolution, he served as a consultant to the Cultural Revolution Group and Vice-Chairman of the CPC Central Committee. He persecuted others and tried to provide theoretical justification for the Cultural Revolution.

Khrushchov, Nikita Sergeyevich (1894-1971) — First Secretary of the Central Committee of the Communist Party of the Soviet Union starting in September 1953 and concurrently Chairman of the Council of Ministers of the USSR from March 1958. He was dismissed from his posts in October 1964.

"Lao Jiu" ("old ninth"): During the Cultural Revolution eight categories of persons were targeted for attack: landlords, rich peasants, counter-revolutionaries, rascals, "Rightists", traitors, spies, and capitalist roaders. Intellectuals were later added as a "stinking old ninth".

Li Fuchun (1900-1975) — Veteran member of the Chinese Communist Party, member of the Politburo of the CPC Central Committee and Vice-Premier of the State Council before the Cultural Revolution.

Li Jingquan (1909-1989) — Veteran member of the Chinese Communist Party. Former member of the Politburo and First Secretary of the CPC Central Committee's Southwest Bureau, he was purged during the Cultural Revolution. Later, he became Vice-Chairman of the Standing Committee of the National People's Congress.

Li Xiannian (1909-1992) — After the founding of the People's Republic of China in 1949, he served as Vice-Premier of the State Council and Minister of Finance for a long time. In August 1977, at the First Plenary Session of the 11th Central Committee of the CPC, he was elected member of the Standing Committee of the Politburo and Vice-Chairman of the Central Committee. In 1979, he served as Vice-Premier of the State Council and deputy head of the Financial and Economic Committee. In 1983, he became President of the People's Republic of China. In 1988, he was elected Chairman of the National Committee of the Chinese People's Political Consultative Conference.

Li Zuopeng (1914-) — Former deputy Chief of the General Staff of the PLA, Political Commissar of the PLA's Navy and a member of Lin

Biao's clique. He was sentenced to 17 years' imprisonment after the Cultural Revolution.

Lin Biao (1906-1971) — Former Vice-Chairman of the CPC Central Committee and member of the Standing Committee of the Politburo and Vice-Chairman of the Central Military Commission. He organized a conspiratorial clique during the Cultural Revolution. When his plot was exposed, he fled in a plane but died when it crashed in Ondorhan, Mongolia on September 13, 1971.

Liu Bang (256-195 BC) — The first emperor of the Han Dynasty (206 BC-AD 220).

Liu Lantao (1904-1982) — Former alternate member of the Secretariat of the CPC Central Committee and First Secretary of the CPC Central Committee's Northwest Bureau. He was purged during the Cultural Revolution. He later became Vice-Chairman of the National Committee of the Chinese People's Political Consultative Conference.

Liu Qingtang (1932-) — A ballet dancer, who became Vice-Minister of Culture and joined the Jiang Qing counter-revolutionary clique during the Cultural Revolution.

Liu Shaoqi (1898-1969) — Former Vice-Chairman of the CPC Central Committee and President of the People's Republic of China. When the Cultural Revolution started in 1966, he was wrongly criticized and accused of being a "capitalist roader" and a renegade by the counter-revolutionary cliques of Lin Biao and Jiang Qing. He suffered physical torment at their hands and died of illness in 1969. In 1980 the Central Committee adopted a resolution clearing his name.

Lu Dingyi (1906-1996) — Veteran member of the Chinese Communist Party. Before the Cultural Revolution, he was alternate member of the Politburo, member of the Secretariat and head of the Publicity

Department of the Central Committee of the Chinese Communist Party.

Lü Zhengcao (1905-) — Veteran member of the Chinese Communist Party, and former Minister of Railways. He was purged and persecuted during the Cultural Revolution. He later became Vice-Chairman of the National Committee of the Chinese People's Political Consultative Conference.

Lu Xun (1881-1936) — Great writer, thinker and revolutionary of the 20th century in China.

Luo Ronghuan (1902-1963) — Former member of the Politburo of the CPC Central Committee and Director of the General Political Department of the Chinese People's Liberation Army.

Luo Ruiqing (1906-1978) — Veteran member of the Communist Party of China, was former member of the Secretariat of the CPC Central Committee and Chief of the General Staff of the PLA. He was severely persecuted during the Cultural Revolution. He became Secretary-General of the CPC Central Military Commission after the Cultural Revolution ended.

Ma Lianliang (1901-1966) — Famous Peking Opera actor.

Nie Er (1912-1935) — Composer of the national anthem of the People's Republic of China.

Nie Rongzhen (1899-1992) — From 1956 to 1975 he was Vice-Premier of the State Council. From 1958 to 1967 he was also Minister in charge of the Commission on Science and Technology for National Defense and Minister in charge of the State Commission on Science and Technology. From 1959 to 1989 he was Vice-Chairman of the CPC Military Commission. He was in charge of research in science and technology and of the manufacture of sophisticated weapons for a long time.

Nie Yuanzi (1921-) — Former secretary of the Party branch of the Philosophy Department of Peking University. She headed the university's rebel group during the Cultural Revolution, inciting violence and persecuting many people. She was subsequently sentenced to 17 years' imprisonment for her criminal activities.

Peng Dehuai (1898-1974) — Marshal of the People's Republic of China, former member of the Politburo of the CPC Central Committee, Vice-Premier of the State Council and Minister of National Defense. At the Eighth Plenary Session of the CPC's Eighth Central Committee held in August 1959, in Lushan, Peng was wrongly designated as a member of a "Right opportunist anti-Party group." He was persecuted to death during the Cultural Revolution. His name was cleared by the "Resolution on Certain Questions in the History of Our Party Since the Founding of the People's Republic of China," which was adopted on June 27, 1981 by the Sixth Plenary Session of the CPC's 11th Central Committee.

Peng Zhen (1902-1997) — A veteran Communist, he was a member of the Secretariat of the CPC Central Committee, First Secretary of the Beijing Municipal Party Committee, and the Mayor of Beijing. During the Cultural Revolution, he was brutally persecuted. After it ended, he was elected Chairman of the Standing Committee of the Sixth National People's Congress in 1983.

Qi Benyu (1931-) — Formerly in the Central Committee General Office. During the Cultural Revolution, he was a member of the Cultural Revolution Group, working to provide theories supporting the Lin Biao and Jiang Qing cliques.

Qian Haoliang — A Peking Opera actor, he was a favorite of Jiang Qing during the Cultural Revolution for his performance in her "model" operas.

464

Qian Xinzhong (1911-) — Veteran member of the Chinese Communist Party and former Minister of Public Health. He was purged during the Cultural Revolution. He later became a member of the Central Advisory Commission in 1982.

Qin Shihuang (259-210 BC) — The first emperor of the Qin Dynasty (221-206 BC), which began feudal dynastic rule in China.

Qiu Huizuo (1914-) — Former Deputy Chief of the General Staff of the PLA, head of the PLA's General Logistics Department and a member of Lin Biao's clique. He was sentenced to 16 years' imprisonment after the Cultural Revolution.

Soong Ching Ling (1893-1981) — Widow of Dr. Sun Yat-sen, pioneer of the Chinese democratic revolution. She was Vice-President and then Honorary President of the People's Republic of China after the Cultural Revolution.

Tan Zhenlin (1902-1983) — Former member of the Secretariat of the CPC Central Committee and member of the Politburo of the CPC Central Committee. He was appointed Vice-Premier of the State Council in 1959.

Tang Wensheng (1943-) — Deputy Director-General of the Department of North American and Pacific Affairs of the Foreign Ministry in the middle of the 1970s.

Tao Zhu (1908-1969) — Veteran member of the Chinese Communist Party and former member of the Secretariat of the CPC Central Committee and Vice-Premier of the State Council. He was hounded to death in 1969 during the Cultural Revolution. He was rehabilitated posthumously in 1981.

The Five Constantly Read Articles (老五篇): — Referring to the

465

five articles of Mao Zedong: "The Three Constantly Read Articles" and two more articles group with them, "Combat Liberalism" (1937) and "On Correcting Mistaken Ideas in the Party" (1929).

The landlords' revanchist militias (还乡团): — The phrase was originally used to describe the armed forces of the landlords in the Kuomintang era. The Gang of Four used the term to sneer the veteran revolutionaries who had been restored to their jobs.

The Three Constantly Read Articles (老三篇) — Referring to the three articles of Mao Zedong: "Serve the People" (1944), "In Memory of Norman Bethune" (1939) and "The Foolish Old Man Who Removed the Mountains" (1945).

Wan Li (1916-) — Veteran Communist and former Vice-Mayor of Beijing, he was purged during the early years of the Cultural Revolution. He served as Minister of Railways in 1975, First Secretary of the Anhui Provincial Party Committee in 1977 and member of the Secretariat of the CPC Central Committee and Vice-Premier of the State Council in 1980. He was a member of the 11th, 12th and 13th CPC Central Committee and member of the Politburo of the 12th and 13th CPC Central Committee. In 1988, he was elected Chairman of the Standing Committee of the Seventh National People's Congress.

Wang Dongxing (1916-) — Former head of the Central Committee General Office. After the Cultural Revolution, he became a member of the Politburo and later a member of the Central Advisory Commission.

Wang Hairong (1942-) — Mao Zedong's niece, was then assistant to the Foreign Minister. She later became Vice-Minister of Foreign Affairs.

Wang Hongwen (1934-1992) — During the Cultural Revolution, he served as a member of the Politburo of the CPC Central Committee, a member of the Standing Committee of the Politburo, and Vice-Chairman of the CPC Central Committee. Together with Jiang Qing, Zhang Chunqiao and Yao Wenyuan, he formed the counter-revolutionary clique, the Gang of Four, and plotted to usurp supreme Party leadership and State power. In July 1977, the Third Plenary Session of the 10th Central Committee of the CPC adopted a resolution, expelling him from the Party and dismissing him from all his posts, both inside and outside the Party. In January 1981, he was sentenced to life imprisonment and deprived of political rights for life.

Wang Li (1900-1986) — Former Vice-Director of the Publicity Department of the CPC Central Committee. During the Cultural Revolution, he was a member of the Cultural Revolution Group.

Wang Liang'en (1918-1973) — Former Vice-Director of the Central Committee General Office.

Wang Ming (1904-1974) — Joining the Communist Party of China in 1926, he and his followers gained the leading position in the CPC Central Committee in 1931. Between 1931 and 1934, Wang carried out a series of "Leftist" political policies and military strategies — which were later called the Wang Ming line or "Left" adventurism — and brought heavy losses to the Party and the whole revolutionary cause. His erroneous policies and strategies were ended in January 1935. He died in Moscow in 1974.

Wang Ruofei (1896-1946) — Veteran member of the Chinese Communist Party and secretary-general of the CPC Central Committee in the late 1920s and late 1930s. Unyielding when he was imprisoned by the Kuomintang between 1931 and 1937. He died in a plane crash in 1946.

Wang Zhen (1908-1993) — Former member of the Politburo of the Central Committee, a Standing Committee member of the Central Military Commission, and Vice-Premier of the State Council.

Wei Guoqing (1913-1989) — Veteran Communist, he was criticized but later restored to his post during the Cultural Revolution as head of the Guangxi Zhuang Autonomous Region government and Party Committee. Before his death, he was Vice-Chairman of the Standing Committee of the National People's Congress.

Wu De (1913-1995) — First Secretary of the Beijing Municipal Party Committee in the middle of the 1970s. He later became a member of the Central Advisory Commission of the CPC.

Wu Faxian (1914-) — Former Deputy Chief of the General Staff of the PLA, Commander of the PLA's Air Force and a member of Lin Biao's clique. He was sentenced to 17 years' imprisonment after the Cultural Revolution.

Wu Han (1909-1969) — Famous historian. Former vice-mayor of Beijing. Persecuted to death during the Cultural Revolution.

Wu Zetian (AD 624-705) — The only woman emperor in Chinese history. She reigned for nine years (674-683) during the Tang Dynasty.

Xian Xinghai (1905-1945) — Composer of the *Yellow River Cantata*.

Xie Fuzhi (1909-1972) — Former Vice-Premier of the State Council and Minister of Public Security. During the Cultural Revolution, he participated in the schemes and activities of the Lin Biao and Jiang Qing cliques and persecuted many people.

Xie Jingyi (1939-) — Former Deputy Director of the Revolutionary Committee of Tsinghua University, Deputy Director of the Beijing Municipal Revolutionary Committee and Secretary of the Beijing Municipal Party Committee.

Xu Xiangqian (1901-1990) — Marshal of the People's Republic of

China and former Vice-Chairman of the CPC Central Military Commission. He was criticized during the Cultural Revolution. In the early 1980s, he became a member of the Politburo of the CPC Central Committee, Vice-Chairman of the CPC Central Military Commission, Vice-Premier of the State Council and Minister of National Defense.

Yang Dezhong (1923-) — Deputy Director of the Central Security Bureau and Deputy Director of the CPC Central Committee General Office.

Yang Chengwu (1914-) — Veteran member of the Chinese Community Party, and Acting Chief of the General Staff of the People's Liberation Army in 1968.

Yang Shangkun (1907-1998) — A senior member of the Chinese Communist Party, he was alternate member of the Secretariat of the CPC Central Committee, and Director of the CPC Central Committee General Office. During the Cultural Revolution, he was brutally persecuted. He later became the President of the People's Republic of China (March 1988-March 1993).

Yang, Yu and Fu — Yang (Chengwu), Acting Chief of the General Staff of the PLA, Yu (Lijin), Political Commissar of the Air Force, and Fu Chongbi, Commander of the Beijing Military Garrison, were purged by Lin Biao and Jiang Qing counter-revolutionary cliques in 1968.

Yao Wenyuan (1932-) — Before the Cultural Revolution he served as a member of the Political Research Bureau of the Shanghai Municipal Party Committee. With Jiang Qing, Zhang Chunqiao and Wang Hongwen, he formed the counter-revolutionary clique, the Gang of Four. In January 1981, he was sentenced to 20 years' imprisonment.

Ye Jianying (1897-1986) — In 1973 he served as a member of the Politburo of the CPC Central Committee, member of its Standing

Committee, Vice-Chairman of the CPC Central Committee and Vice-Chairman of the Central Military Commission. In 1975 he became Minister of National Defense and in 1978 was elected Chairman of the Standing Committee of the National People's Congress.

Ye Qun (1920-1971) — Lin Biao's wife. She became vice-director of the PLA's Cultural Revolution Group and head of Lin Biao's Office. A member of Lin Biao's clique, she died in a plane crash together with him in Ondorhan, Mongolia.

Yu Huiyong (1925-1977) — Former teacher at the Shanghai Conservatory of Music. He won Jiang Qing's favor during the Cultural Revolution and became Minister of Culture in 1975.

Yu Qiuli (1914-) — Former Minister of Petroleum Industry. In the early 1980s, he became a member of the Politburo of the CPC Central Committee and Deputy Secretary-General of the Central Military Commission and Director of the General Political Department of the PLA.

Zhang Chunqiao (1917-) — A member of the Political Bureau of the CPC Central Committee during the Cultural Revolution, he joined the Gang of Four. In January 1981, he was sentenced to death, deferred for two years. In January 1983, his sentence was reduced to life imprisonment.

Zhou Enlai (1903-1976) — Vice-Chairman of the CPC Central Committee and Premier of the State Council of the People's Republic of China.

Zhou Rongxin (1917-1976) — Former Secretary-General of the State Council. He was criticized during the Cultural Revolution and became Minister of Education in 1975. He was hounded to death in 1976.

Zhu De (1886-1976) — Marshal of the People's Republic of China and Vice-Chairman of the CPC Central Committee and Chairman of the Standing Committee of the National People's Congress.

Zhuang Zedong (1940-) — Former world table tennis champion and Minister in charge of the State Physical Culture and Sports Commission (1975-1977).

Index

"A General Outline of the Tasks of the Party and the Nation", 329-31

"A Proclamation and Report on the Crimes of Renegade, Hidden Traitor and Scab Liu Shaoqi", 75

"A Report on Several Problems Concerning Scientific and Technological Work", 328

"A Report on Several Problems", 329

A Synopsis of History Since the Zhou Dynasty, 132

An Ziwen, 51,

Anhui, 34, 72, 96, 107

April 5 Movement, *see "Tiananmen Incident"*

Architectural Engineering Institute, 38

Army headquarters, 34

"attack peaceably, defend by force", 54

Autumn Uprising, 216

Bai Dongcai, 198, 233

Beijing, 3, 5, 7, 8,12, 23, 27, 32, 37, 54, 56, 74, 76, 77, 91, 96-99, 101, 107-16, 122, 130-32, 134, 135, 138, 150, 156, 163, 168-72, 174, 175, 177, 187, 192-95, 200, 201, 203, 205, 206, 208, 211, 230, 232-34, 236-38, 240, 242, 243, 245, 247, 251, 257, 265, 268, 269, 272, 273, 280-82, 284, 286, 287, 295, 300, 302, 309, 312, 314, 316, 321, 335, 338, 344, 356, 359, 362, 364, 366, 370, 373, 374, 377, 389, 392, 395, 404, 410, 412, 413, 422-24, 426, 427, 429, 430, 433, 434, 439, 441-43, 447

Beijing Social Rescue Home, 170, 199, 202

Bhutto, Zulfikar Ali, 270, 417

Big Brother, *see Pufang*

"black gang", 15, 16, 38, 40, 60, 63, 64, 73, 76, 84, 88, 92, 102, 128, 135, 149, 200

Bo Yibo, 7, 149

"Bombard the Headquarters", 20, 45

"bourgeois academic authorities", 14

British legation in Beijing, 54

Cai Chang, 98, 241, 269

"capitalist roader", 23, 35, 36, 38, 50-53, 67, 75, 86, 92, 101, 104, 106, 111, 122, 123, 126-128, 134, 135, 144, 195, 215, 246, 387, 390, 413, 416, 425, 432

Central Academy of Fine Arts, 23, 61, 83, 91, 93, 102, 163, 211

Central Case Bureau, 69, 71, 73

Central Committee, 1-8, 10-13, 16-18, 20-22, 25, 27-29, 31, 33, 35, 37, 38, 44, 45, 51, 71-75, 91, 92, 95, 99, 100, 104, 106, 107, 109-12, 115, 123, 130, 144, 149, 150, 157, 164-66, 169, 173, 174, 182-85, 190, 193, 198, 201, 208-10, 213, 214, 219, 221, 223, 224, 226, 233-36, 240, 241, 243, 250-52, 259, 262, 266, 270, 271, 273, 274, 276, 286, 288, 296, 297, 298, 303, 306, 311-15, 317, 318, 320-23, 325, 334, 338, 339, 342, 344, 348-52, 355, 358, 359, 361-66, 370, 373, 374, 377, 378, 382-87, 392, 393, 398, 399, 402, 405, 407, 409, 417-19, 424-27, 431-36, 439-41, 444, 446, 448, 449

Central Committee General Office (General Office), 4n, 37, 42, 45, 48, 56, 58, 68, 72, 88, 89, 101, 104, 108, 111, 116, 131, 135, 148, 165, 201, 205, 221, 234, 240, 358, 409, 428, 435, 437

Central Conservatory of Music, 23
Central Military Commission, 4, 35, 96, 226, 258-60, 262, 286, 314, 316, 334, 378, 383, 384, 435-37, 440
Central People's Radio Station, 13, 129, 402, 439
Central Soviet Area, 69, 96, 222-225
Central Case Bureau, 69, 71, 73, 160
Chairman Mao, *see Mao Zedong*
"chaos under the heavens", 12, 17, 24
Chen Boda, 8, 11-13, 16, 17, 21, 26, 31, 35, 42, 66, 67, 97, 99, 117, 131, 158, 184, 191
Chen Changfeng, 122
Chen Hongxing, 127, 206
Chen Jingrun, 328
Chen Xilian, 307, 309, 354, 355, 382, 383, 436
Chen Yi, 46, 47, 104, 106, 192, 193, 241
Chen Yonggui, 338, 339, 366
Chen Yun, 33, 106, 107, 109-11, 118, 191, 436, 437, 449
Cheng Huiyuan, 109, 110, 115
Cheng Shiqing, 110, 111, 122, 198, 235
Chengdu, 34, 191, 202
Chi Long, 218, 219
Chi Qun, 262, 350, 353, 356, 364
Chiang Kai-shek, 251, 255
"children who can be educated"
Chinese Academy of Sciences, 257, 325, 329, 343, 368, 421, 422
Chirac, Jacques, 306
Chongqing, 59, 68, 377
Chubby, *see Pufang*
Ciping, 218
Communist Party (the Party), 1, 2n, 4n, 8, 9n, 10, 11, 13-15, 17, 20, 21, 25, 28, 29, 33, 35, 38, 54, 58, 59, 67, 69, 71, 76, 87, 91, 97, 99, 115, 116, 157, 175, 182, 196, 198, 201, 216, 221, 241, 249, 252, 254, 258, 260, 264, 268, 274, 275, 283, 286, 288, 295, 297, 312, 316, 324, 332, 334, 340, 344, 346, 369, 370, 374, 378, 383, 385, 399, 402, 405, 424, 431, 440

Conference of Seven Thousand, 117, 336
"Confucianist", 261n, 271, 324
"conservatives", 16
"continuing the revolution under the dictatorship of the proletariat", 10
"counter-revolutionary revisionists", 8
"Criticize Deng, Oppose the Right-deviationist Attempts to Reverse the Judgments", 365, 371, 380, 385, 386, 421
"Criticize Lin and Confucius", 253, 262
Cultural Revolution, 1, 3-6, 6n, 9, 11, 12, 12n, 13, 14, 16-19, 21-23, 23n, 25-31, 33-35, 37, 39, 47, 51, 54, 56, 62, 63, 67,68, 71, 74, 76, 78-82, 84, 85, 92, 99, 100, 101, 104, 108, 110, 111, 114, 116-18, 122, 125-29, 143, 144, 146, 148, 149, 153, 156, 157, 159, 160, 171, 181-85, 189-96, 199, 200, 206-08, 210-13, 215-19, 232-34, 236, 237, 240-42, 244, 247, 249, 251-54, 258, 260, 261, 263-66, 271-73, 275, 277, 284, 287-91, 298, 299, 315, 316, 318, 321-23, 325, 327, 329, 331, 333n, 334, 340, 344, 351-56, 358, 363-64, 368, 369-71, 375, 377, 381, 383-86, 388, 389, 394, 395, 399, 405, 406, 408-10, 412, 413, 429, 433, 439, 442-44, 450
Cultural Revolution Group, *see Cultural Revolution Leading Group*
Cultural Revolution Leading Group, 11, 15-18, 20, 21, 23, 26, 31, 33, 35, 36, 38, 39, 41, 42, 53, 54, 66, 67, 69, 71, 81, 84, 99, 102, 117, 210, 211, 219, 232, 241-43, 249-51, 253, 260, 264, 265, 276, 288, 289, 292, 369, 383, 399
Dabie Mountains, 69,
Daqing Oilfields, 319
De Gaulle, 305
"defending Chairman Mao's revolutionary line", 24
Deng Case Team, *see Deng Xiaoping Case Team*

Deng Lin, 23, 30, 47, 49, 61, 64, 76, 83, 91, 93, 94, 102, 103, 108, 111, 113, 124, 138, 150, 163-67, 203, 211, 214, 230, 243, 257, 272, 359, 400, 401, 409, 410, 420, 422, 423, 429, 441, 445, 454

Deng Liqun, 329

Deng Nan, 11, 28, 48, 58, 59, 61, 62, 64, 76-78, 80-84, 86-90, 93, 94, 102, 103, 108, 113, 124, 138, 150, 167, 168, 172, 212, 214, 215, 218, 220, 221, 230, 231, 257, 359, 360, 362, 400, 401, 409, 410, 416, 421, 422, 429, 441, 445, 454

Deng Xianfu, 202

Deng Xianqun, 171-73, 200, 202, 203, 230

Deng Xiaoping
beginning of Cultural Revolution, 3-6, 8-19; criticism of Deng, 20-22, 24-32, 35-40, 75; home search, 42-44; denunciation meetings, 45-46; home arrest, 46, 50-54; leave for Jiangxi, 106-14; life in Jiangxi, 115-16, 120-32; 135-55, 161-68, 177-88, 195-206, 208-13, 220-22, 230-39; visit to Jinggang, 214-19; visit to southern Jiangxi, 223-29; back at work as Vice-Premier, 240-48, 250, 253-56, 270, 273-74, 283-84, 322; entered Politburo and Central Military Commission, 258-60, 306-07; attended Special Session of UN General Assembly, 264-68; and "Fengqing Steamer" Incident, 276-77, 279-80, 281-82, 285-87; all-out rectification, 290-301, 311-21, 322-31; visit to France, 304-06; at "Learn fro the Dazhai Production Brigade" conference, 336-38; at conference on agriculture, 338-41; with Zhou Enlai before Zhou's death, 345-48, 372-74; and Zhou's funeral, 374-75, 377-79; second criticism of Deng, 349-50, 351-57, 359-72, 380-88, 390; during and after April 5 Movement, 394-95,

398-404; second home arrest, 405-07, 415-23, 427-30; after smashing of Gang of Four, 440-41; final restoration, 444-49

Deng Xiaoping Case Team (Deng Case Team), 66, 67, 69, 70, 72, 73, 81, 95-98, 111, 114, 116, 121, 122

Deng Xingjun, 257

Deng Yingchao, 243-45, 248, 269, 271, 282, 346, 348, 361, 366, 373, 436

Deng Zhiqing, 407

denunciation meeting, 13, 36, 41, 45, 46, 125

Diaoyutai, 277, 279, 370

Dong Biwu, 106, 282, 283, 300

Dongjiaominxiang, 358-60, 389, 401, 402, 405, 407, 415, 417-19

Dream of Red Mansions, A, 92, 132, 343

Eight Principles, 13

Eighth Party National Congress, 53

Eighth Red Corps, 69

11th Plenary Session of the Eighth Communist Party National Congress, 20

Engels, 448, 449

Enlarged 12th Plenary Session of the Eighth Central Committee, 72, 94

factionalism, 16, 76, 291, 292, 294, 297, 298, 312-14, 317, 324, 325, 327, 328, 333, 368, 371

Fanghuzhai, 56, 57, 60, 62-64, 76-78, 81, 88, 94, 200, 411

"February Countercurrent", 21, 35, 47, 74, 191, 192, 241, 279

"February Mutiny", 21

Feifei, 43, 56, 59-64, 77, 78, 80, 83, 89, 92-94, 102, 103, 113, 124, 138, 140-46, 149, 150, 152, 154, 155, 167, 186, 198, 201, 205, 206, 212, 213, 230, 257, 412-14, 423, 424

Feng Yuxiang, 95, 96

"Fengqing Steamer" Incident, 276-280, 282

Fifth Five-Year Plan, 296

First Front Army (of the Red Army), 219

"First Marxist-Leninist Poster", 11

First Middle School attached to the Beijing Normal University, 92
"five constantly read articles", 340
Foreign Languages Institute, 44
Forum on Literature and Art in the Armed Forces, 6
Four Modernizations, 289, 329, 332, 336, 390
"Four Olds", 23, 24
Fourth Field Army, 26
Fourth Five-Year Plan, 293, 296
Fourth National People's Congress, 157, 283, 285-88, 290, 291
France, 68, 96, 98, 127, 304-306
Fu Chongbi, 259
Fu Lianzhang, 309, 311
Fujian Province, 17, 33, 390
Fuxian County, 133
Fuzhou University, 390
Gang of Four, 252, 261, 274, 285, 286, 291, 293, 299, 301-04, 307-09, 313, 316-21, 323, 324, 330-32, 336-38, 344-48, 350, 351, 354, 356, 361, 362, 366, 367, 370, 373, 375-78, 380-82, 383, 386, 387, 389-99, 402-06, 414, 416, 417, 421, 422, 424, 425, 431, 433-35, 430-43, 444-47, 449
"get in through the back door", 213
Girls High School affiliate of Beijing Normal University, 14
"go up into the mountains and down into the countryside", 92
Grandma (Xia Bogen), 40, 48, 56-64, 77-78, 80, 83, 88, 107, 113, 114, 120-24, 129, 130, 134, 136-38, 141, 143, 146, 152, 154, 162, 164, 178-80, 183, 197, 198, 200, 203-06, 218, 221, 230, 231, 236, 237, 257, 272, 411, 415, 421, 422, 427-29, 445
Great Hall of the People, 18, 66, 71, 73, 193, 246, 274, 288, 304, 321, 366, 378, 399
"Great Leap Forward", 2n, 10, 31, 125
Great Proletarian Cultural Revolution, *see* *Cultural Revolution*

"great revolutionary rebellion", 32
Gu Benhua, 299
Gu Mu, 247, 312
Guan Feng, 191
Guangchang, 228
Guangdong Province, 4, 106
Guangming Daily, 324, 390
Guangming Factory, 235
Guangxi Province, 95
"Hai Rui Is Dismissed from Office", 2
Han Nianlong, 374
Hangzhou, 8, 12, 14, 17, 214, 239, 392
Hao Zhiping, 5,
Hartling, Poul, 280
He Cheng, 311
He Long Case Team, 66, 67
He Long, 21, 33, 67, 192, 259, 273, 322, 323, 358, 359
He Ping, 195-197, 240, 359, 401, 408, 413, 420-24, 430, 440-42, 454
Heath, Edward, 270
Hebei Province, 102, 103, 108, 422, 425
Henan, 34, 50, 107, 125, 136
Hong Xing, 154
Hu Qiaomu, 318, 361, 362, 387
Hu Yaobang, 325, 387, 421
Hua Guofeng, 250, 279, 354, 355, 366, 382-84, 390, 397, 399, 402-06, 416, 417, 424-26, 431, 433, 434, 437, 438-41, 446
Huairentang, 37, 43, 46, 232, 438
Huang Wenhua, 121
Huang Yongsheng, 66, 68, 71, 72, 73, 96, 98, 99, 106
Huangyang (antelope) Crag, 217
Huang Zhizhen, 198, 211
Huichang, 224, 225
Hunan, 34, 75, 96, 106, 136, 196, 197, 250, 253, 254, 417
"inheritance theory", 23
Inner Mongolia, 34,
Internationale, 153, 373, 395
Ji Dengkui, 232, 279, 281, 348, 354, 355, 361, 382
Ji'an, 215, 219, 223

Jian Bozan, 85

Jiang Qing, 2, 3, 4n, 6, 7, 11, 15-17, 21, 25, 31, 35, 36, 38, 42, 54, 66, 67, 70, 74, 75, 81, 84, 95, 97, 99, 101, 116-18, 144, 157-59, 163, 190, 193, 210, 211, 218, 242-44, 251-53, 255, 256, 261-66, 270, 271, 274-82, 285-90, 292, 293, 299-304, 307-09, 316-18, 320-24, 335, 337-39, 344, 345, 345n, 351, 352, 357, 361, 367, 369, 370, 375, 383, 386, 387, 389-91, 395, 397, 399, 402, 403, 425, 432-36, 438, 439,

Jiang Qing clique, 38, 95, 101, 190, 300, 303, 304

Jiangsu, 96, 368

Jin Weiying, 224

Jingdezhen, 234-36

Jinggang Mountains period, 117

Jingxi Hotel, 71, 96

Journey to the West, 43, 132

Kaifeng, 50, 107

Kang Sheng, 6, 6n, 7, 11, 16, 22, 26, 31, 35, 42, 66, 67, 70-72, 74, 97-99, 117, 131, 165, 251, 300, 349, 363, 369, 370

Ke Qingshi, 3

Kim Il Sung, 300

Kissinger, Henry, 254, 255, 268, 283

Kuai Dafu, 31

Kuanjie, 284, 307, 358, 359, 389, 402, 407, 409, 411, 416, 418, 419, 423, 429, 440, 444, 447

Kuomintang, 59, 95, 217, 224, 298, 346, 389, 391

Le Duan, 349

"Learn from the Dazhai Production Brigade", 336

Lee Kuan Yew, 417

"Left" factions, 41

"Leftist", 1, 6, 31, 99, 117, 118, 208, 211, 219, 249, 250, 253, 254, 290, 297, 299, 336, 338, 339, 390, 444

Lei Feng, 391

Lenin, 330, 448

Li Chang, 325

Li Desheng, 251

Li Fuchun, 7, 46, 47, 98, 228, 241, 269

Li Jingquan, 149, 193, 258

Li Lianqing, 439

Li Min, 427

Li Qianming, 202, 203

Li Shuhuai, 236

Li Xiannian, 244, 246, 247, 266, 273, 278-81, 283, 288, 307, 308, 312, 314, 321, 323, 339, 346, 348, 354, 355, 361, 366, 374, 375, 397, 437, 449

Li Zuopeng, 71, 72, 99

Liaoning, 96, 351, 434

Liberation Army Daily, 433

Liberation Daily, 324

Lin Biao, 4, 5, 5n, 6, 8, 10, 16, 21-23, 25, 26, 30, 31, 33, 36, 38, 39, 41, 53, 54, 66, 67, 69, 70, 74, 75, 79, 81, 95, 99, 101, 104, 106, 108, 110, 116-18, 122, 156-60, 163, 164, 181-85, 189-93, 197, 198, 207-10, 216, 219, 232, 235, 241, 246, 249-52, 255, 258-61, 265, 273, 291, 309, 316, 318, 322, 323, 330, 334, 339, 340, 350, 352, 358, 382, 385, 386, 390, 397, 436

Lin Biao clique, 31, 33, 70, 99, 158, 159, 182, 190, 219, 323, 385

Lin Jiamei, 308

Lin Liguo, 159, 160

Lin Qiaozhi, 272, 376

Lin Yueqin, 241

Liu Bing, 350, 351, 353, 356, 362, 364

Liu Bocheng, 193, 209, 300

Liu Jianzhang, 232

Liu Lantao, 149

Liu Qingtang, 366

Liu Shaoqi, 10, 12-18, 20-22, 25, 27, 28, 30, 31, 33, 35, 36, 38-40, 42, 45, 46, 48, 50, 53, 54, 57, 66, 73, 75, 106, 117, 191, 193, 209, 244, 309, 352, 353, 382, 385

"Liu Shaoqi Case Team", 35, 66

Long March, 69, 115, 123, 217, 224, 225, 335, 437

Lu Di, 343, 344

Lu Dingyi, 8, 10, 41
Lu Ping, 85
Lü Tongyan, 195
Lü Zhengcao, 195
Luo Peng, 125, 126, 128, 183, 202
Luo Qingchang, 373
Luo Ronghuan, 241, 339, 358
Luo Ruiqing, 4, 5n, 6, 8, 10, 28, 41, 43, 60, 149, 191, 260
Lushan Conference, 117, 156, 158
Ma Lianliang, 3
Makaries, Archbishop, 270
Mama, see my mother
Mao Yuanxin, 350-57, 359, 361, 362, 370, 372, 380, 382, 383, 385, 397, 398, 434, 439
Mao Zedong, 1, 2n, 3, 4n, 5, 6, 8, 9n, 11, 12, 14, 15, 17, 19, 20, 24, 25, 30, 32, 34-36, 44, 45, 50, 53-55, 66, 69, 74-76, 83, 91, 92, 95, 99, 101, 104, 106-08, 112, 116, 117, 119, 123, 144, 156-59, 164, 182, 184-87, 189-92, 196n, 198, 207, 209, 210, 215, 216, 219, 223, 225, 232, 233, 242-45, 247, 249-54, 256, 258, 259, 261-63, 265, 267, 269, 270, 273-75, 277, 279-85, 287, 290, 291, 297, 299-306, 308, 310, 311, 313, 316, 317, 319-22, 325, 329, 330, 333, 334, 336-40, 342-44, 345n, 346, 349-57, 359-64, 367-70, 372, 374, 381-85, 387, 389, 397, 398, 400-03, 405, 416-18, 426, 427, 431-40, 444, 448, 451, 452
Mao Zedong Thought, 44, 117, 297, 339, 340, 346, 448
Mao Zedong's Three Directives, 292, 352, 365, 372, 377
Mao Zemin, 254, 350
Mao Zetan, 225, 254
Maomao, 103, 113, 124, 149-51, 186, 187, 198, 413
Maoping, 216, 217
Marcos, Ferdinand, 322
Marshal Ye, see Ye Jianying
Marx, 346, 448

Marxism, 263, 297, 301, 303, 330, 344, 385, 448
"mass revolution", 32
May 16 Circular, 1, 8, 9
May Seventh Cadre School, 196, 196n, 197, 230, 234, 236, 257
Miao Faxiang, 202
Mongolia, 34, 160, 181, 182
"Monsters Enclosure", 91, 93, 144, 196, 230
Monument to the People's Heroes, 377, 391, 392, 396
Moscow, 66, 210
my mother (Mama, Zhuo Lin), 5, 11, 22, 23, 28, 29, 37, 40, 42-53, 58-60, 81, 94, 103, 107-09, 114, 120-24, 126-30, 134-38, 141-43, 145, 146, 148, 151, 152, 154, 161-64, 167, 172, 173, 177-80, 182, 183, 194, 196-206, 211-15, 219-21, 223, 224, 226, 228, 230, 231, 234-38, 241, 243, 245, 248, 257, 258, 272, 284, 307, 308, 358-60, 400, 401, 405, 407, 411-13, 415-22, 424, 427-31, 441, 454
Nanchang Uprising, 216, 436
Nanchang, 110, 114, 115, 120, 122, 130, 131, 136, 141, 143, 161, 166, 173, 194, 196, 198, 200, 203-05, 212, 216, 218, 219, 228-30, 234-36, 238, 295, 299, 436
Nanfeng, 228
Nanjing, 295, 377, 391, 392
National Day, 182
Nie Rongzhen, 96, 106, 269, 316, 436, 437
Nie Yuanzi, 11-13, 29, 32, 81, 83-86
Ningdu, 227, 228
Ningxia, 96
Ninth Central Committee, 99
Ninth National Congress of the Chinese Communist Party, see Ninth Party National Congress
Ninth Party National Congress, 53, 73, 74, 76, 99, 101, 109, 111
Nixon, Richard, 254, 255, 384

Old Wu, *see Wu Hongjun*
"On Kuomintang's (in Taiwan) Rumors and Slanders About the So-called 'Wuhao Incident'", 346
"On the Ten Major Relationships", 333
129th Division, 69
Outlaws of the Marsh, 132, 337, 338, 342-44, 345n, 353
"Ox Demons and Venomous Spirits", 16, 33, 76, 442
Paris Commune, 34
Party, *see Communist Party*
Beijing Municipal Party Committee (Beijing Party Committee), 8, 13, 14, 18
Party Constitution, 75, 76, 99, 157, 249, 250, 252
Party rectification, 53
Peking University, 11, 12, 14, 27, 29, 43, 61, 76, 78, 80-89, 92, 94, 102, 104, 108, 109, 113, 124, 138, 147, 150, 165, 166, 169-71, 175, 177, 180, 199, 202, 205, 207, 214, 218, 220, 241, 242, 245, 255, 257, 271, 272, 278-83, 285, 301, 304, 342, 343, 346, 367, 373-76, 416-18, 432, 433, 435, 445-47; Physics Building, 80, 82-83
"Party persons in power taking the capitalist road", 34
"Patriotism or Treason", 35
Peng Dehuai, 2, 2n, 66, 117, 125
Peng Zhen, 3, 6-8, 10, 21, 28, 29, 41, 43, 47, 149, 399
People's Daily, 12, 13, 35, 207, 345, 375, 377, 396, 402, 425, 433
People's University of China, 21
Pinggu County, 434
PLA (the Army), 6, 21, 34, 54, 67, 96, 102, 104, 106, 117, 144, 216, 233, 271, 275, 276, 291, 293, 316, 317, 410
"placing professional work in command", 326
"Policies to Be Observed and Implemented During Struggles Against the Enemy", 92

Politburo, 1, 3, 5, 7, 8, 10, 12, 13, 15, 18, 20, 21, 33, 35, 39, 99, 101, 149, 158, 188, 193, 242, 243, 244, 249, 251, 252, 255, 257-60, 262, 264, 265, 267, 271, 274, 276, 277-81, 286, 288, 292, 300-04, 306, 307, 309, 321, 322, 338, 342, 344, 345, 347, 350, 355, 358, 363, 364, 367, 369, 372, 374, 375, 378, 380-84, 392, 397-402, 417, 418, 427, 434, 437, 438-40,
Political Bureau of the Central Committee of the Chinese Communist Party, *see Politburo*
Ponpidou, Georges, 305
Pufang (Big Brother, Chubby), 61, 64, 76-84, 86-90, 93, 94, 102-05, 108, 109, 113, 124, 138, 150, 165-67, 169-80, 182, 183, 187, 199, 202, 205, 206, 211, 213, 230, 257, 272, 454
Qi Benyu, 35, 36, 45, 191
Qian Xinzhong, 51
Qiao Guanhua, 266, 268, 283, 374
Qiu Huizuo, 71, 99, 104
Rao Yutai, 85
"reactionary bourgeois thinking", 8
"reactionary capitalist line", 25
rebel factions, 21, 32, 34, 39, 45, 51, 52, 54, 64, 85, 92, 99, 110, 143, 211
"rebellion", 15-17, 24, 25, 32, 41, 76, 143, 266, 327
"rebels", 13, 16, 17, 33-36, 42-46, 48-50, 52, 61, 63, 79-90, 92, 298, 327
"rectification through labor", 61
Red Flag, 35, 201, 344, 345, 431, 433
Red Guard, 16-19, 22-24, 27, 28, 32, 81, 110, 127, 300
Red Star, 226
"Resolution on Certain Questions in the History of Our Party Since the Founding of the People's Republic of China", 451
revisionism, 10, 99, 286, 299, 300, 303, 324, 344, 345n, 353, 386, 432
Revolutionary Committee, 34, 109, 110, 115, 120-23, 125, 135, 136, 138, 141,

143, 154, 173, 183, 205, 214, 351, 365, 366
"revolutionary Red Terror", 23
Sanwan, 216
Second Field Army, 26, 51
Selected Works of Mao Zedong, 438
"Self-criticisms", 27, 29, 30, 158, 184, 196n, 303, 307, 380, 381
Seventh Red Corps, 26, 37, 66, 70-72, 95
Shaanxi Province, 94, 133
Shanghai, 2, 3, 5 7, 34, 37, 45, 52, 69, 72, 95, 224, 226, 243, 250, 251, 260, 271, 293, 308, 309, 317, 324, 344, 362, 365, 366, 377, 389, 391, 432, 434, 438
Shanhaiguan Airfield, 160
Shanxi Province, 92, 103, 338, 433
Shaoshan, 253, 254
Shazhou Dyke, 226
Shihezi, 34
Sichuan, 34, 51, 59, 96, 146, 179, 197, 201-05, 220, 230, 231, 358
Sihanouk, Norodon 246
Since the Sixth Party Congress, 209
"small clique of persons in authority taking the capitalist road", 33
"smash first, then build", 12,
"smash the Four Olds", 24
Socialist reform and construction, 1
Soong Ching Ling, 283, 375
Soviet Union, 2n, 42, 106, 160, 255, 256, 264, 268, 304, 305, 369
"Speeding Up Industrial Development", 326
Stalin, 448
State Constitution, 50, 156, 275, 289, 452
State Council, 7, 38, 45, 118, 190, 242, 244, 246, 247, 250, 253, 254, 257, 260, 262, 266, 267, 270, 273, 274, 276, 278, 279, 282-86, 289, 292, 293, 295, 299, 312, 314, 315, 318, 326, 329, 331, 334, 336, 346, 359, 366, 378, 382, 383, 402, 405, 413, 424, 425

"stinking old ninth", 333, 333n
strategic exodus, 106, 118
"Strengthen Party Leadership and Improve the Party's Style of Work", 325
"Strengthen War Readiness Against a Surprise Enemy Attack", 106
struggle meeting, 15, 111
Sun Shaoyu, 268
Sun Yat-sen, 452
Suzhou, 106
"Sweep Away All Ox Demons and Venomous Spirits", 12
Taihang Mountains, 66, 125, 152
Taihe, 218, 219
Tan Zhenlin, 46, 98, 191, 232, 250
Tang Mingzhao, 279
Tang Wensheng, 279-82, 292, 308, 342, 348, 361, 367, 370
Tangshan, 422, 424-26, 430
Tao Duanjin, 126
Tao Zhu, 33, 45, 107
Tea Kettle Lane, 389
Ten Provisions Program, 53,
Ten Thousand Rivers and Mountains, 335
Teng Hesong, 407
10th Party National Congress, 249, 250, 252
the Army, *see PLA*
"The Counter-revolutionary Political Incident at Tiananmen Square", 402
"The Main Crimes of Another Biggest Capitalist Roader Within the Party – Deng Xiaoping", 75
Third Beijing Hospital, 86, 87
Third Five-Year Plan, 2
Third National Games, 335
"three constantly read articles", 340
Three Kingdoms, 343
"three poisonous weeds", 425
Three Unities and One Deletion Policy, 66
"Tiananmen Incident" (April 5 Movement), 398-400, 403, 404, 406, 408, 412, 413, 416, 421, 423, 440, 444, 449

Tiananmen Square, 32, 45, 46, 201, 344, 391, 392, 394-97, 402, 403, 442, 449
Tianjin, 96, 171, 198-200, 202, 203, 205, 206, 230, 271, 295, 377, 424, 432, 435
"to rebel is justified", 19
Tongchuan, 135
Trudeau, Pierre Elliott, 253
Tsinghua University, 31, 32, 36, 253, 350, 353, 356, 364, 365, 432, 434, 435
"Twenty Points in Industry" ("Twenty Points"), 326, 327
Two Lines, 209, 353, 355, 356, 364
"Two Resolutions", 396, 402, 403, 405, (413)
"two whatevers", 444, 445, 448
Ulanhu, 60,
United Nations, 264, 265, 267
"unity, alertness, conscientiousness, liveliness", 317
Verdet, Ilie, 346
"Vice-Chairman Lin Biao's Order Number One" (Order Number One), 106, 108, 219
"Wage the Great Proletarian Cultural Revolution to the End", 33
Wan Li, 298, 312, 387
Wang Dongxing, 37, 38, 44, 53, 66, 68, 72, 101, 104, 107-09, 111, 112, 116, 117, 130, 131, 149, 164-66, 173, 184, 187, 188, 198, 201, 209, 232, 241, 243, 342, 346, 348, 354, 355, 366, 374, 399-402, 405, 418, 437, 438, 441, 446
Wang Guangmei, 36, 50
Wang Hairong, 279-82, 292, 308, 342, 348, 361, 367, 370
Wang Hongwen, 250-52, 256, 260, 261, 265, 270, 271, 274, 276-78, 280-82, 285, 286, 288, 289, 293, 302-04, 307-09, 317, 324, 362, 365-67, 374, 383, 392, 396, 397, 432-35, 438, 439, 447
Wang Li, 17, 39, 72, 107, 108, 111, 131, 187, 191

Wang Liang'en, 72, 107, 108, 111, 131, 187
Wang Ming, 66, 67, 223-25
Wang Ming line, 66, 67, 223, 225
Wang Ruilin, 37, 44, 234, 236, 257, 361, 409
Wang Ruofei, 228
Wang Zhen, 106, 107, 109-11, 118, 200, 250, 436, 437, 449
War of Resistance Against Japan, 69, 125
"weak, lazy and lax", 312
Wei Guoqing, 232
Wen Hui Bao, 2, 7, 324, 391, 392
Western Hills, 440, 447
work team, 13-18, 20, 22, 28, 37, 298, 422
Workers Stadium, 32
World War II, 35, 305
"worship of an individual", 29
Wu De, 250, 348, 356, 397
Wu Faxian, 66, 71-73, 96, 98, 99
Wu Han, 2, 3, 7, 8
Wu Hongjun, 42, 51, 211
Wu Jianchang, 257, 420
Wu Jieping, 245, 446
Wu Weiran, 245
Wuhan, 17, 253, 274, 377, 390, 391
Wuhu, 72
Wuzhou, 228, 229
Xia Bogen, *see Grandma*
Xining, 34
Xie Fuzhi, 26, 45, 66, 97, 99
Xie Jingyi, 102, 262, 350, 353, 364
Xie Tieli, 321
Xingguo County, 223
Xinhua News Agency, 12, 377, 435, 439
Xinhua Printing Press, 432, 433
Xu Lijin, 259
Xu Xiangqian, 316, 436
Xu Yefu, 37
Xuanhua, 102, 163, 165
Xue Ming, 323
Xuzhou, 295, 298, 299, 313, 368
Yan'an Rectification, 66

Yan'an, 6n, 11, 66, 94, 103, 134, 135, 152, 227, 369, 370
Yang Chengwu, 66
Yang Dezhong, 201
Yang Shangkun, 4, 4n, 6, 8, 10, 41, 43, 97, 149
Yang Weiyi, 51
Yao Wenyuan, 2-4, 7, 12, 33, 35, 66, 99, 117, 193, 211, 250-52, 262, 265, 271, 276-80, 288, 309, 331, 344, 375, 377, 393, 398, 399, 403, 425, 433, 438, 439
Ye Jianying (Marshal Ye), 106, 190, 191, 193, 208, 243, 251, 252, 258, 260, 262, 266, 273, 278, 279, 280, 282, 288, 299, 301, 302, 304, 307, 309, 312, 316, 317, 320, 321, 323, 335, 342, 349, 366, 373, 374, 377, 383, 384, 397, 436-39, 440, 442, 446, 447, 449
Ye Qun, 66, 71, 72, 98, 99, 157, 160
Yongxin County, 216
Young He, 121, 122, 129, 130, 152, 162
Youth League, 15, 87, 97, 98
Yu Huiyong, 321, 344, 376, 390
Yu Qiuli, 247, 446
Yudu, 224, 225
Yuqun Lane, 410-12, 418
Zeng Tao, 269
Zhang Baozhong, 44, 408
Zhang Chengxian, 12
Zhang Chunqiao, 3, 7, 12, 31, 33, 35, 99, 117, 211, 242, 245, 250-52, 255, 260, 265, 271, 276-80, 283, 286, 288, 289, 301, 304, 309, 317, 331, 334, 342, 346, 355-57, 366, 370, 377, 383, 384, 386, 391, 392, 399, 402, 403, 433, 434, 438
Zhang Dingcheng, 358
Zhang Qian, 193, 241
Zhang Tianmin, 320
Zhang Xiuchuan, 71
Zhang Xiyuan, 244
Zhang Yuzhen, 257
Zhang Zhongren, 230, 231, 234, 237
Zhangzhou, 214
Zhenbao (Precious Pearl) Island, 106
Zhongnanhai, 31 36-40, 43-45, 48-50, 56-60, 88, 89, 102, 103, 111, 113, 114, 123, 141, 149, 163, 167, 175, 177, 200, 232, 233, 240, 242, 271, 358, 389, 400, 401, 410, 411, 435, 437, 439
Zhou Enlai, 5, 12, 13, 17, 18, 51, 66, 72, 97, 98, 104, 107, 109, 110, 118, 131, 164, 190, 192-94, 201, 207-11, 219, 232, 233, 235, 242-48, 250-56, 259-62, 264-71, 273, 274, 276, 277, 279-83, 285-90, 292, 293, 299, 301, 302, 304-06, 308-11, 318, 320, 322-24, 334, 342, 345-47, 349, 351, 358, 359, 361, 366, 372-80, 390-95, 397, 398, 402-04, 419, 431
Zhou Rongxin, 318, 356, 387
Zhu De, 106, 216, 259, 282, 283, 320, 335, 374, 375, 419, 431
Zhuo Lin, *see my mother*
Zhuang Zedong, 309

图书在版编目（CIP）数据

邓小平文革岁月/邓榕著.— 北京：外文出版社，2002.5
ISBN 7 - 119 - 03040 - X

I. 邓…　II. 邓…　III. 邓小平 - 生平事迹 - 英文　IV. A762

中国版本图书馆 CIP 数据核字（2002）第 019920 号

外文出版社网址：
　http://www.flp.com.cn
外文出版社电子信箱：
　info@flp.com.cn
　sales@flp.com.cn

作　　者	邓　榕	
责任编辑	匡佩华	
封面设计	蔡　荣	
出版发行	外文出版社	
社　　址	北京市百万庄大街 24 号　　　邮政编码　100037	
电　　话	(010)68320579（总编室）	
	(010)68329514/68327211（推广发行部）	
印　　刷	深圳当纳利旭日印刷有限公司	
经　　销	新华书店/外文书店	
开　　本	16 开　　　　　　　　字　　数　390 千字	
印　　数	0001-4,500 册　　　　印　　张　30.75	
版　　次	2002 年 5 月第 1 版第 1 次印刷	
装　　别	平	
书　　号	ISBN 7-119-03040-X/K·140（外）	
定　　价	59.00 元	

版权所有　　侵权必究